The Colonial Bastille

A

Philip E. Lilienthal

■   ■   ■

B O O K

The Philip E. Lilienthal imprint
honors special books
in commemoration of a man whose work
at the University of California Press from 1954 to 1979
was marked by dedication to young authors
and to high standards in the field of Asian Studies.
Friends, family, authors, and foundations have together
endowed the Lilienthal Fund, which enables the Press
to publish under this imprint selected books
in a way that reflects the taste and judgment
of a great and beloved author.

The Colonial Bastille

*A History of Imprisonment
in Vietnam, 1862–1940*

PETER ZINOMAN

University of California Press

BERKELEY   LOS ANGELES   LONDON

University of California Press
Berkeley and Los Angeles, California

University of California Press, Ltd.
London, England

Portions of chapter 1 and the epilogue appear in *Figures of Criminality in Indonesia, the Philippines and Colonial Vietnam,* a collection of essays edited by Vicente Rafael (Ithaca, N.Y.: Cornell University Southeast Asia Program, 1999). A version of chapter 6 appeared in *Modern Asian Studies* 34, pt. 1 (February 2000): 57–99. These materials are reprinted here with the permission of the publishers.

Library of Congress Cataloging-in-Publication Data

Zinoman, Peter, 1965–
    The colonial Bastille : a history of imprisonment in Vietnam,
    1862–1940 / Peter Zinoman
      p.   cm.
    Includes bibliographical references and index.
    ISBN 0-520-22412-4 (cloth : alk. paper)
    1. Prisons—Vietnam—History.   2. National movements—
Vietnam—History.   3. Nationalism—Vietnam—History.   I. Title.

HV9800.5.Z55   2001
365'.9597—dc21

00-31690

Manufactured in the United States of America

09 08 07 06 05 04 03 02 01
10 9 8 7 6 5 4 3 2 1

The paper used in this publication meets the minimum requirements of ANSI / NISO Z39 0.48-1992 (R 1997) (Permanence of Paper). ♾

For Cam

Contents

Maps and Tables

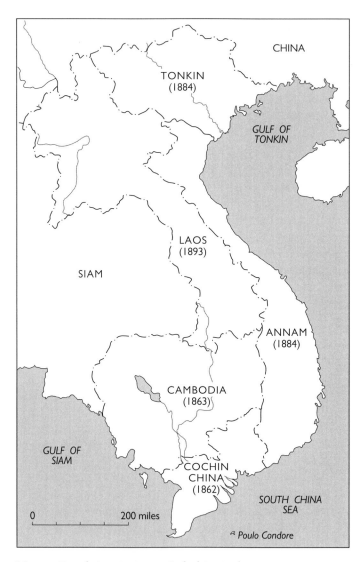

Map 1. French Acquisitions in Indochina in the
        Nineteenth Century

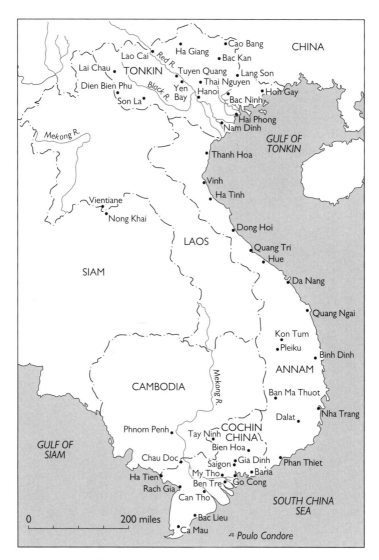

CHINA

Cao Bang
Ha Giang
Bac Kan
Lao Cai
Lang Son
Red R.
Tuyen Quang
Lai Chau
TONKIN
Thai Nguyen
Dien Bien Phu
Black R.
Yen
Bay
Hanoi
Hon Gay
Son La
Bac Ninh
Mekong R.
Hai Phong
Nam Dinh

*GULF OF
TONKIN*

Thanh Hoa

Vinh
Ha Tinh

Vientiane
Nong Khai

Dong Hoi

LAOS

Quang Tri
Hue

SIAM

Da Nang

Quang Ngai

Kon Tum
Pleiku
Binh Dinh

ANNAM

CAMBODIA

Mekong R.

Ban Ma Thuot

Dalat
Nha Trang

Phnom Penh
Tay Ninh
COCHIN
CHINA
Bien Hoa

*GULF OF
SIAM*

Chau Doc
Saigon
Gia Dinh
Phan Thiet
My Tho
Baria
Ha Tien
Ben Tre
Go Cong
Rach Gia
Can Tho

*SOUTH CHINA
SEA*

0   200 miles
Bac Lieu
Ca Mau
Poulo Condore

Map 2.   Colonial Vietnam

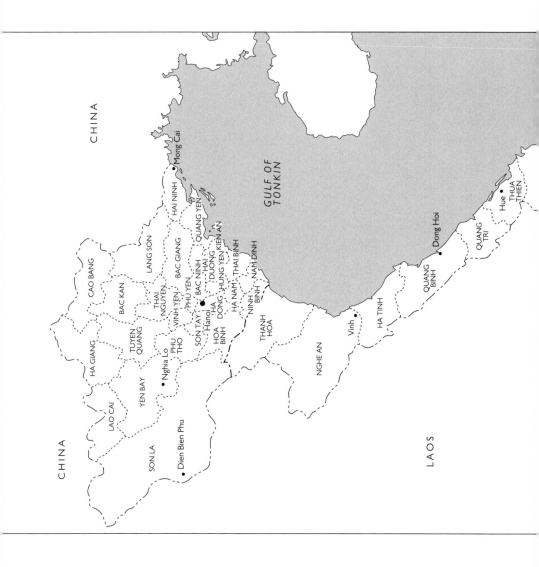

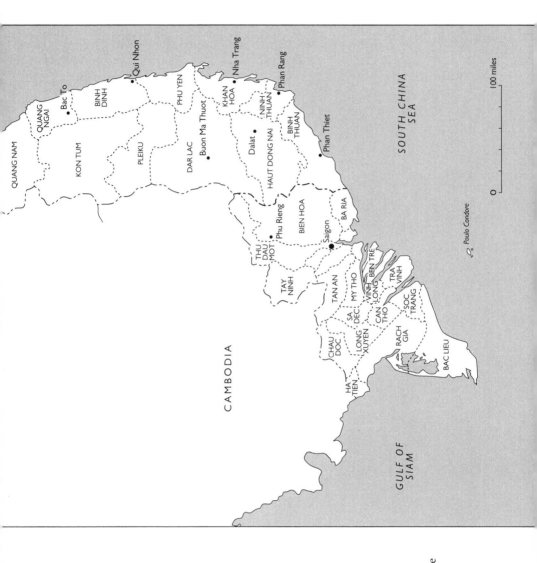

Map 3.
Indochinese
Provinces
in 1945

Acknowledgments

This book could not have been written without the financial assistance of an array of institutions and the intellectual and emotional support of numerous friends, colleagues, teachers, and family members. My language training was facilitated by grants from the Department of Education's Foreign Language Area Studies Fellowship Program, the Southeast Asia Summer Studies Institute, and the University of Hawaii. I carried out the initial archival research in France and Vietnam with financial support provided by the History Department and the Southeast Asia Program at Cornell University and the Mellon Foundation. Fellowships from the American Council on Learned Societies, the Doreen B. Townsend Center for the Humanities, and the Committee on Research of the University of California at Berkeley allowed time off from teaching and administrative duties in order to write and revise the manuscript. I am deeply grateful to Paul Strasburg and Gerry Thompson for graciously permitting me to continue work on the project while employed with Volunteers in Asia and the Council on International Educational Exchange.

This book originated as a research paper for a graduate seminar taught by Benedict Anderson at Cornell University, and I remain grateful to him for his encouragement over the years. The first draft was nurtured to completion by my original dissertation committee at Cornell—David Wyatt, Sherman Cochran, and the late Huynh Kim Khanh. I am especially indebted to Keith Taylor, a later addition to the dissertation committee, whose research and writing have inspired much of my own thinking about the history of Vietnam. Other teachers and scholars who have shaped the final form of this book in various ways include Sugata Bose, Ian Brown, Ralph Smith, Robert Taylor, Takashi Shiraishi, Daniel Hémery, Hy Van Luong, Neil Jamieson, and Hue Tam Ho Tai.

I owe a great deal to friends and colleagues from Cornell and elsewhere who contributed to the stimulating intellectual atmosphere in which the manuscript took shape. I thank Christoph Giebel, Shawn McHale, Micheline Lessard, Patricia Pelley, Bruce Lockhart, Eva-Lotta Hedman, Michael Montesano, Jojo Abinales, Christopher Kern, Chen Yong, Mary Callahan, Tony Nassar, Thaveeporn Vasavakul, Toni Phim, Shaun Malarney, Christopher Goscha, David Del Testa, Owen White, and Dana Sachs. Hans Schodder and Birgit Hussfeld deserve special mention for their exacting criticism, generous counsel, and unfailingly supportive comradeship. Finally, I thank my remarkably tolerant office mate, John Sidel, for his good humor and generous counsel.

Among the friends, sponsors, and colleagues who provided support and assistance to me in Vietnam, I especially wish to acknowledge Phan Quang Minh, Pham Quang Minh, Phan Huy Le, Nguyen Dinh Le, Pham Xanh, Le The Que, Vu The Thach, Vo Van Truc, Hoang Ngoc Hien, Phung Huu Phu, Nguyen Quan, Ho Son Dai, Jim Carlson, Peter Saidel, Mark Sidel, Steve Boswell, Vivienne Lowe, Jonathan Stromseth, and the staffs of the Trung Tam Luu Tru Quoc Gia, I [National Archives, no. 1], Thu Vien Quoc Gia [National Library], Thu Vien Khoa Hoc Xa Hoi [Social Science Library], Bao Tang Cach Mang [Revolution Museum], Bao Tang Nha Tu Hoa Lo [Hoa Lo Prison Museum], Bao Tang Nha Tu Con Dao [Con Dao Prison Museum], and Bao Tang Nha Tu Son La [Son La Prison Museum]. Thanks as well to Nguyen Cong Minh and Le Thi Kim Chi.

I am grateful to Randolph Starn and the participants in the Townsend Center Fellowship Group (1997–98), Thomas Metcalf and the participants in the Imperialism Working Group at UC Berkeley, Tyler Stovall and the participants in the Colonialism and Orientalism Reading Group at UC Santa Cruz, and Priya Joshi and Vashuda Dalmia for reading portions of the manuscript and providing thoughtful feedback. I have greatly appreciated the encouragement and advice that I received during the lengthy revision, submission, and publication process from my Berkeley colleagues: Frederic Wakeman Jr., David Keightley, Mary Berry, Andrew Barshay, Reginald Zelnik, Yeh Wen-hsin, Irwin Scheiner, Gene Irschick, Jon Gjerde, Martin Jay, John Connelly, Nancy Peluso, Aihwa Ong, Robert Reed, David Szanton, and Eric Crystal.

Robert Templer; my wife, Nguyen Nguyet Cam; and my father, Murray Zinoman, read drafts of various chapters and offered pointed and highly constructive criticism that improved the final manuscript in significant ways.

The manuscript has also benefited from the detailed comments, corrections, and suggestions made by Alexandra Sauvegrain and the three outside reviewers for the University of California Press: David Marr, Laura Ann Stoler, and Ken Pomerantz.

A special thanks as well to Sheila Levine, Juliane Brand, Dore Brown, and Peter Dreyer, my editors at the University of California Press.

My deepest debts are to my family and especially my parents, Murray Zinoman and Joy Zinoman, whose constant love and intense devotion to unconventional intellectual and creative pursuits have long been my inspiration.

Finally, I thank my son, Alexander, and my wife, Nguyen Nguyet Cam—objects of my constant love and intense devotion.

Abbreviations

AAPCI	*Les Associations anti-françaises et la propagande communiste en Indochine*
AOM	Centre des Archives d'Outre-Mer, Aix-en-Provence
DRV	Democratic Republic of Vietnam
ICP	Indochinese Communist Party
SLOTFOM	Service de liaison des originaires des territoires français d'Outre-Mer
TTLT	Trung Tam Luu Tru Quoc Gia–1 [National Archives Center, No. 1], Hanoi
VNQDD	Viet Nam Quoc Dan Dang: Vietnamese Nationalist Party

Introduction

Just as idealized accounts of the Long March have played an important role in the political culture of Chinese communism, prison narratives from the French colonial era figure prominently in the Vietnamese Communist Party's official account of its rise to power.[1] After the foundation of the Democratic Republic of Vietnam (DRV) in 1954, scores of Party leaders published revolutionary memoirs (*hoi ky cach mang*) recounting their roles in the "transformation of imperialist jails into revolutionary schools" during the interwar years.[2] Throughout the 1960s, 1970s, and 1980s state publishing houses collected and anthologized a huge body of communist prison poetry from the colonial era, much of which was eventually integrated into

1. David Marr draws this comparison in *Vietnamese Tradition on Trial, 1920–1945* (Berkeley and Los Angeles, 1981), 308. Between 1930 and 1951, the Party was known as the Indochinese Communist Party (ICP). From 1951 to 1976, it was called the Vietnamese Workers' Party (VWP). Since 1976, it has been known as the Vietnamese Communist Party (VCP).

2. See, e.g., Nguyen Tao, *Trong Nguc Toi Hoa Lo* [In the Dark Prison, Hoa Lo] (Hanoi, 1959); Tran Dang Ninh, *Hai Lan Vuot Nguc* [Two Prison Escapes] (Hanoi, 1970); Tran Cung, "Tu Con Dao Tro Ve (hoi ky)" [Return from Poulo Condore (memoirs)], *Nghien Cuu Lich Su* 134, no. 9 (1970): 18–26; Bui Cong Trung, "O Con Dao" [In Con Dao], in *Len Duong Thang Loi* [On the Road to Victory] (Hanoi, 1960); Ly Thi Chung, "Nguoi Phu Nu Cong San Dau Tien O Hoa Lo" [The First Female Communist in Hoa Lo], in *Mua Thu Cach Mang* [Revolutionary Autumn] (Hanoi, 1985); Ha Phu Huong, "O Nha Tu Lao Bao" [In Lao Bao Prison], *Tap Chi Cua Viet* 3 (1990): 34–37. The following (some reprints) can be found in Bao Tang Cach Mang Vietnam and Bao Tang Son La, *Suoi Reo Nam Ay* [The Bubbling Spring That Year] (Hanoi: Van Hoa–Thong Tin, 1993); Dang Viet Chau, "Nguc Son La, 1935–1936" [Son La Prison, 1935–1936]; Van Tien Dung, "Niem Tin la Suc Manh" [Belief Is Strength]; Xuan Thuy, "Suoi Reo Nam Ay" [The Bubbling Spring That Year]; and Nguyen Van Tu, "Toi Lam Cau Doi Tet O Nha Tu Son La" [I Make Rhyming Couplets in Son La Prison].

school curriculums.[3] In addition, the sites of the most notorious Indochinese prisons—the Son La and Poulo Condore penitentiaries and the Hanoi Central Prison—were made over into national museums commemorating the "indomitable struggles" of jailed communists during the 1930s and 1940s.[4] The publication of Ho Chi Minh's colonial-era prison diary, Nhat Ky Trong Tu, in 1960 and its extensive distribution domestically and internationally during the following three decades may be seen as the most far-reaching and high-profile component of the same official project.[5]

The fact that the dissemination of communist prison narratives from the colonial era has long been part of an official propaganda campaign designed to project a heroic image of the founding fathers of the Indochinese Communist Party (ICP) should not obscure the crucial historical role of the colonial prison in the rise of Vietnamese communism. Following the mass incarceration of communists during the repression of an abrupt upsurge of anticolonial activism in 1930–31, the Indochinese prison system provided a curiously stable environment for the reconstitution and expansion of the ICP. For the remainder of the decade, jailed communists established ICP cells and mutual aid associations, organized political education

3. See, e.g., the lengthy chapters on prison poetry in influential anthologies such as Xo-Viet Nghe-Tinh Qua Mot So Tho Van [The Nghe-Tinh Soviets Through Prose And Poetry], ed. Le Trong Khanh and Le Anh Tra (Hanoi, 1959), and Van Tho Cach Mang Viet Nam Dau The Ky XX (1900–1925) [Vietnamese Revolutionary Prose and Poetry from the Early Twentieth Century, 1900–1925], ed. Dang Thai Mai (Hanoi, 1974). In Tho Ca Cach Mang, 1925–1945 [Revolutionary Poetry, 1925–1945], ed. Vien Van Hoc (Hanoi, 1973), a large collection of revolutionary poetry compiled by the Institute of Literature in 1973, half of the 300 poems were written in or about colonial prisons. The Literature Publishing House's 600-page annotated collection of revolutionary verse, Tho Van Cach Mang, 1930–1945 [Revolutionary Prose and Poetry, 1930–1945], ed. Hoang Dung (Hanoi, 1980), and the Social Science Institute's 750-page anthology of colonial-era Vietnamese poetry, Tong Tap Van Hoc Viet Nam, Tap 35 [Anthology of Vietnamese Literature, vol. 35], ed. Hoi Dong Bien Tap, Uy Ban Khoa Hoc Xa Hoi (Ho Chi Minh City, 1985), also devote roughly a third of their space to prison poetry.

4. The Son La and Poulo Condore penitentiaries have both been turned into museums. Plaques mark the sites where colonial prisons once stood at Lao Bao and Kon Tum. In 1996, the museum of the Hanoi Central Prison (known to most Americans as the Hanoi Hilton) opened to the public. See John Rogers, "Hanoi Hilton Heads into History Books," Reuters News Service, November 25, 1994.

5. For a discussion of the checkered publishing history of Nhat Ky Trong Tu, including the suppression of almost two dozen poems in the original manuscript, see Phan Van Cac, "Tu Ban Dich Nam 1960 Den Ban Dich Bo Sung Va Chinh Ly Nam 1983" [From the 1960 Translation to the Supplemented and Corrected Translation of 1983], in Suy Nghi Moi Ve Nhat Ky Trong Tu [New Reflections on the Prison Diary], ed. Nguyen Hue Chi (Hanoi, 1990).

and training programs, and agitated unceasingly against brutal treatment, bad food, and poor sanitary conditions. Not only were communist inmates able to wrest a measure of control over the institutions in which they were held from their captors, but they contributed decisively to the regeneration of the revolutionary movement in the wider community. Throughout the 1930s, French officials uncovered evidence that strategic intelligence and directives were emanating from colonial prisons. In some localities, ICP cells formed in provincial prisons were the first organized manifestation of communist power. Moreover, the gradual seepage of released, escaped, and amnestied activists into civilian society sustained and invigorated the revolutionary movement, providing it with a hardened core of disciplined, experienced, and fiercely loyal cadres skilled in the arts of underground organization.

Nevertheless, in Western historical accounts of the rise of Vietnamese communism, the significance of the era of mass imprisonment during the first half of the 1930s is overshadowed by the movement's early development in Canton between 1925 and 1930, its rapid growth during the Popular Front era in France between 1936 and 1939, and its reorganization under Ho Chi Minh's leadership during World War II.[6] It may be that the capacity of prison walls to convey an illusion of isolation and separation from the wider community has discouraged historical investigations of political developments within colonial prisons. However, a failure to follow Party members into prison during the first half of the 1930s runs the risk of overlooking a crucial stage in the development of Vietnamese communism. There is evidence that the experience of mass imprisonment enhanced the Party's Leninist orientation by highlighting the values of organizational hierarchy, secrecy, and centralization. Moreover, the shared predicament of incarceration generated bonds of loyalty among Vietnamese communists that contributed to the long-term cohesion of the Party at the highest levels.[7] It is no coincidence that colonial-era prison credentials

6. See, e.g., William Duiker, *The Communist Road to Power in Vietnam* (Boulder, Colo., 1996), and Huynh Kim Khanh, *Vietnamese Communism, 1925–1945* (Ithaca, N.Y., 1982).

7. "A key feature of Vietnamese Marxism-Leninism which contributed greatly to the success of the revolution is the unity of the Party and the continuity of its leadership. Large-scale purges are conspicuously absent in the history of the Vietnamese Party," Sean Kelly and Colin Mackerras observe ("The Application of Marxism-Leninism to Vietnam," in *Marxism in Asia*, ed. Colin Mackerras and Nick Knight [New York, 1985], 202–31).

remained an important prerequisite for advancement into the Party's highest echelons well into the postcolonial era.[8]

Even less widely acknowledged is the colonial prison's contribution to the rise of Vietnamese nationalism.[9] During the late colonial era, the prison was an intensely unpopular symbol of state power, which anticolonial activists of various political persuasions exploited successfully to mobilize popular support for their efforts. In addition, the dense patterning of the prison system in Tonkin, Annam, and Cochin China—the three Indochinese territories dominated by ethnic Vietnamese populations—and the constant circulation of inmates within them helped to reify the imagined parameters of a new national space.[10] By subjecting hundreds of thousands of colonial subjects with diverse regional backgrounds, social identities, and political commitments to the same terrifying ordeal, the prison system encouraged fraternal affinities and a sense of shared predicament that contributed to the formation of a national community.[11]

This study examines the subversive transmutation of the Indochinese prison system from a colonial institution, founded to quell political dissent and maintain law and order, into a site that nurtured the growth of communism, nationalism, and anticolonial resistance. While my account is based on the writings of colonial officials and jailed political activists, I do not simply accept their explanations for this extraordinary institutional

8. On May 1, 1960, in a speech commemorating the thirtieth anniversary of the founding of the ICP, Ho Chi Minh declared that the thirty-one current members of the Party Central Committee had been imprisoned in French colonial jails, for a cumulative total of 222 years. See Ho Chi Minh, "Khai Mac Le Ky Niem 30 Nam Ngay Thanh Lap Dang Toi Tai Ha Noi" [Commemoration of the Thirtieth Anniversary of the Establishment of My Party in Hanoi], *Nhan Dan*, May 1, 1960, reprinted in the introduction to *Nhung Nguoi Cong San* [The Communists] (Ho Chi Minh City, 1977). On the importance of jail credentials for Party leaders, see Bui Tin, *Following Ho Chi Minh: Memoirs of a North Vietnamese Colonel* (Honolulu, 1995), 132, 150.

9. A recent allusion to the role of the colonial prison in the rise of Vietnamese nationalism may be found in David Marr, *Vietnam 1945: The Quest for Power* (Berkeley and Los Angeles, 1995), 193.

10. My argument regarding the effects of the prison system on the rise of national consciousness parallels the examination of the significance of maps, transportation networks, and travel writing in the same process of political identity formation by Christopher E. Goscha in *Vietnam or Indochina? Contesting Conceptions of Space in Vietnamese Nationalism, 1887–1954* (Copenhagen, 1995).

11. My understanding of the growth of nationalism in Vietnam owes much to Benedict Anderson's *Imagined Communities: Reflections on the Origins and Spread of Nationalism* (London, 1991).

transformation. For French officials, the metamorphosis of the Indochinese prison into what they frequently referred to as a "school for communism" resulted from the temporary inability of the colonial juridical system to cope administratively with a huge influx of political activists at the start of the 1930s. Communist writers, on the other hand, emphasize the unyielding courage, ingenuity, and endurance of jailed Party members. Although it acknowledges the partial validity of both explanations, this study highlights the significance of certain quasi-structural features of the colonial prison that facilitated its appropriation by the anticolonial movement: communal architecture, haphazard classification systems, murderous forced labor regimes, poorly trained and ethnically divided surveillance staffs, and inadequate health care, provisioning, and sanitation. Together, these features defined a distinct form of colonial institutional power and provided the parameters within which Vietnamese inmates devised and carried out diverse strategies of resistance.

In chapters 1, 2, and 3, I trace the history of these idiosyncratic institutional features of the colonial prison and locate their origins in the exigencies of imperial conquest, the peculiarly racist and tightfisted character of the colonial state, and the continuing influence of the precolonial Sino-Vietnamese penal tradition on colonial punishment. Chapter 4 describes the ways in which inmates adapted creatively to colonial prison conditions on a daily basis and how the experience of incarceration contributed to the modernization of the social and political consciousness of segments of the prison population. In chapters 5 and 6, I suggest that the high frequency of episodes of collective resistance among prisoners during the late nineteenth and early twentieth centuries may be explained with reference to the same constellation of features exhibited by the institution since its foundation, features that eventually facilitated the sustained political struggles in colonial prisons during the 1930s. Finally, chapters 7, 8, and 9 chart the history and significance of these struggles, paying close attention to the coordinated resistance movements spearheaded by communist prisoners during the early 1930s and the highly politicized campaigns for prison reform led by both communist and noncommunist activists later in the decade.

In addition to illuminating the complex relationship between Vietnamese anticolonialism, communism, and nationalism and the Indochinese prison system, this study also contributes to a growing body of scholarly literature about the history of colonial power. Its approach, however, differs from much recent work in the field. Most scholars working within the burgeoning subdiscipline of empire studies take colonial discourse as their primary object of analysis.[12] Such an approach sheds light on the conceptual underpinnings of the imperial project, but it is less illuminating about the impact of colonial regimes of power over the societies that they ruled, or the myriad ways in which colonized subjects experienced and responded to the structures of colonial domination. In contrast, this study seeks to understand the effects of colonialism by reconstructing specific patterns of institutional practice and examining their social and political consequences within the society in which they were deployed. This effort is animated by a conviction that the historical significance of the imperial project may best be understood through an examination of how colonial power functioned in practice, rather than of the ways in which officials represented their actions and motives in discursive form.

Moreover, the picture of French colonialism that emerges from my examination of the Indochinese prison system does not square with prevailing images conveyed in recent scholarship. In contrast to the idea that colonies were "laboratories of modernity," where disciplinary power and the latest techniques of social engineering could be deployed unhindered by the cumbersome political constraints found in France itself, for instance, my research points to the absence of modernist impulses in key sectors of the imperial project.[13] While certain kinds of colonial bureaucrats—architects and urban planners, for example—may well have experimented with new techniques of environmental regulation and social control, colonial prison officials introduced no such innovations and ignored many of the putatively modern methods of prison administration that had been developed in Europe and the United States during the nineteenth century.[14] As

12. Ann Laura Stoler and Frederick Cooper refer to this as the "sharp discursive turn in colonial studies." See "Between Metropole and Colony: Rethinking a Research Agenda," in *Tensions of Empire: Colonial Cultures in a Bourgeois World,* ed. Frederick Cooper and Ann Laura Stoler (Berkeley and Los Angeles, 1997), 18.

13. For treatments of French colonies as "laboratories of modernity," see Paul Rabinow, *French Modern: Norms and Forms of the Social Environment* (Chicago, 1989), and Gwendolyn Wright, *The Politics of Design in French Colonial Urbanism* (Chicago, 1991).

14. My argument about the colonial state in Indochina follows Megan Vaughan's description of the colonial state in Africa: "Colonial states were hardly 'modern states' for much of their short existence, and therefore they relied, especially in their early histories, on a large measure of 'repressive' power. Only in some cases, and then only in the later colonial period, and in their liberal welfarist [*sic*] functions, did they create systems of surveillance and control common in Europe." Megan Vaughan, *Curing Their Ills: Colonial Power and African Illness* (Stanford, Calif., 1991), 10.

Indochinese activists pointed out repeatedly in their campaigns for prison reform, the crude structure and chaotic functioning of the colonial prison recalled the brutality and squalor of the eighteenth-century Bastille more closely than the strict regimentation of the nineteenth-century Euro-American penitentiary.

The coexistence of modern and premodern orientations within different segments of the imperial project undermines recent efforts, animated largely by the pioneering work of Michel Foucault, to locate in colonial environments a system of power relations marked by the pervasive circulation of disciplinary practices throughout the social body.[15] Rather, the simultaneous combination of different modes of power in French Indochina recalls Partha Chatterjee's characterization of the hybridity of power in colonial and postcolonial societies:

> When one looks at the regimes of power in the so-called backward countries of the world today, not only does the dominance of the characteristically "modern" modes of exercise of power seem limited and qualified by the persistence of older modes, but by the fact of their combination in a particular state formation, it seems to open up at the same time an entirely new range of possibilities for the ruling classes to exercise their domination.[16]

While this study supports this emphasis on the complexity of colonial "regimes of power," it does not follow Chatterjee's assertion that the qualitative heterogeneity of colonial power served the hegemonic project of the state or the ruling classes. Indeed, it argues just the opposite. It was the antiquated and ill-disciplined aspects of the colonial prison that facilitated its transformation into an instrument of anticolonial resistance. Murderous forced labor regimes and inadequate provisioning and medical care provoked prisoner rebellions and public outrage against the colonial state that swelled the ranks of the revolutionary movement. Communal architecture coupled with haphazard systems of classification, segregation, and surveillance encouraged intercourse and fraternal bonding among diverse categories of inmates, which, in turn, contributed to the development of modern anticolonial nationalism. Moreover, the distance between the French

15. Michael Salman, "Nothing Without Labor: Penology, Discipline and Independence in the Philippines under United States Rule," in *Discrepant Histories: Translocal Essays on Filipino Cultures*, ed. Vicente L. Rafael (Philadelphia, 1995), 113–32; Timothy Mitchell, *Colonising Egypt* (1988; reprint, Berkeley and Los Angeles, 1991).

16. Partha Chatterjee, "More on Modes of Power and the Peasantry," in *Selected Subaltern Studies*, ed. Ranajit Guha and Gayatri Spivak (New York, 1988), 390.

colonial state's professed commitment to modernization and republican values, on the one hand, and the old-fashioned brutality, squalor, and corruption of the colonial prison system, on the other, highlighted a contradiction within the imperial project that anticolonial activists were quick to exploit.[17] In this way, the ill-disciplined colonial prison gave rise to forces that contributed decisively to the success of the anticolonial project.

SOURCES ON THE COLONIAL PRISON

This study of prisons and imprisonment in colonial Vietnam relies on four kinds of sources, each of which possesses specific strengths and weaknesses as a tool for historical interpretation. The colonial archives contain a huge body of official documentary material, including administrative reports, inspection records, external investigations, interrogation transcripts, architectural plans, and prisoner and personnel files. Such documents are indispensable for understanding the inner workings of the colonial prison, but they suffer from various shortcomings, characteristic of official sources more generally. For example, institutional records tend to reflect the exclusive concerns of upper-level officials, rather than the perspectives of subaltern functionaries, inmates and their families, or society at large. As a result, they can disclose only a one-dimensional, top-down perspective on the colonial prison's complex social history. In addition, administrative reports are shaped by the fact that officials typically prepare them for review and assessment by their superiors. Hence, in addition to the biases of perspective inherent to some degree in all historical sources, their content may reflect bureaucratic and professional imperatives rather than honest appraisals of real historical conditions. Also important is the fact that the existing archive of Indochinese prison administration does not contain equally rich documentation for all periods of the colonial era. As opposed to the voluminous material available for the 1920s and 1930s, data from the nineteenth and early twentieth centuries are spotty and uneven. A glaring example of such inconsistency may be found in the annual statistical compilations published by the colonial state, which provide comprehensive Indochina-wide figures on the workings of the penal and justice systems only for the 1920s and 1930s.[18] Although an image of the prison

17. On the prominence of Republican ideals in the French colonial project, see Alice L. Conklin, *A Mission to Civilize: The Republican Idea of Empire in France and West Africa, 1895–1930* (Stanford, Calif., 1997).
18. Gouvernement général de l'Indochine, *Annuaire statistique de l'Indochine* (Hanoi), 1913–42.

system during the nineteenth and early twentieth centuries may be pieced together from scattered records and reports, the picture that emerges from that era remains blurry and impressionistic.

Contemporary newspaper coverage is a valuable unofficial source of information, offering the observations of outside observers and insights into popular attitudes to the colonial prison not found in the administrative record. However, the relatively late development of widely distributed indigenous printed media in Indochina and the localized ebb and flow of colonial censorship meant that the attention devoted to the prison system in the colonial press varied tremendously over time and space. Prior to the late 1920s, only the French-language press in the directly ruled colony of Cochin China covered colonial prisons, information about which barely figured in the more tightly controlled newspapers published in the indirectly ruled protectorates of Annam and Tonkin. As with the administrative record, media reports are richest during the late 1930s, a period when the Popular Front government in France eased censorship in the colonies and the abysmal state of Indochinese prison conditions emerged as a major story in both the French- and Vietnamese-language press. Media coverage of the prison system also expanded in the 1930s owing to the rise in Indochina of muck-raking investigative journalism, exemplified by Jean-Claude Demariaux's *Les Secrets des îles Poulo-Condore: Le Grand Bagne indochinois*, a vivid exposé of the famous island penitentiary based on several extended trips that the author undertook there during the 1930s.[19] Demariaux commits common journalistic sins—hyperbole and uncomplicated interpretation—but cross-checking corroborates much of his account. The same goes for *Indochine S.O.S.* by Andrée Viollis (Andrée Françoise Caroline d'Ardenne de Tizac), which includes a detailed investigation of colonial prison conditions in the early 1930s, and "Tet Cua Tu Dan Ba" ("Tet for Female Prisoners"), an excellent Vietnamese example of the new journalism, written in 1939 by the novelist Nguyen Hong.[20]

A third source is the vast body of first-person accounts of colonial-era political imprisonment produced in northern Vietnam after the formal establishment of the DRV in 1954. While these communist prison memoirs

---

19. Jean-Claude Demariaux, *Les Secrets des îles Poulo-Condore: Le Grand Bagne indochinois* (Paris, 1956).

20. Andrée Viollis, *Indochine S.O.S* (1935; reprint, Paris, 1949); Nguyen Hong, "Tet Cua Tu Dan Ba," *Tieu Thuyet Thu Bay* [Saturday Novel] 246 (Spring 1939), reprinted in *Tuyen Tap Nguyen Hong, Tap I* [Collected Works of Nguyen Hong, vol. 1], ed. Le Khanh (Hanoi, 1995), 143–57.

appear to offer possibilities for the recovery of an array of inmate perspectives, the fact that most were written as part an official project to celebrate the heroic early struggles and sacrifices of the Communist Party means that they typically provide more insight into the political culture and imperatives of the postcolonial state than into the history of the colonial prison. The same goes for a handful of quasi-academic histories of the colonial prison produced in postcolonial northern Vietnam, which rely almost exclusively on communist prison memoirs for their empirical data.[21]

Despite the interpretive pitfalls posed by postcolonial prison memoirs, several works within the genre deserve attention because of their unusual precision or originality. A good example is the series of contemplative accounts of colonial-era prison life by the brilliant journalist, revolutionary activist, and historian Tran Huy Lieu, written from Viet Minh liberated zones in the 1950s.[22] Lieu's recollections are all the more valuable in that Party intellectuals enjoyed a limited freedom to write expressively during this era. Another worthwhile postcolonial memoir is Nguyen Hai Ham's *Tu Yen Bay Den Con Lon, 1930–1945* (From Yen Bay to Poulo Condore, 1930–1945), published in Saigon in 1970.[23] Reflecting his allegiance to the Vietnamese Nationalist Party, or Viet Nam Quoc Dan Dang (VNQDD), Ham's account is strongly colored by anticommunism, but it remains useful for its intimate tone and close attention to detail.

The most valuable "inside" information on colonial prisons and prisoner society may, however, be found in memoirs published by former political prisoners immediately following their release from jail during the late 1920s and 1930s. One of the earliest and most compelling examples, Phan Van Hum's *Ngoi Tu Kham Lon* (Sitting in the Big Jail), was serialized

21. See, e.g., Ban Nghien Cuu Lich Su Dang Dac Khu Vung Tau—Con Dao, *Nha Tu Con Dao, 1862–1945* [Con Dao Penitentiary, 1862–1945] (Hanoi, 1987); Vien Mac-Lenin and Vien Lich Su Dang, *Nguc Son La: Truong Hoc Dau Tranh Cach Mang* [Son La Prison, the School of Revolutionary Struggle] (Hanoi, 1992); Tinh Uy Dak Lak and Vien Lich Su Dang, *Lich Su Nha Day Buon Ma Thuot, 1930–1945* [History of Buon Ma Thuot Penitentiary] (Hanoi, 1991); and So Van Hoa Thong Tin Ha Noi and Vien Lich Su Dang, *Dau Tranh Cua Cac Chien Si Yeu Nuoc Va Cach Mang Tai Nha Tu Hoa Lo* [The Struggle of Patriotic and Revolutionary Fighters in Hoa Lo Prison] (Hanoi, 1994).

22. These accounts were recently collected in *Tran Huy Lieu: Hoi Ky* [Tran Huy Lieu: Memoirs] (Hanoi, 1991). See "Tren Dao Hon Cau" [On Hon Cau], 99–126; "Xuan Hong" [Pink Spring], 127–33; "Tinh Trong Nguc Toi" [Love in the Dark Prison], 134–41; "Phan Dau De Tro Nen Mot Dang Vien Cong San" [Striving to Become a Communist Party Member], 155–67; "Duoi Ham Son La" [In the Son La Hole], 252–76; and "Xuan No Trong Tu" [Spring Blooms in Prison], 222–51.

23. Nguyen Hai Ham, *Tu Yen Bay Den Con Lon, 1930–1945* (Saigon, 1970).

in the Saigon periodical *Than Chung* (Morning Bell) immediately follow-ing the author's release from the Saigon Central Prison in 1929.[24] Another especially valuable text is Huynh Thuc Khang's *Thi Tu Tung Thoai* (Prison Verse), which provides a meticulous eyewitness description of the Poulo Condore Penitentiary between 1908 and 1921.[25]

Colonial-era prison memoirs are valuable sources for several reasons. Because they tended to be written soon after the events they describe, they are less subject to unintentional inaccuracies than memoirs produced decades later. Unlike colonial documents or communist genre works, they were produced more or less free from state control. As opposed to post-colonial communist memoirs, which focus almost exclusively on political education and resistance behind bars, colonial-era memoirs pay close at-tention to the quotidian details of prison life, an emphasis reflecting the in-fluence of *phong su*, a genre of realist reportage that became popular in In-dochina during the 1930s. Proponents of *phong su* advocated a method of participant observation in which the writer would infiltrate and describe a subaltern social milieu while simultaneously providing an intensely per-sonal account of going undercover.[26] The influence of the genre on Phan Van Hum is apparent early in the introduction to *Ngoi Tu Kham Lon:*

> Recently, a friend challenged the value of this project. But I disagree. The truth as seen through my eyes, heard through my ears, and felt by my conscience is a truth worth writing about. I invite readers to form their own opinions about the truth placed on exhibit here. . . . I ob-served only one prison, and although I lived with the other prisoners, I really only knew my own thoughts. I shall refer to myself, therefore, so as to fill in those unknowable spaces, the internal worlds of others.[27]

The value of colonial-era prison memoirs as historical sources is also heightened by the diverse political commitments of their authors. Mem-bers of the VNQDD—Nhuong Tong, Nguyen Duc Chinh, and Tran Van Que, for example—were especially fastidious recorders of prison life.[28] When Phan Van Hum penned his idiosyncratic prison memoir, his political sympathies lay with a mysterious anticolonial sect known as the Nguyen

---

24. Phan Van Hum, *Ngoi Tu Kham Lon* (1929; reprint, Saigon, 1957).
25. Huynh Thuc Khang, *Thi Tu Tung Thoai* (Hue, 1939).
26. See Greg Lockhart, "First Person Narratives from the 1930s," in *The Light of the Capital: Three Modern Vietnamese Classics,* ed. id. (Kuala Lumpur, 1996), 1–49.
27. Phan Van Hum, *Ngoi Tu Kham Lon,* 15.
28. Nhuong Tong, *Doi Trong Nguc* [Life in Prison] (Hanoi, 1935); Tran Van Que, *Con-Lon Quan-Dao Truoc Ngay, 9–3–1945* [The Con Lon Archipelago before March 9, 1945] (Saigon, 1961); Nguyen Duc Chinh, *Thu Con Lon* [Con Lon Let-ters] (Hanoi, 1937).

An Ninh Secret Society. In 1933, an unusually detailed account, *Cai Than Tu Toi* (My Life as a Prisoner), was published by Hoang Minh Dau, a middle-class southerner of indeterminate political orientation.[29] Prior to the mass production of officially commissioned prison narratives in the 1950s and 1960s, prominent communists (or, in some cases, future communists) such as Hai Trieu, Tran Huy Lieu, Ton Quang Phiet, and Le Van Hien also produced unconventional, highly personal accounts.[30] It is on these diverse, idiosyncratic, and contemporaneous sources, above all, that attempts to reconstruct the internal world of the colonial prison in Indochina must be based.

29. Hoang Minh Dau, *Cai Than Tu Toi* (Saigon, 1933).
30. See Hai Trieu, "Su Thuc Trong Tu" [Truth in Prison], *Bao Doi Moi* [New Life], March 24, 1935; Tran Huy Lieu, "Con Lon Ky Su" [Con Lon Memoir], serialized in the newspaper *Anh Sang*, nos. 24–52 (May 4–October 26, 1935), reprinted in *Tran Huy Lieu: Hoi Ky*, 417–50; Ton Quang Phiet, *Mot Ngay Ngan Thu (Lan Thu Nhat O Nha Nguc)* [The Eternal Day (My First Time in Prison)] (Hue, 1935); and Le Van Hien, *Nguc Kontum* [Kontum Jail] (1938; reprint, Hanoi, 1958).

1 The Origins of the Ill-Disciplined Prison

Most of our prisons in Indochina include only one room, in which all detainees, both the accused and the convicted, are held together indiscriminately. From a moral point of view, such cohabitation gives rise to numerous regrettable consequences. Legally, it is inexcusable. During my visit, I was told that the administration was simply unable to finance the segregation of prisoners by category. . . . I also noted that the insufficiency of surveillance and the carelessness with which the prison registers are kept make it impossible to acquire a comprehensive understanding of the true situation of the prison population.

Inspector of the Administrative and Financial Services of the Ministry of the Navy and Colonies, October 28, 1885[1]

The detainees have, for a long time, been involved in abusive practices that cannot be stamped out with occasional punishments. Most notably, the rules of silence and prohibitions against gambling and opium are not observed. During the night I have visited the *bagne* and overheard conversations between guards and inmates coming from the wards. Searching guards returning from corvée, I found lumps of opium hidden in their belts. Indeed, most of the guards are drunkards and opium addicts who are, with rare exceptions, involved in various forms of collusion with the inmates. The degree of corruption is so extensive and the number of negative elements so large that it seems foolish to attempt a moral and material reorganization of the penitentiary.

Director of the Poulo Condore Penitentiary, March 1, 1910[2]

These detailed observations apply to all the prisons that I have visited in Indochina: a chronic disorder in bookkeeping, an ignorance or disregard of the most elementary administrative rules, the confinement together of detainees from all categories, minors included, without any observation of legal prescriptions for

---

1. AOM, H Colonies, 2026, Rapport sur le Service pénitenciaire en Cochinchine, August 28, 1885.
2. AOM, Indochine, Gouvernement général, 4248, Régime pénitenciaire, M. Cudenet, Administrateur des Services civils, Directeur des îles et du pénitencier de Poulo Condore, à Monsieur le Lieutenant-gouverneur de la Cochinchine, March 1, 1910.

each order of penalty. Given the extent of such practices, the regulations are little more than a façade.

Inspector of the Ministry of Colonies, January 30, 1932[3]

The establishment of a colonial prison system in French Indochina during the nineteenth century coincided with the emergence of the modern penitentiary in Europe and the United States. Unlike eighteenth-century prisons, which were largely custodial, modern Western penitentiaries endeavored to modify inmate behavior through a series of coercive and corrective practices that historians of modern punishment, following Michel Foucault, commonly refer to as disciplinary power.[4] As Michael Ignatieff puts it, the modern penitentiary embodied the notion of "confinement as a coercive education . . . the idea of recasting the character of the deviant by means of discipline."[5]

Although the structure and functioning of nineteenth-century penitentiaries varied over time and space, the indispensable principle of discipline gave modern carceral practice a number of core features.[6] First, because it

3. AOM, Indochine, Affaires politiques, 1728, Rapport fait par M. Le Gregam, Inspecteur des colonies, sur la Maison centrale de Saigon, January 30, 1932, 1.

4. During an interview in 1975, Foucault said: "My hypothesis is that the prison was linked from its beginning to a project for the transformation of individuals. People tend to suppose that the prison was a kind of refuse-dump for criminals, a dump whose advantages became apparent during use, giving rise to the conviction that the prisons must be reformed and made into a means of transforming individuals. But this is not true: such texts, programmes and statements of intention were there from the beginning. The prison was meant to be an instrument comparable with—and no less perfect than—the school, the barracks, or the hospital, acting with precision upon individual subjects." "Prison Talk," in *Power/Knowledge: Selected Interviews and Other Writings, 1972–1977*, ed. Colin Gordon (New York, 1980), 40–41.

5. Michael Ignatieff, *A Just Measure of Pain: The Penitentiary in the Industrial Revolution, 1750–1850* (New York, 1978), 11. In *The Promise of Punishment: Prisons in Nineteenth-Century France* (Princeton, N.J., 1982), 48, Patricia O'Brien makes a similar argument with reference to the penitentiary in nineteenth-century France: "Another organizing principle of the modern penitentiary was the concept of rehabilitation. The new nineteenth-century prisons promised the elimination of crime through the moral reformation of criminals. Deprivation of liberty was to serve the double role of deterrent and corrective. Through an ordered and disciplined life in prison, the inmate was expected to internalize the dominant social values and to carry them out with him into society." On the role of "utopian" and "rehabilitative" impulses in the development of the American penitentiary, see David Rothman, *The Discovery of the Asylum: Social Order and Disorder in the New Republic* (Boston, 1971), 79–109.

6. The most elaborate discussion of these features can be found in Michel Foucault, *Discipline and Punish: The Birth of the Prison*, trans. Alan Sheridan (New York, 1979), 135–230.

aspired to maintain a radically continuous surveillance, the penitentiary employed an architecture that distributed prisoners in space so as to increase their visibility.[7] Second, rather than targeting the inmate's body as the site of penal intervention, it attempted to transform his or her behavior or character through the regimentation of activity and mandatory labor.[8] Third, to ensure physical well-being and to sever the inmate from potentially "unhealthy" external influences, the penitentiary introduced the concept of "total care"—supplying the prisoner with food, clothing, medicine, instruction, and religion.[9] And, fourth, the penitentiary gave rise to systems of behavioral accountancy, manifest in the proliferation of reports and dossiers, as well as in the gradual hegemony of social-scientific "experts" (penologists, criminologists, psychologists) over the management of punishment.[10] These disciplinary techniques never succeeded in completely replacing older forms of incarceration, but they made significant inroads in both Europe and the United States during the nineteenth

7. The most famous exponent of architecture as a reformative force was Jeremy Bentham, whose utopian vision of the perfectly ordered prison, *Penitentiary Panoptican*, was published in 1791. Bentham wrote: "Morals reformed—health preserved—industry invigorated—instruction diffused—public burthens lighted—economy seated as if it were upon a rock—the gordian knot of the Poor law not cut but untied—all by a simple idea in architecture" (quoted in Ignatieff, *Just Measure of Pain*, 112). See also Robin Evans, *The Fabrication of Virtue: English Prison Architecture, 1750–1840* (Cambridge, 1982). For another extensive discussion of architecture's role in the disciplinary penal institution, see Foucault, *Discipline and Punish*, 141–48, 170–76.

8. An especially detailed account of the history of the uses of prison labor in France is Jacques-Guy Petit, *Ces peines obscures: La Prison pénale en France, 1780–1875* (Paris, 1990), 377–418. See also U. R. Q. Henriques, "The Rise and Decline of a Separate System of Prison Discipline," *Past and Present* 54 (1972); Dario Melossi and Massimo Pavarini, *The Prison and the Factory: Origins of the Penitentiary System* (Totowa, N.J.: 1981); John A. Conley, "Prisons, Production and Profit: Reconsidering the Importance of Prison Industries," *Journal of Social History* 14, no. 2 (1980): 257–75; Foucault, *Discipline and Punish*, 149–69; O'Brien, *Promise of Punishment*, 150–89; Rothman, *Discovery of the Asylum*, 102–5.

9. For the meaning of "total care" in the nineteenth-century French context, see O'Brien, *Promise of Punishment*, 42–48.

10. For the rise of the various systems of penal accountancy, see Foucault, *Discipline and Punish*, 184–93. The history of the professionalization of penal management is examined in Stanley Cohen, *Visions of Social Control: Crime, Punishment and Classification* (Oxford, 1985), and David Garland, *Punishment and Welfare: A History of Penal Strategies* (Aldershot, Hants, 1985).

century and, at very least, produced new standards by which prison officials measured their work.[11]

Given that France was at the center of the global penological revolution in the nineteenth century, one of the most remarkable aspects of the prison system in French Indochina was its utter failure to deploy disciplinary practices. Indochinese prisons never employed cellular or panoptic architecture and held the vast majority of inmates in undifferentiated, overcrowded, and unlit communal rooms. On questions of rehabilitation, behavioral modification, and the reformative effects of mandatory labor, the archive of colonial penal discourse is virtually silent. Instead of serving as a moralizing force within the institution, guards in colonial prisons were entangled in webs of collusive and coercive relations with inmates and frequently facilitated intercourse between prisoners and the outside world. Far from the body being eschewed as a target for punitive intervention, all accounts confirm that a brutal regime of corporal punishment figured ubiquitously behind the walls of Indochinese prisons. One is equally struck by the absence of technical experts and the dominant role played by that supreme administrative generalist the provincial resident in the management of incarceration in colonial Indochina. In view of the prominence accorded the *mission civilisatrice* in colonial discourse and the fact that French officials came from a metropolitan milieu in which the disciplinary penal institution was closely associated with new notions of modern governance, the remarkably ill-disciplined character of Indochinese prisons requires some explanation.

During the era in which disciplinary techniques were gradually infiltrating and transforming penal institutions across Europe and the United States, a multitude of factors discouraged their deployment in Indochinese prisons. In this chapter, three preliminary considerations are examined. First, Indochinese prisons were penetrated and shaped by preexisting Sino-Vietnamese carceral traditions in which discipline played only a minor role. Second, unlike the European penitentiary, which traced its genealogy to the monastery, the hospital, and the workhouse—institutions concerned fundamentally with salvation, rehabilitation, and reformation—the colonial prison evolved directly out of the prisoner-of-war camp, an institution that was repressive, not corrective. And, third, the essentially racist orientation of

---

11. As Patricia O'Brien has argued with reference to nineteenth-century France, discipline was never a pervasive reality within the new penitentiaries, but it did serve as a "code of action for institutional efficiency" (O'Brien, *Promise of Punishment*, 304).

the colonial state, coupled with the growth of a conviction in nineteenth-century French criminology that some lawbreakers were innately incorrigible, discouraged belief in the value or indeed the feasibility of employing discipline to modify the behavior of non-European lawbreakers. A fourth important consideration, to be explored at length in chapter 2, was the extremely tightfisted character of the colonial state and its stubborn refusal to provide the resources necessary for the creation of a truly disciplinary penal system. A consequence of these factors was the creation of a hybrid prison system in Indochina, in which disciplinary practices were overshadowed by a host of ill-disciplined and exclusively repressive methods of coercion and control.

THE VIETNAMESE CARCERAL TRADITION

In precolonial Vietnam, the prison was rarely used as a penal instrument. In 1825, the Nguyen dynasty's system of imperial detention houses held fewer than a thousand inmates.[12] The relative insignificance of imprisonment as a form of punishment reflected the influence of a Confucian juridical culture that promoted the idea that penal sanctions were best enforced informally within the lineage or village. For cases in which local penalties were deemed inadequate, the state had recourse to a penal arsenal made up of five principal types of punishment: light flogging, heavy flogging, indentured servitude, exile, and death (*xuong, truong, do, luu,* and *tu*).[13] As in Europe, executions and floggings were staged publicly for deterrent effect.[14] Because mechanisms of social control in precolonial Vietnam were embedded in hierarchical networks of blood and clan relations, public rituals of punishment served the additional purpose of enacting a "spectacle of family disgrace."[15] Likewise, banishment, which severed individuals from their clan groups, native places, and ancestral cults was intended to "identify the culprit forever as a source of family shame and dis-

12. Alexander Woodside, *Community and Revolution in Modern Vietnam* (Boston, 1976), 24.

13. The system of five punishments originated in the Kaihuang Code of the Sui Dynasty (A.D. 581–617). See Joanna Waley-Cohen, *Exile in Mid-Qing China, 1758–1820* (New Haven, Conn., 1991), 141.

14. For a history of public punishment in Europe, see Pieter Spierenburg, *The Spectacle of the Scaffold: Executions and the Evolution of Repression, from a Preindustrial Metropolis to the European Experience* (Cambridge, 1984).

15. For a similar argument with regard to China, see Michael R. Dutton, *Policing and Punishment in China: From Patriarchy to the People* (Cambridge, 1992), 83–84, 108.

honour."[16] Excluded from the state's inventory of juridical punishments, imprisonment was used merely to hold defendants awaiting trial or to warehouse convicts prior to the execution of their real punishments.

Prisons were probably introduced into Vietnamese territory by Chinese officials sometime between 111 B.C. and A.D. 939, the millennium in which the Middle Kingdom ruled the Red River Delta as the frontier protectorate of Giao Chi.[17] After breaking away from China in the tenth century, the Vietnamese elite continued to organize their legal and penal institutions according to Chinese models.[18] Hence, premodern Vietnamese prisons were regulated by a Chinese-style board of justice (*hinh bo*) and administered by Confucian-educated provincial and district mandarins.[19]

One of the first references to a carceral institution run by an independent Vietnamese dynasty comes from the eleventh century. According to the *Dai Viet Su Ky Toan Thu,* Emperor Ly Thanh Tong instructed court officials to distribute blankets, mats, and rice to prisoners during the harsh winter of 1055:

> Living in the palaces heated with coal stoves and wearing plenty of warm clothing, I still feel this cold. I am quite concerned about the prisoners [*nguoi tu*] in jails [*nguc*] who are miserably locked up in stocks and manacles [*gong cum*], without enough food to eat and without clothes to warm their bodies, some even undeservedly dying before their guilt or innocence has been determined. I feel a deep compassion for them.[20]

The emperor's comments reveal several important features of juridical incarceration in premodern Vietnam. The words for prisoner (*nguoi tu*) and jail (*nguc*) used by the emperor were borrowed directly from Chinese, highlighting the Sinic roots of Vietnamese penal institutions.[21] The refer-

16. Ibid., 78.

17. For a history of Chinese administration in Giao Chi during this era, see Keith Weller Taylor, *The Birth of Vietnam* (Berkeley and Los Angeles, 1983).

18. The history of Vietnamese institutional borrowing from China is treated in Alexander Woodside, *Vietnam and the Chinese Model: A Comparative Study of Vietnamese and Chinese Government in the First Half of the Nineteenth Century* (Cambridge, Mass., 1971).

19. Ibid., 68.

20. Ngo Si Lien, comp., *Dai Viet Su Ky Toan Thu, Tap I* [The Complete Book of the Historical Records of Great Viet, vol. 1] (Hanoi, 1972), 284.

21. Dao Duy Anh, *Han Viet Tu Dien* [Sino-Vietnamese Dictionary] (1932; reprint, Ho Chi Minh City, 1994), 43, 313.

ence to prisoners "dying before their guilt or innocence has been determined" supports the notion that prisons functioned primarily as way stations prior to trials or other juridical procedures. The emperor's anxiety that prisoners possessed inadequate food and clothing suggests that traditional Sino-Vietnamese carceral institutions assumed little responsibility for the welfare of their inmates.

Additional evidence about imprisonment in early Vietnam comes from penal regulations found in the *Hong Duc* code, a fifteenth-century Vietnamese legal text, partially derived from Tang law.[22] Many articles concerning penal administration in the code aimed to check the power of prison officials and ensure decent sanitary conditions. For example, article 707 sanctioned jail officers who "mistreat or strike prisoners and inflict injury on them without reason."[23] Article 660 ordered that "all houses of detention will be carefully inspected four times a year by the Office of the Provincial Judicial Commissioner," and that "detention rooms must be spacious, well-ventilated, swept, and washed clean."[24] Article 717 targeted corruption and extortion by warders: "Jail officers and judicial clerks who compel payment of a lamp fee [*dang hoa tien*] or a paper fee [*chi tin*] . . . shall receive fifty strokes of the light stick and a one grade demotion."[25]

For some legal historians, the code's benevolent prison regulations and Emperor Ly Thanh Tong's sympathy for imperial prisoners suggests the existence of a "Vietnamese tradition of humanitarian treatment of detainees and lenient punishment for convicts heavily influenced by Buddhism."[26] However, because much of it was borrowed directly from Chinese texts, the *Hong Duc* code's capacity to illuminate a distinct Vietnamese carceral tradition is limited. As Alexander Woodside has pointed out, Vietnamese rulers frequently adopted blueprints for Chinese institutions that they were unable or unwilling to implement.[27] Hence, while the code contains clues about the history of Vietnamese institutional

---

22. Nguyen Ngoc Huy and Ta Van Tai, *The Lê Code: Law in Traditional Vietnam: A Comparative Sino-Vietnamese Legal Study with Historical-Juridical Analysis and Annotations*, vol. 1 (Athens, Ohio, 1987). See articles 650, 651, 658, 659, 660, 661, 663, 664, 695, 707, and 717.

23. Ibid., 290.

24. Ibid., 332.

25. Ibid., 292.

26. Ta Van Tai, *The Vietnamese Tradition of Human Rights* (Berkeley, Calif., 1988), 70.

27. This a major theme of Woodside, *Vietnam and the Chinese Model.*

borrowing from China, it may not provide a reliable guide to how imprisonment in early Vietnam actually functioned in practice.

The earliest eyewitness accounts of prisons in Vietnam come from European travelers and missionaries who were imprisoned by the imperial court during the first half of the nineteenth century.[28] For example, M. Miche, a member of the Société des Missions étrangères left a vivid description of his four-month stay in Hue's Kham Duong prison during the winter of 1842:

> The prison in which we two missionaries were confined was a large walled building covered with tiles. In appearance, it was just like other public buildings or the houses of the great mandarins. In France, it might have passed for a fine stable. It had a frontage of 130 feet with a depth of 40. It was divided into three compartments, a captain with 50 soldiers being in charge of each. Each compartment had a further subdivision: one behind walls; which was confined and dark, and the smaller, which was the prison; the other more large and commodious, with more light and air, in front, which was reserved for the gaolers and soldiers and such prisoners who could obtain the favor.[29]

Miche's portrayal of Kham Duong's internal structure corresponds to pictures painted by colonial scholar-bureaucrats who investigated traditional Vietnamese penal practices in the late nineteenth century. Around the turn of the century, Alfred Schreiner remarked that "early Annamite prisons" were composed of two spatial components: an enclosed hardwood chamber known as the *nguc that* and an open courtyard adjacent to it called the *trai la*. The *nguc that*, which he referred to as "a kind of dark dungeon," was reserved for serious criminals, while the *trai la* held minor offenders. He also noted that premodern prisons were constructed to allow for the physical segregation of women.[30]

---

28. There also exists an earlier Sino-Vietnamese tradition of poetic writing from confinement, but its thematic emphasis on the internal life of the poet limits its capacity to contribute to historical reconstructions of the premodern prison. For translations of premodern prison poetry by Nguyen Trai (1380–1442) and Cao Ba Quat (1809–53), see *Vietnamese Literature: Historical Background and Texts*, ed. Nguyen Khac Vien and Huu Ngoc (Hanoi, 1979), 247, 383.

29. John Shortland, *Persecutions of Annam: A History of Christianity in Cochin China and Tonking* (London, 1875), 234. On the activities of French missionaries in nineteenth-century Annam, see also Patrick Tuck, *French Catholic Missionaries and the Politics of Imperialism in Vietnam, 1857–1914: A Documentary Survey* (Liverpool, 1987).

30. Alfred Schreiner, *Les Institutions annamites en Basse-Cochinchine avant la conquête française* (Saigon, 1900), 148–49.

The evidence presented by Miche and Schreiner suggests that premodern prisons in Indochina employed some of the same mechanisms of differentiation and classification that are associated with the advent of modern prisons in the West. However, compared with the myriad distinctions of age, sentence, judicial status, and political orientation that structured the nineteenth-century European penitentiary, the taxonomy by which early Vietnamese penal administration classified prisoners was relatively uncomplicated. For example, because neither the *nguc that* nor the *trai la* contained individual cells, all prisoners lived collectively in communal settings. Not only were juveniles and adults mixed together, but infants were allowed to accompany their mothers into jail. In addition, premodern Vietnamese prisons made no provision for segregating defendants from convicts, or recidivists from first-time offenders.[31]

Moreover, the chaotic, poorly supervised atmosphere of the *trai la*, in particular, contrasted sharply with the strict regimentation of incarceration in nineteenth-century Europe. According to the English seaman Edward Brown, who spent several months in a central Vietnamese prison during the 1850s, inmates lived and worked much as they pleased within the unstructured environment of the *trai la*:

> The prisoners had free access to every part of the outer jail. They were allowed to follow their trade, which was chiefly making baskets, or other fancy wicker-work, of bamboo or rattan. The bamboo was supplied to them gratuitously, but the rattan they had to purchase for themselves; and each was allowed to dispose of his own work as he saw fit, in a small bazaar within the precincts of the jail. . . . A few of them made fans, umbrellas or embroidery. [32]

The lively randomness depicted by Brown was enhanced by the fact that the institution furnished little in the way of food, clothing, or medicine. As a result, prisoners were supplied by friends or family, who enjoyed wide access to the *trai la*. Schreiner observed that most prisoners "are not sealed off from the outside world and can communicate easily with relatives who provide them with food."[33] Visitation rights were granted to parents, uncles, brothers, spouses, children, grandchildren, and even concubines.[34]

---

31. Ta Van Tai, *Vietnamese Tradition of Human Rights*, 68, 77.

32. Edward Brown, *Cochin-China, and my experience of it; a seaman's narrative of his adventures and sufferings during a captivity among Chinese pirates on the coast of Cochin-China, and afterwards during a journey on foot across that country, in the years 1857–8*, by Edward Brown (1861; reprint, Taipei, 1971), 186.

33. Schreiner, *Institutions annamites*, 148.

34. Ibid., 150.

Father Miche described sympathetic Catholic villagers penetrating the prison regularly to provide him with "gifts, fruit and money."[35]

Given the porous character of prison walls, it is not surprising that guards were well positioned to act as predatory middlemen between prisoners and their families. They were known to extract extortionate fees in return for petty privileges, services, and protection.[36] During an interview with the colonial scholar-bureaucrat J. B. Roux, one veteran of Hue's Tran Phu prison described the guard corps there as a "gang of bloodsuckers" who constantly demanded bribes of betel nut and liquor.[37]

Another commonly noted feature of precolonial prison life was the ubiquity of corporal punishment. On a visit through Tonkin in the late seventeenth century, William Dampier observed that "prisoners in publick Prisons are used worse than a Man would use a Dog, they being half starved, and soundly beaten to boot."[38] Over a century and a half later, Edward Brown painted a picture of similar conditions:

> The warden of the prison was a Canton man by birth. It appears that the Cochinchinese government generally choose these men to fill situations where severity is required, and truly this man was severe, and even brutal, for he kept the rattan going on the unfortunate prisoners' hides from sunrise to sunset, and for the most trivial of offenses. . . . He used to sit on a couch, in the middle of the cottage floor, and there award the daily punishment to the poor prisoners of whom there were more than 200. About 20 of them were flogged daily on average.[39]

Miche followed Brown in his observation that the training of Cochin Chinese prison guards "was confined to a single practice—the use of the rattan—so as to lay it on with dexterity."[40] He described the training he witnessed within the prison compound in Hue:

> A stuffed figure was placed in the midst of the courtyard and one after the other, the soldiers took their turn in elaborately thrashing it. The

---

35. Shortland, *Persecutions of Annam*, 238–39.

36. The *Lê* code punished guards who accepted bribes. See, e.g., article 664: "A guard who takes bribes from detainees in order to advise them about changing their statements or to communicate what other people say about their case . . . shall be punished" (Nguyen Ngoc Huy and Ta Van Tai, *Lê Code*, 278).

37. J. B Roux, "Les Prisons du vieux Hué," *Bulletin des amis du vieux Hué* 1 (January–March 1915): 114.

38. William Dampier, *Voyages and Discoveries*, ed. C. Wilkinson (1699).

39. Brown, *Cochin-China*, 186.

40. Shortland, *Persecutions of Annam*, 256.

great art was to administer the blows so that they left a single wheal. He who hit best in this manner carried off the prize of skill. . . . In Cochin China, indeed, the rattan is the universal remedy and the soldier feels it as often as he uses it.[41]

The routine flogging of the confined suggests that imprisonment in Vietnam functioned to facilitate, rather than to substitute for, more corporal forms of punishment. The widespread use of chains, fetters, and *cangues* (yokes) further supports the notion that imprisonment operated in tandem with penal practices that worked directly on the bodies of the condemned. A French doctor studying prison conditions in Annam in the late nineteenth century expressed dismay at the repeated sight of "inmates with purulent wounds or skin ulcerations at places where they wore cangues or stocks."[42]

It is striking how closely Western descriptions of incarceration in precolonial Vietnam resemble historical reconstructions of imprisonment in eighteenth-century Europe. Prior to the nineteenth century, most European prisoners were confined while awaiting trial or sentencing, rather than as a form of punishment. Miche's portrait of the randomness and heterogeneity of Vietnamese prison life corresponds with Alexander Smith's famous description of Newgate in 1714 as "a confused Chaos without any distinction, a bottomless pit of violence and a Tower of Babel. . . . There is mingling the noble with the ignoble, the rich with the poor, the wise with the ignorant, and debtors with the worst malefactors."[43] A resemblance to premodern Vietnamese incarceration can also be found in the liability of prisoners in eighteenth-century France to obtain their own food "either through friends and relatives outside the prison or by purchasing it from guards."[44] Another parallel may be observed in the "easy traffic of visitors" characteristic of old English prisons.[45]

41. Ibid.

42. Ta Van Tai, *Vietnamese Tradition of Human Rights*, 73.

43. Alexander Smith, *A Complete History of the Lives and Robberies of the Most Notorious Highwaymen* (London, 1933), 108. The mixing of diverse categories of detainees in Vietnamese prisons also mirrors Patricia O'Brien's observation that old-regime prisons in France were "teeming with people of all ages and both sexes, those awaiting trial and those convicted, for all types of crimes, beggars, murderers, pickpockets and prostitutes" (O'Brien, *Promise of Punishment*, 18).

44. O'Brien, *The Promise of Punishment*, 18.

45. John Bender, *Imagining the Penitentiary: Fiction and the Architecture of Mind in Eighteenth-Century England* (Chicago, 1987), 29.

Although such correlations point to real similarities between premodern European and Vietnamese carceral practices, it is also true that the imperial project encouraged European observers to draw such comparisons. Like much Orientalist discourse, colonial writing on "traditional" punishment was crafted to authenticate claims that imperial conquest had been undertaken to deliver subject populations from the despotism of indigenous *anciens régimes*.[46] Such an impulse is evident in J. B. Roux's lurid scholarly essay "Les Prisons de vieux Hué," which contrasts the "humane and scientific" methods of incarceration practiced in Europe with the savage forms of beating, extortion, and food deprivation characteristic of traditional Annam. "The ghastly description offered here shows the profound distance between European and Annamite prisons," Roux explains. "There are many points of contrast, as the facts demonstrate, but they can be summarized briefly as follows: in Europe, the prisoner is treated as a man; in Annam, he is not."[47] It is easy to see how Roux's conclusions could function ideologically to celebrate the distance between benevolent colonial governance and the "barbaric" local rule it had displaced.

THE ENDURING INFLUENCE OF TRADITIONAL PRACTICES

Although the French moved quickly in the late nineteenth century to replace existing sites of detention with new prisons, traditional Vietnamese carceral practices continued to shape the development of the colonial system. Such continuity was most apparent in the protectorate of Annam, where the royal court and imperial bureaucracy continued to control a system of "native" tribunals and provincial prisons until the end of the colonial era.[48] The French tolerated the old system in Annam as part of an ef-

46. David Arnold makes a similar point about the ideological function of the colonial criminal justice system in British India. "While exemplary punishments were in times of crisis and rebellion deemed necessary and legitimate, the British sought to demonstrate a superiority over pre-colonial 'barbarity' by condemning torture, mutilation and indefinite imprisonment without trial" (Arnold, "Touching the Body: Perspectives on the Indian Plague, 1896–1900," in *Selected Subaltern Studies*, eds. Ranajit Guha and Gayatri Chakravorty Spivak [New York: Oxford University Press, 1988], 393).
47. Roux, "Prisons du vieux Hué," 119.
48. "The only legislation applied in Annam by the indigenous tribunals is the code of Emperor Gia Long (1820). In Annam, the indigenous justice system is administered without interference by or participation of the French juridical authorities" (Gouvernement général de l'Indochine, *Annuaire statistique de l'Indochine* [Hanoi, 1929], 118).

fort to shore up the flagging prestige of the collaborationist monarchy and mandarinate and to draw attention away from the foreign character of colonial rule.[49] Hence, other than the Tourane Civil Prison and the penitentiaries at Lao Bao and Buon Ma Thuot, which were under the direct authority of French officials, Annam's smaller provincial prisons were run by mandarins appointed by the puppet court in Hue.[50] As in the precolonial era, they were staffed by imperial soldiers and structured according to regulations laid down in the Nguyen dynasty's *Gia Long* code, promulgated in the early nineteenth century. The autonomy of prison administration in colonial Annam is further evidenced by the fact that the protectorate's prison records were not integrated with those from the rest of Indochina until the early 1930s.[51]

The high volume of amnesties and sentence reductions issued to prisoners in colonial Annam also points to the persistence there of older juridical practices. In traditional Sino-Vietnamese jurisprudence, amnesties gave the emperor an opportunity to demonstrate the beneficence characteristic of good rulership.[52] Statistics from the 1930s reveal huge numbers of amnesties for prisoners in colonial Annam relative to the handful in Tonkin or Cochin China. In 1933, for example, 2,078 prisoners from Annam were amnestied, compared to 334 from Tonkin and 8 from Cochin China.[53] As during the precolonial era, amnesties in colonial Annam came directly from the emperor.[54]

Despite the fact that colonial discourse tended to vilify traditional Vietnamese punishment as barbaric and archaic, officials were not above romanticizing the paternalistic nature of the old system when doing so

49. Bruce Lockhart, *The End of the Vietnamese Monarchy* (New Haven, Conn., 1993).

50. On prison administration in colonial Annam, see Tinh Uy Dak Lak—Vien Lich Su Dang, *Lich Su Nha Day Buon Ma Thuot, 1930–1945* [History of Buon Ma Thuot Penitentiary, 1930–1945] (Hanoi, 1991), and Le Kim Que, "Tim Hieu Ve Nha Tu Lao Bao" [Understanding Lao Bao Prison], *Tap Chi Lich Su Dang* 10 (1985): 71–74.

51. Gouvernement général, *Annuaire statistique de l'Indochine,* 1913–42.

52. See Brian McKnight, *The Quality of Mercy: Amnesties and Traditional Chinese Justice* (Honolulu, 1981).

53. Gouvernement général, *Annuaire statistique de l'Indochine,* 1932–33, 118.

54. Throughout the 1930s, amnesties issued by Emperor Bao Dai were covered extensively in the colonial press. See, e.g., the article "O Trung Ky Cung Co Nhieu Chinh Tri Pham Va Thuong Pham Duoc Tha Cung Duoc Giam Toi" [In Annam, Many Political Prisoners and Common-Law Prisoners Receive Amnesties or Sentence Reductions], *Dong Phap,* June 19, 1936.

served their purposes. During the mid 1930s, as Annam's antiquated prison system came under sustained attack from anticolonial activists, French officials put forward a more positive picture of the precolonial carceral tradition. In 1935, a colonial inspector explained: "Political and common-law prisoners in Annam enjoy a treatment founded on the natural generosity that flows from the essence of the Annamese political system. Here, the sovereign is known as the 'father and mother of the people,' and the more scientific penal methods employed in our other territories are never applied."[55]

That colonial prisoners frequently attempted to avoid serving sentences in Annam suggests, however, that the "natural generosity" of the old system impressed them less than its brutality, corruption, and squalor. In his memoir *Mot Ngay Ngan Thu* (The Eternal Day), the nationalist political activist Ton Quang Phiet recalled that his greatest anxiety following his arrest in 1934 was that he might be turned over to prison authorities in Annam.[56]

The persistence of traditional carceral practices in Tonkin and Cochin China, on the other hand, reflected the endurance there of precolonial cultural notions about institutional confinement. Although prisons in these territories were structured according to slightly modified versions of metropolitan penal regulations and managed by French officials, the culture of imprisonment could not be changed overnight. Colonial prisons were staffed by native guards whose occupational habits stubbornly resisted transformation to the modern institutional ideal. Since imperial prison guards had always supplemented meager salaries with bribes and petty fees, it is not surprising that their equally underpaid colonial-era counterparts carried on with the practice in colonial prisons. In 1909, an official noted that guards in Tonkin surreptitiously charged prisoners "surveillance money," which permitted them to receive special supplies from their families, including clothes, medicine, and opium.[57] Virtually all prison memoirs from the 1930s describe guards selling tobacco and food to prisoners at inflated prices.[58] According to the French journalist Jean-Claude

55. AOM, Indochine, Affaires politiques—Détenus politiques, January 5, 1935.
56. Ton Quang Phiet, *Mot Ngay Ngan Thu (Lan Thu Nhat O Nha Nguc)* [The Eternal Day (My First Time in Prison)] (Hue, 1935), 32.
57. TTLT, Résidence supérieure au Tonkin, 71793, correspondances diverses, September 1, 1909.
58. See, e.g., Le Van Hien, *Nguc Kontum* [Kontum Prison] (Hanoi, 1958), 27.

Demariaux, guards on Poulo Condore were known to auction easy prison work assignments to the highest bidder.[59]

For Vietnamese guards, images of traditional juridical confinement in popular culture may have reinforced beliefs about the propriety of older forms of occupational behavior. For example, cultural representations in which the keepers beat the kept as matter of course may have prompted guards to enter colonial service with inflated notions about the legitimate extent of their power. Indeed, a prison scene of considerable brutality figures in an early nineteenth-century version of a much older Vietnamese verse fable, *The Catfish and the Toad*. In the story, a toad's bogus lawsuit lands a catfish in jail. There, he is chained and beaten repeatedly by his abusive keepers:

> "Well, let the Toad go home," the prefect said.
> "For further hearings bolt the Catfish in!"
> The zealous bailiffs did as they were told
> and promptly clapped the Catfish into jail.
> Alas, they kept him under lock and key—
> ten men closed in on one to bleed him white.
> From mandarin to bailiffs orders flowed:
> they cangued his neck by day and chained his legs
> by night, they cut his hide to rags and shreds,
> plying a twin-lash whip with diligence.[60]

The brutalization of the catfish prisoner corresponds with pictures of the routinization of beating in colonial prisons. Following thirteen years in the penitentiary on Poulo Condore, Huynh Thuc Khang wrote that "beatings follow a prearranged plan: the French beat the guards, the guards beat the *caplans* [inmates employed as overseers], and the *caplans* beat the prisoners."[61] Likewise, in 1929, the former political prisoner Phan Van Hum noted: "[P]rison recalls two dominant images: rotten food and incessant beatings."[62]

Cultural representations linking judicial confinement and corporal punishment were sustained and deepened by the routine brutality of French penal officials to prisoners and native guards alike. Episodes featuring the

---

59. Jean-Claude Demariaux, *Les Secrets des îles Poulo-Condore: Le Grand Bagne indochinois* (Paris, 1956), 52.

60. *The Heritage of Vietnamese Poetry: An Anthology*, ed. Huynh Sanh Thong (New Haven, Conn., 1979), 61.

61. Huynh Thuc Khang, *Thi Tu Tung Thoai* [Prison Verse] (1939; reprint, Saigon, 1951), 68.

62. Phan Van Hum, *Ngoi Tu Kham Lon* [Sitting in the Big Jail] (1929; reprint, Saigon, 1957), 78.

indiscriminate flogging of both prisoners and guards occur regularly in colonial-era prison memoirs and appear repeatedly in internal reports.[63] Beatings of guards, in particular, tended to exacerbate inclinations to cruelty. It is not surprising that victimized guards tended to take out their frustrations on vulnerable prisoners, creating an extraordinarily brutal institutional culture. Here, colonial racism and the persistence of precolonial carceral practices coalesced to create a prison system that functioned through the dramatic deployment of terror and violence.

IMPERIAL CONQUEST AND THE ORIGINS OF THE COLONIAL PRISON

The institutional character of the colonial prison in Indochina was also shaped by the peculiar circumstances of its birth and early development. Historians of European punishment have shown how putatively emblematic features of the modern penitentiary evolved gradually out of older institutional patterns. For example, Edward Peters has demonstrated how the idea of behavioral modification through segregation and regimentation, so integral to the modern penitentiary, was rooted in the early medieval *ergastulum*, "a disciplinary cell within monasteries in which forced labor took place."[64] J. T. Sellin and more recently Pieter Speirenburg have traced the nineteenth-century penitentiary's emphasis on reformative labor to the early modern workhouse, first established in northern European towns in the late sixteenth century.[65] In Indochina, on the other hand, the colonial prison system grew directly out of the camps that the French had established to hold prisoners of war during the initial period of military conquest.

The conquest and pacification of Indochina occurred gradually over a forty-year period.[66] It took five years for French troops to defeat the impe-

---

63. For a graphic official account of the routinization of beating in prison, see AOM, Indochine, Affaires politiques, 7F51, Affaire de Thai Nguyen: Rapport confidentiel 2547, December 24, 1918, on the violent behavior of the director of the Thai Nguyen Penitentiary.

64. Edward M. Peters, "Prisons Before the Prison: The Ancient and Medieval Worlds," in *The Oxford History of the Prison: The Practice of Punishment in Western Society,* ed. Norval Morris and David Rothman (New York, 1995), 28.

65. J. T. Sellin, *Pioneering in Penology: The Amsterdam House of Correction in the Sixteenth and Seventeenth Century,* (Philadelphia, 1944); Pieter Speirenburg, *The Prison Experience: Disciplinary Institutions and Their Inmates in Early Modern Europe* (New Brunswick, N.J., 1991).

66. For the initial French attacks, see John Cady, *The Roots of French Imperialism in Eastern Asia* (Ithaca, N.Y., 1954), Mark W. McLeod, *The Vietnamese Response to*

rial Vietnamese army and a host of irregular guerrilla forces before they secured control over Cochin China in 1867.[67] The consolidation of colonial authority over Annam and Tonkin in 1885 followed a decade of military skirmishes and the painstaking repression of a widespread royalist resistance movement.[68] Although the French had eliminated most residual pockets of opposition by the late 1880s, sporadic fighting continued, in northern Tonkin especially, until the close of the nineteenth century.[69]

For the French, the intensity of Vietnamese resistance generated demands for fortified camps where anticolonial leaders and prisoners of war could be locked away. Indeed, camps of confinement were constructed in Indochina prior to virtually any other colonial institution.[70] On February 1, 1862, four months before the Treaty of Saigon ceded the eastern half of Cochin China to France, Admiral Louis-Adolphe Bonard ordered the establishment of a *bagne* (penal colony) on Poulo Condore, an archipelago 180 kilometers off the southern Vietnamese coast.[71] According to Bonard's decree:

French Intervention, 1862–1874 (New York, 1991) and Georges Tabulet, *Le Geste français en Indochine,* 2 vols. (Paris, 1955). For French pacification efforts and Vietnamese anticolonial insurgency during the late nineteenth century, see David Marr, *Vietnamese Anticolonialism, 1885–1925* (Berkeley and Los Angeles, 1971), and Truong Buu Lam, *Patterns of Vietnamese Response to Foreign Intervention, 1858–1900* (New Haven, Conn., 1967).

67. Mark W. McLeod, "Truong Dinh and Vietnamese Anticolonialism (1859–1864): A Reappraisal," *Journal of Southeast Asian Studies* 24, no. 1 (March 1993).

68. Charles Fourniau, *Annam-Tonkin (1885–1896): Lettrés et paysans vietnamiens face à la conquête coloniale* (Paris, 1989).

69. See, e.g., Kim Munholland, "The French Army and the Imperial Frontier, 1885–1897," in *Proceedings of Third Annual Meeting of the French Colonial Historical Society* (Montréal, 1977), 82–107, and Ella Laffey, "The Tonkin Frontier: The View from China, 1885–1914," in ibid., 108–18.

70. Indochina was not unique in this respect. "Prisons are often among the earliest examples of colonial architecture with large central prisons in the distant towns not to mention a large number of lock-ups attached to the courts," E. Coldham observes ("Crime and Punishment in British Colonial Africa," in *Punishment: Transactions of the Jean Bodin Society for Comparative Institutional History,* LVIII [Brussels, 1989], 60).

71. The Poulo Condore (Con Lon) Archipelago comprises fourteen islands. In Vietnamese, the island group is alternatively referred to as Con Non or Con Son. The largest island in the chain is Con Dao. Following the Malay name, the French referred to Con Dao as Poulo Condore (or occasionally la Grande Condore); "Poulo" obviously derives from *pulao,* the Malay word for island, and "Condore" may be from *kundur,* the Malay word for gourd. Poulo Condore is mentioned by Marco Polo, who passed through Champa in 1285. See Tran Van Que, *Con-Lon*

> There will be set up on Poulo Condore an Annamite penitential establishment, where dangerous men, prisoners, and malefactors will be deported. The men will be divided into two categories: (1) prisoners incarcerated for rebellion or common crimes; (2) prisoners of war. The two categories will, as much as possible, be separated. The prisoners of war will be granted land concessions. The prisoners for rebellion and common crimes will be used for work of public utility. [72]

The overlap between the two categories of inmates imagined by Bonard—"prisoners of war" and "prisoners incarcerated for rebellion and common crimes"—confirms that Indochina's first colonial officials anticipated a prison population dominated by enemy soldiers and anticolonial insurgents. Indeed, Poulo Condore played a key role in the repression of anticolonial resistance throughout the early decades of its existence.[73] It was the final destination for captured troops involved in Truong Dinh's Southern Uprising (Khoi Nghia Nam Ky) in the 1860s, the Scholars' Movements (Phong Trao Van Than) in the 1870s, and the defense of Hanoi against French attacks in 1873 and 1882.[74] The repression of the Save-the-King Movement (Phong Trao Can Vuong) in the 1880s drew more anticolonial rebels into the prison population, including such eminent resistance figures as Nguyen Van Tuong, Pham Thuan Duat, and Ton That Dinh.[75]

Quan-Dao Truoc ngay 9–3–1945 [The Con Lon Archipelago Before September 3, 1945] (Saigon, 1961), 13.

72. AOM, H Colonies, 2026, Fondation à Poulo Condore d'un établissement pénitencier, January 2, 1862.

73. The names of numerous nineteenth-century anticolonial rebels were seen scrawled on the walls during a visit to the *bagne* in the 1930s by Demariaux (*Secrets des îles Poulo-Condore*, 184).

74. Vietnamese historians have stressed Poulo Condore's early role as a repository for anticolonial rebels. See Ban Nghien Cuu Lich Su Dang Dac Khu Vung Tau—Con Dao, *Nha Tu Con Dao, 1862–1945* [Con Dao Penitentiary, 1862–1945] (Hanoi, 1987), 58, and Tran Van Que, *Con-Lon Quan-Dao Truoc Ngay 9–3–1945*, 105–7.

75. For lists of nineteenth-century rebels sent to Con Dao, see Ban Lien Lac Tu Chinh Tri So Van Hoa Thong Tin, *Con Dao Ky Su va Tu Lieu* [Con Dao: Reports and Documents] (Ho Chi Minh City, 1996), 85–86. See also Le Huu Phuoc, "Lich Su Nha Tu Con Dao, 1862–1930" [History of Con Dao Prison, 1862–1930] (master's thesis, Ho Chi Minh City Institute of Social Science, 1992), 85–93. Both works mention the incarceration on Poulo Condore of the rebel leaders Le Xuan Oai, Pham Huy Du, Dang Ngoc Kiem, Tran Thien Tinh, Nguyen Thien Ke, Lanh Dat, and Tran Trong Cung.

During this protracted era of colonial conquest, captives were shepherded into prison by a tangle of irregular procedures and juridical institutions.[76] Initially, most prisoners were sentenced by military councils under the authority of the French Army.[77] Thereafter, deliberations were handled by mixed tribunals, presided over by a Vietnamese judicial mandarin (*quan an*) in collaboration with a French resident. As mixed tribunals gradually displaced military councils, imprisonment replaced the scorched-earth tactics and collective punishments favored by the French military. For example, in 1888, the acting resident of Tonkin persuaded military officials not to raze thirty villages suspected of sheltering rebels but to send the leaders of the communities in question to Poulo Condore instead.[78]

The combination of Tonkin's infant judicial system with the French Army's aggressive military pacification campaign in the 1880s and 1890s resulted in the indiscriminate imprisonment of hundreds of suspected rebels. The haphazard workings of this piebald system were revealed in 1890, following an investigation into the arbitrary internment of Tonkinese prisoners on Poulo Condore.[79] The investigator, Attorney General Daurand Forgues, detailed fifteen separate instances in which apparently innocent civilians had been seized by colonial troops, turned over to corrupt or inept local authorities, and sent to the islands, in many cases without intervening court proceedings, as exemplified by the following excerpts from his report:

> Pham Van Bao from Nam Sach district, Hai Duong Province, was fourteen when he was arrested. During a search of his village, someone informed the authorities that he had served as the domestic servant of a rebel chief. He was sent to a French resident, who passed him on to the

76. "French administrators did not hesitate to make legal decisions on the basis of expediency. Execution of rebels or suspected rebels or their deportation to Poulo Condore, which was soon used as a place of detention for the opponents of the French, were countenanced because of the unsettled conditions that prevailed" (Milton Osborne, *The French Presence in Cochinchina and Cambodia: Rule and Response, 1859–1905* [Ithaca, N.Y., 1969], 76).

77. AOM, Gouvernement général 22791, Tentative de révolte au penitencier de Poulo Condore, 1890, Saigon, September 27, 1890.

78. Munholland, "French Army and the Imperial Frontier," 103.

79. For an extended analysis of the 1890 revolt, consult AOM, Indochine, Fonds du Gouverneur général, 22791, Révolte au pénitencier de Poulo Condore, Rapport adressé à M. le Procureur général, Chef du Service judiciare, par M. Daurand Forgues, juge-président du tribunal de première instance de Saigon délégué, afin de procéder à une enquête sur les faits criminels commis au pénitencier de Poulo Condore le 19 juin dernier, July 26, 1890.

indigenous authorities. Without ever being questioned, he was sentenced to ten years' hard labor by a mixed tribunal.[80]

The case of 21-year-old Nguyen Pham Tu from Thuan Thanh district, Bac Ninh province, is particularly remarkable. He told me that the wife of a rebel chief had lived in his village. When soldiers searched the village, they seized him and five other inhabitants, but not the woman in question. After several days, four of the six paid a bribe and were released. He and Trinh Duc Pham, however, were too poor to afford the bribe. They were sentenced by the Bac Ninh mixed tribunal to life in prison. I have corroborated this story with Trinh Duc Pham, who is currently deathly sick in the prison hospital.[81]

The fact that the colonial penal system traced its origins to camps for captured enemy soldiers shaped the evolution of colonial incarceration. Whereas prison officials in France may have conceived of prisoners as fundamentally antisocial, their colonial counterparts saw them as antistate. Hence, colonial officials tended to conceptualize imprisonment in terms of repression rather than rehabilitation and displayed little overt interest in the possibility of the behavioral modification of prison inmates. This early repressive orientation launched the colonial prison on an institutional trajectory that would continue to influence its development until the end of the colonial era.

CRIMINOLOGY, RACISM, AND THE LIMITS
OF COLONIAL DISCIPLINE

It has been argued that the concept of penal rehabilitation in nineteenth-century France "was posited on the assumption that the inmate was a malleable object who could be shaped by institutional experience."[82] Faith in this idea was shared by successive generations of French prison

80. AOM, Indochine, Gouvernement général, 22791, Révolte au pénitencier de Poulo Condore, Rapport au Gouverneur général, Saigon, September 27, 1890, 7.
81. Ibid., 10.
82. Patricia O'Brien traces this idea to an eighteenth-century "environmentalism" believing "that properly administered institutions could reform and correct individuals in their care" (*Promise of Punishment*, 32, 48). In "The Rise and Decline of Solitary Confinement: Socio-Historical Explanations of Long-Term Penal Changes," *British Journal of Criminology* 32, no. 2 (Spring 1992): 136–37, Herman Franke links its origins to early Christian notions of sin, redemption, and salvation, and to the idea of *homo clausus* expressed in the experiments with babies carried out by Frederick II of Hohenstaufen (1194–1250) and the Scottish king James IV (1472–1513).

reformers—from the classical jurists who championed the ideas of Cesare Beccaria in the late eighteenth century to the Philanthropists who founded the Royal Prison Society in 1819 to medical men and social scientists connected with the new positivist disciplines of public hygiene, moral science, utilitarian statistics, and legal medicine.[83] In Indochina, however, several factors prompted colonial officials to view "native" prison inmates as intrinsically less susceptible to institutional manipulation.

The first was a growing anxiety in France about criminal incorrigibility. As the nineteenth century progressed, the French public grew increasingly concerned about the "habitual criminal," a figure considered both "incurable of vice" and a "species apart from normal men."[84] The concept of the "habitual criminal" gained momentum in conjunction with heightened fears about the problem of recidivism and the growing influence of medical experts over questions of social deviance.[85] In 1885, anxiety about the rise of a "separate race" of incorrigible criminals led to the notoriously harsh Relegation Law, which stipulated that recidivists would be deported to penal colonies overseas rather than subjected to expensive and apparently fruitless programs of rehabilitation in metropolitan prisons.[86] The historian Michelle Perrot has argued that the passage of the 1885 law signified a significant erosion of public faith in the efficacy of moral engineering.[87]

Just as the growth of recidivism promoted the idea that there existed a category of chronic criminals, the development of a French school of criminal sociology in the late nineteenth century suggested that the origins of this category could be found in discrete "environments" that nurtured incorrigibility.[88] Under the leadership of Alexandre Lacassagne, a doctor of legal medicine at the University of Lyon, the French school sought to provide an alternative to the biological determinism of Cesare Lombroso's criminal anthropology. Whereas Lombroso emphasized the existence of

83. Petit, *Ces peines obscures*, 183–205.
84. Robert A. Nye, *Crime, Madness, and Politics in Modern France: The Medical Concept of National Decline* (Princeton, N.J., 1984), 75, 79.
85. For discussions of recidivism and its social interpretation in nineteenth-century France, see ibid., 74–96; O'Brien, *Promise of Punishment*, 287–96; Foucault, *Discipline and Punish*, 264–68.
86. An instructive account of the politics of the 1885 law can be found in Nye, *Crime, Madness and Politics in Modern France*, 49–96.
87. Michelle Perrot, "Delinquency and the Penitentiary System in Nineteenth-Century France," in *Deviants and the Abandoned in French Society: Selections from the « Annales, économies, sociétés, civilisations », Volume IV*, ed. Robert Forster and Orest Ranum (Baltimore, 1978), 234.
88. Nye, *Crime, Madness and Politics in Modern France*, 97–131.

morphological characteristics in "hereditary criminals," Lacassagne and his colleagues looked to the "social milieu" as the "mother culture of criminality."[89] This position led French criminologists to highlight essential differences in criminal behavior across cultures and societies, as suggested by Lacassagne's best-known aphorism: "Societies get the criminals they deserve."[90]

In Indochina, Lacassagne's theories shaped ideas about the unique nature of "yellow" criminality. In 1887, Louis Lorion, a Navy doctor, provided a systematic examination of this question in his study *Criminalité et médecine judiciaire en Cochinchine*.[91] To establish the preeminent influence of the social and physical environment on criminal behavior in Cochin China, Lorion opened with a discussion of its exotic geography, climate, and demography.[92] The heart of his study consisted of an examination of the idiosyncratic character of crime in the colony. Crimes of passion were rare, Lorion claimed, because the Annamite "does not know the violent emotions of European social life: neither exquisite joy nor profound misery. . . . He is fickle, very patient, easy to please, and extremely easygoing."[93] Murder rarely followed conflicts over principle, but rather occurred in conjunction with theft or disputes over money, especially gambling debts.[94] Rape was rare, because the "licentious and very active imagination" of Annamite women left few men unsatisfied.[95] Bestiality was not unusual, however; it was practiced by both sexes with pigs or dogs.[96] Poisonings were also common, which the environmentally minded Lorion attributed to "the wealth of venomous plants" in the region.[97] Although Lorion offered detailed instructions about the proper way to conduct autopsies and criminal investigations in the colony, he provided no suggestions regarding penal corrections. Nevertheless, by stressing fundamental differences between the forces driving "yellow" and "white" criminality, his study implied that metropolitan penal methods would have little effect

89. Ibid., 104.

90. Gordon Wright, *Between the Guillotine and Liberty: Two Centuries of the Crime Problem in France* (New York, 1983), 121.

91. Louis Lorion, *Criminalité et médecine judiciare en Cochinchine* (Lyon, 1887).

92. Ibid., i–iv. Not only did Lorion dedicate the study to Lacassagne, he acknowledged adopting the doctor's "method and organization" in his research.

93. Ibid., 44.

94. Ibid., 58.

95. Ibid., 118.

96. Ibid., 117.

97. Ibid., 76.

in the foreign criminological terrain of Cochin China.[98] Years of "arbitrary and antiquated government" had dulled the capacity of the Annamite to respond to the inducements and disincentives that had long shaped behavior in the West.[99] "His satisfactions, like his punishments," Lorion argued, "are experienced on a purely material plane; his life is more vegetative than intellectual."[100] The doctor concluded by providing an implicit justification for the introduction of a colonial juridical and corrections system that was qualitatively distinct from its metropolitan counterpart: "This short examination will suffice to show that owing to its racial diversity, different morals and institutions, and the particularity of its milieu and conditions, Cochin China's medico-judicial practices should exhibit special characteristics."[101]

Lorion's conclusions reflected a widely held belief that modern technologies (disciplinary or otherwise) were inappropriate to effect fundamental changes in the nature of colonial subjects. How could one expect significant "improvements" in a people considered to be, in the words of one governor-general, "mentally retarded, more or less asleep"?[102] Even avowedly anticolonial French observers such as Roland Dorgelès tended to see in the "yellow races" an essential cultural incorrigibility:

> Some people believe that European inventions are going to produce a revolution in the old world. This is a great mistake. The old world adopts, but is not astonished. Give the yellow race the telegraph and they send telegrams; the phonograph, and they listen to songs; the railway and they buy tickets. But *they do not change fundamentally* for these trifles. As a matter of fact, it is the machine and not they, that is metamorphosed.[103]

CONCLUSION

While disciplinary power never dominated the workings of the colonial prison system in Indochina, it would be an overstatement to deny its existence

---

98. Such an argument was made more explicitly by the criminal ethnographer Dr. A. Corre, who cautioned against the naive belief that distinctly French penal methods could "modify the criminal tendencies of all races." Corre was expecially pessimistic about the deterrent capacity of the guillotine in Indochina. "The guillotine," he wrote, "will not change habits." A. Corre, *L'Ethnographie criminelle* (Paris, 1894), 382.

99. Lorion, *Criminalité et médecine judiciare en Cochinchine*, 45.

100. Ibid., 46.

101. Ibid., 133.

102. Conseil de gouvernement de l'Indo-Chine, *Session ordinaire de 1923: Discours prononcé par M. Martial Merlin* (Hanoi, 1923), 13.

103. Roland Dorgelès, *On the Mandarin Road* (New York, 1926), 52. My emphasis.

there altogether. Like their metropolitan counterparts, colonial wardens devised daily schedules, set standards for inmate conduct, attempted to monitor behavior, punished petty infractions, maintained individual dossiers, and tabulated statistics. Still, we should be wary of the fact that such disciplinary techniques reveal themselves today at the site most accessible to historians: the archive of penal directives and regulations. These institutional blueprints and decrees were typically imported directly from France, modified (more or less) for colonial conditions, and eventually published in annual collections of administrative documents. Consequently, historians have little difficulty finding Indochinese analogues to the metropolitan texts that historians cite as evidence for discipline's abrupt ascendance in European and American juridical punishment.

However, as colonial officials pointed out repeatedly, the gulf between prison policy and practice could be vast. "At this moment," remarked one colonial inspector in 1932, "the prisons of Tonkin reveal so much overcrowding and promiscuity, and such a melange of different categories of condemned of all sorts that I am led to the conclusion that there is no longer any observation of legal texts."[104] A report on the Poulo Condore Penitentiary expressed a similar view: "Indochina possesses decrees and local texts that constitute an imposing arsenal of penalties: prison, reclusion, detention, deportation, forced labor, banishment, etc., . . . which are ill-adapted to the conditions of the colony. On Poulo Condore, the *bagne* receives convicts of all categories and sensibly subjects them to an identical regime."[105]

Although the distance between colonial penal policy and practice poses problems for historians, the discrepancy itself can be interpreted as embodying the very disorder of the system. The failure of colonial prison administration to conform to written regulations reflected deeper problems: badly kept records, incompetent management, disobedient personnel, and the general failure of the colonial prison to meet metropolitan standards.

Despite the paucity of sustained scholarly research on colonial prisons in other contexts, anecdotal evidence suggests that, in this regard, the Indochinese system was not unique. In a discussion of the colonial justice system in late nineteenth-century East Sumatra, Ann Laura Stoler cites

104. AOM, Indochine, Affaires politiques, 1728, Rapport fait par M. Chastenet de Géry, Inspecteur de colonies, concernant l'organisation du régime pénitenciaire au Tonkin, April 26, 1932.

105. AOM, Indochine, Affaires politiques, 1728, Observations de M. l'Inspecteur des colonies Demongin, April 23, 1932.

the example of a newly appointed Dutch assistant resident who found "prison ledgers in such disarray that he could neither find records of the number of people in the prison nor dossiers detailing the length of their sentences nor even their crimes."[106] In British Indian penal documents, Anand Yang reports finding neither a "voice of humanitarianism" nor a discourse "about reformation or rehabilitation."[107] In British Burma, John Furnivall remarks, "the jails were continually being enlarged and continually overcrowded," whipping was "freely used," and "a prisoner could have anything he wanted except women; some said he could even have women."[108] Viewed alongside the prison system in Indochina, the images conjured by Stoler, Yang, and Furnivall suggest that despite the historical convergence of high imperialism and the birth of disciplined penal institutions in Europe, colonial prisons rarely embodied modern disciplinary technologies. It is likely that the forces impeding the spread of discipline in Indochinese jails discouraged its deployment in other colonial prison systems as well.

Of course, the enduring power of precolonial penal traditions, the legacy of imperial conquest, and the effects of colonial racism were not the only factors shaping the Indochinese prison. The institution must also be seen as one component of a larger colonial administration that exhibited distinctive organizational and operational characteristics. As chapter 2 will show, both the Indochinese prison and the social and political developments to which it gave rise reflected the peculiar administrative, financial, and legal workings of the French colonial state.

106. Ann Laura Stoler, "'In Cold Blood': Hierarchies of Credibility and the Politics of Colonial Narratives," *Representations* 37 (Winter 1992): 178. Stoler continues that Assistant-Resident Valck's predecessor "may have never kept a register, but neither did Valck take it upon himself to start one. Faber reported that among the few dossiers he found was one for a prisoner who had been interned for over eleven months for a four month sentence."

107. Anand Yang, "Disciplining 'Natives': Prisons and Prisoners in Early Nineteenth-Century India," *South Asia* 10, no. 2 (1987): 30.

108. J. S. Furnivall, *Colonial Policy and Practice: A Comparative Study of Burma and Netherlands India* (Cambridge, 1948), 137, 173, 268.

2 The System
Fragmented Order and Integrative Dynamics

The chaotic and irregular character of the prison system in Indochina reflected the fragmented and decentralized nature of the French colonial state. In spite of periodic attempts to rationalize and homogenize administration within the five territories that came to make up the Indochinese Union, the state bureaucracies of Annam, Tonkin, Cochin China, Cambodia, and Laos retained considerable autonomy until the end of the colonial era. As a result, prisons in each territory functioned within their own distinct legal, bureaucratic, and financial frameworks. Moreover, the system included different kinds of institutions, each of which followed its own staffing policies and internal regulations. The fact that Indochina's largest prisons were situated in frontier regions, far from administrative centers, contributed to the heterogeneity of the system by endowing wardens with extraordinary power to run their institutions free from external oversight. "The Indochinese prison system is not an administrative organism whose different elements are coordinated in a single direction," commented one colonial official in 1931; "rather it is an ensemble of formations spread throughout the territories, with only weak ties between them, and dependent on different authorities."[1]

Despite the fact that the colonial prison exhibited few of the qualities typically associated with modern administration (i.e., rationalization, centralization, standardization), the structure and functioning of the institution contributed inadvertently to the emergence in Indochina of another key element of modernity: political nationalism. As with colonial capitalist enterprises, administrative bureaucracies, school systems, and transporta-

1. J. de Galembert, *Les Administrations et les services publics indochinois* (Hanoi, 1931), 897.

38

tion and media networks, the prison system blanketed every corner of Indochina, and, despite its inconsistent structure, it was experienced by inmates and their families in the different territories in fundamentally similar ways. It also functioned to channel prisoners from various regional
backgrounds throughout the same far-flung institutional network. The geographical expanse of the system allowed prisoners passing through its internal channels to imagine and experience, often for the first time, the vast
extent and connectedness of Indochinese political space. Moreover, the fact
that colonial prisons mixed different categories of inmates indiscriminately
together in large communal wards created conditions for otherwise discon-
nected men and women to forge enduring bonds and collective identities. In
this way, the colonial prison system served as an institutional mainspring
for the development in Indochina of a modern political identity.

THE LEGAL FRAMEWORK

The heterogeneity of prison administration in French Indochina reflected
the uneven development and distribution of colonial power in its five ter-
ritories, Cochin China, Tonkin, Annam, Cambodia, and Laos. The French
Navy attacked Cochin China in 1859 and turned it into a formal French
colony through treaties signed with the imperial court in 1862 and 1867.[2]
In 1863, France established a protectorate over the kingdom of Cambodia.[3]
Over twenty years later, Annam and Tonkin also became protectorates of
France.[4] Laos was added officially in 1893 and split into the protectorate of
Luang Prabang and the rest of the country, which was ruled directly as a
colony.[5] Each territory had a separate administrative apparatus, which was
headed by a lieutenant-governor in Cochin China and by residents superior in Annam, Tonkin, Cambodia, and Laos. Provincial administration was
in the hands of French residents, who reported directly to the lieutenant-
governor and the residents superior.

Although the component parts of Indochina were integrated formally
into the Indochinese Union in 1887 and placed under the authority of a

2. John F. Cady, *The Roots of French Imperialism in Eastern Asia* (Ithaca, N.Y.,
1954), 272–74; Mark McLeod, *The Vietnamese Response to French Intervention,
1862–1874* (New York, 1991), 57–59.

3. Milton Osborne, *The French Presence in Cochinchina and Cambodia: Rule
and Response (1859–1905)* (Ithaca, N.Y., 1969), 175–206.

4. Pierre Brocheux and Daniel Hémery, *Indochine: La Colonisation ambiguë,
1858–1954* (Paris, 1995), 46–54.

5. Martin Stuart-Fox, "The French in Laos, 1887–1945," *Modern Asian Studies*
29, no. 1 (1995): 112–21.

powerful governor-general based in Hanoi, the nature of colonial administration continued to vary from territory to territory. A fundamental distinction concerned the degree of application of French laws in areas governed directly as colonies—Cochin China and most of Laos—and those
ruled indirectly as protectorates—Annam, Tonkin, Cambodia, and Luang
Prabang.[6] In Cochin China, for example, the colonial state introduced the
Napoleonic Code and established courts in which French judges adjudi-
cated all criminal cases.[7] In criminal matters involving native litigants exclusively, local authorities assisted the judge and suggested minor modifications that took local practices into account.[8] Nevertheless, all persons in
Cochin China, regardless of race, were subject to French criminal law.[9]

In the protectorates, French officials exercised power less directly and
relied to a greater extent on indigenous law. In the extreme case of Annam,
the monarchy was retained and the precolonial juridical administration
was preserved almost in its entirety.[10] This consisted of a three-tiered court
system made up of prefectural (*phu*) and district (*huyen*) tribunals, run by
village heads; provincial (*tinh*) tribunals, headed by provincial mandarins;
and special deliberative bodies within ministries (*bo*) under the authority
of superior mandarins.[11] Laws and decrees from the old Nguyen code were
applied at every level.[12] The emperor and the Imperial Council of Ministers
reviewed all judgments involving death penalties and highborn defendants.[13] Important decisions were conveyed to provincial residents, who

---

6. M. B. Hooker, *A Concise Legal History of South-East Asia* (Oxford, 1978),
153–75.

7. Milton Osborne, "The Debate on the Legal Code for Cochin China," *Journal
of Southeast Asian History* 10, no. 2 (1969): 224–35.

8. E. A. F. Garrigues, "Cochinchine," in *La Justice en Indochine*, ed. H. Morché
(Hanoi, 1931), 44–48.

9. Civil matters, on the other hand, were handled by a system of ethnically segregated courts. Civil cases involving "native" parties were tried in "indigenous tribunals," which applied to the laws of the old Nguyen code. French codes and courts
were used for cases in which French litigants were involved. Indigenous tribunals,
known as *justices de paix indigènes*, were only created by a decree of February 16,
1921. See Hooker, *Concise Legal History of South-East Asia*, 156.

10. The best general overview of justice in colonial Annam is Albert Bonhomme,
"Annam," in *La Justice en Indochine*, ed. H. Marché (Hanoi, 1931), 155–74.

11. Ibid., 158–59.

12. The Nguyen code comprised (1) the uncodified precepts contained in the
Book of Rites, (2) the constitutional edicts of the emperor, (3) the regulations of the
six ministries, and (4) the laws and decrees dealing with punishments. See Hooker,
Concise Legal History of South-East Asia, 169.

13. Ibid., 170.

could investigate serious or controversial cases.[14] Judgments involving imprisonment or physical punishment required the authorization of French officials, but only in extraordinary instances would they act to modify the decisions of judicial mandarins.[15]

Between fossilized Annam and frenchified Cochin China lay the protectorate of Tonkin. It exhibited such a tangled mixture of juridical features that one legal scholar referred to it as a hybrid "colony-protectorate."[16] As in Annam, the Nguyen code was applied in criminal and civil cases, but the law was radically modified in Tonkin and reorganized along the lines of French law.[17] Minor crimes were tried before provincial mandarins, appointed, as in the past, by the imperial court at Hue. More serious cases were brought before provincial tribunals headed by a French resident and a native official working in tandem. As in Cochin China, French courts served the protectorate's French and resident alien populations.[18]

Separate legal frameworks led to differences in the forms of punishment employed in each territory. For example, torture, corporal punishment, and death by strangulation were discontinued in Cochin China following the introduction of the French penal code in 1877.[19] In Annam, on the other hand, such practices were only abolished (by royal ordinance) in 1913.[20] Likewise, the antiquated Sino-Vietnamese sentence of exile endured in Annam throughout the 1930s, despite the gradual disappearance of frontier areas to which exiles could be sent. As a result, exiles from Annam were forced to serve their sentences alongside hard-labor convicts on Poulo Condore.[21] Since the Nguyen code made no distinction between political and common-law prisoners, neither courts nor prisons in Annam provided for separate or qualitatively distinct carceral regimes for political

14. Ibid., 171.

15. Ibid.

16. Paul Couzinet, "La Structure juridique de l'Union indochinoise," in *La Revue indochinoise juridique et economique* (Hanoi, 1939), 329, cited in Alexander Woodside, *Community and Revolution in Modern Vietnam* (Boston, 1976), 24.

17. L. A. Habert, "Le Tonkin," in *La Justice en Indochine*, ed. H. Morché (Hanoi, 1931), 175–210.

18. Hooker, *Concise Legal History of South-East Asia*, 172–75.

19. Ibid., 158. Jean-Claude Demariaux reports that the beating of inmates was banned on Poulo Condore by Director Félix Faure in 1896. This suggests that the ban of 1887 was not enforced. See Demariaux, *Les Secrets des îles Poulo-Condore: Le Grand Bagne indochinois* (Paris, 1956), 183.

20. Ibid., 171.

21. AOM, Affaires politiques, 1728, Rapport fait par M. Chastend de Géry, Inspecteur des colonies, concernant l'organisation du régime pénitentiaire au Tonkin, April 26, 1932.

offenders. Hence, imprisoned political activists in Cochin China merited a milder punitive regime than thieves and murderers, but such was never the case in Annam.

Moreover, the asymmetrical growth of French authority over the territories meant that colonial institutions in Cochin China enjoyed a twenty-year head start, at least, over those in the rest of Indochina. By the time the colonial state established Annam's first penitentiary, at Lao Bao, in 1896, prisons in Cochin China had undergone over thirty years of administrative development. In addition, the earlier annexation of Cochin China led to a larger and more established French community there, which in turn resulted in a denser European presence at the lower levels of the state bureaucracy. Hence, Cochin Chinese prisons employed a significantly higher percentage of European personnel than their counterparts in Annam and Tonkin.

THE FISCAL FRAMEWORK

The lack of uniformity in Indochina's penal order was magnified by its decentralized fiscal structure. Following reforms devised by Governor-General Paul Doumer in 1898, Indochina adopted a federal-style budget. Fiscal authority was divided between five autonomous "local" budgets (for Cochin China, Annam, Tonkin, Laos, and Cambodia) and a "general" budget (for all of Indochina) under the authority of the governor-general in Hanoi.[22] Local budgets drew revenue from personal taxes, while the general budget was funded by customs tariffs and state opium, alcohol, and salt monopolies. Under the new system, prisons were financed by local budgets exclusively, which meant that a penitentiary like Poulo Condore, which received inmates from all five Indochinese territories, could only draw funds from the budget of Cochin China. This tended to leave prison officials financially strapped and discouraged even the most modest restructuring or reform.

Almost immediately following the fiscal reforms of 1898, officials complained that the inadequacy of local budgets and their inability to tap the superior resources of the general budget constrained their capacity to maintain and upgrade the prison system. For example, in 1901, the resident superior of Annam reported to the governor-general that male and female

22. Brocheux and Hémery, *Indochine*, 83–99.

prisoners in Tourane (Da Nang) were being held together in the same room and requested supplementary funds from the general budget to build a separate female ward. He pointed out that the local budget was insufficient to pay for renovations and that the central government in France routinely granted subventions to local authorities for similar projects. The governor-general, however, rejected the request. Referring to the 1898 decree stipulating local responsibility for such matters, he admonished the resident superior "not to be preoccupied with metropolitan legislation that is neither applicable nor appropriate in the colony."[23]

During the 1930s, overcrowding and an acute shortage of funds for the operation of Poulo Condore prompted the governor-general himself to criticize the fact that local budgets bore the entire burden of prison administration in Indochina. "It is evident," he wrote to the minister of colonies, "that because Poulo-Condore receives prisoners condemned to heavy sentences from every territory in the Union, it is illogical to leave the responsibility for all administrative costs to the budget of Cochin China."[24] The governor-general called for a study to examine transferring fiscal responsibility for Poulo Condore to the general budget, but no action was ever taken.

Compounding the problem was the fact that prisons had never merited high priority as a budgetary item. In 1885, an inspection mission from the Ministry of Colonies chided the inequitable distribution of funds by the Colonial Council of Cochin China, which, it claimed, "was absurdly generous towards favored groups but tight-fisted towards everyone else."[25] Inspectors complained that the council's "niggardliness in providing prison facilities" resulted in "frightful conditions" and "promiscuous" mixing of untried defendants with sentenced convicts.[26] From 1913 to 1934, only 2 to 6 percent of annual state expenditures in Tonkin and Cochin China went to prison administration.[27] In spite of Ho Chi Minh's provocative charge in

23. AOM, Gouvernement général, carton 247, 4216, Régime pénitentiaire, August 24, 1901.

24. AOM, Affaires politiques, 1728, Gouverneur général de l'Indochine à M. le Ministre des colonies, December 1, 1932.

25. Quoted in Reuben Garner, "The French in Indochina: Some Impressions of the Colonial Inspectors, 1867–1913," *Southeast Asia: An International Quarterly* 2 (1969): 832.

26. Ibid.

27. Figures are calculated from Gouvernement général de l'Indochine, *Annuaire statistique de l'Indochine* (Hanoi), 1913–34.

the Vietnamese Declaration of Independence that France "built more prisons than schools" in Indochina, the colonial state in fact earmarked two to seven times more resources annually for education than for the prison system.[28] Indeed, prisons received significantly smaller budgetary allocations than medical services, offices of public works, civil service bureaus, transportation agencies, and police and paramilitary forces. Among the budgetary items with annual funding roughly on par with the prison services were the Office of Forestry, the provincial courts, and the bureaus in charge of cadastral and topographical surveying.

Another notable feature of state expenditure on prison administration was its invariability over time. In 1922, 515,000 piasters out of Cochin China's total budget—roughly 12,000,000 piasters—went to the Penitentiary Service.[29] By 1928, the colony's local budget had almost doubled (to roughly 20,000,000 piasters), but allocations for prison administration rose only a little more than 10 percent (to 584,000 piasters).[30] This inflexibility was even more apparent following the social and political disorder that coincided with the onset of the Great Depression. Despite the fact that the economic slump gave rise to a massive crime wave and an acute upsurge in anticolonial political agitation, spending on prisons remained more or less constant (as a percentage of the total budget) throughout the 1930s.

Table 1 shows that Indochina's various police and paramilitary forces absorbed a much greater percentage of local budgets than prisons. In 1934, 26 percent of Tonkin's budget went to the police and the paramilitary Garde indigène, while only 3 percent went to prisons. Moreover, unlike prisons, police forces received dramatic increases in state funding during periods of social unrest. These differences reflect colonial attitudes to the relative value of each institution as an instrument of state security policy. Officials at the highest levels exhibited a single-minded preoccupation with catching lawbreakers rather than with treating or reforming them. The unvarying character of state funding for prison administration points to the crude function that prisons were expected to play in the maintenance of social order. In contrast to the police, the colonial prison was not conceived as an institution that could be reinvigorated financially or refashioned structurally to solve complex social problems. Free from the utopian baggage carried by their counterparts in metropolitan France,

28. For a copy of the text, see *Vietnam Documents: American and Vietnamese Views of the War*, ed. George Katsiaficas (New York, 1992), 32.

29. Gouvernement général, *Annuaire statistique de l'Indochine*, 1922.

30. Ibid.

Table 1. Selected Annual Expenses, Local Budgets, 1929–1934
(thousand of piasters)

	1929		1930		1931		1932		1933		1934	
	Amount Spent	% of Total	Amount Spent	% of Total	Amount Spent	% of Total	Amount Spent	% of Total	Amount Spent	% of Total	Amount Spent	% of Total
Tonkin												
Garde indigène	2,321	12	2,346	11	2,422	19	2,361	19	2,009	19	2,012	21
Penitentiary Services	446	2	570	3	462	4	576	5	386	4	273	3
Police	1,101	5	1,282	6	639	5	596	5	583	5	462	5
Public Instruction	2,719	14	3,068	14	1,060	8	1,139	9	905	8	804	8
Public Works	3,845	20	3,941	18	1,746	14	1,195	9	1,190	11	1,223	13
Total Local Budget	19,429		21,736		12,924		12,716		10,683		9,715	
Cochin China												
Civil Guard	310	1	381	2	546	3	546	4	425	4	403	4
Penitentiary Services	632	3	800	4	800	5	827	6	602	6	568	5
Police	1,793	12	2,106	10	2,165	14	1,144	8	961	9	912	8
Public Instruction	2,429	11	2,287	11	2,453	15	2,314	17	1,835	17	1,659	15
Public Works	6,422	30	5,592	26	3,039	18	1,916	14	1,232	11	1,259	11
Total Local Budget	21,414		21,205		16,528		13,919		10,760		11,042	

SOURCE: Gouvernement général de l'Indochine, *Annuaire statistique de l'Indochine*, various years.

colonial prisons simply removed lawbreakers from civilian society and tried to keep them from stirring up trouble by putting them to work.

THE INSTITUTIONAL FRAMEWORK

The Indochinese prison system was made up of a complex hierarchy of penal institutions, densely patterned in the eastern Indochinese territories of Annam, Tonkin, and Cochin China, but extending much further afield. It was dominated by three kinds of institutions—provincial prisons, central prisons, and penitentiaries—but it also included houses of correction for minors and civil prisons. In addition, the Indochinese system was integrated into a vast penal network that stretched over France's global empire into South America, Africa, and the South Pacific. Given the diversity of the system, an understanding of its workings requires attention to several discrete institutional forms as well as to the patterned circulation of prisoners between them.

Provincial Prisons

The smallest institutions in the system were provincial prisons, typically constructed to hold from 50 to 100 prisoners. Their inmate populations were dominated by convicts sentenced to from one to three years' simple imprisonment. Most had been convicted of small-time crimes—petty theft, vagabondage, abuse of confidence, extortion, and assault. Provincial prisons also held defendants awaiting trial at local courts and individuals held under administrative detention for state monopoly violations, loan defaults, or tax evasion.[31] They were not authorized to hold political prisoners, European offenders, or inmates serving terms in excess of three years.

The modest capacity of the provincial prisons and the fact that their inmate populations were dominated by petty criminals should not obscure their importance in the penal arsenal of the colonial state. At the local level, the provincial prison was a fundamental pillar of state power. When French naval officers created the six original provinces of Cochin China in 1867, they promptly erected six provincial prisons.[32] In 1938, the colonial state continued to maintain provincial prisons in every province: 21 in Annam, 29 in Tonkin, 21 in Cochin China, 14 in Cambodia, and 9 in

---

31. De Galembert, *Administrations et les Services publics indochinois*, 901–902.
32. The six provinces were Ben Tre, Chau Doc, My Tho, Sai Gon, Soc Trang, and Vinh Long. See *Annuaire de la Cochinchine française*, 1880 (Saigon), 122–26.

Laos.[33] As table 2 demonstrates, the total number of prisoners held in provincial prisons at any one time was three to four times as great as that in colonial Indochina's larger and more elaborate penal institutions.[34] During the decade between 1913 and 1922, provincial prisons held an average of 15,925 prisoners on the last day of each year. Penitentiaries and central prisons, on the other hand, averaged a combined total of 4,566. Moreover, many more inmates entered provincial prisons annually than any other kind of penal institution. In 1935, for example, the provincial prison system ingested a startling total of 86,741 inmates, almost seven times the number processed by penitentiaries and central prisons combined.[35]

Unlike larger penal institutions, provincial prisons were neither run by professional wardens nor staffed by trained guards. Instead, each was managed by a French resident, the most powerful civil official in the province, and staffed by members of the provincial militia (the Garde indigène in Tonkin and Annam; the Garde civile in Cochin China).[36] Infantrymen stationed in the provincial capital supervised prisoners employed at external work sites. Given that they were run by administrative generalists and guarded by militiamen and soldiers rather than professional warders, provincial prisons exhibited significant diversity in organization and operations. As one observer noted, "the fidelity of provincial prisons to the official decrees that govern them is, in general, more theoretical than real."[37]

Administrative variation aside, provincial prisons were typically located in the center of provincial capitals, alongside the courthouse, the police station, the post office, and the office of the resident. In small or backwater provinces, this cluster of state offices might be little more than a handful of red-tiled, single-storied buildings lining a dusty central avenue. Consider Roland Dorgelès's description of Buon Ma Thuot Town during the early 1920s: "A few palms, a few huts, a fountain, the school, the prison, the

33. Gouvernement général, *Annuaire statistique de L'Indochine,* 1937–38, 88–90.

34. Gouvernement général, *Annuaire statistique de L'Indochine,* provides detailed statistical breakdowns of the penal system and population from 1929 to 1942. For the period from 1913 to 1921, more abbreviated records can be found in a retrospective summary in the *Annuaire statistique* of 1922. The *Annuaire statistique* for the period from 1922 to 1928 curiously and unfortunately does not include prison statistics. Prior to 1913, statistics on the prison system must be gathered piecemeal from different sources.

35. Ibid.

36. Léon Mossy, *Principes d'administration générale de l'Indochine* (Saigon, 1918), 68.

37. De Galembert, *Administrations,* 902.

Table 2. The Indochinese Prison Population on 31 December, 1913–1941

Year	Provincial Prisons	Central Prisons	Penitentiaries	Total
1913	13,914	2,125	2,301	18,340
1914	14,485	2,434	2,415	19,334
1915	15,590	2,327	2,317	20,234
1916	16,299	2,336	2,219	20,884
1917	15,755	2,012	2,460	20,227
1918	15,422	1,754	2,392	19,568
1919	18,204	1,880	2,638	22,722
1920	17,483	1,719	2,987	22,189
1921	15,693	1,796	2,778	20,267
1922	16,413	1,962	2,810	21,185
1930	13,270	3,294	3,297	20,312
1931	16,226	3,423	3,666	23,719
1932	19,416	3,440	4,895	28,097
1933	17,422	2,990	4,723	25,388
1934	16,754	2,755	4,242	24,031
1935	16,550	2,282	4,279	23,388
1936	14,225	2,159	3,850	20,515
1937	14,608	2,236	3,648	20,842
1938	15,292	2,594	3,767	22,064
1939	14,542	2,444	4,043	21,441
1940	17,721	3,760	4,349	26,233
1941	19,274	3,356	6,813	29,871

SOURCE: Gouvernement général de l'Indochine, *Annuaire statistique de l'Indochine*, various years. No statistics are available for 1923 through 1929.

barracks for four hundred militia-men—and then farther on, the forest once again."[38] No matter how remote the province or superficial the colonial presence there, the provincial prison was a familiar feature of the Indochinese landscape.

From the outside, provincial prisons conveyed an impression of strength and order. Most were encompassed by thick concrete walls, three and a half meters in height and studded on top with shards of broken glass.

38. Roland Dorgelès, *On the Mandarin Road*, trans. Gertrude Emerson (New York, 1926), 267.

The walls were cleaned and whitewashed at regular intervals by prison work teams. The façade of the prison was typically part of a two-story rectangular building that housed administrative offices, storage rooms, visiting areas, and, in some cases, the headquarters of the provincial police. Access to the inner courtyard was provided by a single arched entryway, located midway along the façade. The French flag hung above the entryway, as did a sign on which the institution's name was printed in capital letters. Watchtowers positioned at opposite corners of the walls facilitated surveillance of both the prison compound and the surrounding area.

Once inside, any visions of total institutional power conjured by the sturdy façade and whitewashed walls gave way before the cramped and ramshackle residential buildings where prisoners were kept. Lighter, less durable materials, such as bamboo and corrugated tin, were often used for doors, window bars, and ceilings. Inadequate ventilation, makeshift latrines, and an absence of running water gave rise to a stench of musty air and human waste. Poor maintenance left many of the residential buildings in chronic disrepair. "The buildings of the provincial prison are falling into ruins," complained the resident of Son Tay in 1910. "Several appear unlikely to withstand a violent gust of wind and are clearly too dangerous to inhabit."[39] The interior compounds of provincial prisons typically consisted of a communal residential ward, a rudimentary kitchen, an infirmary, and an open courtyard, where prisoners ate, bathed, and exercised. They often included separate living quarters for guards and their families. Some prisons had a small separate room for female inmates and a handful of solitary cells for prisoners considered dangerous, disruptive, or suicidal.

Owing to the small number of residential units, most inmates lived together in the communal dormitory, typically the largest edifice in the prison compound. There, all the prisoners lay side by side, on elevated concrete platforms that ran along the walls. Embedded at the foot of these platforms were rows of iron rings, through which a metal bar, known as the *barre de justice*, was threaded. To prevent them from moving around freely in the open chamber, prisoners slept with their ankles shackled to the *barre*. While the *barre* restricted physical mobility within the dormitory, however, it could not prevent social intercourse among prisoners. Recalling his

39. TTLT, Résidence supérieure au Tonkin, L'Administrateur de 3ème classe Gaillard, Résident de France à Son Tay, à M. le Résident superieur au Tonkin, October 18, 1910.

imprisonment in the Yen Bay Provincial Prison during 1929, Nguyen Hai Ham noted that inmates often found solace in the prison's communal setup. "Despite being immobilized by the chains around our feet, we were glad because we were next to each other and could share happy and sad memories."[40]

Because penal regulations imported into Indochina from France called for the segregation of prisoners based on gender, age, sentence, juridical status, and number of offenses, the crude communal structure of provincial prisons induced considerable anxiety among colonial officials. "The Yen Bay Prison is completely inadequate," the provincial resident wrote in 1908. "It consists of two residential buildings, one of which is flimsy and insecure. We are therefore forced to keep all our prisoners, including the accused, together in a single room."[41] The following year, the resident of Hai Phong wrote: "Owing to the absence of space, it is not possible to group the inmates following the degree of their penalties. As a result, smugglers and tax evaders of both sexes are imprisoned in the same space along with all the common-law offenders."[42] Twenty years later, the resident superior of Tonkin rehearsed a familiar critique of the system's enduring communal character. He expressed dismay at the frequency with which "prisoners of both sexes are confined side by side," bemoaned the "inconvenient arrangement of space" that prevented "the separation of diverse categories of prisoners," and pointed to the dangers posed by an architectural configuration that subjected "impressionable juveniles" to the "corrupting influences of hardened criminals."[43]

Although disenchantment with the crude communal structure of provincial prisons figures unceasingly in the correspondence of prison of-

---

40. Nguyen Hai Ham, *Tu Yen Bay Den Con Lon, 1930–1945* [From Yen Bay to Con Lon, 1930–1945] (Saigon, 1970), 108.

41. TTLT, Résidence supérieure au Tonkin, 79540, L'Administrateur résident de France à Yen Bay à M. le Resident supérieur au Tonkin, February 9, 1909.

42. TTLT, Gouvernement général, Rapports des commisions de surveillance de la prison de Hanoi et Haiphong pour 1908.

43. "Their crude setup does not allow provincial prisons to serve as places of treatment for morally abandoned minors. It is only through a physical and moral regime judiciously graded and adapted to the great diversity of cases that we can fulfill the social duty we have assumed. Only by making the prison into a house of education can we hope to struggle successfully against the worrisome growth of Annamite juvenile criminality" (TTLT, Maire de Hanoi, Le Résident supérieur au Tonkin à Messieurs les Résidents chefs de province et Commandants de territoire militaire au Tonkin, June 30, 1926).

ficials, the colonial state never committed resources to rectify the problem. In almost every case, administrative inaction was blamed on budgetary constraints. The significance of this bureaucratic imperative may be seen in negotiations that took place between the resident of Son Tay and the resident superior of Tonkin over the construction of a new provincial prison in 1911.

Chronic overcrowding and a series of mass escapes during the preceding decade had prompted the resident to propose building a new prison at an estimated cost of 28,000 piasters. This modest proposal called for the construction of two small communal dormitories, an infirmary, a paved courtyard, a room for female inmates, a kitchen, and a handful of solitary cells. Citing budgetary considerations, the resident superior responded with a scaled-down counterproposal that slashed the original budget by half. He rejected the paved courtyard, calling it "inessential in a prison in which inmates leave the buildings daily to work." The kitchen was also unnecessary, he explained, because "food has always been prepared by an outside contractor." He dismissed the proposal for a separate room for women, claiming that "there are rarely more than five or six female prisoners at any one time." Finally, in the "interests of economizing," he cut the number of proposed solitary cells from eight to four.[44]

The resident superior's tightfisted counterproposal was emblematic of the colonial state's skinflint approach to provincial prison administration. Although frequent episodes of overcrowding, epidemic disease, and institutional disorder revealed the shortsightedness of such an approach, financial imperatives consistently overrode attempts to modernize the system. Underfunded local budgets, however, were only part of the story. After all, the colonial state routinely reallocated scarce resources to police and paramilitary forces in response to crime waves and upsurges in anticolonial political agitation. Had colonial officials believed that prisons possessed the capacity to produce a more docile and law-abiding subject population, they might have supported more elaborate institutional designs. Instead, the colonial state's failure to endow provincial prisons with the physical capacity to classify and segregate different categories of inmates points to the relative weakness of the disciplinary impulse within the colonial penal project as a whole.

44. TTLT, Résidence supérieure au Tonkin, 5127, M. Le Résident supérieur au Tonkin au Résident de France à Son Tay, October 16, 1891.

Central Prisons

The colonial state maintained central prisons in Saigon, Hanoi, Phnom Penh, and Vientiane. Compared with provincial prisons, they were larger, structurally more complex, and responsible for a wider array of juridical functions. Construction on Indochina's first central prison, known in Vietnamese as Kham Lon (the Big Jail), began in Saigon in 1862. The walls, central dormitory, and main administrative offices were completed late in 1863 and refurbished following a fire in 1885.[45] New wings were erected in 1894 and 1902, and workshops and punitive cells were added between 1885 and 1911.[46] Periodic renovations and expansions gradually doubled Kham Lon's original capacity from 400 in 1863 to 800 by 1930.[47] Hoa Lo (the Oven), Indochina's second central prison (later known as the Hanoi Hilton), was completed on the outskirts of Hanoi's French quarter in 1898.[48] Its original capacity increased from 460 to 600 following a renovation completed in 1913.[49] As with provincial prisons, central prisons suffered from chronic overcrowding. Hoa Lo, for example, averaged 730 prisoners per day in 1916, 895 in 1922, and 1,430 in 1933.[50]

An important distinction between central prisons and provincial prisons lay in the professionalization of their staff. In 1916, Governor-General Albert Sarraut ordered the creation of a centralized Penitentiary Service to recruit a permanent administrative corps to staff the colony's larger penal institutions. Thereafter, central prisons were headed by a director and manned by guards drawn directly from this professional corp.[51] External oversight was provided by a Commission of Surveillance, made up of one

45. AOM, Indochine, Affaires politiques, 1728, Mission d'Inspection, Service de la Maison centrale de Saigon, January 30, 1932, 17.

46. Ibid.

47. *Annuaire de la Cochinchine*, 1880, 134; Gouvernement général, *Annuaire statistique de l'Indochine*, 1930, 213.

48. Hoa Lo was named after the kilns traditionally produced by the communities displaced during construction of the new prison. It was built in the Phu Khanh hamlet in the Tho Xuong district. See So Van Hoa Thong Tin Ha Noi and Vien Lich Su Dang, *Dau Tranh Cua Cac Chien Si Yeu Nuoc Va Cach Mang Tai Nha Tu Hoa Lo (1899–1954)* [The Struggle of Patriotic and Revolutionary Fighters in Hoa Lo Prison (1899–1954)] (Hanoi, 1994), 27.

49. Ibid., 34.

50. Figures for 1922 and 1933 come from Gouvernement général, *Annuaire statistique de l'Indochine*. For the 1916 figures, see TTLT, Résidence supérieure au Tonkin, 81781, Rapport annuel sur le fonctionnement de la Maison centrale de Hanoi, January 12, 1917.

51. De Galembart, *Administrations*, 895.

doctor and several municipal officials, who visited central prisons monthly and issued periodic reports.[52]

Like its metropolitan counterpart, the colonial central prison served as both a *maison de correction* and a *maison pour peine*.[53] This meant that convicts sentenced to at least one year's simple imprisonment could serve out their terms there. However, the Indochinese central prison was expected to play the additional roles of a *maison d'arrêt*, a *maison de justice*, and a *maison de detention par mesure administrative*.[54] In France, the two former institutions held defendants awaiting trial. The latter was reserved for debtors, smugglers, and tax-evaders. In addition, central prisons were the only colonial penal institutions that maintained facilities for European defendants and convicts.[55]

Because of the diversity of their inmate populations, central prisons featured a more elaborate internal structure than provincial prisons. In Hanoi, for example, the central prison featured separate wards for defendants, convicts, common-law inmates, and political prisoners. Special wards were reserved for European men, who were kept apart from the natives. There were three residential units for female prisoners: one for natives, one for Europeans, and a small cell block for incorrigibles. In addition, Hanoi Central Prison possessed fifty cells for death-row convicts, high-profile political prisoners, and inmates considered dangerous or disruptive.

Despite being equipped with a multitude of discrete spaces in which different categories of prisoners might be held separately, central prisons resembled provincial prisons in their failure to enforce rules of classification and segregation. After visiting Hanoi Central Prison in 1916, the resident superior of Tonkin complained that, "according to regulations, different categories of prisoners should occupy different rooms. However, the arrangement of the buildings does not permit the observation of the letter of these prescriptions. The different quarters of the prison do not correspond to the categories of prisoners as fixed by the law."[56] Likewise, in

---

52. AOM, Nouveaux fonds, Gouvernement général, 4235, Rapport de la Commission de surveillance de la prison de Hanoi pour l'année 1908.

53. See *Arrêté portant réglementation des prisons de l'Indochine*, May 17, 1916. The copy consulted here can be found in TTLT, Résidence supériere au Tonkin, 81781.

54. Ibid.

55. European convicts sentenced to over six months were sent to serve out their sentences in France (De Galembert, *Administrations*, 902).

56. TTLT, Résidence supérieure au Tonkin, 81781, Services pénitentiaires, Tonkin, 1916.

1932, a ministerial inspection team observed that "most of the rooms in the Saigon Central Prison hold, at the same time, defendants with convicts, political with common-law prisoners, and children with adults."[57]

The institutional character of central prisons was also shaped by the fact that they were situated in the heart of Indochina's largest cities and their inmates were well integrated into urban life. During the day, convicts worked on city streets and in state office buildings. Sick prisoners were routinely transferred to municipal hospitals for the duration of their maladies. The continual motion of inmates, guards, and visitors entering and leaving the institution gave rise to a constant exchange of information and contraband across prison walls. Guards in Kham Lon were known to frequently visit the relatives of prisoners throughout Saigon in order to transmit letters and arrange secret provisioning.[58] In 1911, the director of Hoa Lo posted sentries outside the prison to prevent street peddlers from smuggling messages through the barred windows. "These merchants," the director complained, "are, for the most part agents of communication between inmates and their families."[59] In 1913, sentries reported a rash of small packages containing tobacco, opium, and "Annamite pastries" being tossed over the wall into the prison compound.[60] The following year, the resident superior commented that letters and packets, apparently thrown from within Hoa Lo, routinely littered the path surrounding the outer wall.[61] Similar practices were observed well into the 1930s.[62]

The urban location of central prisons provoked anxiety among French officials and city residents, especially during periods of overcrowding. Following a massive wave of arrests during the early 1930s, officials in Saigon worried that disorder within prisons might spill out into the city. During a mass protest against the execution of a Communist Party member, Ly Tu

---

57. AOM, Affaires politiques, Mission d'Inspection, 1728. Rapport fait par M. Le Gregam sur la Maison centrale de Saigon, January 30, 1932.

58. Phan Van Hum, *Ngoi Tu Kham Lon* [Sitting in the Big Jail] (1929; reprint, Saigon, 1957), 86.

59. TTLT, Résidence supérieure au Tonkin, 81824, July 25, 1911.

60. Ibid., August 4, 1913.

61. Ibid., 81826, May 16, 1914.

62. See, e.g., "Vut Thuoc Phien vao Nha Pha Hoa Lo Cho Tu" [Throwing Opium into Hanoi Central Prison for Prisoners], *Dong Phap*, March 17, 1937, 7. See also Hoang Dao's 1938 account of a court case in Hanoi in which two opium addicts imprisoned in Hoa Lo are tried and convicted for attempting to retrieve small packets of opium lobbed over the prison wall. Hoang Dao, *Truoc Vanh Mong Ngua* [In the Court of Justice] (Hanoi, 1938), reprinted in *Phong Su Chon Loc* [Selected Reportage], ed. Vuong Tri Nhan (Hanoi, 1994), 409–11.

Trong, in November 1931, the chanting of disgruntled prisoners could be heard for hours echoing throughout the surrounding neighborhood.[63] "Several incidents have occurred over the past month at the Saigon Central Prison," a colonial official remarked in early 1932, "nothing excessively grave—but troubling in that they give rise to a clamor of disorder in the very heart of the town."[64] A similar nightmare haunted officials at Hoa Lo: "What is the worst that can happen? Imagine the horrible spectacle, unfolding in the center of the capital, of inmates becoming masters of the prison after reducing guards and prison officials to impotence. What will follow? An American-style siege of the establishment."[65]

In his memoir of life in the Saigon Central Prison during the late 1920s, Phan Van Hum described the strange sensation of being confined within permanent earshot of a rich symphony of urban noise. In the morning, prisoners could hear the low din of cars driving by and street vendors hawking pâté, cream cakes, sweet bean pudding, and grilled meat. During the afternoon, they overheard headlines chanted by itinerant newsboys and snatches of *cai luong* opera and French music played on a nearby phonograph. At night, prisoners listened to the echoes of Saigon nightlife: cars honking, couples laughing, and "the clattering of high heels over the pavement outside."[66]

Penitentiaries

If central prisons were quintessentially urban institutions, penitentiaries were distinguished by their geographical remoteness from large population centers. Several, like Poulo Condore and the short-lived penitentiaries on Phu Quoc and the Ile de la Table, were located on islands completely isolated from the mainland.[67] Annam's two penitentiaries, Lao Bao and Buon

63. For a brief French account, see AOM, SLOTFOM, 3d ser., carton 49, November–December 1931, 8. For two Vietnamese descriptions of the event, see Tran Thanh Phuong, *Day Cac Nha Tu My Nguy* [Here, the Prisons of the American Puppets] (Ho Chi Minh City, 1995), 111, and Han Song Thanh, *Nhung Ngay Tu Nguc* [Prison Days] (Ho Chi Minh City, 1995), 42–43.

64. AOM, Indochine, Affaires politiques, 1728, Rapport fait par M. Le Gregam sur la Maison centrale de Saigon, January 30, 1932, 23. Le Gregam commented that "the only advantage gained by the positioning of the prison is its immediate proximity to the court."

65. Ibid., Rapport fait par M. Chastenet de Géry concernant l'organisation du régime pénitentiaire au Tonkin, April 26, 1932, 15.

66. Phan Van Hum, *Ngoi Tu Kham Lon*, 148.

67. Phu Quoc was identified by the Saigon police commissioner as a special site for prisoners sentenced to *relégation* in 1881. In January 1882, 30 prisoners were

Ma Thuot, were situated in isolated mountainous areas near the Lao border.[68] In Tonkin, penitentiaries were built along the Chinese frontier at Cao Bang, Ha Giang, and Lai Chau, and in upland regions dominated by ethnic minority communities, such as Thai Nguyen and Son La.

In choosing such remote sites, several considerations shaped the thinking of colonial officials. The isolation of penitentiaries from French and Vietnamese population centers served to diminish security concerns. The transfer of serious offenders to remote outposts was seen as a deserved intensification of punishment for serious offenders. Moreover, officials believed that Vietnamese convicts were less likely to escape in regions peopled by "hostile" ethnic minority communities. Each of these arguments may be found in the following report:

> Lai Chau Penitentiary should be maintained because it is situated far enough away from the Red River Delta that imprisonment there represents a real punishment for the condemned. Its location also ensures that movements or revolts there will have as small a repercussion as possible in the provinces of the Delta. Moreover, the surrounding population, Thai and Meo, is completely devoted to us. Consequently, Lai Chau is inhospitable for escape attempts.[69]

In addition, frontier regions and upland areas lacked the manpower necessary for infrastructural development. Hence, colonial officials in remote outposts looked to prison labor to meet a pressing administrative need. The decision to convert the provincial prison at Thai Nguyen into a penitentiary in 1908 confirms that labor demands played a key role in the selection

---

sent there and placed under his supervision. Prisoners on Phu Quoc were compelled to work on land owned by this same police commissioner. By 1885, 120 prisoners were held there. The penitentiary was closed in 1929. AOM, Anciens fonds H Colonies, 2026, Prisons Cochinchine—affaires générales, August 28, 1885.

68. For European travelers who happened upon them, penitentiaries cut a dramatic figure against the jungle and frontier landscapes into which they were awkwardly inserted. Consider the following description of the Lao Bao Penitentiary in the British reporter Harry Hervey's *Travels in French Indochina* (London, 1928), 259: "I remember the scene so well. . . . Fireflies stitched the dusk like luminous needles, and behind them a few bats reeled in drunken embroidery. The evening had a soft, fantastic quality. Suddenly a bugle call seemed to inject a momentary glitter into the quiet. Ahead, where the red road entered a stockade, a native soldier appeared, and following him was an irregular line of half-naked prisoners, chained and some wearing the cangue. In the background rose the whitewashed prison building, grim as a medieval fortress."

69. AOM, Affaires politiques, 7F54, Révolte de Lai Chau—Rapport de M. Roux, July 20, 1927, 60.

of geographic sites. At the center of the provincial resident's case for up-grading the prison was an argument about the "anticipated utility of penal labor for road building and excavation in Thai Nguyen."[70]

Like central prisons, penitentiaries were managed by officials recruited from the Penitentiary Service. The staff consisted of a director, a chief warder, a registrar, a medical doctor, and a clerk in charge of storage and supplies.[71] Medical postings and clerkships were occasionally filled by ethnic Vietnamese, but the supreme posts of director and chief warder were reserved for Europeans. Officials acknowledged, however, that ethnic exclusivity was no guarantee of administrative competence:

> The choice of director of Poulo Condore has not always been a happy one. Before 1917, the penitentiary was run by M. O'Connell whose administration, if certain echoes are to be believed, was far from model—negligence being the rule. He was replaced by Lieutenant Andouard from the Customs Office, who, during a revolt in 1918, brutally machine-gunned seventy-one convicts. He was assassinated in 1919. His successor, Captain Lambert, was dismissed in 1927 after being tried and convicted for assault. Based on a report prepared by M. De Tastes in June 28, 1927, Lambert was also guilty of numerous miscarriages of justice and an astonishing accumulation of other charges.[72]

A major difference between penitentiaries and central prisons was the ethnic composition of their surveillance staff. Most guards in central prisons were Vietnamese. In penitentiaries, on the other hand, they were recruited from ethnic minority communities that lived in the surrounding area. Ede, Jarai, and Mnong tribesmen staffed the penitentiaries at Buon Ma Thuot and Lao Bao. Tai and Mnong villagers manned the penitentiaries at Son La and Lai Chau, and most guards at the Cao Bang Penitentiary were ethnic Tay. Staffing the penitentiaries with minorities was one of the conventional divide-and-rule tactics of colonial administration. Because inmate populations were dominated by Vietnamese lowlanders, officials hoped that ethnic rivalries between guards and prisoners might reduce collusion between the two groups. This may well have been true. On the other hand, an enduring French belief in the innate inferiority of upland minority groups relative to Vietnamese lowlanders generated reservations about

70. TTLT, Résidence supérieure au Tonkin, 79552.
71. AOM, Indochine, Affaires politiques, 1728, Arrêté portant le règlement des îles du pénitencier de Poulo-Condore, May 17, 1916, 1–3.
72. Ibid., Rapport fait par M. Le Gregam, Inspecteur des colonies, sur les îles et le pénitencier de Poulo Condore, February 23, 1932, 42–43.

the wisdom of minority staffing policies. In 1913, the resident of Cao Bang speculated that a recent wave of escapes from the penitentiary was owing to "the fact that the Tho [Tay] guards were easily deceived by crafty Annamite detainees from the Delta."[73]

Such anxiety was compounded by the fact that penitentiaries typically held the most dangerous categories of prisoners. Most numerous were felons serving lengthy sentences (five years to life) of forced labor.[74] Courts issued forced-labor sentences for murder, manslaughter, rape, pillage, highway robbery, grand larceny, counterfeiting, fraud, and embezzlement.[75] Penitentiaries also received prisoners sentenced to detention and deportation—punishments applied exclusively to political crimes.[76] They could also hold convicts serving longer terms of simple imprisonment. In addition, penitentiaries were expected to accommodate prisoners sentenced to *relégation* (banishment, or transportation), a special punishment reserved for recidivists.[77]

In terms of architecture and design, penitentiaries were simply larger versions of provincial prisons. Although they held Indochina's most menacing inmates, penitentiaries housed the majority of their prisoners in large, undifferentiated communal rooms. The first *bagne* built on Poulo Condore (1875), Bagne I, had ten dormitories (150 m² in area), each of which held 80 prisoners.[78] One hundred inmates could fit comfortably into the two main dormitories (75 m² in area) of the Lao Bao Penitentiary (1896).[79] Poulo Condore's second (1916) and third (1928) *bagnes* had twelve and eight dormitories respectively, with dimensions similar to those of Bagne I.[80] Buon Ma Thuot Penitentiary (1930) consisted of six large dor-

73. TTLT, Résidence supérieure au Tonkin, 81781, Rapport sur la fonctionnement des établissements pénitentiaires du Tonkin et du service de l'identité, 1913–16.

74. De Galembert, *Administrations*, 897–99.

75. Benjamin Martin, *Crime and Criminal Justice under the Third Republic: The Shame of Marianne* (Baton Rouge, La., 1990), 256–57.

76. De Galembert, *Administrations*, 905–6.

77. Ibid., 907. In Indochina, those sentenced to *relégation* were occasionally sent to a special camp on Phu Quoc Island.

78. Ban Nghien Cuu Lich Su Dang Dac Khu Vung Tau—Con Dao, *Nha Tu Con Dao, 1862–1945* [Con Dao Penitentiary, 1862–1945] (Hanoi, 1987), 32.

79. Le Kim Que, "Tim Hieu Ve Nha Tu Lao Bao" [Understanding Lao Bao Prison], *Tap Chi Lich Su Dang* 10 (1985): 71.

80. Ban Nghien Cuu Lich Su Dang Dac Khu Vung Tau—Con Dao, *Nha Tu Con Dao, 1862–1945*, 34–35.

mitories (100 m² in area), each with enough capacity for 100 prisoners.[81] The five dormitories of the Son La Penitentiary (1930) each held 80 inmates.[82]

As in provincial prisons and central prisons, communal architecture and the heterogeneity of the inmate population led to unauthorized category mixing in penitentiaries. According to an inspection of Poulo Condore in 1910, the penitentiary was "characterized by a constant interpenetration of convicts serving different sentences."[83] An assessment conducted six years later reported little improvement: "Convicts on Poulo Condore are not divided into categories based on the nature of their penalty. Instead, they are mixed pell-mell, so that those sentenced to *relégation* or to short terms of forced labor mingle freely with those condemned to life sentences. In fairness, material inadequacies have prevented adherence to legal prescriptions."[84]

Several factors made the problem especially acute in penitentiaries. The concentration of political prisoners in penitentiaries magnified fears of "promiscuity" and "contamination." Also troubling was the fact that their inmate populations included prisoners who, according to penal codes, simply did not belong there. Although prisoners sentenced to *relégation* were held in penitentiaries, these sentences did not, in fact, entail physical confinement. Rather, they called for quarantining convicts in secluded regions, where they were supposed to be provided with seed, farming tools, and agricultural land. In 1896, the minister of colonies remarked that "the incarceration of such prisoners in the prison buildings on Poulo Condore constitutes a cruel and illegal aggravation of [their] punishment."[85] Such protests were ignored, however, and identical complaints resurfaced habitually throughout the 1930s.

81. Tinh Uy Dak Lak and Vien Lich Su Dang, *Lich Su Nha Day Buon Ma Thuot, 1930–1945* [History of Buon Ma Thuot Penitentiary, 1930–1945] (Hanoi, 1991), 25.

82. Vien Mac-Lenin and Vien Lich Su Dang, *Nguc Son La: Truong Hoc Dau Tranh Cach Mang* [Son La Prison, The School of Revolutionary Struggle] (Hanoi, 1992), 10.

83. AOM, Nouveaux fonds du Gouvernement général, 4248, M. Cudenet, Administrateur des Services civils, Directeur des îles et du pénitencier de Poulo Condore à Monsieur le Lieutenant-gouverneur de la Cochinchine, March 1, 1910.

84. Ibid., 4260, Inspection de Poulo Condore, September 23, 1916, 3.

85. TTLT, Résidence supérieure au Tonkin, 7272, Le Ministre des colonies à M. le Gouverneur général de l'Indochine, March 31, 1896.

Civil Prisons, Houses of Correction, and Penal Colonies

In addition to provincial prisons, central prisons, and penitentiaries, Indochina possessed two other kinds of penal institutions: civil prisons and
houses of correction. Civil prisons, located in Hai Phong and Tourane (Da
Nang), functioned as miniature central prisons under the authority of municipal officials.[86] Houses of correction were used to incarcerate juvenile
delinquents. In 1904, the colonial state constructed a house of correction
adjacent to the Ong Yem agricultural station in Cochin China's Thu Dau
Mot Province.[87] A similar installation was completed in 1925 in Tonkin's
Bac Giang province in the district of Tri Cu.[88] As in France, juvenile facilities in Indochina were organized as large collective farms, and delinquents
were compelled to perform agricultural labor.[89]

Third, Indochinese convicts could be sent abroad to penal colonies in
other parts of the French empire. Such was often the fate of Vietnamese
monarchs who fell out of favor with the colonial regime. Following his role
in the Save-the-King Movement during the mid 1880s, the young rebel
king Ham Nghi was exiled for life to Algeria.[90] In 1916, the deposed king
Thanh Thai and his son Duy Tan were shipped off to the penal colony on
Réunion Island in the Indian Ocean.[91] The former died there, and the latter
was released in 1945.[92]

86. De Galembert, *Administrations*, 900. From the early 1920s on, for purposes
of statistical calculation, the municipal prison at Tourane was often categorized as a
central prison, while the one at Hai Phong was classed as a provincial prison. See
Gouvernement général, *Annuaire statistique de l'Indochine*, 1922 on.

87. TTLT, Résidence supérieure au Tonkin, 72060, Note du Directeur de l'Administration de la Justice en Indochine relative au régime pénal applicable aux
mineurs en Indochine, March 28, 1927, 4.

88. Ibid., 7.

89. French "utopic thought had long valued agricultural pursuits as a means of
eliminating poverty and vice," Patricia O'Brien notes in *The Promise of Punishment: Prisons in Nineteenth-Century France* (Princeton, N.J., 1982), 137–40. By
1880, sixty agricultural colonies for minors were operating in France, many run by
private charitable groups.

90. David Marr, *Vietnamese Anticolonialism, 1885–1925* (Berkeley and Los Angeles, 1971), 55.

91. "Everyone knows that King Ham Nghi is currently in Algeria and that kings
Thanh Thai and Duy Tan are on Réunion Island," observed the Hue newspaper
Tieng Dan [The People's Voice], "3 Vua Ham Nghi, Thanh Thai Va Duy Tan Se
Duoc An Xa Chang?" [Will Our Three Kings, Ham Nghi, Thanh Thai, and Duy Tan
Be Amnestied?], August 1, 1936.

92. Bruce Lockhart, *The End of the Vietnamese Monarchy* (New Haven, Conn.,
1993), 27.

Less exalted convicts were sent to New Caledonia in the South Pacific, where the French had set up a large penal colony in 1857.[93] According to one source, Indochinese convicts were first deported to the island in 1864 and continued to be sent there well into the twentieth century.[94] A more distant but nevertheless more frequent destination for Indochinese convicts was French Guiana. Between 1867 and 1887, most of the prisoners sent to the South American penal colony were Vietnamese or Algerians, who, it was argued, could withstand the humid tropical climate better than Frenchmen.[95] Transportation from Asia to French Guiana continued sporadically until 1931, when the French National Assembly created a special territory there, called Inini, exclusively for Indochinese convicts.[96] On June 3, 1931, after a 35-day voyage, 523 Indochinese prisoners arrived at Inini, where they were put to work opening up the hinterland for economic exploitation.[97] Owing to protests against conditions in the South American *bagne*, deportations to Guiana slowed considerably during the mid 1930s, and they stopped completely when the Popular Front assumed power in France in 1936.[98]

THE EXPANSION OF THE SYSTEM

Prior to World War II, the growth of the Indochinese prison system progressed through four general phases. During the twenty years following the Treaty of Saigon in 1862, it consisted of the Poulo Condore Penitentiary, the Saigon Central Prison, and six provincial prisons connected to the

93. In 1887, New Caledonia held 9,700 convicts; in 1901, 10,500; and in 1931, still 5,700. Most were Frenchmen sentenced to hard labor. See Robert Aldrich, *The French Presence in the South Pacific, 1842–1940* (Honolulu, 1990), 144. I have found no figures for the number of Indochinese sent to New Caledonia, but see an interesting memoir by a Vietnamese ex-prisoner, Pham Binh Ry, "Tan The Gioi Hay La Nam Nam O Numea" [The New World, or, Five Years in Noumea], *Tieng Dan*, May 2–July 4, 1939.

94. Pham Binh Ry describes finding the grave of Nguyen Van Truyen in the cemetery on New Caledonia. An original participant in Phan Boi Chau's Eastern-Travel Movement, Truyen was arrested in Hong Kong in 1913 and deported to the island the following year. He died on January 24, 1915. See ibid., May 20, 1939.

95. Gordon Wright, *Between the Guillotine and Liberty: Two Centuries of the Crime Problem in France* (New York, 1983), 95.

96. Hy V. Luong, *Revolution in the Village: Tradition and Transformation in North Vietnam, 1925–1988* (Honolulu, 1992), 117.

97. Ibid.

98. Daniel Ballof, "La Déportation des Indochinois en Guyane et les établissements pénitentiaires spéciaux, 1931–45," *Revue guyanaise d'histoire et de géographie* 10 (April–May–June 1979): 21.

six original provinces of Cochin China.[99] Between 1882 and 1896, the colonial state consolidated its control over Cochin China and annexed the protectorates of Annam and Tonkin. The annexations were followed by rapid administrative expansion that entailed the establishment of 51 new provinces and 51 new provincial prisons: 20 in Tonkin, 15 in Annam, and 16 in Cochin China. During the third phase, between 1896 and 1917, the colonial state constructed a series of larger prisons in an effort to rationalize the system. In 1896, Annam's first penitentiary was built at Lao Bao, with adequate space for 250 convicts.[100] Three years later, Governor-General Paul Doumer oversaw the completion of Hanoi Central Prison, built to hold 460 prisoners.[101] In 1904, a civil prison for 200 inmates was constructed at Hai Phong.[102] The Cao Bang Penitentiary was completed in 1905 and equipped for 400.[103] In 1908, the provincial prison at Thai Nguyen was expanded to hold 300 inmates and transformed into a penitentiary.[104] And in 1917, a second *bagne* was added to Poulo Condore, with a capacity of 600.[105]

Prison construction slowed during the 1920s, but picked up again in the early 1930s in response to an upsurge of anticolonial political activity. In 1931, the colonial state erected a camp for 250 inmates in the central highlands at Kon Tum.[106] In 1932, it transformed the small provincial prison at Son La into a huge maximum security penitentiary, which soon became

---

99. The six provincial prisons were Ben Tre, Chau Doc, My Tho, Sai Gon, Soc Trang, and Vinh Long. See *Annuaire de la Cochinchine*, 1880, 126.

100. Le Kim Que, "Tim Hieu Ve Nha Tu Lao Bao," 71. During the first decade of its existence, Lao Bao doubled as a provincial prison, and then began admitting predominately long-term hard-labor convicts following the antitax movements of 1908. While Lao Bao typically held fewer than one hundred prisoners per day prior to the 1920s, it averaged over two hundred throughout the 1930s.

101. So Van Hoa Thong Tin Ha Noi and Vien Lich Su Dang, *Dau Tranh Cua Cac Chien Si Yeu Nuoc Va Cach Mang Tai Nha Tu Hoa Lo, 1899–1954*, 28.

102. Ngo Thi Thanh, "Hoat Dong Cua Nhung Tu Nhan Cong San Trong Nha Tu Hai Phong, 1930–1945" [Activities of Communist Prisoners in Hai Phong, 1930–1945] (Undergraduate honors thesis, 1987, History Department, Vietnam National University, Hanoi).

103. AOM TTLT, Résidence supérieure au Tonkin, 81781, Note sur le fonctionnement des établissements pénitentiaires du Tonkin et du Service de l'identité pendant l'année 1912–1913.

104. See chapter 5.

105. Ban Nghien Cuu Lich Su Dang Dac Khu Vung Tau—Con Dao, *Nha Tu Con Dao, 1862–1945*, 31.

106. See Le Van Hien, *Nguc Kontum* [Kontum Prison] (1938; reprint, Hanoi, 1958), 4–20.

Tonkin's most important detention center for political prisoners.[107] That same year, a penitentiary was built at Buon Ma Thuot with a capacity of 700, making it Indochina's second largest penitentiary, after Poulo Condore.[108] Hence, at the start of 1933, the colonial prison system comprised ten penitentiaries (4,895 prisoners), five central prisons (3,440 prisoners), and eighty-nine provincial prisons (19,416 prisoners).[109] Including 346 juvenile delinquents at two houses of correction, the entire system held 28,097 prisoners.[110]

The extraordinary level of punitiveness in colonial Indochina may be seen by comparing its rate of incarceration with other countries. Following the first comprehensive census at the end of 1936, 117 people were in jail in Indochina for every 100,000 members of the population.[111] During roughly the same era, the ratio of prisoners to population was 77:100,000 in the Dutch East Indies (1927), 75:100,000 in Japan (1935), and 50:100,000 in France (1932). Assuming a slightly lower population figure for Indochina in 1932, the ratio that year was 160:100,000. As table 3 suggests, the rate of incarceration in Indochina during the late colonial era was two to three times higher than in France and significantly greater than in Japan and the Dutch East Indies.

Equally instructive is the number of people who entered the colonial prison system annually. While such figures fail to consider the duration of incarceration or the fact that recidivists may have been jailed multiple times in a single year, they still convey something of the extraordinary number of lives touched by colonial imprisonment. In 1936, for example, 91,118 individuals were processed and held by the prison system (see table 4). Given that Indochina's population in 1936 was roughly 17.6 million, more than one of every 200 people that year served some time behind bars.

Integrative Dynamics

Despite its regional, fiscal, and legal fragmentation, the colonial prison system contributed to the emergence of a modern national consciousness among the Vietnamese. Prior to the French conquest, a precolonial history

107. Vien Mac-Lenin and Vien Lich Su Dang, *Nguc Son La: Truong Hoc Dau Tranh Cach Mang*, 10.

108. Tinh Uy Dak Lak and Vien Lich Su Dang, *Lich Su Nha Day Buon Ma Thuot, 1930–1945*, 23.

109. For statistical purposes, the Hai Phong Civil Prison is classified as a provincial prison and the Tourane Civil Prison is classified as a central prison.

110. Gouvernement général, *Annuaire statistique de l'Indochine*, 1932–33.

111. Ibid., 1936.

Table 3.   Comparative Rates of Incarceration: Indochina, Japan, the Dutch
East Indies, and France, 1930s

	No. of Prisoners	Rate of Incarceration
Indochina, 1932	28,097	160
Indochina, 1936	20,515	117
Japan, 1935	51,094	75
Dutch East Indies, 1927	46,000	77
France, 1932	18,954	50

SOURCES: Indochina: Gouvernement général de l'Indochine, *Annuaire statistique de l'Indochine*, vol. 6: *1934–1935–1936* (Hanoi, 1937), 88; Charles Hirshman, "Population and Society in Twentieth-Century Southeast Asia," *Journal of Southeast Asian Studies* 25, no. 2 (September 1994): 381–416; Japan: Elmer Johnson, *Japanese Corrections: Managing Convicted Offenders in an Orderly Society* (Carbondale, Ill., 1996), 2; France: Franklin Zimring and Gordon Hawkins, *The Scale of Imprisonment* (Chicago, 1991), 9; Dutch East Indies: Anne Marie Christien Bruinink-Darlang, *Het penitentiair stelsel in Nederlands-Indie van 1905 tot 1940* (Alblasserdam, 1986), 411.

Table 4.   Number of Prisoners Entering the Indochinese Penal System,
1930–1941

Year	Provincial Prisons	Central Prisons	Penitentiaries	Total
1930	50,275	12,894	1,707	64,876
1931	55,645	13,065	1,749	70,459
1932	66,986	12,574	1,959	81,519
1933	67,524	12,877	1,733	82,134
1934	83,455	12,218	694	96,367
1935	86,741	11,732	1,098	99,571
1936	78,228	11,945	1,071	91,118
1937	65,357	12,348	663	78,368
1938	62,844	14,219	752	77,815
1939	54,618	13,204	1,512	69,334
1940	56,514	16,248	1,346	74,108
1941	64,629	21,086	4,281	89,996

SOURCE: Gouvernement général de l'Indochine, *Annuaire statistique de l'Indochine*, various years.

marked by territorial division, cultural heterogeneity, and economic diversity along its north-south axis discouraged the formation of a single political identity among ethnic Vietnamese.[112] Indeed, since the late sixteenth century, Vietnamese inhabiting the narrow strip of coastal land between the highlands of eastern Tonkin and the mountains of southwestern Cambodia had lived under the political authority of a single government for only a few decades between 1802 and 1862. And even during this brief period of unity, political identity among the elite appears to have been deeply fragmented along regional and family lines.[113]

As with many institutions put into place by the colonial state, the prison system unleashed integrative forces that countered the historical tendency toward the fragmentation of Vietnamese political identity. It did so by penetrating into every administrative center of Indochina, where it subjected individuals from widely divergent social and regional backgrounds to the same terrifying ordeal. For murderers from My Tho, smugglers from Son La, and vagabonds from Vinh, the system's brutal and erratic mode of operation generated a common set of experiences and a similar cluster of antagonistic attitudes toward the colonial state. The same was true for millions of spouses, parents, children, relatives, lovers, and friends whose relations were caught up in its internal network. "Families with imprisoned members are desperately afraid for them," remarked Phan Van Hum in 1929; "some do nothing but wait anxiously for their safe release."[114] Vietnamese prisoners and their families came to see themselves as part of a vast community of victims, stretching from southern Cochin China to northern Tonkin, and the common interests of an emergent national community gradually came into focus.

Just as the brutality of the prison system contributed to the formation of a unified political identity, the constant circulation of prisoners through

112. See Keith Taylor, "Nguyen Hoang and the Beginning of Viet Nam's Southward Expansion," in *Southeast Asia in the Early Modern Era*, ed. Anthony Reid (Ithaca, N.Y., 1993), 42–65; Li Tana, "An Alternative Vietnam? The Nguyen Kingdom in the Seventeenth and Eighteenth Centuries," *Journal of Southeast Asian Studies* 29, no. 1 (March 1998): 111–21; and Nola Cooke, "Regionalism and the Nature of Nguyen Rule in Seventeenth-Century Dang Trong (Cochinchina)," *Journal of Southeast Asian Studies* 29, no. 1 (March 1998): 122–61.

113. Nola Cooke, "Nineteenth-Century Vietnamese Confucianism in Historical Perspective: Evidence from the Palace Examinations (1463–1883)," *Journal of Southeast Asian Studies* 25, no. 2 (September 1994): 270–311; id., "The Composition of the Nineteenth-Century Political Elite of Pre-Colonial Nguyen Vietnam (1802–1883)," *Modern Asian Studies* 29, no. 4 (1995): 741–64.

114. Phan Van Hum, *Ngoi Tu Kham Lon*, 86.

its component parts encouraged inmates to internalize the parameters of a new national space. Lawbreakers were typically held in local jails following arrest, sent to provincial prisons before trial, transferred to a central prison while awaiting appeal, and deported to a remote penitentiary after sentencing. Hard-labor convicts and political prisoners were almost always severed from their native places and transported either to the distant southern islands of Poulo Condore, the remote northern provinces of Cao Bang, Lai Chau, Ha Giang, and Son La, or the secluded eastern highland towns of Buon Ma Thuot and Lao Bao. Inmates sentenced to *relégation* in Cochin China, Cambodia, and Laos were compelled to serve their sentences in the Tonkinese penitentiaries at Cao Bang and Lai Chau, while those from Annam and Tonkin were sent south to Poulo Condore.

Labor shortages in undeveloped provinces also encouraged the mobility of the colonial prison population. Two to three times a year, residents drew up lists of "healthy and robust" prisoners who could be furnished temporarily to provinces in need of manpower. In a letter sent to all residents in 1904, the resident superior of Tonkin announced his "intention to send to the High Region the most prisoners possible, in order to make up for a severe insufficiency of labor."[115] In 1920, 1,365 Tonkinese inmates were transferred from institutions in the Delta to prisons in the northern provinces for road construction and other "work of general interest."[116] Prisoners were also moved to relieve overcrowding, to break up clandestine plots and prison gangs, and to evacuate sites infected by epidemic disease.

What was the impact of the constant traffic of inmates through the prison system's serpentine network of communal wards? In certain respects, the flow of lawbreakers through the colonial prison system generated changes in popular consciousness similar to the changes in elite consciousness triggered by the circulation of students through the Franco-Vietnamese school system.[117] Both systems uprooted individuals from their native places, removed them from their families and shepherded them through a hierarchical network of institutions that blanketed a new administrative landscape. During their journeys, they formed intimate at-

---

115. TTLT, Résidence supérieure au Tonkin, 76541, le Résident supérieur au Tonkin à Messieurs les Maires de Hanoi, de Haiphong et les Résidents-Chefs de Provinces au Tonkin, May 5, 1904.

116. Ibid. 81781. Rapport annuel sur la situation générale de la Maison centrale de Hanoi au cours de la période du 1ᵉʳ janvier au 31 décémbre 1920.

117. Gail Kelly, "Franco-Vietnamese Schools, 1918–1938" (Ph.D. diss., University of Wisconsin, 1975).

tachments with fellow sojourners who came from faraway regions and spoke in unfamiliar accents. As a result, prisons, like schools, nurtured bondings that supported the development of what Benedict Anderson has described as "imagined communities."[118] After release, escape, graduation, or expulsion, many ex-students and ex-prisoners (especially political prisoners) attempted to promote the sensations of connectedness that they had experienced during their journeys as the ideology of modern nationalism. In contrast to schools, however, prisons were neither exclusive nor elitist institutions. Whereas mere thousands completed educational pilgrimages from local primary schools to urban secondary schools and on to higher educational opportunities in Hanoi, Saigon, and Paris, millions undertook the equally extensive but involuntary carceral journey. Hence, large segments of the colonial underclass participated in the formation of a national community through the shared experience of penal imprisonment.

Because the prison system blanketed Cambodia and Laos, in addition to Annam, Tonkin, and Cochin China, the nationalism it promoted was perhaps more Indochinese than Vietnamese. After all, Vietnam as a modern geopolitical concept did not emerge until the establishment of the Democratic Republic of Vietnam by Ho Chi Minh's Viet Minh in 1945.[119] Until then, French efforts to integrate the three dominant ethno-linguistic components of Indochina—Cambodia, Laos, and Annam–Tonkin–Cochin China—by creating common bureaucratic and infrastructural frameworks had created an unresolved tension within local nationalist thinking. For many Vietnamese officials assigned to posts in Phnom Penh and Cambodian students attending university in Hanoi, the postcolonial nation-state that they imagined was Indochinese, not Cambodian or Vietnamese. This was only natural given that colonial bureaucracies penetrated all five territories of the Union and functioned to channel elite boys throughout the diverse ethno-linguistic terrain of Indochina. The same was true, of course, for the colonial prison system, which occasionally transferred Lao murderers to Cochin China and Vietnamese recidivists to Cambodia.

However, the system's dense patterning in Annam, Tonkin, and Cochin China meant that the bodies of sojourning Vietnamese prisoners more

118. Benedict Anderson, *Imagined Communities: Reflections on the Origins and Spread of Nationalism* (London, 1991), 119–32.

119. Christopher E. Goscha, *Vietnam or Indochina? Contesting Conceptions of Space in Vietnamese Nationalism, 1887–1954*, Nordic Institute of Asian Studies Report Series, no. 28 (Copenhagen, 1995), 74–96.

often than not traced the outlines and crisscrossed the area of a geopolitical space that coincided with the parameters of the future postcolonial Vietnamese nation-state. For example, before being deposited on Poulo Condore in 1908, Huynh Thuc Khang passed through prisons in Hue, Tourane (Da Nang), Hoi An, Quang Ngai, and Saigon. [120] Following his arrest in July 1926, Ton Quang Phiet was routed through ten different penal institutions, stretching from Mong Cay on the Sino-Tonkinese border down to Nha Trang along the southern coast of Cochin China, and eventually up to Buon Ma Thuot in western Annam.[121] In a memoir describing his arrest, incarceration, and deportation in 1929, Nhuong Tong charted changes in climate, scenery, and regional dialect as he traveled, under armed guard, between Hue, Vinh, Hanoi, and Poulo Condore.[122] Such itineraries served to reinforce a sense of the reality of a Vietnamese national space.

An illustration of the role of imprisonment in the formation of a national identity may be found in the prison memoir of the anticolonial Confucian scholar Huynh Thuc Khang. Like many patriotic activists of his generation, he became involved in local movements for modern schooling during the first decade of the twentieth century. Although Western-style schools were founded throughout Tonkin, Annam, and Cochin China, Huynh Thuc Khang's own efforts were relatively parochial, being confined to the region around Hue where he had been born and grown up. In 1908, he was arrested following a wave of antitax and anticorvée labor riots in Annam and sentenced to life imprisonment on Poulo Condore. On his way to prison, he encountered a group of unfamiliar prisoners who had been jailed under identical circumstances:

> At the Han Cua Dock in Tourane, on the way to Poulo Condore, a Western officer led us to the back of the ship, where we came upon a group of nine prisoners chained together. Immediately, I recognized these Nghe An scholars as political prisoners like myself. We gazed at each other and smiled. For several years, Dang Nguyen Can, Thai Son, and Ngo Duc Ke and I had been spiritually connected through our common efforts to promote new schooling, but before that instant we had never met.[123]

120. Huynh Thuc Khang, *Thi Tu Tung Thoai* [Prison Verse] (1939; reprint, Saigon, 1951), 11–40.
121. Ton Quang Phiet, *Mot Ngay Ngan Thu (Lan Thu Nhat O Nha Nguc)* [The Eternal Day (My First Time in Prison)] (Hue, 1935), 1.
122. Nhuong Tong, *Doi Trong Nguc* [Life in Prison] (Hanoi, 1935), 2–32.
123. Huynh Thuc Khang, *Thi Tu Tung Thoai*, 32.

The passage shows how incarceration functioned to intensify sensations of connectedness among anticolonial activists who had long struggled, in isolation from one another, for similar goals against a common enemy. Although Huynh Thuc Khang insisted that a "spiritual connection" had existed previously between him and his fellow prisoners, it is clear from their gleeful reaction to each other that their physical encounter aboard the prison ship served to deepen their sense of comradeship.

In the remainder of his memoir, Huynh Thuc Khang chronicled the close relationships he formed over the following thirteen years with an array of political prisoners from different regions and generations. He met the surviving leaders of the Save-the-King campaigns of the 1880s and the rebels who spearheaded the Duy Tan uprising during World War I. He also came into contact with lower-class anticolonial agitators, such as the soldiers and criminals who launched the mutiny at Thai Nguyen in 1917, and anti-French outlaws who followed the celebrated social bandit De Tham. Through these encounters, Huynh Thuc Khang was able to situate himself within a movement that may be characterized as nationalist by virtue of the fact that its members recognized the existence of deep cultural and historical commonalities among themselves that transcended much older regional and social divisions.

If Huynh Thuc Khang went to prison for protesting against local taxation and corvée labor policies in rural Annam, his political activities following his release thirteen years later focused on national objectives. In 1927, he founded the newspaper *Tieng Dan* (Voice of the People), which became the longest-running paper in the new romanized Vietnamese script (*quoc ngu*) in the history of Indochina.[124] Highlighting the nationalist project of *Tieng Dan*, he argued that the paper's primary goal was to help the people "take cognizance of being Vietnamese."[125] The paper's national orientation may also be seen in its relentless promotion of *quoc ngu* as the "national language" and its preoccupation with the establishment of a national literary canon. During the late 1930s, *Tieng Dan* served as a forum for a seminal debate over whether Nguyen Du's brilliant early nineteenth-century verse narrative *Truyen Kieu* (The Tale of Kieu), ought to be considered

124. The reference to "the people" in the newspaper's title represented a standard convention of early Vietnamese nationalist discourse that first appeared in the writings of Phan Boi Chau. See Greg Lockhart, *Nation in Arms: The Origins of the People's Army of Vietnam* (Boston, 1989), 41–51.

125. Cited in Nguyen The Anh, "A Case of Confucian Survival in Twentieth-Century Vietnam: Huynh Thuc Khang and His Newspaper *Tieng Dan*," *Vietnam Forum* 8 (Summer–Fall 1986): 182.

the "embodiment of Vietnam's national soul and national essence."[126] In 1939, it sponsored a poetry contest on the theme "this S-Shaped territory," a prophetic allusion to what was to become the cartographical archetype of the postcolonial nation.[127]

CONCLUSION

The decentralized and heterogeneous character of the Indochinese prison system embodied the chaotic and unsystematic workings of the colonial state. Just as Indochina comprised an irregular hodgepodge of colonies, protectorates, and hybrid colony-protectorates, the components of the prison system varied significantly from territory to territory. Different legal systems and separate financial frameworks in Tonkin, Annam, and Cochin China gave rise to a variety of institutional forms and administrative procedures. If centralization and rationalization are seen as hallmarks of the modern state, the French colonial state, as viewed through its prison bureaucracy, would seem to be a particularly crude variant of the genre.

The Indochinese prison's indiscriminate treatment of different categories of prisoners also points to the limits of colonial modernity. As John Bender has observed, the capacity to "categorize and differentiate" was "a defining feature of the new penitentiaries."[128] In the early nineteenth century, the French penal reformer Thomas Le Breton identified "classification" as "the very basis of prison reform."[129] This increasingly taxonomic approach, all but absent from the colonial environment, was expressed in the construction of cellular prisons, the first of which was completed in Paris in 1836.[130] By 1853, a regime of classification and segregation, known as the "system of separation by quarters," structured the 150 prisons run by the French Ministry of the Interior. The system provided for "the grouping in distinct quarters of men and women, condemned and accused, adults and minors and first-time offenders and recidivists."[131]

Nevertheless, in view of its contribution to the rise of a national consciousness among the Vietnamese in Indochina, the colonial prison system

---

126. Nguyen The Anh, "Case of Confucian Survival," 185.

127. Ibid., 182.

128. John Bender, *Imagining the Penitentiary: Fiction and the Architecture of Mind in Eighteenth-Century England* (Chicago, 1987), 61.

129. Robin Evans, *The Fabrication of Virtue: English Prison Architecture, 1750–184* (Cambridge, 1982), 261.

130. Wright, *Between the Guillotine and Liberty*, 68.

131. Robert Badinter, *La Prison républicaine, 1871–1914* (Paris, 1992), 34.

may have played an inadvertent role in the emergence of a key aspect of Vietnamese modernity. To the extent that the success of the Vietnamese revolution was based on its ability to harness the power of Vietnamese nationalism, the ill-disciplined colonial prison may be seen, paradoxically, as one powerful engine that propelled the Vietnamese political community into the modern era.

3 The Regime
Surveillance, Forced Labor, and Total Care

Life inside the colonial prison was powerfully shaped by three factors: the conduct of the guards, the conditions of forced labor, and the quality of food and health care. Indeed, it was innovations in these three areas (in addition to architectural changes) that marked the transition to a modern prison system in nineteenth-century France. In the utopian visions of French prison reformers, the role of the guard corps in the modern penitentiary was to instruct and educate inmates. The forced-labor regime was intended to help them internalize industrial discipline. And food and medical care were supposed to provide a healthy physical foundation for moral rehabilitation. These reforms were implemented only partially and with limited success in France, but they remained significant as "a code of action" against which institutional performance was measured.[1]

In Indochina, on the other hand, modern forms of prison surveillance, forced labor, and institutional provisioning and health care were virtually absent. French colonial officials' distrust of and contempt for the indigenous prison staff discouraged the idea that guards might act as a moralizing force within the institution. Faith in the power of industrial-style work to reform prisoners paled beside a more compelling view of the labor power of the Indochinese inmate as a motor for infrastructural development. And support for the socializing virtues of a good diet and sound health care gave way before the financial imperatives of the colonial state and its callous indifference to the fate of native inmates.

1. Patricia O'Brien, *The Promise of Punishment: Prisons in Nineteenth-Century France* (Princeton, N.J., 1982), 304.

COLONIAL PENAL SURVEILLANCE

Although the duties of colonial prison guards were defined in prison regulations, the nature of penal surveillance was determined by the social and ethnic composition of the inmates and staff. At every level of the prison system, the vast majority of inmates were Vietnamese. On the other hand, with outside of a handful of upland penitentiaries staffed by members of ethnic minority communities, prison personnel were divided between a small European administrative elite and a large corps of Vietnamese warders. Not only did Vietnamese prisoners and Vietnamese warders share a common language and culture, but members of both groups tended to come from similar class and regional backgrounds. It is not surprising, therefore, that a host of informal relations—some collusive and some predatory—developed between surveillants and inmates. Such unauthorized interactions were not unknown in prisons in France, but the characteristically colonial ethnic dynamic within Indochinese prisons served to heighten their scope and intensity. Indeed, the social distance separating European prison officials from Vietnamese guards and inmates created space for the development of a relatively autonomous indigenous social domain in the colonial prison that European officials could never penetrate or control.

Matas *and* Linhs

During the late nineteenth and early twentieth centuries, colonial prison administration was highly decentralized, and wardens recruited guards for their own institutions. In 1916, Governor-General Albert Sarraut attempted to standardize and improve the quality of colonial penal surveillance by setting up a centralized Penitentiary Service responsible for staffing penitentiaries and central prisons in Indochina.[2] Separate bureaucratic hierarchies were established for European and indigenous personnel, with different job titles and pay scales. Key positions in the European chain of command included those of the prison director, the chief guard, and three classes of ordinary guards. Members of the indigenous staff, known colloquially as *matas*, were divided into four classes of "surveillants."

---

2. J. de Galembart, *Les Administrations et les services publics indochinois* (Hanoi, 1931), 895. Institutions affected by the change included the *bagne* on Poulo Condore; the penitentiaries at Thai Nguyen, Cao Bang, Lai Chau, and Lao Bao; the central prisons of Hanoi, Saigon, and Pnomh Penh; the provincial prisons at Nam Dinh, Battambang, and Kampot; and the civil prison at Haiphong.

Consistent with the grossly unequal salary structure of the colonial bureaucracy as a whole, the wages of the lowliest European guards were
roughly five times greater than those of the highest class of indigenous
surveillants.[3]

Matas were always subordinate to the European staff. In most institutions, they were prohibited from handling keys, and, instead of bearing
firearms like European guards, they were permitted to carry only truncheons.[4] *Matas* stood guard at various locations within and around the
prison and monitored inmates whenever they left their dormitories to eat,
wash, go to the toilet, or receive visitors. They also supervised inmates employed at forced labor, usually at external work sites. They were assisted in
their duties by *caplans*, prisoners who took on surveillance responsibilities
in return for special privileges.[5]

Like guards in nineteenth-century French prisons, most *matas* were de-
mobilized or retired soldiers.[6] As early as 1898, all *matas* were required to
have served at least four years in French or Indochinese regiments.[7] In addition to engendering obedience, discipline, and respect for authority, military training was thought to provide good preparation for the mundane
rigors of guard duty. Like soldiering, surveillance entailed lots of idle time,
and tasks tended to be monotonous and repetitive. As in the army, *matas*
were divided into ranks based on seniority and paid on a graded scale.[8]
Matas of different ranks were distinguished by emblems stitched into their
uniforms. And just as soldiers were trained to exhibit unwavering respect
for and obedience to their superiors, prison guards were expected to behave
in a uniformly correct and courteous manner toward prisoners under their
authority.[9]

While local warders at penitentiaries and central prisons were recruited
from the ranks of retired soldiers, indigenous guards in provincial prisons,
known as *linhs*, were drawn directly from provincial militias—the Garde

3. TTLT, Résidence supérieure au Tonkin, 81795, Services pénitentiaires, Etats de
solde du personnel indochinois et européen, April 30, 1916.
4. Ibid., Arrêté portant le règlement des prisons de l'Indochine, May 17, 1916.
5. For a more detailed discussion of *caplans*, see chapter 4.
6. On the military backgrounds of French prison guards, see Benjamin Martin,
Crime and Criminal Justice under the Third Republic: The Shame of Marianne
(Baton Rouge, La., 1990), 263–64.
7. TTLT, Maire de Hanoi, 3929, Réorganisation de la prison de Hanoi, 1898.
8. TTLT, Résidence supérieure au Tonkin, 81795, Arrêté portant règlement des
prisons de l'Indochine, May 17, 1916.
9. Ibid.

indigène in Tonkin and Annam, and the Garde civile in Cochin China.[10] Guard duty was among a number of paramilitary tasks that militiamen carried out in provincial outposts.[11] According to a 1915 decree, the main responsibilities of militiamen included "escorting convoys, protecting government offices, policing roads, and guarding provincial prisons."[12] Again, militiamen were thought to possess the requisite martial skills and institutional orientation necessary for work in penal surveillance.

If guard duty was similar to soldiering, it was also a little like being a prisoner. In large prisons, *matas* were often compelled to live with their families in special quarters within the institution. As a result, their lives were circumscribed by some of the same regulations that structured the lives of inmates. In Hanoi Central Prison, for example, guards and their families were subjected to bodily searches upon entering and leaving the prison grounds.[13] Visitors needed to be approved in advance and were not allowed between the hours of 9:00 P.M. and 5:00 A.M.[14] In addition, *matas* themselves were to be kept under surveillance by European personnel. The first regulation in the professional handbook for the European staff read: "European employees must report all infractions committed by prisoners and indigenous surveillants."[15]

Superficially at least, colonial penal surveillance in Indochina resembled the routinized "hierarchical observation" that historians have identified as a crucial innovation of modern disciplinary institutions in Europe. The fact that guards were themselves under surveillance recalls panoptic features that Foucault emphasizes in his account of the emergence of the modern prison, and the militarization of colonial penal surveillance squares with his concept of the circulation of disciplinary techniques throughout the social body.[16] However, firsthand accounts of surveillance practices in colonial

---

10. The militias were founded in the late nineteenth century and modeled on British India's Bengal police. See E. Daufès, *La Garde indigène de l'Indochine de sa création à nos jours* (Avignon, 1933), vi.

11. Kim Munholland, "The French Army and the Imperial Frontier, 1885–1897," in *Proceedings of Third Annual Meeting of the French Colonial Historical Society* (Montréal, 1977), 92.

12. Léon Mossy, *Principes d'administration générale de l'Indochine* (Saigon, 1918), 68.

13. Phan Van Hum, *Ngoi Tu Kham Lon* [Sitting in the Big Jail] (1929; reprint, Saigon, 1957), 89.

14. TTLT, Résidence supérieure au Tonkin, 81795, Arrêté portant le règlement des prisons de l'Indochine, May 17, 1916, 7.

15. Ibid.

16. Michel Foucault, *Discipline and Punish: The Birth of the Prison*, trans. Alan Sheridan (New York, 1979), 302–3.

prisons suggest a significantly more ill-disciplined picture. Indeed, the image of colonial penal surveillance conveyed through memoirs and administrative reports recalls patterns of informal corruption, collusion, and predation more typically associated with premodern systems of incarceration.

Predation and Collusion

According to numerous sources, indigenous guards regularly extorted money from prisoners and their families. *Matas*, for example, were notorious for demanding a wide array of illicit payments from prisoners, known as "surveillance money." In 1909, an inmate named Pham Van Thu wrote to the resident superior claiming that prisoners who refused to pay guards in Hanoi Central Prison were routinely beaten or punished falsely for bogus disciplinary infractions.[17] Prisoners who paid promptly, on the other hand, stood to enjoy perks such as extra rations and exemptions from the rigors of the forced labor. "Such prisoners may receive special supplies from their families, including opium," Pham Van Thu complained, "and they are allowed to relax for long periods at work sites."[18]

In 1929, Phan Van Hum claimed that *matas* in the Saigon Central Prison demanded bribes directly from the families of prisoners:

> When a new prisoner arrives, the Annamite guard orders the *caplan* to record his name, profession, residence, home village, sentence, and registration number. With all this information, the guard picks a day off and visits the prisoner's house. Members of his family are typically starved for information about the condition of their imprisoned loved one. Hence, the guard can lie that their imprisoned relation has been severely beaten, is weak, and has no one to care for him. He then offers to look after the prisoner in exchange for money. If the family does not believe the guard's lie and refuses to pay, then the guard makes sure that the lie is no longer a lie.[19]

The fact that *matas* and prisoners came from the same background facilitated this particular form of corruption. It is difficult to imagine European guards in Indochina furtively blackmailing prisoners' families this way.

---

17. "When a prisoner is initially put in prison, the *quan, doi,* or one of the *linhs* demands a small payment for the cost of surveillance" (TTLT, Résidence supérieure au Tonkin, 71793, Correspondances diverses: letter of complaint from inmate Pham Van Thu, September 1, 1909).

18. Ibid.

19. Phan Van Hum, *Ngoi Tu Kham Lon*, 86.

Not only would it have entailed considerable risks, but it would have been difficult for Europeans to practice such intimidation and extortion in the Vietnamese cultural context.

The institution of "surveillance money" was little more than a crude form of extortion, but *matas* devised more subtle methods as well. On Poulo Condore, they developed an ingenious scheme that entailed soliciting bribes from prisoners to facilitate escapes, while simultaneously tipping off bounty hunters in return for a cut of their reward money. Although this practice was eventually discovered and the *matas* involved dismissed, the high frequency of escapes and recaptures on the island suggests that similar arrangements may have persisted throughout the colonial era.[20] In addition, *matas* collected a wide variety of petty bribes and informal fees from prisoners. Le Van Hien describes *matas* at Kon Tum Prison selling fresh fruit and cakes to prisoners at inflated prices.[21] On Poulo Condore, *matas* were known to auction off easy work assignments to the highest bidder, to organize gambling in return for a percentage of the winnings, and to tolerate opium smoking in exchange for small quantities of the drug.[22]

Just as bribery and petty extortion upset the scripted formalities of penal surveillance, collusive and recreational fraternization between Vietnamese guards and Vietnamese prisoners undermined institutional norms as well. Illicit intercourse was often based on a common enthusiasm for narcotics and alcohol. In 1889, the warden of the Hanoi Civil Prison discovered that guards and prisoners were regularly sneaking away from hard-labor work sites together in order to "smoke opium in a den on the rue des Cartes."[23] In 1925, the warden of the Kien An Provincial Prison reported that a guard and a group of bootleggers he was escorting to the prison had "arrived, after an unusually long time, in a state of utter drunkenness."[24] Similar episodes were cited regularly on Poulo Condore: "In addition to their proclivities for vices such as drunkenness and opium smoking,

20. AOM, Gouvernement général, 4248, Régime pénitentiaire—M. Cudenet, Administrateur des Services civils, Directeur des îles et du pénitencier de Poulo Condore à Monsieur le Lieutenant-gouverneur de la Cochinchine, March 1, 1910.

21. Le Van Hien, *Nguc Kontum* [Kontum Prison] (1938; Hanoi, 1958), 47.

22. Jean-Claude Demariaux, *Les Secrets des îles Poulo-Condore: Le Grand Bagne indochinois* (Paris, 1956), 52.

23. TTLT, Maire de Hanoi, 3931, Le Commissaire central de police de la ville de Hanoi au Résident Maire de la ville de Hanoi, March 10, 1889.

24. TTLT, Résidence supérieure au Tonkin, 81833, Résident de Kien An au Résident supérieur au Tonkin, March 25, 1925.

indigenous personnel rarely report irregularities concerning the activities and conditions of convicts under their authority. One reason is that they often befriend the latter so as to jointly indulge their vices and together commit misdeeds."[25]

Gambling was another common interest. In 1910, the warden on Poulo Condore reported that "three convicts were found at eight yesterday morning at the camp of the *matas* gambling for large sums of money with the wife of the surveillant assigned to guard them."[26] In 1925, a guard in the Kien An Provincial Prison was caught "gambling in the main dormitory while several prisoners were wandering unsupervised in the yard."[27] In 1928, the warden of Poulo Condore included chronic gambling in a litany of complaints against the Vietnamese staff: "Frankly speaking, most *matas* are drunks, opium addicts, and gamblers. They collude with the prisoners and steal from the regime. In short, their mentality is no better than [that of] the prisoners."[28]

On Poulo Condore, prisoners and *matas* were mixed up in a thriving sex industry, a fact the warden bemoaned in 1910: "I call your attention to the demoralized state of the *matas*. These agents, a large percentage of whom are drunkards and opium addicts, are, with rare exceptions, involved in pimping and collusion with the detainees."[29] The warden eventually expelled from the island the wives of two *matas*, "who, despite persistent warnings, had continued to organize gambling and prostitution for guards and prisoners."[30] Acknowledging the pervasiveness of prostitution within the prison, the warden expressed hope that "these expulsions may intimidate others involved in similar ventures."[31]

25. AOM, Indochine, Affaires politiques, 1728, Rapport fait par M. Le Gregam, Inspecteur des colonies, sur les îles et le pénitencier de Poulo Condore, March 11, 1932, 52.

26. AOM, Indochine, Gouvernement général, 4248, M. Cudenet, Administrateur des Services civils, Directeur des îles et du pénitencier de Poulo Condore à Monsieur le Lieutenant-gouverneur de la Cochinchine, Saigon, March 1, 1910.

27. TTLT, Résidence supérieure au Tonkin, 81833, Résident de Kien An au Résident supérieur au Tonkin, March 26, 1925.

28. AOM, Indochine, Affaires politiques, 1728, Mission d'inspection, Rapport fait par M. Le Gregam, Inspecteur des colonies, sur les îles et le pénitencier de Poulo Condore, March 11, 1932, 52. The 1932 report cited references from an earlier investigation completed in 1928.

29. AOM, Indochine, Gouvernement général, 4248, M. Cudenet, Administrateur des Services civils, Directeur des îles et du pénitencier de Poulo Condore à Monsieur le Lieutenant-gouverneur de la Cochinchine, March 1, 1910.

30. Ibid.

31. Ibid.

To explain the prevalence of illicit social intercourse between prisoners and surveillants, French officials pointed to the powerful pull of racial solidarity. "It seems ridiculous," explained the warden of Poulo Condore in 1916, "to entrust the security of indigenous prisoners to individuals of their own race. It is only natural that indigenous surveillants should sympathize with indigenous prisoners."[32] In 1932, a colonial inspector cited "nationalism" to explain such collusion: "The complacency and compassion that *matas* display toward the condemned derives from either a spirit of gain or a latent nationalism within all Annamites."[33]

For French officials, intensified contact between prisoners and surveillants during Tet confirmed suspicions about the power of racial and national affinities. Intelligence reports note increases in fraternization connected to customary Tet activities such as gambling, drinking, and fortune-telling. Because members of each group grew increasingly homesick around Tet, both escape attempts and resignations from the guard corps always rose sharply as the New Year approached. There is even evidence that *matas* sometimes helped prisoners to escape in order that they might celebrate Tet at home with their families. In 1906, the resident of Hung Hoa raised the issue with the resident superior: "The goodwill guards feel toward prisoners is so excessive that they finished their mutual celebration of Tet by helping some prisoners escape. There is no question that these escapes only occurred through the complicity of the *linhs*. In general, orders are rarely executed, and *linhs* have frequently been discovered smoking opium with those they are charged to guard."[34]

Although French officials stressed racial and national solidarity to explain collusion between prisoners and surveillants, regional and class affinities may have been equally significant, especially in provincial prisons. Just as inmates in these institutions were drawn overwhelmingly from local populations, recruitment into the provincial militias that staffed them was carried out "on the spot."[35] As the resident of Kien An suggested in

32. TTLT, Résidence supérieure au Tonkin, 81781, Services pénitentiaires, March 11, 1916.

33. AOM, Indochine, Affaires politiques, 1728, Rapport fait par M. Chastenet de Géry, Inspecteur des colonies concernant l'organisation du régime pénitentiaire au Tonkin, April 26, 1932, 5.

34. TTLT, Résidence supérieure au Tonkin, 79549, Résident de Hung Hoa au Résident supérieure au Tonkin, February 12, 1906.

35. To recruit militiamen, the provincial resident would order canton chiefs from the province to provide quantities of men proportionate to the number of taxpayers in their village (Mossy, *Administration générale de l'Indochine*, 70).

1925, this policy meant that surveillants often found themselves guarding prisoners from their native villages, or even from their own families: "I have asked the commandant of the brigade about the spirit of his men, and he admits that bad elements bear responsibility for infractions regarding penal surveillance. As for the *linhs*, they are often completely without authority within the prison, inasmuch as their parents and friends may often be found among the inmates."[36]

Military recruitment also functioned to ensure that militiamen (and hence prison guards) came overwhelmingly from the same subaltern social orders as the vast majority of the inmate population. According to Phan Van Hum, recruitment at the local level was in the hands of corrupt canton chiefs, who targeted boys too poor or too poorly connected to bribe their way out of military service.[37] The resident of Hung Hoa made a similar point in 1906: "It is unclear exactly why, but conscription has been especially difficult in the province. Villages send their worst subjects or men unfit for serious service to the enrollments. It follows that the majority of these men are gamblers and thieves, who merit frequent punishments."[38]

While the lower-class social origins of *matas* may help explain why their relations with inmates were so often based on pastimes such as gambling and opium smoking, they also shed light on their predatory behavior toward prisoners. Given their meager family resources and modest salaries, *matas* saw bribes and surveillance money as a crucial source of supplementary income. Phan Van Hum characterized *matas* in the Saigon Central Prison as "de-classed peasants," who squeezed inmates for bribes in order to secure an "urban lifestyle."[39] For Hum, the social-climbing pretensions of the *matas* were apparent in their insistence that prisoners address them with exalted personal pronouns such as *thay* (master) and *chu* (uncle):

> Who are the *thay/chu*? *Thay/chu* are Annamese jailers. After returning from military service and finding themselves unemployed, ex-soldiers often apply for work within the prison system. Jailers constitute a separate and distinct cadre of officials. A man will enter this service under

36. TTLT, Résidence supérieure au Tonkin, 81833, Résident de Kien An au Résident supérieur au Tonkin, March 26, 1925.

37. Phan Van Hum, *Ngoi Tu Kham Lon*, 83.

38. TTLT, Résidence supérieure au Tonkin, 79540, Résident de Hung Hoa au Résident supérieur au Tonkin, February 12, 1906.

39. Phan Van Hum, *Ngoi Tu Kham Lon*, 84–85.

the rank *tay tron* [3d class] and then be promoted to the rank of *cai* [2d class] and then *doi* [1st class]. Prisoners are expected to refer to the *cai* as *chu*, while the *doi* must be called *thay*. The *tay tron* are called *anh* [elder brother]. However—and in life it's the same—to be truly polite, one must use pronouns that are excessively exalted, so *tay tron* are often called *chu*, while *cai* are called *thay* and the term *ong* [grandfather] is used when addressing a *doi*. In short, elevated pronouns such as *thay* and *chu* must be used in order to indulge the pretensions of the jailers.[40]

Violence and Surveillance

The brutality of guards and the ubiquity of corporal punishment are common themes in colonial-era prison memoirs. According to Phan Van Hum, inmates in Kham Lon were beaten mercilessly for tiny violations of rules: misplacing a sleeping mat, tearing one's clothes, or eating too slowly. To Hum, it seemed that "clairvoyance" was the only way to avoid daily beatings, because "guards expected orders to be followed before they had been issued."[41] Hoang Minh Dau claimed that guards in the Ha Tien Provincial Prison commonly responded to specific complaints from individual prisoners with collective beatings of the inmate population as a whole.[42]

It is likely that the dense patterning of predatory, recreational, and collusive relations between prisoners and surveillants heightened violence between the two groups. Disputes over gambling or business deals, rivalry over contraband, late payments of bribes, jealousy over sexual partners, failure to honor verbal agreements—all of these contributed to the potential for vendettas, contract killings, and explosive outbursts of violence within the institution. Prisoners were most frequently the victims of such violence, but guards were targeted too. During a visit to Poulo Condore in the mid 1930s, Jean-Claude Demariaux was struck by the numerous graves of murdered *matas* in the island's cemetery.[43] Huynh Thuc Khang's 1939 memoir *Thi Tu Tung Thoai* (Prison Verse) evokes a tense atmosphere in which guards were periodically singled out by vengeful inmates and assassinated, observing: "In prison there are groups of scoundrels so violent-tempered that a dirty look or minor comment will provoke them to fight

40. Ibid., 79
41. Ibid.
42. Hoang Minh Dau, *Cai Than Tu Toi* [My Life as a Prisoner] (Saigon, 1933), 16.
43. Demariaux, *Secrets des îles Poulo-Condore*, 53.

and often kill those around them."[44] After detailing several dramatic cases involving murdered guards from 1905, 1910, and 1918, Khang noted that "in prison, such killings are . . . everyday stories."[45]

The archival record chronicles numerous instances in which guards were set upon by prisoners. An interesting example dates from 1914, in which a *mata* at Kham Lon was clubbed to death by Nguyen Van Bong, a prisoner serving a life sentence for murdering another guard on Poulo Condore several years earlier. In regard to the more recent murder, investigators pointed to a pattern of professional negligence on the part of the guard as a factor contributing to the attack: "It must be reported that the sense of danger that their job should instill in surveillants frequently fades through force of habit. Guards and surveillants who over many years have never been the target of sudden violence tend to become less careful, less vigilant, and less respectful of the regulations designed to protect their own personal safety."[46] The investigation noted that the same surveillant had been attacked and wounded by a prisoner four years earlier, in what was officially dubbed "an act of personal vengeance." Implying a similar explanation for the recent attack, the investigator reported that "a close relationship had once existed between Bong and his victim."[47]

Seven months later, while awaiting execution for the murder described above, Nguyen Van Bong struck again. With help from a Cambodian convict condemned to die the following day, he killed one guard and wounded three others with a homemade knife. An enquiry into the death of the third surveillant in five years to die at Bong's hands again highlighted dangers arising from "permanent contact" between keepers and kept: "The permanent contact between guards and prisoners expunges in the former the appropriate sense of danger. It is thus that the most explicit rules are violated, ironically by those whom they were intended to protect. What level of compulsion can we expect from rules, guidelines, or advice when the risk of death itself proves insufficient?"[48]

---

44. Huynh Thuc Khang, *Thi Tu Tung Thoai* [Prison Verse] (1939; reprint, Saigon, 1951), 50.

45. Ibid., 100–104. Hoang Minh Dau makes the same point in *Cai Than Tu Toi*, 13: "Because of their brutality, indigenous surveillants are often killed by prisoners."

46. AOM, Gouvernement général, 4252, Régime et Service pénitentiaire, Le Directeur de la Maison centrale de Saigon à Monsieur le Gouverneur de la Cochinchine, June 15, 1914.

47. Ibid.

48. AOM, Gouvernement général, 4255, A.S. attentat commis à la Maison centrale de Saigon, February 5, 1915.

Divide and Rule: Minority Communities
and Penal Surveillance

If common regional and class identities complicated relations between the keepers and the kept in provincial prisons, ethnic rivalry shaped relations between guards and prisoners in upland penitentiaries. As mentioned earlier, the French built penitentiaries in mountainous regions such as Cao Bang, Son La, Lai Chau, Buon Ma Thuot, and Lao Bao because they were easy to staff with provincial militiamen recruited from surrounding Thai, Tay, Hmong, Ede, and Jarai communities. The use of non-Vietnamese soldiers to guard Vietnamese prisoners was consistent with what has been called a "divide-and-rule-policy on the basis of ethnographic knowledge."[49] The French hoped that ethnic hostility between lowland prisoners and upland guards would prevent the illicit intercourse that they observed frequently in provincial prisons, central prisons, and on Poulo Condore. While minority staffing policies may indeed have discouraged unauthorized fraternization, however, they may also have intensified levels of institutional brutality.

There is some evidence that the lack of a common language between guards and prisoners in upland penitentiaries resulted in harsher institutional conditions. In 1905, inmates from the Son La Penitentiary complained in a letter smuggled to the resident superior of Tonkin that the linguistic gulf between themselves and their keepers exacerbated the hardships of confinement: "What makes us most miserable is that the *linhs* of this region are all Thos, none of whom can understand our language. They never let us rest, and they beat us even if we are sick. At night, they lock us in iron stocks and put rags in our mouths to silence our screams."[50]

In 1938, in *Nguc Kontum* (Kontum Prison), Le Van Hien suggested that the language barrier between Vietnamese prisoners and Ede guards there contributed to the exceptional brutality of the prison regime. "Few of the Ede guards knew Vietnamese, and those who did were unfamiliar with our Nghe Tinh dialect," he wrote, "hence we could not communicate, and every time we opened our mouths to ask a question or explain ourselves, we

---

49. Oscar Salemink, "Mois and Maquis: The Invention and Appropriation of Vietnam's Montagnards from Sabatier to the CIA," in *Colonial Situations: Essays on the Contextualization of Ethnographic Knowledge,* ed. George Stocking Jr. (Madison, Wis., 1991), 247.

50. TTLT, Résidence supérieure au Tonkin, 795655, Requête des prisonniers condamnés aux travaux forcés à Son La, protestant contre le mauvais traitement, January 5, 1905.

would be whipped or beaten."[51] Hien claimed that Ede guards were especially cruel to prisoners who could speak French, because they feared that they might inform French officials about their misbehavior. Prisoners fluent in Ede, and consequently able to follow conversations among the guards, were subject to similar mistreatment.[52] Detailing the deterioration of relations between the two groups over time, Hien recounted a series of atrocities perpetrated by Ede guards, including episodes in which prisoners were tortured, starved, forced to eat excrement, bludgeoned to death, and buried alive.[53]

PRISON LABOR

As with penal surveillance, the organization and objectives of forced labor were conceptualized in fundamentally different ways by colonial and metropolitan prison officials. Whereas in nineteenth-century France, forced labor was seen as a way of reforming inmates and preparing them to enter the industrial workforce, it was valued solely as an economic resource in Indochina. The colonial state's attitude to prison labor may be viewed as a response to chronic labor shortages, especially in remote provinces far from the densely populated river deltas.[54] It also reveals the colonial state's disregard for rehabilitation as a goal of Indochina's prison system.

Prisoners were first put to work in Indochina immediately following the establishment of the penitentiary on Poulo Condore in 1862.[55] In the late 1870s, the administration attempted to boost the productivity of prison labor by providing hard-labor convicts with a modest monthly salary. During the early 1880s, inmates from Cochin China's six provincial prisons were used to build roads and public buildings, secure embankments, and dig irrigation canals. During the late 1890s, thousands of convicts from

51. Le Van Hien, *Nguc Kontum*, 15.

52. Ibid., 35–37.

53. Although Le Van Hien's *Nguc Kontum* is written in a polemical idiom, the story it tells is more or less verified in an official investigation undertaken immediately following the suppression of a rebellion there in 1932. For example, the statistics it offers concerning the number of prisoners and the number of deaths are consistent with figures found in the French report. See AOM, Indochine, Affaires politiques, 1728, Rapport fait par M. Chastenet de Géry, Inspecteur des colonies, concernant le Service pénitentiaire au Kontum, February 26, 1932.

54. Charles Robequain, *The Economic Development of French Indo-China* (London, 1944), 53–73.

55. Ban Nghien Cuu Lich Su Dang Dac Khu Vung Tau—Con Dao, *Nha Tu Con Dao, 1862–1945* [Con Dao Penitentiary, 1862–1945] (Hanoi, 1987), 49–55.

Poulo Condore and provincial prisons in the Mekong Delta built the new port city of Cap Saint-Jacques (Vung Tau).[56] Prison labor continued to be used primarily for public works projects until the end of the colonial era. In 1903, the mayor of Hanoi reported that convicts provided 2,871 work-days for road maintenance and light construction work in and around the capital.[57] In 1906, three-quarters of the convicts in Tonkinese provincial prisons were employed at construction, ditch-digging, or road work.[58] In 1929, it was reported that 1,022 short-term inmates from the Saigon Central Prison "were put at the disposal of provincial residents for road construction and other work of public utility."[59]

The high proportion of prisoners employed at roadwork reflected administrative, military, and economic considerations. From the turn of the century on, most transportation funds from the General Budget of Indochina went to finance Paul Doumer's elaborate and costly north-south railway. As a result, responsibility for road construction fell to those local officials—the provincial residents—who were also in direct control of provincial prisons. Given chronic labor shortages, it is not surprising that residents came to rely on prison labor. Moreover, because working conditions for convicts were not regulated by Indochinese labor legislation, prisoners could be used to build roads in insalubrious, malaria-infested upland areas where high mortality rates discouraged the recruitment of wage laborers.[60]

The military value of road building was especially significant in northern Tonkin, where endemic banditry prevented the replacement of military administrators with civilian officials until well into the twentieth century. During the 1880s and 1890s, roads were seen as a key component of bandit suppression campaigns. In 1897, Commander Bichot explained that "an important element of our pacification strategy has been the timely opening of roads that crisscross the territories and make it more difficult for bandits

56. Ibid., 29.

57. TTLT, Maire de Hanoi, 3945, Emploi de la main-d'oeuvre pénale, November 27, 1903.

58. Of the remainder, ten worked in the resident's garden, ten cleaned public latrines, six worked in a stone quarry, two carried water to public buildings, and a handful were assigned kitchen duties and odd jobs around the prison (TTLT, Résidence supérieure au Tonkin, 79546, February 2, 1906).

59. Gouvernement général, *Annuaire statistique de l'Indochine*, 1929–30, 41.

60. Jean Goudal, "Labor Legislation in Indo-China," *Asiatic Review* 30 (January 1934): 136–45.

to elude our pursuit."[61] Bichot praised provincial residents in Tonkin for "making large numbers of prisoners available for roadwork, not only around provincial capitals but in areas far from population centers as well."[62]

Road building was also an important aspect of official efforts to promote the growth of trade and the development of mining and plantation agriculture.[63] Officials believed that an expanded network of roads in northern Tonkin would provide access to the Chinese market. It is no coincidence that two of the four principal Indochinese roads converging on the Chinese frontier originated in Cao Bang and Ha Giang—towns with large penitentiaries that could provide reserves of convict labor for construction and maintenance.[64] In the 1920s, European colonization of the central highlands in southern Annam stimulated demand for new roads and for prison labor to build them.[65] Hence, the French erected penitentiaries in Kon Tum and Buon Ma Thuot as well as penal work camps at Dark Lak and Dark Mil.[66] During the 1930s, prisoners from these sites built Strategic Road #14 from Buon Ma Thuot to Quang Nam and roads #5, #24, #27, and #33, which eventually linked Kon Tum, Plei Ku, Ban Me Thuot, Qui Nhon, Ninh Hoa, and Nha Trang.[67]

Although comprehensive statistics are unavailable, there is no question that roadwork contributed to high rates of death and disease among prisoners. Laying roads entailed physically laborious work, such as breaking rocks and clearing away the jungle. Corporal punishment and food deprivation were common instruments to enforce labor discipline. To save time and transport costs, prisoners often slept, completely exposed to the elements, along the roads on which they worked. Conditions were worst, perhaps, in remote upland areas, where beatings and overwork combined with high rates of malaria and dysentery to ravage prison work teams. In one

61. TTLT, Résidence supérieure au Tonkin, 7269.
62. Ibid.
63. Martin Murray, *The Development of Capitalism in Colonial Indochina, 1870–1940* (Berkeley and Los Angeles, 1980), 315–74.
64. Robequain, *Economic Development of French Indo-China*, 101.
65. Ibid., 103.
66. For a firsthand account of the conditions for penal laborers working on roads in the central highlands during the 1930s, see Nguyen Tao, *Vuot Nguc Dark-Mil* [Escape from Dak Mil] (Hanoi, 1976).
67. Tinh Uy Dak Lak and Vien Lich Su Dang, *Lich Su Nha Day Buon Ma Thuot (1930–1945)* [History of Buon Ma Thuot Penitentiary, 1930–1945] (Hanoi, 1991), 33.

extreme example, 135 prisoners from Kon Tum Penitentiary died during a six-month period in 1931 while working on strategic road #14. To explain the Kon Tum Penitentiary's outrageously high mortality rate, an inspector from the Ministry of Colonies pointed directly to "the dreadful balance sheet of the preceding work campaign."[68]

Although most inmates were employed at roadwork, they could also be assigned menial jobs in provincial post offices, hospitals, police stations, army barracks, and forestry stations. In provincial towns, they swept the streets, tended parks and gardens, and delivered water to public buildings. They were also leased to charitable organizations, commercial associations, and schools. In 1911, the Société de protection des enfants métis abandonnés was granted twenty convicts to help construct an orphanage outside of Haiphong.[69] In 1923, the committee organizing a Hanoi trade fair received thirty convicts to erect tents and prepare fairgrounds for an upcoming exhibition.[70] In 1925, the Indochinese Fine Arts Academy requested two "young and vigorous" prisoners to serve as nude models for an entrance exam.[71]

In rare cases, inmates might work inside the prison at light manufacturing: basket-weaving, rice-husking, woodworking, and hat-making. Women prisoners were often employed as seamstresses. Profits from such prison industries were used to defray institutional costs. Shortage of space discouraged such arrangements, however, and prison workshops were always among the first rooms converted into dormitories during periods of overcrowding. In 1914, the resident of Lang Son wrote that "the provincial prison no longer has adequate space to maintain workshops, hence all of our 180 prisoners work at corvée sites in and around the town."[72] During

68. AOM, Indochine, Affaires politiques, 1728, Rapport fait par M. Chastenet de Géry, Inspecteur des colonies, concernant le Service pénitentiaire au Kontum à la date du 26 Février, 1932 et transmis à Monsieur le Résident supérieur en Annam. See marginal comments by Inspecteur des colonies Demongin, March 25, 1932.

69. TTLT, Résidence supérieure au Tonkin, 81823, M. J. Blanc, Président de la Société de protection des enfants métis abandonnés à M. le Résident supérieur au Tonkin, August 19, 1911.

70. TTLT, Résidence supérieure au Tonkin, 81833, Le Président du Comité d'organisation de la foire de Hanoi à M. le Résident supérieur au Tonkin, October 29, 1923.

71. TTLT, Résidence supérieure au Tonkin, 81833, Directeur de l'Instruction publique en Indochine au Tonkin à M. le Résident supérieur au Tonkin, October 15, 1925.

72. TTLT, Résidence supérieure au Tonkin, 81826.

the 1930s, with officials trying to find room for the huge influx of new inmates at the start of the decade, virtually all prison workshops were closed. The most sustained experiment with prison industries was carried out on Poulo Condore.[73] Because the island had almost no civilian population, many inmates were housed at semi-permanent work camps, known as *services*, located away from the main prison buildings. There, they were engaged in specialized enterprises under the supervision of foremen and armed guards. For example, a fishery *service* built boats, wove nets, and employed dozens of prisoners as fishermen. A livestock *service* raised cows, pigs, and fowl and produced meat and milk for consumption on the islands. Building materials were provided by *services* responsible for rock breaking, logging, and lime production. A general construction *service* used prisoners as carpenters, bricklayers, blacksmiths, mechanics, and painters. Several *services* used unskilled manual laborers to load and unload ships and collect garbage. There were also agricultural *services* that tended paddy fields, vegetable gardens, fruit orchards, and small vanilla and pepper plantations.

The poor quality of living and working conditions at *services* contributed to Poulo Condore's menacing reputation. Because *services* were located far from the central prison buildings, there was little administrative oversight, leaving prisoners subject to the autocratic whims of relatively low-level guards. Moreover, inmates at many *services* were not equipped with proper tools for the tasks they were supposed to perform, increasing the risks of serious injuries. Loggers were often mutilated on the job, and prisoners assigned to collect coral for lime production frequently drowned or sustained serious injuries.[74]

A dramatic example of the murderous labor conditions on Poulo Condore dates from 1882, when 150 prisoners from the construction *service* were sent to build a lighthouse on Bai Canh Island, several kilometers west of Poulo Condore. After six weeks, the prisoners launched a violent uprising, during which two French officers were killed and a third seriously wounded. To explain the revolt, investigators pointed to the brutality of

73. For descriptions of the forced-labor system on Poulo Condore, see Ban Nghien Cuu Lich Su Dang Dac Khu Vung Tau—Con Dao, *Nha Tu Con Dao, 1862–1945*, 49–55; Tran Van Que, *Con-Lon Quan-Dao Truoc ngay 9–3–1945* [The Con Lon Archipelago Before March 9, 1945] (Saigon, 1961), 90–105; Ban Lien Lac Tu Chinh Tri So Van Hoa Thong Tin, *Con Dao: Ky Su va Tu Lieu* [Con Dao: Reports and Documents] (Ho Chi Minh City: Tre, 1996), 49–51.

74. Ban Nghien Cuu Lich Su Dang Dac Khu Vung Tau—Con Dao, *Nha Tu Con Dao, 1862–1945*, 49–50.

the labor regime supervised by a French guard named Dulong: "Prisoners at Bai Canh were exposed to the rain and sun all day while they worked on the lighthouse. There have been no days off in the past six weeks. Even on Sundays, they worked from 5 to 11 in the morning and from 1 to 6 in the afternoon. Those who complained of exhaustion or illness were whipped or beaten by M. Dulong."[75]

Without noting the precise number of prisoners who died working on Bai Canh prior to the revolt, officials acknowledged that the construction of the lighthouse was the main reason that mortality on Poulo Condore jumped from 54 in 1881 to 158 in 1882. "We must admit," concluded an annual report, "that labor conditions for prisoners working on the lighthouse at Bai Canh represent a determinate cause of the recent rise in mortality."[76]

While *services* helped feed the inmate population and contributed to infrastructural development on the island, they never came close to making the penitentiary self-sufficient. Monsoons destroyed 30 to 50 percent of the rice crop each year, and the fishing *service* never yielded more than one-third of the total catch required to feed the prison population. In 1882, the value of all products produced by inmates on Poulo Condore was estimated to be 3,257 piasters, a mere fraction of the 21,235 piasters needed to run the prison.[77] Financial reports reveal that local budgets continued to foot the bill for the vast majority of the penitentiary's operating expenses well into the 1930s.[78]

Prisoners could also be rented out to mining companies, construction firms, and plantations. Such arrangements entailed sending inmates to live outside of the prison near the enterprises in which they worked. For prison officials, the practice was an easy and efficient way to generate income. Not only did entrepreneurs pay the prison a fee for the inmates they employed, but they assumed full responsibility for their food, clothing, and shelter. For prisoners, however, the privatization of punishment left them vulnerable to exploitation and abuse by contractors. During the 1890s, hundreds

75. Nguyen Phan Quang and Le Huu Phuoc, "Cuoc Noi Day Cua Tu Nhan Con Dao Tai Hon Bay Canh, 8/1883" [The Uprising of Con Dao Prisoners on Bay Canh Island, August 1883], *Nghien Cuu Lich Su* 2, no. 261 (March–April 1992): 73.

76. Gouvernement général de l'Indochine, *Annuaire statistique de la Cochinchine*, 1882, 102.

77. Ibid.

78. See Gouvernement général, *Annuaire statistique de l'Indochine* (Hanoi), 1922–42.

of Tonkinese prisoners were leased to the Société nouvelle de Ke Bao, a private coal-mining company operating in northeastern Tonkin.[79] In 1895, more than 600 inmates worked full-time in mines owned by the company on Ke Bao Island.[80] They were supervised by private security guards and fed and clothed at company expense. Housing consisted of flimsy bamboo barracks with dirt floors and thatched roofs, which provided little protection from wind and rain. In violation of prison regulations, inmates on Ke Bao worked in the mines seven days a week, either at day shifts from 5:30 A.M. to 6:30 P.M. or at night shifts from 7:00 P.M. to 4:00 A.M. Given the heavy workload, poor diet, and effects of malaria, anemia, cachexia, dysentery, and untreated infections, 161 prisoners died on Ke Bao during the three months between December 1897 and March 1898. "Morale among prisoners at Ke Bao is bad," a colonial doctor wrote in 1898; "a cloud of utter despondency hangs over the locale."[81]

It may be argued that the murderous work conditions connected with the coal mines of Ke Bao, the lighthouse at Bai Canh, and the strategic road at Kon Tum were extreme cases. Still, these episodes point to certain emblematic features of the organization of colonial prison labor in Indochina. In all three cases, labor was performed outdoors rather than in enclosed work spaces. Not only did this increase the harshness of the work, by leaving inmates exposed to the elements, but it made an unappealing public spectacle of punishment.[82] Moreover, all three cases entailed backbreaking physical labor, rather than skilled or semi-skilled factory-style production. Hence, unlike in nineteenth-century Europe, there appears to be little con-

79. TTLT, Résidence supérieure au Tonkin, 7269, Pénitencier de Ke Bao, Province de Quang Yen, September 15, 1897.

80. Ibid. The numerical breakdown of convicts by prison of origin was as follows: Ninh Binh, 26; Hung Yen, 9; Phu Ly, 10; Thai Binh, 32; Hai Duong, 40; Nam Dinh, 45; Son Tay, 30; Thai Nguyen, 30; Bac Ninh, 40; Hung Hoa, 60; Quang Yen, 45; Phu Lang Thuong, 50; Hanoi, 100; Haiphong, 100.

81. Ibid. Rapport sur l'état sanitaire des prisonniers employés aux mines de Ke Bao—Causes de morbidité et de mortalité, September 15, 1897.

82. The Résident supérieur at Tonkin notified residents on May 30, 1890: "The European population complains with reason about the disgraceful but all too common spectacle presented by indigenous prisoners working within full public view. Many of the men are almost completely naked and the women often work while carrying their children. Not only is this contrary to decency and to public morals but it undermines the very dignity of the French administration" (TTLT, Maire de Hanoi, 3953). On July 5, 1914, it was noted: "The detainees employed at corvée are clothed in rags, which expose them to the inclemencies of the season" (TTLT, Résidence supérieure au Tonkin, 79453, Habillement des prisonniers).

nection between systems of colonial prison labor and efforts to inculcate industrial discipline. Finally, evidence that prisoners were often worked to the point of complete exhaustion or death points to the absence of a meaningful rehabilitative orientation within colonial punishment. This point was acknowledged implicitly by a colonial inspector in 1932. "It is incontestable," he wrote, "that the current regime of convict labor in Indochina should be completely modified so that the work actually contributes to the improvement of the prisoners."[83]

TOTAL CARE

In nineteenth-century French prisons, the notion of "total care"—provision by the institution of all daily needs—was based on the idea that an unsanitary social milieu led to a life of crime.[84] Prison reformers believed that inmates needed to be isolated from their corrupt moral and material environment if rehabilitation were to occur. The central innovation in this regard was the furnishing of a regular diet. With the state providing their nourishment, inmates would be severed from the outside world of family, friends, and peddlers, who would no longer enjoy access to the institution.[85] In Indochina, on the other hand, the job of provisioning prisons was farmed out to local businessmen. As a result, the quality of prison food was based on economic rather than rehabilitative considerations. Although comprehensive data are lacking in this area, there is scattered evidence that many inmates became malnourished in prison, and mortality was often the result of dietary-related illnesses. Far from contributing to the reform of inmates, in other words, the process of provisioning colonial prisons was more likely to help kill them.

According to regulations, inmates in Indochina were provided with two meals per day. Native prisoners were to receive 750 grams of rice, 60 grams of green vegetables, seven grams of salt, 20 centiliters of chili, 15 grams of green tea, and 60 grams of meat, fish, or tofu. The diet of European prisoners consisted of 600 grams of bread, 400 grams of soup, 400 grams of beef or pork, 300 grams of vegetables, 10 grams of Chinese tea, 30 grams of

83. AOM, Indochine, Affaires politiques, 1728, Mission d'Inspection, M. Le Gregam a M. le Gouverneur de la Cochinchine, March 11, 1932.

84. For a discussion of the concept of "total care," see O'Brien, *Promise of Punishment*, 42–48.

85. Michael Ignatieff, *A Just Measure of Pain: The Penitentiary in the Industrial Revolution, 1750–1850* (New York, 1978), 101.

sugar, and a portion of seasonal fruit.[86] While the size of rations was fixed by the regime, the preparation and service of prison food were contracted out to local entrepreneurs.[87] Concessions were awarded to whoever offered to supply the designated rations at the lowest cost. In every province, Chinese, Vietnamese, and Europeans competed in annual public auctions for the right to supply specific institutions. In 1893, for example, Pierre Bedier, Jaques Labeye, James François, Le Ngoc Thieu, Nguyen My Loi, and Ahmed Ben Tassi vied to provision the Hanoi Civil Prison. Bedier won the concession in this case, but auction records reveal that Vietnamese and Chinese entrepreneurs were just as likely to win prison contracts.[88] The following year, the concession was awarded to a Chinese pharmacist named Lai Ky.[89]

By allowing private businessmen to provision prisons, the colonial state relinquished control over a key component of a regime of total care. As a result, the quality of prison food was never a manifestation of rehabilitative ideas about the relationship between a reformed mind and a healthy body. More often, it simply reflected illicit efforts by contractors to cut costs. According to the journalist Nguyen Van Nguyen, vegetable rations on Poulo Condore consisted of banana stalks, sweet potato leaves, purslane, and a variety of unpalatable mountain weeds. Contractors met quotas for fresh fish by serving "pinkie-size" minnows typically used by fishermen as bait. Fish sauce, a crucial element of the Vietnamese diet, came watered down and was often stinking and rotten. Rice servings were "padded with sand, pebbles, unhusked paddy, and potsherds."[90]

The fact that officials permitted contractors to illegally prepare meals away from the prison grounds contributed to the poor quality of prison food. In 1920, a doctor inspecting the Hai Duong provincial prison linked

86. TTLT, Résidence supérieure au Tonkin, 7269, Cahier des charges pour la fourniture des vivres nécessaires des Européens et Asiatiques détenus à la Prison de Hanoi du 1er janvier 1905 au 31 décembre 1905.

87. At the end of each fiscal year, provincial residents and municipal mayors would place advertisements in local newspapers announcing an auction for the right to supply the penal establishments under their jurisdiction. For example, in early August 1897, the following notice appeared in three different newspapers in Tonkin: "On August 20, 1897, at 3:30 P.M., there will take place, at the residence of the mayor of Hanoi, an auction for the right to provide the necessary nourishment for the prisoners at the Hanoi Civil Prison. All interested parties are invited to attend" (TTLT, Résidence supérieure au Tonkin, 3952).

88. TTLT, Maire de Hanoi, 3952.

89. TTLT, Résidence supérieure au Tonkin, 7229.

90. Nguyen Van Nguyen, "Poulo Condore: La Terre des damnés," *Le Travail,* November 20, 1936, 2.

an outbreak of dysentery to the fact that external food preparation prevented effective oversight by prison officials.[91] Collusion between contractors and prison officials was another problem. In 1929, *Tieng Dan* exposed a plot by a warden and contractor in Quang Tri to secretly cut prison rations and split the excess profits. "When people are confined in prison," the article began, "the administration must provide money for their daily rations. This money is given to wardens, who are supposed to turn it over to contractors responsible for food. . . . Unfortunately, this particular setup gives rise to numerous opportunities for vice and collusion between the warden and contractor."[92]

Another problem was that poorly paid guards often stole food destined for prisoners. Hoang Minh Dau described guards ransacking kitchen pantries at night and stealing supplemental milk and meat rations intended for sick prisoners.[93] On Poulo Condore, guards in charge of *services* often pilfered prison food in order to sell it or consume it themselves. According to one eyewitness account: "In the exterior work camps, rice is entrusted to a *mata*, who distributes it among the prisoners. One can easily imagine the abuses that can be committed at the prisoners' expense. In 1933, for example, Sergeant Dau was caught stealing rice intended for the prisoners under his care. His only penalty was to be reassigned to the *bouverie* [cattle shed]."[94]

In 1918, a scandal came to light that dramatized many of the problems associated with the system of outside provisioning. On July 24, the resident superior of Tonkin received a letter from two prisoners who worked in the kitchen of Hanoi Central Prison. The inmates complained that a warden named Limousin regularly pilfered rice, meat, and coal for his personal use. Following a denial by Limousin, the resident superior dismissed the allegations, asserting that "the claims of ten Annamite prisoners will never prevail over the word of one honest Frenchman." A subsequent investigation into the matter revealed the involvement of the contractor who provisioned the prison. According to the investigator, Limousin had angered the

91. TTLT, Résidence supérieure au Tonkin, 3421. "November has seen many cases of dysentery. The prison has been overcrowded and because food is prepared outside, it is difficult to inspect its quality. For the same reason, it is suspected that the drinking water provided the prisoners has been defective."

92. "Cau Chuyen Com Tu" [A Story of Prison Food], *Tieng Dan*, November 12, 1929, 2.

93. Hoang Minh Dau, *Cai Than Tu Toi*, 12.

94. Nguyen Van Nguyen "Poulo Condore: La Terre des damnés," *Le Travail*, November 13, 1936, 2.

contractor by his "zealous surveillance over the delivery and preparation of the prison meals." Limousin had rejected "rancid meat" on several occasions and reprimanded the contractor for providing "light rations." Hence, the contractor plotted to rid himself of this troublesome prison official by bribing two inmates to testify against him. Instead, Limousin was vindicated, the prisoners were disciplined, and the contractor's concession was terminated.[95]

This mini-scandal reveals important consequences of the system of provisioning used in Indochinese prisons. References to "rancid meat" and "light rations" point to what may have been widespread efforts by contractors to cut costs by providing food of poor quality and insufficient quantity. The accusation of theft by a guard, whether true or not, squares with allegations that food intended for prisoners was often stolen by the prison staff. Finally, the conspiracy against Limousin involving the contractor and prisoners suggests that the system of provisioning did not work to sever inmates from pernicious influences from the outside world. Rather, it could function to entangle them in a complex web of interests involving outside contractors and prison staff.

The privatization of provisioning in colonial prisons thus served to undermine the original objectives of "total care," but its greater significance lay in its devastating impact on the health of the inmate population. That diet played an important role in the abysmal health conditions prevailing in Indochinese prisons may be seen in the ubiquity of diet-related diseases among inmates. For example, beriberi, a thiamine deficiency that often accompanies malnutrition, was a prolific killer in colonial prisons. In 1880, it was reported that "beriberi is the dominant cause of morbidity on Poulo Condore."[96] In the 1890s, an "appalling epidemic" of beriberi struck Poulo Condore, peaking in 1897, during which 405 prisoners died from the disease.[97] Although the introduction of unpolished brown rice into prison diets around the turn of the century prevented a recurrence of the murderous epidemics of the 1890s, dietary diseases continued to strike inmate

95. TTLT, Résidence supérieure au Tonkin, 81831, Rapport pour Monsieur le Résident supérieur au Tonkin, March 29, 1918.

96. *Annuaire statistique de la Cochinchine française,* 1880.

97. "Over the past two years, death has descended on the penitentiary and struck without mercy. It has been much more pitiless than the justice of men. . . . In its utter blindness, it has perverted any sense of justice or balance" (report cited in Demariaux, *Secrets des îles Poulo-Condore,* 145).

populations well into the twentieth century. In 1908, 24 of the 48 deaths reported in Hanoi Central Prison were owing to beriberi.[98] Between 1908 and 1913, beriberi accounted for 83 out of the 856 deaths that occurred throughout the provincial prison system in Cochin China.[99]

Scurvy, a severe deficiency of vitamin C, was also common. In 1930, a "grave epidemic of scurvy" on Poulo Condore was triggered by consecutive typhoons that struck the island during 1929 and 1930, destroying its entire crop of fruit and vegetables.[100] Scurvy was a major cause of the 338 deaths that occurred on Poulo Condore that year, the highest annual mortality figure on the island since the beriberi epidemic of 1897.[101] Poor sanitation and contaminated water led to other fatal diseases, such as dysentery and cholera, "the great patron of the first cemetery on Poulo Condore," according to Jean-Claude Demariaux.[102] Hanoi Civil Prison had to be evacuated in 1888 and again in 1890 owing to cholera epidemics.[103] Between May and June 1904, a cholera epidemic killed 30 prisoners there.[104] Huynh Thuc Khang mentions an outbreak on Poulo Condore in 1909 that killed three of his cell mates.[105] In 1915, cholera epidemics struck several prisons in Tonkin, including Hai Phong, which suffered 8 fatalities, and Hanoi Central Prison, where 60 prisoners died.[106]

Other common diseases included typhoid, tuberculosis, and malaria. In 1926, 21 inmates in Hanoi Central Prison died of typhoid.[107] On Poulo Condore, 18 deaths were attributed to tuberculosis in 1927, 16 in 1928, 14 in 1929, and 23 in 1930. Malaria appears to have been especially widespread in upland penitentiaries like Son La and Buon Ma Thuot and on Poulo

98. AOM, Indochine, Gouvernement général, 4235.

99. Ibid., 4251, Mortalité dans les prisons et pénitenciers, October 24, 1913.

100. AOM, Indochine, Affaires politiques, 1728, Rapport fait par M. Le Gregam, Inspecteur des colonies, sur les îles et le pénitencier de Poulo Condore, March 11, 1932.

101. Ibid.

102. Demariaux, *Secrets des îles Poulo-Condore*, 124.

103. TTLT, Maire de Hanoi, 3918, October 20, 1880, and Marie de Hanoi, 3961, June 6, 1890.

104. AOM, Indochine, Gouvernement géneral, 4231, Compte-rendu des travaux de la commission de surveillance des prisons pendant l'année 1904.

105. Huynh Thuc Khang, *Thi Tu Tung Thoai*, 62.

106. TTLT, Résidence supérieure au Tonkin, 81781, Rapport annuel sur la situation générale du service de la Prison civile de Hanoi December 31, 1915.

107. Ibid., Rapport annuel sur la situation générale du service de la Maison centrale de Hanoi au cours de la période du 1er janvier au 31 décembre 1926.

Table 5. Mortality in Prison: Indochina and Poulo Condore,
1925–1940

	No. of Deaths	
Year	Indochina	Poulo Condore
1925	—	129
1926	—	58
1927	—	69
1928	—	103
1929	—	117
1930	927	338
1931	1,100	154
1932	1,155	100
1933	1,096	78
1934	1,045	76
1935	865	37
1936	—	50
1937	791	26
1938	654	22
1939	741	41
1940	729	48

SOURCE: Gouvernement général de l'Indochine, *Annuaire statistique de l'Indochine*, various years.

Condore. There were 14 deaths from malaria on Poulo Condore in 1927 and 19 in 1928.[108]

High rates of death and disease in colonial prisons were doubtless owing to a combination of poor food, inadequate sanitation, unresponsive medical services, overcrowding, and overwork. Unfortunately, prison records on sickness and mortality are fragmentary and incomplete prior to the 1930s, and even during that decade, annual reports do not include data on causes of death. What we do know is that 9,826 prisoners died in prison in Indochina between 1930 and 1940, an average of about 900 a year (see table 5).[109]

108. AOM, Indochine, Affaires politiques, 1728, Rapport fait par M. Le Gregam, Inspecteur des colonies, sur les îles et le pénitencier de Poulo Condore, February 23, 1932.
109. Gouvernement général, *Annuaire statistique de l'Indochine*, 1930–40.

We can also identify certain extreme cases of institutional mortality during the decade. For example, 338 prisoners died on Poulo Condore in 1930, and 197 deaths were recorded there the next year.[110] In 1934, 168 inmates died at Hanoi Central Prison.[111] Another 108 prisoners died at the Ha Giang penitentiary in 1933, and 51 died in Buon Ma Thuot.[112] In 1934, 63 prisoners perished in the Lai Chau Penitentiary, and 76 died there the following year.[113]

There is no reason to think that most prisoners who died in captivity were sick or on the verge of death at the time of their arrests. Rather, it was the brutality and squalor of the prison system itself that weakened and ultimately killed them. The fact that so many inmates died in Indochina without ameliorative measures ever being introduced is perhaps the most persuasive indication of the complete absence of modern ideas of rehabilitation and behavioral modification in French colonial prisons.

110. Ibid., 1930–31.
111. Ibid., 1934.
112. Ibid., 1933.
113. Ibid., 1934–35.

4 Prisoners and Prison Society

Some three decades ago, Michelle Perrot bemoaned the fact that prisoners had "disappeared from their own history" and urged historians to rectify this neglect by investigating the "daily life of this group" at "its most hidden level."[1] Although scholarly research on the history of the prison has since expanded rapidly, a preoccupation with strategies and discourses of institutional domination has discouraged historians from following Perrot's advice.[2] As a consequence, prisoners rarely appear in histories of the prison except when rising in revolt. This chapter attempts to take up Perrot's challenge by offering a rough sociological sketch of the inmate population and a reconstruction and analysis of the dominant structures and practices that shaped their everyday lives within the colonial prison.

Once in prison, Indochinese inmates appear to have existed within two parallel social hierarchies. The first, imposed formally by the prison regime, ranked and treated prisoners differentially according to their juridical status, their capacity for work and their behavior within the institution. Although this hierarchy functioned explicitly to serve the administration, prisoners learned to manipulate and maneuver through it in

---

1. Michelle Perrot, "Delinquency and the Penitentiary System in Nineteenth-Century France," in *Deviants and the Abandoned in French Society: Selections from the « Annales, économies, sociétés, civilisations », Volume IV,* ed. Robert Forster and Orest Ranum, trans. Elborg Forster and Patricia M. Ranum (Baltimore, 1978), 217.

2. See, e.g., *The Birth of the Penitentiary in Latin America: Essays on Criminology, Prison Reform and Social Control,* ed. Ricardo Salvatore and Carlos Aguirre (Austin, Tex., 1996). The editors write: "This dimension—prisoners' lives and experiences—receives less emphasis in this volume. In part, this neglect obeys our focus on the discourse of reform, its appropriation, and its uses" (xvii).

pursuit of their own individual aims. A second social hierarchy, created by the inmates themselves, was structured around seniority, social class, and gang affiliation. It represented a relatively autonomous social domain within the institution that the administration could never fully monitor or control.

At the same time, prison gave rise to communal sentiments among inmates driven by common subcultural adaptations to institutional life and similar emotional predicaments. Communal identity may be located in the collective use of prison argot, in a common culture of leisure, and in the intensity of social and homosexual relationships among prisoners. While these common subcultural adaptations brought inmates together, group identity was rarely powerful enough to transcend divisions within the prison population or to serve as a foundation for collective resistance to the regime. Despite the relatively high frequency of prison rebellions in Indochina, it must be remembered that acts of collective resistance were still exceptional—abrupt breaks in periods of calm that typically stretched on for years. Nevertheless, the relative autonomy and vitality of prisoner subculture reveal the failure of the prison regime to impose on the inmate population a hegemonic vision of institutional life. It was in this same interstitial space occupied by prison subculture that the Communist Party was able to cultivate a powerful insurgent movement behind bars during the late colonial era.

This chapter also examines the ways in which the experience of imprisonment encouraged the growth of characteristically modern forms of social and political consciousness among certain segments of the inmate population. Although ordinary lawbreakers left few accounts of how prison may have changed them, there is substantial evidence that many educated inmates left prison with heightened apprehensions of themselves as autonomous individuals on the one hand and as members of modern social classes on the other. Alongside these new sensations of individual and group identity emerged a powerful modernist faith in the possibility of radical personal and social transformations. Finally, prison seems to have encouraged in certain inmates an unusual degree of confidence in their ability to understand the true nature of colonial society at large and, by implication, in their capacity to transform it.

THE PRISON POPULATION

Throughout the colonial era, the Indochinese inmate population was dominated by thieves. In 1880, the first year for which data are available,

65 percent of those imprisoned in Saigon Central Prison were convicted thieves, as were 35 percent of all inmates in provincial prisons.[3] Twelve years later, 60 percent of the prison population in Poulo Condore had been convicted of theft.[4] Trial statistics also confirm the prominent place of robbery in colonial criminality: 24 percent of all convictions handed down by provincial tribunals in Tonkin between 1919 and 1942 involved theft, the highest percentage for any category of offense.[5] Likewise, theft accounted for the largest percentage (31 percent) of sentences issued by the correctional courts in Hanoi and Saigon between 1913 and 1931.[6] During the same period, 44 percent of convictions secured at the criminal courts of Hanoi and Saigon also involved some sort of robbery.[7] Given that the vast majority of Vietnamese lived in the countryside during the colonial era, it is safe to assume that in nineteenth-century Indochina, theft was a largely rural phenomenon. Indeed, 20 percent of all thefts prosecuted during 1882 were identified as cases of "buffalo rustling."[8]

Following the turn of the century, the growth of so-called "clever offenses" in trial statistics—swindling, abuse of confidence, counterfeiting, and forgery—points to an expansion of capitalist economic relations and to a related urbanization of theft.[9] An impressionistic picture of urban crime in late-colonial Indochina may be found in Hoang Dao's "Truoc Vanh Mong Ngua" (Before the Court of Justice), a lengthy piece of nonfiction reportage that documents fifty cases brought before the correctional tribunal in Hanoi during a three-day period in 1937.[10] Roughly consistent with the proportions cited above, one-third of the cases Hoang Dao observed concerned acts of illegal appropriation. Most involved modest sums of money or small items seized in an opportunistic fashion: a bottle of perfume, a bracelet, or a pair of socks. Another common type of theft involved employees stealing from their employers: a maid palming jewelry from her mistress or a rickshaw driver failing to return a wallet left in his vehicle.

3. *Annuaire de la Cochinchine française,* 1880.

4. Ibid., 1892.

5. Gouvernement général de l'Indochine, *Annuaire statistique de l'Indochine* (Hanoi), 1919–42.

6. Ibid., 1913–31.

7. Ibid.

8. *Annuaire de la Cochinchine française,* 1882.

9. On the "clever offenses," see Perrot, "Delinquency and the Penitentiary System in Nineteenth-Century France," 224.

10. Hoang Dao, "Truoc Vanh Mong Ngua" (Before the Court of Justice), in *Phong Su Chon Loc,* ed. Vuong Tri Nhan, 400–450.

After theft, vagabondage was the next most common crime for which people were imprisoned in Indochina.[11] Vagabonds were defined as persons who had "no certain domicile," or "means of subsistence."[12] The growth of vagabondage during the twentieth century may be linked to the growth of cities and to an acute increase in rural-urban migration. It is estimated that Hanoi had a floating population of 75,000 in 1921, and of 180,000 during 1937 in the wake of the Depression.[13] Living from job to job and enduring frequent periods of unemployment, members of this transient group tended to be arrested after they turned to begging in the streets. Although typically seen as an urban problem, vagabondage had a significant rural dimension as well. There were numerous "unemployed individuals who wander from village to village and fall into gangs of criminals and secret societies," Maurice Chautemps noted.[14]

In 1882, the number of convicted vagabonds in Saigon Central Prison was second only to thieves, accounting for 7 percent of the inmate population.[15] That same year, vagabonds in provincial prisons were outnumbered only by thieves, bandits, and smugglers.[16] Between 1913 and 1931, only thieves and murderers were convicted more often than vagabonds by the Correctional Tribunals of Hanoi and Saigon.[17] From 1919 to 1942, roughly 14 percent of convictions issued by the Provincial Tribunal of Tonkin targeted vagabonds, again placing them second only to thieves as objects of legal persecution.[18] In 1928, Phan Van Hum noted the prominence of vagabonds among the inmate population of Saigon Central Prison:

11. Critics of French policy often pointed to the unfair prosecution of vagrancy to indict the colonial regime. "The inappropriateness of French law is nowhere more clearly seen than in the regulation of vagrancy. In a highly organized society, vagrancy is punished as a preventative measure. A resourceless man is almost bound to commit crimes when his life is hard, his needs numerous and the weather inclement. Such is not the case in Indochina, where for the most part, the climate is agreeable, native needs reduced to the minimum and easy to satisfy—in short it is not likely that the vagabond will become a social menace." Virginia Thompson, *French Indochina* (London, 1937), 263.

12. Robert Nye, *Crime, Madness and Politics in Modern France: The Medical Concept of National Decline* (Princeton, N.J., 1984), 56.

13. Greg Lockhart, "First Person Narratives from the 1930s," in *The Light of the Capital: Three Modern Vietnamese Classics*, ed. id. (Kuala Lumpur, 1996), 11.

14. Maurice Chautemps, *Le Vagabondage en pays annamite*, thèse pour le doctorat, Université de Paris, Faculté de droit (Paris, 1908), 201.

15. *Annuaire de la Cochinchine française*, 1882.

16. Ibid.

17. Gouvernement général, *Annuaire statistique de l'Indochine*, 1913–31.

18. The figure here must be an inexact estimate as the *Annuaire statistique*'s tabulation of crimes successfully prosecuted at the Tonkin Provincial Tribunal from 1919 to 1942 contains an unexplained four-year gap between 1932 and 1935.

You may ask: "Where do all these prisoners come from?" Many are sentenced for a single month for "lacking gainful employment"—also known
as vagabondage—or for several days for failure to pay the head tax. People
lose their jobs and become vagrants. They are then thrown into prison.
Some people call them lazy, but I see them as victims of circumstance.[19]

Violations of state monopolies for opium, alcohol, and gambling were
another category of frequently prosecuted offenses. While monopoly infractions (bootlegging and smuggling, for example) do not appear in annual trial statistics, the prevalence of such offenses may be discerned
from scattered sources.[20] It is tempting to assume that such infractions
were statistically covered under the mysterious generic category "other
crimes," the figures for which perennially dwarfed all offenses except
theft. Data from 1882 and 1894 indicate that illegal gambling ranked
third behind theft and vagabondage as the reason inmates were jailed in
Saigon Central Prison.[21] Also in Saigon Central Prison, the category
"contraband opium and alcohol" ranked fourth in 1882 and sixth in
1894, slipping behind public drunkenness and assault.[22] Between 1915
and 1917, 21 percent of the prisoners admitted to Hanoi Central Prison
were arrested for monopoly infractions.[23] In 1936, Bui Quang Chieu
charged that "tens of thousands of illiterate peasants are now languish-
ing in jail for violating state monopolies."[24] According to the historian
Ngo Vinh Long, the high number of monopoly violators in prison was
owing to the use of collective punishments.[25] He pointed out that in
1917, the French resident of Thanh Hoa had ordered a whole village
jailed for "alternate periods throughout the year" because of evidence
that several families had been making rice wine illegally.[26] Joseph Buttinger has argued that "thousands of innocent people were sentenced

19. Phan Van Hum, *Ngoi Tu Kham Lon* [Sitting in the Big Jail] (1929; reprint,
Saigon, 1957), 135–36.
20. Between 1919 and 1942 (1932–35 excepted), the provincial tribunals of
Tonkin sentenced 40,405 convicts for "other crimes." The figure for theft was
36,140 and 22,108 for vagabondage. Gouvernement général, *Annuaire statistique
de l'Indochine*, 1919–42.
21. *Annuaire de la Cochinchine française*, 1882, and *Annuaire de l'Indo-Chine
française*, pt. 1: *Cochinchine et Cambodge*, 1894.
22. Ibid.
23. TTLT, Résidence supérieure au Tonkin, 81781.
24. "Nous demandons l'amnistie en faveur des condamnés pour infractions aux
règlements douaniers et forestiers," *La Tribune indochinoise*, August 24, 1936, 1.
25. Ngo Vinh Long, *Before the Revolution: The Vietnamese Peasants under the
French* (New York, 1991), 66–67.
26. Ibid.

to jails" as a result of the corrupt and unscrupulous methods employed to enforce the monopolies.[27]

After theft, vagabondage, and monopoly infractions, the most common crimes for which people were incarcerated were assault, murder, attempted murder, public drunkenness, and violence or threats of violence against state officials.[28] During the military pacifications of the nineteenth century, anti-French combatants were often imprisoned for piracy, rebellion, and banditry. Rape and sexual assault, on the other hand, were rarely prosecuted during the colonial era. In 1880, only 6 of the 905 inmates who entered the Cochin Chinese prison system had been convicted of rape.[29] Poulo Condore incarcerated only three rapists during all of 1892.[30] During the nineteen years between 1913 and 1931, the criminal courts in Hanoi and Saigon secured an average of ten rape convictions per year.[31] And between 1919 and 1942, accusations of rape were among the least common type of case brought before the Provincial Tribunal of Tonkin—along with infanticide, poisoning, and selling false lottery tickets.[32]

While we have significant (albeit fragmentary) information about the crimes prisoners committed, there are fewer data on their social backgrounds. One useful source is a brief sociological survey carried out on the provincial prison population of Cochin China during 1896. In that year, 95 percent of all prisoners were men, and 95 percent were Vietnamese (the remaining 5 percent were classified as Chinese, Cambodians, Indians, and Malays).[33] Sixty-four percent were between 20 and 40 years of age, 3 percent were under 16, and 3 percent were over 60. Thirty-six percent of the inmate population were single or widowed, and 64 percent were married.[34]

---

27. "In its efforts to protect the monopolists against losses due to illegal distilling, the administration mobilized the scum of society by offering bonuses for denunciations. Penalties were extremely severe. On the basis of a single denunciation, a person could be arrested, heavily fined, put in prison, or deported to forced labor on public works in the most desolate regions of the country. Each year, thousands of completely innocent people were sentenced to prison." Joseph Buttinger, *Vietnam: A Dragon Embattled*, vol. 1: *From Colonialism to the Vietminh* (London, 1967), 58. A similar argument is put forward in Pham Cao Duong, *Vietnamese Peasants under French Domination: 1861–1945* (Berkeley, Calif., 1985), 105.

28. Gouvernement général, *Annuaire statistique de l'Indochine*, 1919–42.

29. *Annuaire de la Cochinchine française*, 1880.

30. Ibid., 1892.

31. Gouvernement général, *Annuaire statistique de l'Indochine*, 1913–31.

32. Ibid., 1919–42.

33. *Annuaire de l'Indo-Chine française*, pt. 1: *Cochinchine et Cambodge*, 1896. Because all European prisoners in Cochin China were held in the Saigon Maison centrale, there were none in provincial prisons.

34. Ibid.

In terms of occupational background, the survey divided the inmate population into nine categories. The largest of these, cultivators and day laborers, made up 67 percent of the prison population; the next, domestic servants and security guards, 12 percent.[35] The prevalence of cultivators in prison is unsurprising, given that over 95 percent of all Vietnamese lived in the countryside during the colonial era. The relatively large number of servants and security guards may reflect the expanding number of rural landlords and an urban middle class prosperous enough to hire domestic help. It also points to the frequency with which domestic servants stole (or were accused of stealing) from their employers. Rounding out the occupational survey were landlords, at 3 percent; skilled workers, at 2 percent; merchants, at 1.5 percent; and state employees and janitors, at 1 percent apiece. Finally, in the lowest category, only eight members of the liberal professions—doctors, lawyers, teachers, and artists—spent time in provincial prisons during 1896.

Although comparable data are unavailable for any other single year, scattered evidence indicates that members of the rural and urban lower classes made up the majority of the Indochinese prison population until the end of the colonial era. A subplot of virtually every colonial-era prison memoir concerns the efforts of self-consciously middle-class narrators to assimilate into the lower-class culture of prison life. "In jail, most prisoners are workers," explained Hoang Minh Dau following his release from Ha Tien Provincial Prison in 1931, "and they are constantly shaking down the few middle-class inmates for coins to buy liquor and extra food."[36] Hoang Dao's depiction of Indochina's criminal class paints a similar picture. Composed primarily of peasants, rickshaw pullers, prostitutes, coolies, domestic servants, and vagabonds, the ensemble of unsuccessful defendants depicted in his account suggests that Hanoi's prison population was dominated by poor cultivators, members of the urban underclass, and recent rural migrants to the city.

Women in Prison

Like all data on the inmate population, evidence about female prisoners is fragmentary and impressionistic. What figures do exist confirm that their numbers were relatively small. On December 31, 1880, only 6 percent

---

35. There was also a miscellaneous category that comprised 12 percent of the total population.

36. Hoang Minh Dau, *Cai Than Tu Toi* [My Life as a Prisoner] (Saigon, 1933), 15.

(25 out of 410) of the prisoners in Saigon Central Prison were women.[37] During 1882, women made up 4 percent (311 out of 8,131) of all inmates processed by Cochin Chinese provincial prisons and Saigon Central Prison.[38] On December 31, 1894, 2 percent (10 out of 439) of the prisoners on Poulo Condore were women.[39] During 1895, women constituted 5 percent (556 out of 10,700) of the prisoners entering provincial prisons in Cochin China and Saigon Central Prison.[40] Although these odd figures are insufficient to paint a comprehensive portrait of the female prison population, they do reveal a significant contrast between Indochina and France, where women made up roughly 20 percent of the inmate population in 1850, and 12–13 percent at the end of the century (see table 6).[41]

More extensive statistics from the twentieth century (presented in table 7) indicate that women continued to make up an extremely modest proportion of the Indochinese inmate population until the end of the colonial era. Between 1929 and 1942, only 5 percent of the inmates in provincial prisons (9,589 out of 163,686) were women. During the same period, women made up roughly 13 percent (4,253 out of 29,450) of the inmate population in central prisons. The higher proportion of women in these institutions can be explained by the fact that overcrowding led the wardens of provincial prisons to convert female dormitories to male ones and send their female inmates to central prisons.

Since numerous penal institutions for women and adolescent girls were established in nineteenth-century France, it is unclear why the colonial state never built prisons for female inmates in Indochina. Financial considerations probably played some role, as did perceptions that female lawbreakers in Indochina were nonviolent, unlikely to join male-dominated secret societies and anticolonial parties, and hence less threatening to social and political order than their male counterparts. It is also possible that women were not viewed as a useful source of prison labor, because the work reserved for inmates in Indochina entailed laborious tasks such as road-building and ditch-digging, which women were considered ill-equipped physically to perform.

37. *Annuaire de la Cochinchine française*, 1880.
38. Ibid., 1882.
39. Ibid., 1894.
40. Ibid., 1895.
41. Patricia O'Brien, "The Prison on the Continent, 1865–1965," in *The Oxford History of the Prison: The Practice of Punishment in Western Society*, ed. Norval Morris and David Rothmand (New York, 1995), 200.

Table 6.   Number of Men and Women in Indochinese Central
Prisons on 31 December, 1922–1940

| Year | Saigon | | Hanoi | |
	Men	Women	Men	Women
1922	223	17	771	122
1929	691	60	400	117
1930	1,485	89	1,065	147
1931	1,662	128	913	164
1932	1,197	132	1,144	227
1933	753	117	1,155	261
1934	673	188	1,130	226
1935	636	143	838	183
1936	651	82	880	113
1937	692	111	831	88
1938	621	129	977	124
1939	980	126	662	112
1940	2,109	155	825	93

SOURCE: Gouvernement général de l'Indochine, *Annuaire statistique de
l'Indochine*, various years.

Whatever the reason, the absence of prisons for women in Indochina
meant that female convicts were often kept in small, cramped rooms away
from the main dormitories, or, in more unfortunate cases, locked up together with men. Few women were sent to remote upland penitentiaries,
where the climate was thought to be too severe. While Poulo Condore held
a handful of women during the late nineteenth and early twentieth centuries, female prisoners were no longer sent to the island after 1910.[42] With
no prisons reserved specifically for women, the administration was unable
to segregate female convicts from defendants, political from nonpolitical
offenders or prisoners with different sentences. Moreover, as Indochina's
two juvenile detention centers accepted only boys, adolescent girls were incarcerated alongside adults. The fact that women were allowed to keep
infants with them in prison further intensified the social heterogeneity

42. Jean-Claude Demariaux, *Les Secrets des îles Poulo-Condore: Le Grand
Bagne indochinois* (Paris, 1956), 134.

Table 7.   Number of Men and Women in Indochinese Provincial Prisons
on 31 December, 1929–1940

Year	Annam		Cochin China		Tonkin	
	Men	*Women*	*Men*	*Women*	*Men*	*Women*
1929	1,490	150	2,469	78	3,129	374
1930	1,670	180	3,313	69	4,190	418
1931	3,203	163	3,892	182	4,168	332
1932	4,034	139	3,986	239	5,496	432
1933	3,087	188	3,225	229	5,454	502
1934	2,330	108	3,063	269	5,706	626
1935	2,341	143	3,094	155	5,750	417
1936	2,123	88	2,633	97	4,666	358
1937	2,149	146	2,336	90	5,280	244
1938	2,443	123	3,117	137	4,960	287
1939	2,638	187	3,365	139	4,439	194
1940	2,834	195	4,922	171	5,065	233

SOURCE: Gouvernement général de l'Indochine, *Annuaire statistique de l'Indochine,*
various years.

within female dormitories. Consider, for example, the following description of the female dormitory in Hanoi Central Prison in 1932:

> From a hygienic and moral point of view, and from the standpoint of
> simple humanity, the women's quarter presents a revolting spectacle.
> Two hundred and twenty-five of these miserable creatures are locked
> up in a space meant for a hundred. They form an incredible mob, nei-
> ther classed nor categorized, composed of political prisoners, common-
> law convicts incarcerated for various crimes, defendants, and minors,
> not to mention twelve women with infants.[43]

A survey of inmates from 1896 reveals few significant differences between the male and female prison populations. As with male prisoners,
most female prisoners were ethnically Vietnamese and were classified as

43. AOM, Indochine, Affaires politiques, 1728, Rapport fait par M. Chastenet de
Géry, Inspecteur des Colonies concernent l'organisation du régime pénitencier au
Tonkin, April 26, 1932, 9.

"cultivators or day laborers."[44] The vast majority were between 20 and 40 years old; 63 percent were married, and 48 percent had children. Women also tended to be imprisoned for the same crimes as men. Statistics from 1882 and 1894 indicate that well over half of the female inmates in Cochin Chinese provincial prisons and Saigon Central Prison had been convicted of theft, with vagabondage a distant second, and illicit gambling third. Conviction figures from 1929 to 1931 suggest that theft remained the main reason women were jailed well into the twentieth century.[45]

Fragmentary statistical data suggest that women, like men, tended to be incarcerated for various kinds of robbery, but both official and popular attitudes toward crime in Indochina emphasized fundamental differences between male and female criminality. Dr. Louis Lorion claimed erroneously and without a shred of evidence in the 1880s that Cochin Chinese women were most often incarcerated for poisoning. Women frequently poisoned, he argued, out of "cupidity, jealousy, or revenge."[46] Jean-Claude Demariaux suggested that most women sent to Poulo Condore prior to 1910 had been convicted of counterfeiting or of buying and selling children for immoral purposes.[47] Phan Van Hum offers a different but equally unsubstantiated claim that most of the hundred or so women incarcerated with him in Saigon Central Prison were being punished for murdering their husbands or children, citing the cases of a street singer serving a twenty-year sentence for pouring molten zinc into the mouth of her sleeping husband and a "light-skinned college girl" convicted of murdering her newborn baby because it had been conceived out of wedlock.[48]

Political Prisoners

The legal definition of political prisoners was unclear in Indochina and gave rise to confusion and anxiety within the French administration.[49] Officially, political prisoners were convicts who had been sentenced to depor-

44. *Annuaire de l'Indo-Chine française*, pt. 1: *Cochinchine et Cambodge, 1896*.

45. Gouvernement général, *Annuaire statistique de l'Indochine, 1929–31*.

46. Louis Lorion, *Criminalité et médecine judiciaire en Cochinchine* (Lyon, 1887), 78.

47. Demariaux, *Secrets des îles Poulo-Condore*, 139.

48. Phan Van Hum, *Ngoi Tu Kham Lon*, 125.

49. In the words of one colonial inspector, "the definition of a political convict and the regime to be applied to him is a subject of grave uncertainty for the administration" (AOM, Indochine, Affaires politiques, 1768, Détenus politiques—Régime spécial, July 22, 1939).

tation and detention. Such sentences were given for acts that violated article 91 of the Indochinese criminal code, a wide-ranging statute comprising a number of borrowed French laws that had been passed in the 1890s.[50] These laws regulated press freedoms, assemblies, elections, and the activities of collective labor, and restricted membership in "anarchist groups."[51] Article 91's vague language—it prohibited "acts of a nature that compromise public security or occasion political troubles"—allowed it to be broadly applied in a wide range of circumstances.[52] Because it was only introduced into Indochina in the 1890s, anticolonial rebels arrested during the 1860s, 1870s, and 1880s were charged with criminal offenses, most often banditry and piracy.

This meant that members of the Southern Resistance, the Scholars' Movement, and the Save-the-King campaigns were sentenced to hard labor and incarcerated together with common criminals.[53] During the early twentieth century, some activists connected to the Eastern Travel Movement, the Dong Kinh Free School, the Reform Society (Duy Tan Hoi), and the Restoration Society (Quang Phuc Hoi) were charged with violating article 91 and issued political sentences, but they did not enjoy special rights, a better diet, or exemptions from forced labor.[54] Instead, they lived together with common criminals and were subjected to an identical regime. In effect, political prisoners were legally designated as such by the courts through the handing out of political sentences, but they were not separately distinguished in any meaningful way by the prison system.

The origins of a special regime for political prisoners in Indochina dates from the mass arrests of reformist scholars who spearheaded antitax riots in Annam during 1908.[55] Following the restoration of order, hundreds of scholars who participated in the movements were deported to Poulo Condore and Lao Bao. Huynh Thuc Khang, a reformist Confucian scholar who

50. For a concise discussion of article 91, see Albert Serol, "Amnistie première," *Le Travail*, September 30, 1936.

51. Ibid. The law forbade "meetings of people organized in order to prepare measures contrary to law; outrages of speech, writing, or gesture; threats against magistrates, juries, officers, employees with the public service ministries; destruction of monuments; and attempts to disrupt work or industry."

52. For a reprint of law 91, see "Pour Tao et Thau," *La Lutte*, October 10, 1937.

53. See David Marr, *Vietnamese Anticolonialism, 1885–1925* (Berkeley and Los Angeles, 1971), 22–77.

54. Ibid., 77–185.

55. Ibid., 185–212.

worked as a prisoner clerk on Poulo Condore in the early twentieth century and became the great chronicler of the Poulo Condore deportees, describes how, during the first two years on the island, he and his fellow political prisoners were subjected to the same arduous penal regime as common criminals.[56] Even Indochina's most famous political prisoner was subjected to forced labor: Phan Chu Trinh's well-known poem "Breaking Rocks on Con Lon" dates from this period.[57]

In 1910, Huynh Thuc Khang and his fellow political prisoners successfully petitioned Director Cudenet to isolate them from the common-law prisoners and to grant them a special, more lenient penal regime.[58] Thereafter, political prisoners on the island were kept segregated from the general population, served better food, and allowed to engage in less onerous work, such as gardening and mat-making.[59] This continued until the late 1920s and early 1930s. Activists arrested for their role in the Reform Society and the Restoration Society, students jailed for activities connected with Phan Boi Chau's trial in 1925 and Phan Chau Trinh's funeral in 1926, and individuals prosecuted for their membership in protorevolutionary parties such as the Revolutionary Youth League (Viet Nam Thanh Nien Cach Menh Dong Chi Hoi) and the New Viet Revolutionary Party (Tan Viet Cach Mang Dang) were granted mattresses, special visitation and mail privileges, larger rations, and access to paper, pens, newspapers, and books.[60] In the early 1930s, however, massive overcrowding, brought on by the Yen-Bay Uprising and the Nghe-Tinh soviet movement, plus a new, hardline reticence by courts to grant political sentences to violent revolutionaries led to an erosion of the benefits afforded political prisoners.

Tran Huy Lieu, who served a six-month political sentence in 1927 and a six-year sentence during the 1930s, expressed dismay at how conditions for

56. Huynh Thuc Khang, *Thi Tu Tung Thoai* (Prison Verse) (1939; reprint, Saigon, 1951), 53–54, reports that approximately sixty scholar-gentry activists were deported to Poulo Condore in late 1908 and early 1909. Khang describes fellow political prisoners involved in masonry, carpentry, rock breaking, wood gathering, and unloading cargo from ships (ibid., 47–49).

57. Marr, *Vietnamese Anticolonialism*, 242.

58. Huynh Thuc Khang, *Thi Tu Tung Thoai*, 65–66.

59. "From then on we began to have a more interesting life and turned dormitory B into a school and a poetry club [*thi dan*]. The study of science in this natural school begins from this point" (ibid., 66).

60. For instructive accounts of the special regime for political prisoners prior to 1930, see "Pour l'application du régime politique," *La Lutte*, August 24, 1935, 1, and "La Vie des condamnés politiques dans les pénitenciers," *Le Travail*, December 14, 1936, 1.

political prisoners had deteriorated by the time of his second incarceration.[61] In 1927, Lieu was not forced to shave his head like the common-law prisoners or confined during the day. Instead of the light blue prison uniform worn by most inmates, he was allowed to wear white cotton clothes sent by his family. He could also receive mail and reading material. By 1930, however, all of these petty privileges had been rolled back. "The lone thing that distinguished political and nonpolitical regimes after 1930," Lieu explained, "was that the prisoners were kept physically separate."[62] Only following aggressive agitation in the colonial press during the mid 1930s was a more lenient regime for political prisoners reintroduced into Indochina.[63]

FORMAL SOCIAL HIERARCHIES

In most Indochinese prisons, there was a formal pecking order of prisoners, headed by special inmate-overseers known as *contremaîtres* or *caplans*. Jean-Claude Demariaux described the *caplan* as "a social hybrid created by the French administration: one half prisoner, one half guard." In theory, *caplans* were to be given limited supervisory authority over prison work teams. In practice, however, they served the administration in a broad variety of ways. As officials on Poulo Condore explained to Demariaux, *caplans* functioned simultaneously as "informers, guards, and valuable auxiliaries."[64] In many institutions, they were issued rattan whips and charged with maintaining order in communal dormitories.[65] *Caplans* also oversaw the custody of prisoners confined temporarily at work camps outside of the main prison buildings.[66]

61. Tran Huy Lieu, "Tren Dao Hon Cau" [On Hon Cau Island], in *Hoi Ky Tran Huy Lieu*, ed. Pham Nhu Thom (Hanoi, 1991), 100.
62. Tran Huy Lieu, "Tu Hoc Trong Tu" [Self-Study in Prison], in ibid., 144.
63. See chapter 8.
64. Demariaux, *Secrets des îles Poulo-Condore*, 54.
65. Ton Quang Phiet, *Mot Ngay Ngan Thu (Lan Thu Nhat O Nha Nguc)* [The Eternal Day (My First Time in Prison)] (Hue, 1935), 14; Huynh Thuc Khang, *Thi Tu Tung Thoai*, 67.
66. AOM, Indochine, Affaires politiques, 1728, Rapport fait par M. Le Gregam concernant la vérification de M. Bouvier, Chef de bureau de l'administration pénitentiaire, en service détaché en Indochine, Directeur de pénitencier de Poulo Condore, February 23, 1932, 53. "All the detainees situated at work camps, including those isolated on Hon Cau, are placed under the direct control of *matas* when they are not simply under *caplans*, prisoners who take on the functions of guarding their comrades."

Prisoners were recruited to serve as *caplans* based on their fitness, initiative, and competence in French. Demariaux claimed that they were chosen from among "the most energetic and robust prisoners."[67] Ton Quang Phiet reported that *caplans* in Hoa Lo were known for their "cleverness and fluency in the Western language [*tieng tay*]."[68] Other accounts suggest that officials looked for evidence of ruthlessness in selecting *caplans* and favored prisoners incarcerated for violent crimes. On Poulo Condore, Huynh Thuc Khang was struck by their casual predilection for brutality, and Nguyen Hai Ham describes them as "robbers, murders, and hooligans" recruited explicitly for their merciless personalities.[69] Indeed, the first *caplan* encountered by Ton Quang Phiet in Hoa Lo had been convicted of the brutal murder of his wife and child.[70]

In addition to the explicit authority that stemmed from their official duties, *caplans* derived informal power from the fact that they earned double the daily stipend of hard-labor convicts.[71] Not only did this facilitate greater access to supplemental food, medicine, and supplies but it allowed them to bribe guards and maintain clientalist networks within the institution. More important, because they were often responsible for allocating work assignments, *caplans* were well positioned to receive kickbacks and favors from other inmates. On Poulo Condore, a chief *caplan*, known as the *memento*, apportioned all labor postings for the head warder.[72] He also visited work sites and prepared reports for French superiors on discipline, surveillance, and labor conditions. Eyewitness accounts suggest that the *memento's* close working relationship with the head warder invested him with extraordinary power over inmates and indigenous guards alike. Because he was often consulted about rivalries and conflicts within the institution, the *memento* received a huge number of bribes and illicit gifts, especially on the occasion of Tet and New Year's Day. Tran Van Que likened the informal jockeying prior to the selection of a new *memento* to the

---

67. Demariaux, *Secrets des îles Poulo-Condore,* 54.

68. Ton Quang Phiet, *Mot Ngay Ngan Thu,* 14.

69. Huynh Thuc Khang, *Thi Tu Tung Thoai,* 67. Nguyen Hai Ham, *Tu Yen Bay Den Con Lon, 1930–1945* [From Yen Bay to Con Lon, 1930–1945] (Saigon, 1970), 192, writes that "the more brutal the prisoner, the greater the odds that he would be selected to guard other prisoners."

70. Ton Quang Phiet, *Mot Ngay Ngan Thu,* 14.

71. Tran Van Que, *Con-Lon Quan-Dao Truoc ngay 9–3–1945* [The Poulo Condore Archipelago before March 9, 1945] (Saigon, 1961), 94–95.

72. Ibid.

back-room deal-making that accompanies any election in which patron-client networks are at stake.[73]

Along with *caplans,* members of the formal prisoner elite included convicts employed as clerks (*tho ky*), servants (*boi*), cooks (*bep*), messengers (*tuy phai*), and medical assistants (*tro-y-ta*).[74] Inmates recruited to work as live-in servants for prison officials also enjoyed a privileged status. Most were employed as maids, gardeners, and cooks; some worked as nannies, known as *coolies-bébé.*[75] In remote locales, it was not unusual for guards to take on several inmates to fulfill a variety of domestic tasks. In 1905, the resident superior of Tonkin criticized this practice in an open letter to all provincial residents:

> It has been brought to my attention that in numerous residencies, a number of prisoners are granted to each functionary, who uses them as servants. This usage warrants severe critique, both because of the inadequacy of the surveillance to which these prisoners are subjected and because of the improper appropriation of penal labor, which is exclusively reserved for work in the public interest. It is important to put an end to this abuse. I request, therefore, that you take measures so that in the future, prisoners will only be employed at roadwork and not used to fulfill the domestic needs of our functionaries.[76]

Official efforts to curtail the practice met with limited success. In 1910, the resident of Yen Bay chided prison officials for allowing prisoner domestics to sleep in their homes.[77] And a 1932 report noted that many European staff on Poulo Condore employed "the permanent domestic services of no fewer than four prisoners."[78]

Among the most important perks enjoyed by the prisoner elite was the right to move around within the institution, or, in the case of domestics, to leave the prison on a daily basis. Clerks had access to storerooms and offices; cooks circulated in and out of pantries, dining areas, and kitchens; and medical assistants spent their days at the infirmary or visiting sick inmates

73. Ibid.

74. Ibid., 90–96.

75. Demariaux, *Secrets des îles Poulo-Condore,* 115.

76. TTLT, Maire de Hanoi, 3945, Emploi de la main-d'oeuvre pénale, October 10, 1905.

77. TTLT, Résidence supérieure au Tonkin, 79540, Le Résident de Yen Bay à M. le Résident supérieur au Tonkin, September 17, 1910.

78. AOM, Indochine, Affaires politiques, 1728, Rapport fait par M. Le Gregam, Inspecteur des Colonies, sur les îles et le pénitencier de Poulo Condore, February 23, 1932.

in dormitories throughout prison. Servants and messengers traveled widely within the institution transporting supplies, delivering documents, and carrying out custodial and maintenance work.[79]

If their physical mobility enhanced the power and livelihood of the prisoner elite, so too did access to scarce resources. It is no surprise that cooks and food servers appeared better-fed than other inmates.[80] Those who worked in the infirmary supplied active black markets for medicine, milk, and sugar. Clerks took advantage of their role managing prison storerooms and processing new inmates to engage in embezzlement, petty thievery, and extortion.[81] Servants and messengers received payoffs for trafficking in smuggled goods and facilitating illicit correspondence between inmates. Domestics enjoyed many benefits, including home-cooked meals and temporary relief from communal living.

Below the prisoner elite, additional status hierarchies structured relations among the remainder of the inmate population. In theory, an important dividing line separated hard-labor convicts from those prisoners not compelled to work: untried defendants, nonviolent recidivists, and convicts sentenced to simple imprisonment. However, faced with high demands for penal labor, most institutions ignored this distinction. On Poulo Condore, prisoners were classified according to a tripartite scheme in which seniority determined differences in status and treatment rather than sentence.[82] According to this system, all new prisoners were placed in the lowliest category—category 3—and given the most hazardous labor assignments. After two years, prisoners graduated to category 2, which entailed onerous but less dangerous work. Finally, prisoners who completed one-half of their terms (or served twenty years of a life sentence) were moved to category 1 and assigned light chores such as gardening, laundry, and dishwashing. Although seniority acted as the primary determinant of mobility within this system, changes in behavior or acute physical deterioration could also trigger the transfer of prisoners from one category to another.[83]

While formal status distinctions were structured around labor assignments, they were displayed and amplified through differential markings on the bodies of the condemned. In most prisons, the institutional and juridi-

79. Phan Van Hum, *Ngoi Tu Kham Lon,* 134.
80. Ibid., 72.
81. Huynh Thuc Khang, *Thi Tu Tung Thoai,* 145. Khang recounts the story of a clerk on Poulo Condore who embezzled a large sum from the prison treasury.
82. AOM, Indochine, Affaires politiques, 1728, Rapport fait par M. Le Gregam concernant la pénitencier de Poulo Condore à la date du 23 février 1932, 23.
83. Ibid.

cal status of each inmate was inscribed on a small wooden placard, known in Vietnamese as a *dinh bai*, which prisoners wore around their necks at all times.[84] In Kham Lon, the *dinh bai* came in different shapes and sizes to allow prison officials to recognize quickly the category of prisoner to whom it belonged.[85] Huynh Thuc Khang sarcastically likened the function of the *dinh bai* to that of a *bai nga*, a square insignia worn by imperial mandarins to signify their educational credentials and bureaucratic rank.[86]

Clothing and hairstyles in prison also functioned as status markers. Most members of the prisoner elite dressed in white to distinguish themselves from ordinary prisoners, who wore blue.[87] *Caplans* were distinguished from other prisoners by the bright red insignia C.M. (for *contremaître*) stitched into their clothes.[88] The myriad meanings conveyed through compulsory prison hairstyles on Poulo Condore prompted Demariaux to remark that "the scissors represents an important weapon in the arsenal of the prison regime."[89] Because shaved heads were mandatory for new convicts and for inmates in category 3, bald prisoners could be identified as neophytes or as inmates who had failed somehow to conform to behavioral standards. Prisoners serving the final year of their terms were allowed to grow their hair out, presumably to help ease reintegration in civilian society. Prisoners with chronic discipline problems and recaptured escapees had one-half of their heads shaved, a policy designed both to humiliate them and to stimulate a heightened vigilance towards them on the part of the guards.[90]

The creation and exhibition of formal status hierarchies among inmates served the prison regime in several ways. Most important, the prisoner elite helped run the institution at every level. Not only did this privileged caste play important roles in bookkeeping, surveillance, provisioning, health care, building maintenance, and the enforcement of labor discipline but it provided officials with valuable "inside" information on the state of the inmate population. Moreover, although the prisoner elite received

84. Phan Van Hum, *Ngoi Tu Kham Lon*, 25; Huynh Thuc Khang, *Thi Tu Tung Thoai*, 40. According to Khang, on Poulo Condore the *dinh bai* was referred to as the *the bai*.

85. Phan Van Hum, *Ngoi Tu Kham Lon*, 25.

86. Huynh Thuc Khang, *Thi Tu Tung Thoai*, 41.

87. Demariaux, *Secrets des îles Poulo-Condore*, 45–49.

88. AOM, Arrêté portant les règlements des prisons de l'Indochine, 12.

89. Demariaux, *Secrets des îles Poulo-Condore*, 43.

90. Ibid. Demariaux claimed that Vietnamese viewed a shaved head as "a mark of mortification."

higher monthly stipends than ordinary hard-labor convicts, they were cheaper to employ than civilians.[91] Hence, the prisoner elite facilitated the smooth operation of the prison at minimal cost. The system also contributed to the preservation of institutional order. As a fluid social hierarchy, it created incentives for individuals to demonstrate "good behavior." Prisoners hoping for "promotion" into desirable categories or powerful positions were more likely to follow the rules and to cooperate with officials. While colonial prisons gave rise to high degrees of collective violence, formal status hierarchies probably served to dampen levels of resistance and disorder.

Another effect of the system was to divide inmate populations against themselves. Attitudes of ordinary inmates to the prisoner elite ranged from nagging envy to murderous (literally) animosity, directed especially at *caplans*. Intense hatred of *caplans* provides subtext in virtually every colonial-era prison memoir. The nocturnal execution-style killing of a *caplan* on Poulo Condore was described to Demariaux as "a routine event."[92] In *Nguoi Cap Rang Cua Ham Xay Lua* (The *Caplan* of the Rice-Mill Stockade), Nguyen Cong Hoan claimed that *caplans* assigned to the punitive dormitory on Poulo Condore, known as the rice-mill stockade, rarely survived more than six months.[93]

It is also likely that the recruitment of talented inmates into the prisoner elite functioned to co-opt potential leaders of internal resistance movements. Evidence to this effect can be found in the prison memoir of Huynh Thuc Khang. Jailed for anti-French activity in 1908, Khang spent his first five years on Poulo Condore confined together with a supportive brotherhood of political activists. Much of Khang's memoir consists of affectionate profiles of his fellow inmates and recollections from memory of the bittersweet Sino-Vietnamese poetry that they composed and recited together. The memoir also recalls Khang's efforts, immediately following his incarceration, to persuade prison officials to implement a special, more lenient regime for political prisoners.

In 1912, Khang's competence in French drew the attention of the chief warder, who recruited him to work as an office clerk. Reflecting on the opportunity, Khang wrote: "To work as a clerk in prison is the highest honor,

---

91. According to Huynh Thuc Khang, prisoners who worked as secretaries on Poulo Condore in the early 1920s were paid 2–3 piasters per month, while civilian clerks made roughly twenty-five times as much (Huynh Thuc Khang, *Thi Tu Tung Thoai*, 143).

92. Demariaux, *Secrets des îles Poulo-Condore*, 54.

93. Nguyen Cong Hoan, *Nguoi Cap Rang Cua Ham Xay Lua* (Hanoi, 1978), 7.

not unlike being a great mandarin on the mainland. Clerks are exempt from hard labor; *matas* and guards treat them very well. Plus, in terms of food, clothing, and salary, they are better off than other prisoners."[94]

Thereafter, Khang spent his days in the office and his afternoons wandering relatively unsupervised around the island. At night, he slept, together with a small group of clerks and kitchen aides, in segregated quarters outside of the main prison building. These new circumstances appear to have triggered a change in Khang's posture toward the prison administration: "I never made any mistakes and always remembered to check my figures. I answered all questions and requests immediately. Although Chief Warder Campion had been skeptical at first, he soon realized that the so-called 'big mandarins' [*bon quan to*] were not as dishonest as the common-law prisoners, and he began to treat us better."[95]

Whereas before, Khang had worked tirelessly to raise the morale of his fellow prisoners and pressure the regime for reforms, afterward, he endeavored to impress prison officials with his trustworthiness, competence, and diligence. He did not take part in any of the prisoner rebellions that occurred during his incarceration, including a massive uprising in 1918 that left eighty inmates dead. While he does not explore the reasons for his apparent disengagement from the resistance efforts of his fellow inmates, he admits that his improved fortunes seem to have sapped his capacity to compose poetry—an oblique reference, perhaps, to the politically enervating effects of promotion into the prisoner elite.

SUBCULTURAL HIERARCHIES

Inmates also existed within a subcultural social order of their own making. Prison subcultures are often interpreted as manifestations of collective resistance to the power of the total institution. Evidence from Indochina suggests, however, that social and cultural formations initiated by prisoners were as likely to divide inmate populations against themselves as to bring them together. While some fault lines structuring the subcultural order in Indochinese prisons mirrored fundamental divisions in civilian society (i.e., regional and ethnic identities), others were an exclusive product of institutional life. Examples include rifts between old and new prisoners, the structure of prison gangs, and class antagonism between political and nonpolitical prisoners.

94. Huynh Thuc Khang, *Thi Tu Tung Thoai*, 143.
95. Ibid., 145.

As in penal institutions the world over, conflict between "old-timers" and neophytes represented a basic structural division in colonial prisons. According to Nhuong Tong, the split was manifest in a regular hazing ordeal known as *khao cua,* during which veteran prisoners harassed, beat, and robbed new inmates. Immediately following his arrest and incarceration in Hue in 1926, Tong was subjected to a *khao cua* in which four old-timers set upon him and seized his belongings.[96] Ton Quang Phiet pointed out that old prisoners were often threatened by new ones, whom they saw as potential rivals for jealously protected patron-client relationships with guards.[97]

Social divisions based on seniority tended to be fluid—this month's victim might be next month's bully. More durable status distinctions in prison derived from underworld gangs. The *anh chi,* or criminal gang leader, appears repeatedly in prison memoirs. According to Phan Van Hum, *anh chi*s enjoyed remarkable power in prison for two reasons: the devotion of their followers, known as *em ut*s (baby brothers), and the alliances they formed with corrupt guards.[98]

In Hum's analysis, the remarkable devotion of *em ut*s for their *anh chi*s derived from the hegemony in the Indochinese underworld of traditional Sino-Vietnamese notions of political authority. "Our *anh chi*s model themselves after heroes in Chinese novels and operas," he wrote. "Such figures have long served as moral examples in our country. Most of our *anh chi*s are monarchists at heart. . . . They consider themselves petty kings and adopt an autocratic posture toward their *em ut*s. Since the *em ut*s know nothing but dictatorship, they follow their *anh chi*s faithfully and rarely even think off deposing them."[99]

As Hum's discussion makes clear, such "monarchist" tendencies in underworld gangs provided imprisoned *anh chi*s with selflessly dedicated foot soldiers. The power of an *anh chi,* therefore, was a product of the size of his following and the fact that his devotees were "more than ready to die for him."[100] Hum observed that *em ut*s were "steadfastly loyal":

> They will kill a man or even take responsibility for a murder they did not commit if so ordered by their *anh chi. Em ut*s often go to jail in

96. Nhuong Tong, *Doi Trong Nguc,* 6.
97. Ton Quang Phiet, *Mot Ngay Ngan Thu,* 21.
98. Phan Van Hum, *Ngoi Tu Kham Lon,* 90–100.
99. Ibid., 94–95.
100. Ibid., 91.

place of their *anh chi*. Owing to their power and connections, *anh chi*s are able to arrange early releases, reduced sentences, or light work assignments for *em ut*s who make this sacrifice for them. At very least, they are able to bribe guards to "nurture" their *em ut*s and treat them well. *Anh chi*s who cannot avoid prison are looked after by their *em ut*s. Their lawyers provide cigarettes and food, but it is the *em ut*s who really take care of them. As a result, jail for them is not really so bad.[101]

*Anh chi*s enjoyed additional authority because of their personal connections with guards. Because jailers and gang members came from a common lower-class urban milieu, it was not unusual for powerful *anh chi*s to cultivate collusive bonds with guards prior to as well as during their jail terms:

> Because the *anh chi*s crave certain amenities, they purchase the allegiance of guards in exchange for tobacco, liquor, and opium. Not only do they form such relationships in prison but many befriend guards on the outside prior to their convictions. They do this as a precaution, because they expect to go prison, the way we expect to "go to market"— they just never know when their "invitation" will arrive. Because the *anh chi*s grow dependent on these relationships, they do not interfere when guards beat other prisoners. They listen impassively as fellow prisoners are beaten. . . . This can lead to divisions between *anh chi*s and *em ut*s in prison.[102]

If underworld gangs injected a structure of discrete vertical relationships into prison society, the presence of several gangs added an element of horizontal rivalry. As Hum explained:

> Another division occurs when territory is staked out around rival parties and factions. An *anh chi* with martial skills and a strong following can easily dominate and dislodge other prison cliques. Such internal struggles are natural when men are locked up together in a cage. . . . After struggles for supremacy are concluded, victorious *anh chi*s absorb the *em ut*s of their vanquished foes.[103]

Just as formal attributions of status in prison were recorded on the bodies of the condemned, informal social distinctions were made manifest corporally through the medium of tattoos. The popularity of tattooing in

101. Ibid., 95.
102. Ibid.
103. Ibid.

prison is typically understood as a form of inmate resistance to overbearing demands for compliance with institutional norms.[104] Tattoos are seen as providing an opportunity for prisoners to fashion and represent their own identity independent of the status labels imposed on them by the prison regime. Because the process can involve considerable discomfort, the decision to get tattooed highlights the persistence of a capacity on the part of inmates to assert and express their own individuality. While similar dynamics of individual self-representation may have been at work in Indochinese prisons, tattooing there was as likely to mark inmates off as members of rival collectivities—generational groupings, religious movements, and criminal gangs.

Pham Van Hum described tattooing as a common form of "recreation" (*cuoc choi*).[105] It involved fastening a needle to a chopstick, heating its tip over an open flame and soaking it in a pot of dark Chinese ink. The needle was then inserted under the surface skin of the subject's thigh, back, or chest and manipulated until the desired image appeared. Hum noted that the process appeared painful and left a lingering soreness for over a week.[106]

For colonial observers, tattoos in prison pointed to an intensely spiritual culture of criminality. Demariaux remarks that while the tattoos of French criminals focused on erotic scenes and tributes to loved ones, the bodily art favored by Indochinese lawbreakers depicted deities and mythical beasts.[107] According to one of his informants, dragons and phoenixes were believed to furnish protection from evil spirits and enjoyed a special popularity with members of secret societies.[108] In contrast to Demariaux, Phan Van Hum interpreted the tattoos he observed in Kham Lon as evidence of the erosion of traditional beliefs and the growth of a crass fetishism of sex and consumer goods among criminals. While acknowledging that the tattoos of older *anh chi*s often depicted "classical" imagery—"the four mythical beasts," "the eight fairies," or "two dragons fighting over the sun"—he pointed out that young delinquents favored images of modern objects of desire—limousines, opium pipes, expensive hats, and nude Western women.[109] Hum saw a similar trend in the increase in the number of

104. Patricia O'Brien, *The Promise of Punishment: Prisons in Nineteenth-Century France* (Princeton, N.J., 1982), 80–86.

105. Phan Van Hum, *Ngoi Tu Kham Lon*, 150.

106. Ibid.

107. Demariaux, *Secrets des îles Poulo-Condore*, 29.

108. Ibid., 86–87.

109. Phan Van Hum, *Ngoi Tu Kham Lon*, 92.

"fashionable" tattoo messages in French, such as "Vive la France!" and "Liberté–Egalité–Fraternité."[110] Although he allowed that such slogans might signify the presence of French ideals among the Vietnamese masses, he believed that few of the largely illiterate prisoners who featured them understood even their literal meanings. The real attraction of French-language tattoos, Hum surmised, was the aura of modernity and European sophistication that they conveyed. Hence, he concluded, "the spread of such faddish slogans means that the time of the traditional *anh chi* is coming to an end."[111]

Class divisions also structured the society of Indochinese captives. Such distinctions obviously preceded institutional life, but colonial prisons placed members of different social classes in intimate proximity to one another, a living arrangement that appears to have heightened the sense of class identity. Much contemporary Vietnamese writing depicts class distinctions in prison in terms of divisions between political and nonpolitical prisoners. However, colonial prisons also ingested white-collar criminals, whom they integrated indiscriminately with their largely lower-class inmate populations. It is difficult to recover from historical evidence how lower-class prisoners experienced communal incarceration with upper-class inmates, but memoirs by elite political prisoners are preoccupied with class issues and suggest that relations between the groups were marked by animosity.

In prison, social class could be apprehended in a variety of ways. Demariaux reports being able to pick out the sole political prisoner from a large convoy of common criminals on route from Kham Lon to Poulo Condore: "He was the only one not tattooed. His features were distinct, his hands very fine, and he spoke impeccable French."[112] Vietnamese, too, looked at physical characteristics to determine class difference, but speech patterns, table manners, and comportment provided equally instructive barometers of social distinction. According to Huynh Thuc Khang: "When Phan Chu Trinh arrived on Poulo Condore, he spoke, ate, and behaved in such a distinct way that guards and prisoners called him 'the big mandarin.'"[113]

Inmates from elite backgrounds were frequently subjected to verbal and physical abuse. Huynh Thuc Khang recounted how common-law prisoners

110. Ibid., 92, 95.
111. Ibid., 92.
112. Demariaux, *Secrets des îles Poulo-Condore*, 31.
113. Huynh Thuc Khang, *Thi Tu Tung Thoai*, 42.

on Poulo Condore chided him mercilessly because of his physical weakness and ineptitude at corvée labor.[114] Ton Quang Phiet recalled being ridiculed by an illiterate petty thief with whom he shared a cell temporarily in Vinh Prison: "How did you get here, master [*thay*]?" the thief asked mockingly. "You have devoted your life to studying and yet have ended up no better than I."[115]

Whereas discrimination against upper-class inmates is a common theme in prison memoirs written by men, power relations may have been reversed in female dormitories. In 1939, the brilliant realist novelist Nguyen Hong spent his New Year's holidays observing the lives of roughly 200 female prisoners at the Nam Dinh Provincial Prison. He published his observations in an essay entitled "Tet for Female Prisoners" in the popular Hanoi weekly *Tieu Thuyet Thu Bay* (Saturday Novel). Hong reported that female convicts at Nam Dinh were divided into two categories: a wealthy clique of crooked pawnbrokers and drug smugglers, and a larger, poorer group, most of whom had been convicted for violating state alcohol and salt monopolies.[116] The better part of Hong's account details the unequal treatment of the two groups. Poor prisoners, many in tattered clothes and caring for infants, carried out hard labor in the neighboring countryside. Rich inmates worked in relative comfort within the prison at embroidery and knitting. On the first day of Tet, poor women were served a simple meal, unexceptional save for a few scraps of meat. In contrast, rich prisoners feasted on *banh chung*, betel nut, and candied fruit sent to them by their families. During their meal, rich prisoners adopted what Hong referred to as "aristocratic airs" as poor prisoners served their food and massaged their limbs.[117] It is possible that access to wealth conferred greater power within female dormitories because physical intimidation figured less there as a social equalizer.

SLANG AND COLLECTIVE SADNESS

Although no less hierarchical than the order imposed on inmates by the regime, the prison subculture also included communal elements that served to mark off inmate populations as a whole from civilian society. One such element was the development of prison argot, a specialized vocabu-

114. Ibid., 47.
115. Ton Quang Phiet, *Mot Ngay Ngan Thu*, 31.
116. Nguyen Hong, "Tet Cua Tu Dan Ba," 150.
117. Ibid., 154.

lary and set of idioms shared by all inmates. Prison argot probably originated in the jargon of secret societies and the urban underworld, but it
eventually came to be used by inmates from all backgrounds and social
classes. When first sent to Poulo Condore, Tran Huy Lieu was struck by the
strangeness of prison usage, such as calling the warden Ong Lon ("Mr.
Big"). "This sort of language sounded funny when I arrived on the islands," he notes, "but after a while, it became familiar, and I used it regularly."[118]

Colorful examples of argot can be found throughout prison memoirs.
The intrusive strip search in which new prisoners were forced to spread
wide their arms, legs, and various bodily cavities was called the "phoenix
dance" (*mieng phung hoang*).[119] Because every new inmate was provided
with a sleeping mat, release from prison came to be known as "returning
the mat" (*lay chieu*).[120] Inmates responsible for serving prison food were
called *mat cat* (macaques), after the short-tailed, fat-cheeked jungle mon-
keys famous for snacking surreptitiously while gathering food.[121] Prisoners referred to a five-year sentence as a "peacock note" (*con cong*), because
the Bank of Indochina's five-piaster bill featured a picture of the bird.[122] A
sour broth served on Poulo Condore, made from dried fish and fermented
rice, was known as "motorcycle soup" because of the flatulent sounds
heard afterward in the latrine.[123]

In addition to a common language, prisoners shared a collective emotional experience conditioned by their loss of freedom and disengagement
from family ties. As Tran Van Que explained, feelings of despondency were
most intense for long-term prisoners:

> Prisoners serving 20- or 30-year sentences have many reasons to be
> sad. Twenty or thirty years is a long time to survive in these conditions.
> Even if your health holds up, release may be as devastating as incarcer-
> ation. Families and villages will have changed drastically. Parents will
> be dead; wives and children will have moved away. Surviving relatives
> will be old and feeble. What hope will be left? Most likely, you will be
> on the verge of death yourself.[124]

---

118. Tran Huy Lieu, "Con Lon Ky Su," 425.
119. Phan Van Hum, *Ngoi Tu Kham Lon,* 31.
120. Ibid., 71.
121. Ibid., 72.
122. Tran Van Que, *Con-Lon Quan-Dao Truoc ngay 9–3–1945,* 120.
123. Hoang Quoc Viet, "Our People, a Very Heroic People," in *A Very Heroic People: Memoirs from the Revolution* (Hanoi, 1965), 167.
124. Tran Van Que, *Con-Lon Quan-Dao Truoc ngay 9–3–1945,* 119.

Of course, depression was an ordinary reaction even for short-term inmates and for those held temporarily while awaiting trial. Describing his first night in jail following arrest, Nhuong Tong wrote of a "vast sadness":

> The sadness was like a tightly woven net encasing my heart. My cell was pitch black. I struck a match, lit a candle and placed it in the corner of the floor. I sat stone-still staring at the flame. I tried to compose a poem, but my mind was a blank. I wanted to recite some old verse but couldn't utter a sound. The sadness had paralyzed my brain, placed a stranglehold on my throat.[125]

While most narrators of prison memoirs wallow in their own sadness, Phan Van Hum described the despondency he observed in other neophyte prisoners. He related the story of a "newly imprisoned barber who cried like a baby whose mother had just died. I tried to comfort him but he only grew sadder and cried more."[126] Another episode involved a recently imprisoned clerk who grew so miserable during his first day in prison that he "refused food and drink and became weak and sick. All day he sat silently, as grief-stricken as a bird locked in a cage."[127] Tran Van Que described the case of one prisoner who literally died of grief, unable to bear the prospect of long-term separation from his wife and child. Que recounted the pitiful deathbed scene, during which the man cried out over and over, "Where is my wife?! Where is my child?! Come here, child!"[128]

The emotional gloom of imprisonment was intensified by a condition known among inmates as "fortune lost, family dispersed" (*tang gia bai san*). According to Hoang Minh Dau (quoting a famous line from Nguyen Du's *The Tale of Kieu* [*Truyen Kieu*]), "In cases where the wife is weak, the children small, and the prisoner unable to provide even a meager subsistence, the wife is often forced to 'reorient her heart and play her lute in another's vessel.'"[129] Phan Vam Hum relayed the story of Xa Thu, a pathetic cellmate whose land and belongings had been confiscated following his arrest. Not only did his wife take up with a neighbor for financial support but his eighteen-year-old daughter became the mistress of a predatory French lawyer who promised falsely to appeal her father's case. Eventually, Xa Thu

125. Nhuong Tong, *Doi Trong Nguc*, 8.
126. Phan Van Hum, *Ngoi Tu Kham Lon*, 146.
127. Ibid.
128. Tran Van Que, *Con-Lon Quan-Dao Truoc ngay 9–3–1945*, 121.
129. Hoang Minh Dau, *Cai Than Tu Toi*, 17. See also Nguyen Du (1765–1820), *The Tale of Kieu: A Bilingual Edition of Truyen Kieu*, translated and annotated by Huynh Sanh Thông, with a historical essay by Alexander B. Woodside (New Haven, Conn., 1983).

discovered traces of poison in the homemade pastries that his wife had been sending him, a betrayal he interpreted as an attempt on his wife's part to secure a commitment from her new lover. "Only after this episode," Hum remarked, "did I understand the true meaning of 'fortune lost, family dispersed.' "[130]

COPING WITH INCARCERATION:
AMUSEMENTS AND INTIMACIES

To cope with despair, inmates devised games and diversions, which in turn contributed to the rich subcultural texture of prison life. Prisoners used odds and ends to make crude sets of cards, dice, and chessmen. Many grew addicted to games of chance, which they played for monthly stipends, cigarettes, matchsticks, and sporting slaps on the cheek.[131] Pham Hung recalled:

> In the cell, we played with cards and dice that we made ourselves. We glued scraps of paper together to make cards. We moulded bread-crumbs to make dice. We smoked and applied cigarettes to the wall to get some tar for the black spots on the dice. We crumpled wrapping paper from cigarette packets and inlaid it in the dice to make red spots. [132]

Fortune-telling was also popular, including an elaborate ritual of spirit possession known as *cau tien*.[133] Phan Van Hum recalled prisoners predicting the future by randomly flipping through pages of a Bible that had been donated to the dormitory by a French missionary.[134] Educated prisoners spent free time reading, writing letters, improving their French and Chinese, and composing and reciting poetry. While such activities may have improved the morale of prisoners in the moment, Phan Van Hum likened their forced joviality at play to the "hollow laugh of a prostitute who secretly pities herself while sleeping with a customer."[135]

Theater provided another diversion. Numerous memoirs describe the production of Molière plays—*Le Bourgeois Gentilhomme, L'Avare, Les*

130. Phan Van Hum, *Ngoi Tu Kham Lon*, 147.
131. Tran Huy Lieu, "Tet Trong Tu" [Tet In Prison], *Ngay Nay* [Today], February 1939.
132. Pham Hung, "Never to Give Up Working So Long As One Lives," in *A Heroic People: Memoirs from the Revolution* (Hanoi, 1965), 73.
133. Ton Quang Phiet, *Mot Ngay Ngan Thu*, 25.
134. Phan Van Hum, *Ngoi Tu Kham Lon*, 150.
135. Ibid.

Fourberies de Scapin, and *Le Malade imaginaire*—coinciding with work holidays on Tet and Bastille Day.[136] Nguyen Duc Chinh reported that political prisoners on Poulo Condore once staged an elaborate rendition of Alexander Dumas's *La Dame aux camélias.*[137] Inmates also put on traditional (*hat tuong*) and reformed operas (*cai luong*), as well as original spoken plays that portrayed familiar scenes from the outside world. Nguyen Hai Ham described a bitter satire of colonial society produced on Poulo Condore entitled *Cho Phien* (The Seasonal Market).[138] Also on Poulo Condore, Tran Van Que saw an original play entitled *Di Con Dao* (To Poulo Condore), which depicted the arrest, trial, and deportation to the islands of an innocent man. He reported that "prisoners broke into tears" during a farewell scene between the main character and his family.[139]

While such amusements helped mitigate the tedium and misery of prison life, inmates found greater solace in the relationships they formed with each other. The uncommon intensity of friendship among inmates is a theme explored in virtually every prison memoir. Nguyen Hai Ham wrote that prisoners felt "extraordinary love and sympathy for each other . . . many times we would embrace each other's necks and prattle on endlessly through the evening."[140] Huynh Thuc Khang was struck by the speed with which total strangers developed inordinately sentimental attachments in prison.[141] Nhuong Tong noted that inmates barely acquainted with one another on the outside greeted each other in prison with intimate pronouns typically reserved for relatives, lovers, or lifelong friends.[142]

Fraternal closeness in prison was also evident in the feelings of sadness and guilt inmates experienced upon liberation. When Phan Van Hum learned of his imminent release from Kham Lon, he reported that teary-eyed cellmates "laughed, cried and hugged me tightly around the waist and shoulders."[143] Tran Huy Lieu recounted a similar scene, during which an abrupt announcement of upcoming amnesties generated an emotional

136. See, e.g., Ha Huy Giap, *Doi Toi, Nhung Dieu Nghe, Thay Va Song: Hoi Ky Cach Mang* [My Life—Things Heard, Seen, and Lived: Revolutionary Memoirs] (Ho Chi Minh City, 1994), 129–33.

137. Nguyen Duc Chinh, *Thu Con Lon,* 15.

138. Nguyen Hai Ham, *Tu Yen Bay Den Con Lon, 1930–1945,* 167–70.

139. Tran Van Que, *Con-Lon Quan-Dao Truoc Ngay 9–3–1945,* 127.

140. Nguyen Hai Ham, *Tu Yen Bay Den Con Lon, 1930–1945,* 156.

141. Huynh Thuc Khang, *Thi Tu Tung Thoai,* 31.

142. Nhuong Tong, *Doi Trong Nguc,* 20.

143. Phan Van Hum, *Ngoi Tu Kham Lon,* 159.

whirlwind in his dormitory: "The sudden revelation induced feelings of pain, embarrassment, and shame. We parted with tears in our eyes."[144]

Needless to say, intense homosocial sentiments in prison could evolve into homosexual relations. While there is evidence that prisoners had sex and formed unions with one another in the single-sex communal environment of colonial prisons, observers disagree about the nature and frequency of such practices. As communist writings tend to suppress representations of sexuality in general, the absence of homosexuality from postcolonial northern Vietnamese prison memoirs reflects long-term patterns of censorship and self-censorship. It is also possible that homosexuality does not figure in communist prison memoirs because ascetic and homophobic norms within Vietnamese communist and early nationalist culture discouraged its practice. Indeed, the most candid account of homosexuality in an Indochinese prison, Tran Van Que's memoir *Con-Lon Quan-Dao Truoc ngay 9–3–1945* (The Poulo Condore Archipelago before March 9, 1945), insists that it did not occur among political prisoners.[145]

Whereas few ex-convicts acknowledged the presence of homosexuality in their memoirs, French observers found it wherever they looked. According to Dr. Louis Lorion:

> Pederasty is widespread in Cochin China, but it rarely falls under judicial purview. . . . It is above all practiced by Annamites and Chinese; the latter, more vigorous and audacious, seem to play the active role. It is in markets, opium dens, gambling houses, and theaters that this shameful industry is practiced and where one would meet those searching for this genre of debauchery. One also observes pederasty in all agglomerations where individuals of the same sex live communally, such as barracks where populations of workers, coolies, guards, and servants swarm together, and in the penitentiaries, notably Poulo Condore.[146]

Lorion's comments are echoed in official reports that allude suggestively to the fact that communal architecture encouraged "promiscuity" among inmates. On Poulo Condore, the famous gentleman bandit Thomas Phuoc told Demariaux that he preferred solitary confinement to the "promiscuous obscenity" of the communal dormitories. Another of Demariaux's informants forthrightly reported that prisoners routinely traded gay sex for opium or cash.[147]

144. Tran Huy Lieu, "Tet Trong Tu," 2.
145. Tran Van Que, *Con-Lon Quan-Dao Truoc ngay 9–3–1945*, 130.
146. Lorion, *Criminalité et médecine judiciaire en Cochinchine*, 115–16.
147. Demariaux, *Secrets des îles Poulo-Condore*, 160.

In the writings of prisoners themselves, furtive allusions to homosexual desire most frequently appear in accounts of prison theater. For example, *Thu Con Lon* (Letters from Poulo Condore), a collection of missives written from prison by Nguyen Duc Chinh and published in 1937, contains a provocative passage linking homoerotic desire in prison to plays in which female roles were performed by young male prisoners in drag:

> In the play performed this Tet, there was a brothel and the young girls who work there hug their "guests" and dance with them. If I had known before that Tho was to play a prostitute, I would have volunteered immediately to take the part of the libertine youth [*cong tu*]. That way, I could have hugged the one to whom everyone's been writing letters this year—the one about whom we often joke: "If there was a flower garden in the prison, I would risk several days of punishment in the hole to pluck a flower and present it to her."[148]

A remarkably similar episode appears in Tran Huy Lieu's "Tinh Trong Nguc Toi" (Love in the Dark Prison), a posthumously published prison memoir originally written in 1950, which describes Lieu's loneliness and unrequited longings while incarcerated on Poulo Condore during the early 1930s. In one passage, Lieu admits to a temporary attraction for "brother T," a fellow prisoner who had performed a female role in a play staged within the ward; "After viewing the play performed during Tet in Bagne II, I sent a letter over ten pages long to brother T, who, on that day, had played the role of a female courtesan. As the prison regime suppressed family sentiments and petty bourgeois romantic sentiments, we were often forced to seek other outlets."[149]

It is instructive that "Tinh Trong Nguc Toi" was only published in 1991, after the cultural liberalization that accompanied the Communist Party's Renovation Policy in 1986. This contrasts with roughly a dozen other prison memoirs written by Lieu, all of which were published during the 1950s and 1960s. It is tempting to conclude that the decision to put off the publication of "Tinh Trong Nguc Toi" derived from its candid allusion to homosexual impulses among political prisoners, during a period in

148. Nguyen Duc Chinh, *Thu Con Lon,* 30. The suggestion of homoerotic yearning is implicit in the passage. While "Tho" can occasionally be a woman's name, it is much more commonly used for men. Moreover, there is no evidence from other accounts that female prisoners were allowed to participate in theatrical productions with male prisoners. Also, women convicts were no longer sent to Con Dao after 1910.

149. Tran Huy Lieu, "Tinh Trong Nguc Toi" [Love in the Dark Prison], in Tran Huy Lieu, *Tran Huy Lieu: Hoi Ky,* 137.

which the Party was promoting a distinctly sexless image of the "new socialist man."

The only first-person account to address the presence of homosexuality in Indochinese prisons directly is Tran Van Que's hybrid memoir/history *Con-Lon Quan-Dao Truoc ngay 9–3–1945*. Que devotes considerable attention to the *em nuoi*, an ambiguous term that may be translated as "adopted younger brother," "adopted younger sister," or "adopted beloved," depending on the meaning attributed to the intimate personal pronoun *em:*

> Because members of the weaker sex were absent on Poulo Condore, the common prisoners were plagued by the problem of *"em nuoi."* Far from their wives and children for long periods, gang leaders [*anh chi*] and *caplans* at different work camps needed a way to share love with others and to chase away their boredom. As a result, they provided protection, money, and clothes for pretty young prisoners known as *"em nuoi."*[150]

Que's account suggests that homosexual relations were integrated into the colonial prison's formal and subcultural social hierarchies. It is significant that the inmates who "kept" *em nuoi*—*caplans* and *anh chis*—were situated at the apex of the prison's twin pecking orders. According to Que, control over *em nuoi* could provoke conflicts between rival members of the prisoner elite. "Sometime before 1940," he wrote, "competition over an *em nuoi* led one prisoner to kill his love rival [*tinh dich*]. Before he was guillotined, the murderer begged to see his *em nuoi* one last time before he died."[151] Que's account implies that just as *anh chis* struggled to control *em uts* and *caplans* competed over patronage networks, so too powerful members of the prisoner elite vied with one another for the affections of the most desirable *em nuois*.

THE PRISON SUBCULTURE AND THE COMMUNIST MOVEMENT

Inmate society and the institutional forces that nurtured its development shed light on the process whereby the Communist Party reconstituted itself and expanded its operations in prison during the 1930s. The same communal living arrangements that enabled inmates to develop elaborate subcultural social formations sustained ICP efforts to transform prison

150. Tran Van Que, *Con-Lon Quan-Dao Truoc ngay 9–3–1945*, 124.
151. Ibid., 127.

dormitories into centers of revolutionary activity. As one colonial inspector pointed out in 1932:

> Because political and common-law prisoners are not compartmentalized and live in intimate contact with each other, the dormitories in Hoa Lo give rise to constant exchange of ideas, both oral and written. This is no surprise when dealing with individuals imbued with a doctrine that instills a mental exaltation and a quasi-sick need to make propaganda.[152]

The formal social hierarchies imposed on inmate populations by the prison regime provided a modular power structure that communist inmates could infiltrate and control from within. In 1933, Ton Duc Thang, a Communist Party member (and future president of the Democratic Republic of Vietnam), managed to get himself chosen *caplan* in the rice-mill stockade on Poulo Condore.[153] He proved so successful at protecting fellow communist inmates under his authority that other imprisoned Party members were encouraged to vie for *caplan* positions. Thereafter, many communists on Poulo Condore, including Dao Gia Luu and Ngo Gia Tu, secured similar postings, which they used to further the interests of the Party.[154]

Just as extreme personal discipline and a rigidly autocratic command structure allowed underworld prison gangs to achieve hegemony over informal prisoner hierarchies, similar attributes of communist organization led to the dominance of the Communist Party in prison. In certain respects, the ICP's "democratic centralism" mirrored the top-down authoritarianism and corporate discipline characteristic of underworld gangs. Like powerful *anh chis*, imprisoned Party officials relied on a cadre of devoted foot soldiers to buttress their authority. These low-level cadres exhibited a willingness to make profound sacrifices for the sake of their leaders and for the movement as a whole.

Communist inmates also proved adept at appropriating and employing leisure activities associated with the prison subculture for their own purposes. Just as educated inmates used free time in prison to brush up their knowledge of literature and foreign languages, communist prisoners studied nationalist history and Marxist theory. Given the popularity of prison

---

152. AOM, Indochine, Affaires politiques, 1728, Rapport fait par M. Chastenet de Géry, Inspecteur des Colonies concernant l'organisation du régime pénitentiaire au Tonkin, April 26, 1932, 13.

153. Ban Nghien Cuu Lich Su Dang Dac Khu Vung Tau—Con Dao, *Nha Tu Con Dao, 1862–1945*, 84–85.

154. Ibid., 91.

theater among the inmate population, communist inmates displayed a keen interest in it as well:

> Several times a month, propaganda is spread through theatrical repre-
> sentations complete with costumes and sets. The sets are made from
> mats smeared white with rice starch. Pieces of bricks or carbon are used
> to sketch the scenery. The costumes are made of paper. A makeshift or-
> chestra accompanies the performance. Rudimentary instruments are
> fashioned from cans of condensed milk. The plays often depict scenes of
> the "barbarous institutions of the capitalist regime." They include rep-
> resentations of criminal tribunals or Sûreté interrogation sessions.[155]

In addition, the profound emotional attachments that inmates experienced as a result of their incarcerations prefigured the intense devotion and
partisan commitment that imprisoned Party members maintained toward
each other in jail and following release. As David Marr has argued:
"Friendships forged behind bars were often the closest of any in the revolutionary movement. Thus, it is not entirely coincidental that a number of
subsequent ICP Political Bureau members were together on Con Son island in the early 1930s, or that another group of ICP leaders worked with
each other inside Son La prison in the early 1940s."[156]

IMPRISONMENT AND MODERN CONSCIOUSNESS

In addition to its visceral impact on the emotional state of prisoners, incarceration promoted certain characteristically modern attitudes toward society and human nature, at least among the highly educated inmates who
left accounts of their experience. Like foreign travelers, observant inmates
came to perceive familiar social norms and institutions in a different light.
Prisoners separated from their relatives for the first time were encouraged
to reassess the strengths and weaknesses of the traditional family unit. The
primitive conditions of prison life, coupled with constant exposure to underworld elements, generated intensified sensations of social class. Moreover, many upper-class prisoners came away from prison with a heightened
confidence in their powers to analyze society and to shape their own individual destinies. In retrospect, prison appeared to them as an exclusive
school whose graduates had shared in a life-shaping ordeal and enjoyed a
restricted insight into the human condition.

---

155. AOM, SLOTFOM, 3d. ser., carton 52, *AAPCI*, February 3, 1932.
156. David Marr, *Vietnamese Tradition on Trial, 1920–1945* (Berkeley and Los Angeles, 1981), 315.

The capacity of incarceration to erode certain traditional social formulations was manifest in the attitudes of prisoners toward their families. Although it was usually depicted as a source of intense grief, the long-term isolation of inmates from spouses, children, and parents could also be experienced as a liberation from burdensome family obligations. This sensation corresponded with a broad-based social movement during the interwar era that promoted individualism and rejected the conventions of traditional family life.[157] Recalling an important theme of the movement, Phan Van Hum claimed that prison helped him to conquer a crippling fear of disappointing family expectations. This anxiety materialized immediately after his arrest, when an old woman scolded him on route to the police station for bringing shame upon his kin and native village.[158] After four months in prison, however, Hum came to the realization that obsessive fears about dishonoring one's family induced negative personality traits such as moral cowardice and passivity: "I came to realize that my own fears are the biggest barrier to achieving my goals: fear of losing my fortune, fear of leaving my family—my mother, father, and children, fear of risks, fear of misery, fear of failure, fear of the future, fear of public ridicule and scorn."[159] In a similar vein, Tran Van Que noted that prison taught inmates that their survival depended on individual resources and personal endurance, not family support. He argued that survival in prison required prisoners to stop relying on relatives and to learn to take care of themselves instead.[160] Seen in this light, the colonial prison may have contributed to the general erosion of traditional familial commitments in colonial Indochina and to the related rise of individualism.

Prison also heightened consciousness of class membership. For inmates from elite social backgrounds, the hardships of prison life served to confirm the extent to which they had been shaped and circumscribed by their upbringings. The absence of amenities in prison prompted guilty acknowledgments of privileged childhoods and inflated living standards. Nhuong Tong interpreted his deep distaste for prison food and extreme embarrassment at communal nudity as a shameful indication of his own gentility.[161]

157. See Hue-Tam Ho Tai, *Radicalism and the Origins of the Vietnamese Revolution* (Cambridge, Mass., 1992), 89–92, and Neil Jamieson, *Understanding Vietnam* (Berkeley and Los Angeles, 1993), 106–7.
158. Phan Van Hum, *Ngoi Tu Kham Lon*, 20.
159. Ibid., 145.
160. Tran Van Que, *Con-Lon Quan-Dao Truoc ngay 9–3–1945*, 124.
161. Nhuong Tong, *Doi Trong Nguc*, 25, 32.

Likewise, Ton Quang Phiet explained the uncommon difficulty he encountered coping with an absence of toilet paper in prison as a product of the "comfortable lifestyle" to which he had grown accustomed.[162] Sensations of class identity were stimulated further by the way in which the rigid Vietnamese pronominal system was inverted in prison. For Ton Quang Phiet, the fact that uneducated guards addressed him with subordinate pronouns was among the worst humiliations of prison life: "I found it especially irritating that the warder called me *anh* [brother]. Outside, people call me *thay* [teacher] or sometimes *quan* [mandarin]. To be called *anh*, *may*, or *ten* in prison was painful to my ears."[163] Later in the memoir, Phiet described the disgrace of being "continually cursed, kicked in the ass, and referred to as *thang*."[164]

Such complaints aside, some elite inmates experienced the coarse informality of prison life as a mode of transgressive liberation. The normally prim Huynh Thuc Khang boasted of "an unforgettable experience" in which he and a fellow prisoner chatted casually while emptying their bowels.[165] Others were titillated by the opportunity to go slumming with colorful characters—gangsters, thieves, pimps, and con artists—whom they had encountered before only in books or films. Indeed, Nguyen Hai Ham compared living in prison to "being in a novel," and Nhuong Tong likened it to "acting on stage."[166] During his incarceration, Ton Quang Phiet exhibited a deep fascination for the various underworld figures with whom he came in contact. Concluding his memoir, he claimed that extended exposure to ordinary criminals had made him more tolerant and less affected:

> Prison changed me. Before my imprisonment, I ate and spoke in a
> proper and pretentious way, but afterward, I became much less formal.
> Before, I considered thieves to be a rotten and wicked group in society;
> they barely seemed human. I looked down on young men who spent all

---

162. Ton Quang Phiet, *Mot Ngay Ngan Thu*, 20.

163. *May* and *ten* are both extremely low-status pronouns for which there are no English equivalents. Ton Quang Phiet, *Mot Ngay Ngan Thu*, 37.

164. Ibid., 16.

165. Huynh Thuc Khang, *Thi Tu Tung Thoai*, 19: "Following the meal, I asked the guard to take me to the latrine. . . . This latrine had three shit holes surrounded by a wall. Inside the latrine, I met Mr. Tieu, who had been escorted there by another guard. The two of us sat merrily over our shit holes chatting and exchanging news. This was truly an unforgettable memory of prison."

166. Nguyen Hai Ham, *Tu Yen Bay Den Con Lon, 1930–1945*, 93; Nhuong Tong, *Doi Trong Nguc*, 1.

their money on gambling, wine, and whores. Now, after my incarceration, these stories no longer shock me; in fact, I find no fault in them at all.[167]

Phan Van Hum expressed a related sentiment in response to critics who chided his account for its unvarnished realism and emphasis on the gritty underside of prison life. Such criticism, he argued, was the product of a "false sense of morality." "To ignore the filth of prison," he wrote, "is to behave like a rich man who refuses to enter the miserable slums where parents and children live together among pigs and dogs, piss and shit."[168]

The connection between short-term transgressive behavior in prison and more durable personal transformations can also be seen in attitudes towards public nudity. A compelling illustration is found in Hai Trieu's essay "Su Thuc Trong Tu" (Truth in Prison) published in the newspaper *Doi Moi* (New Life) in 1935:

> When I first entered prison, I saw a mass of naked men and felt very afraid, almost dizzy. My mind—my morality was unprepared for such a crude and forthright truth. I couldn't bring myself to discard my shabby clothes even though my trousers were missing a leg and my sleeves were in tatters. I continued to wear my filthy clothes for many days. After several weeks, I threw away my stinking shirt but kept my pants. Only later, did I dare to take them off, but only in the cell, never outside. Eventually, I felt comfortable enough to walk around, dance, eat, chat, and joke stark naked with my friends in the cell.[169]

Hai Trieu's feelings about nudity suggest how imprisonment could intensify the way well-educated prisoners perceived the elite culture in which they had been born and raised. To survive in prison, one needed to literally strip away the modesty and mannered civility that came with good breeding. Once it was discovered that many of the courtesies and conventions of polite society could be profitably discarded in prison, elite culture itself was revealed to be artificial and unstable:

> In life I see countless truths that like my body are hidden by layers of tattered and dirty "clothes." These "clothes" include morality, politeness, dignity, an elevated spirit, and a heroic will. Like everyone else, I must wear clothes, either elegant or threadbare, in order to maintain normal relations with other people. When people see that I am moral, polite, dignified, and possess a heroic will, they respect me, and I, in

---

167. Ton Quang Phiet, *Mot Ngay Ngan Thu*, 36.
168. Phan Van Hum, *Ngoi Tu Kham Lon*, 17.
169. Hai Trieu, "Su Thuc Trong Tu," 4.

turn, respect them. The world is full of lies and duplicity, which we must employ in order to maintain social relations. Gradually, we forget about these lies and this duplicity; we forget that we, ourselves, are lies and duplicity. In prison, however, I newly see my behavior, feelings, and imagination—like my body and my friends' bodies—nakedly exposed. Are you a hero? Enter prison and you'll know. Are you moral and humane? Enter prison and find out. Are you human? In prison, you'll know for sure. Prison is a place to distinguish right from wrong, appropriate from inappropriate, the important parts of life from things that are merely trivial.[170]

Hai Trieu's changing attitudes to public nudity point to another common theme in prison narratives: the ability of incarceration to reveal fundamental truths about the character of men and the nature of humanity. He asserted the connection in the following way: "A friend of mine with whom I had been in prison recently said to me, 'Only in prison can I find truth.' This may seem daring, but as fate has forced me to eat the stale rice of many prisons, I now see the validity of my friend's words."[171] Ton Quang Phiet expressed a similar viewpoint:

You can really recognize other people's true natures in prison. On the outside, people are rarely honest; they deny feelings of competition and never show their true faces. In prison, explicit conflicts of interest occur every day. Hence, it becomes rapidly apparent who is big-hearted and who is stingy. People have numerous flaws that become clear only in prison. . . . Who would imagine that teachers, students, and government clerks could come to blows over tiny morsels of food? In life, people conceal their true desires. Appearing self-interested can hurt one's reputation. . . . Ten years of contact with someone on the outside is less revealing than a single month in prison together.[172]

As Phiet's comments demonstrate, the colonial prison could be understood as a place where the artificial trappings of a status-obsessed society were temporarily cast off. The experience of confronting the colonial state without its duplicitous veneer of civility and "slumming it" with the colonial underclass invested imprisonment with a sobering sense of "authenticity." For elite boys, the experience was disorienting, but also liberating and invigorating. For those who went through it together, prison forged close relationships and a sense of shared secret knowledge inaccessible to nonprisoners.

170. Ibid.
171. Ibid.
172. Ton Quang Phiet, *Mot Ngay Ngan Thu*, 35.

5 · Colonial Prisons in Revolt, 1862–1930

Just as colonial and metropolitan prisons exhibited significant disparities in their structure, functioning, and administrative orientation, they also provoked remarkably different levels of collective resistance. Historians of French prisons have found little documentary evidence of large-scale prisoner revolts. Indeed, Michelle Perrot observes that the nineteenth-century archive of the French prison system "conveys an impression of calm" and "nothing that would qualify as an 'event.'"[1] In regard to the colonial prison in Indochina, on the other hand, the archival record is nothing if not eventful.

Between 1862 and 1930, episodes of collective violence such as riots and mass uprisings occurred regularly in Indochinese prisons.[2] Colonial archives record no fewer than eight major episodes during the second half of the nineteenth century and at least two dozen between 1900 and 1930. There were certainly more. During World War I, perhaps the most turbulent period in the history of the prison system, seven major incidents took place, including insurrections at Thai Nguyen and Lao Bao that resulted in the complete destruction of the largest penitentiaries in Tonkin and

1. Michelle Perrot, "Delinquency and the Penitentiary System in Nineteenth-Century France," in *Deviants and the Abandoned in French Society: Selections from the « Annales, économies, sociétés, civilisations »*, Volume IV, ed. Robert Forster and Orest Ranum, trans. Elborg Forster and Patricia M. Ranum (Baltimore, 1978), 216–17.
2. Collective violence here includes the following types of actions carried out or abetted by groups of prisoners: assaults or murders of prison personnel, mass escape attempts, attacks on prison property, or attempts to seize total or partial control of the institution by force. I am excluding solitary escapes or cases in which individual prisoners targeted individual guards. Such low-level violence occurred so regularly that it scarcely disrupted the operation of the colonial prison.

Annam. Prisoner revolts occurred so frequently that colonial officials came to view them as a routine by-product of the functioning of the prison system. Consider the tone of inevitability and resignation in the following official attempt to account for a bloody revolt on Poulo Condore in 1918:

> In reality, there was only one cause of the recent revolt on Poulo Condore. It is a general cause that has existed and will continue to exist as long as there are penitentiaries and men who are confined there for all or part of their life. It is the desire to be free, the urge to return home to one's country and family that provokes prisoners to risk one or several escapes and that prompts them also from time to time, when they are the most dangerous men who don't recoil before the consequences, to risk a violent *coup de force* in the hope of escaping.[3]

Although undeniable on one level, this interpretation fails to explain why prisons in Indochina, as distinct from their counterparts in France, generated so much collective violence.[4] A consideration of this question requires attention to unique features of colonial prisons that may have promoted or facilitated movements of resistance among inmates. One was the indigenous population's profound ignorance and mistrust of the colonial legal system. During the nineteenth century especially, few Vietnamese knew the law or understood the most basic colonial juridical procedures. As the lawyer-journalist Hoang Dao explained, the situation was especially bad in the countryside: "The people of the countryside have absolutely no knowledge of the tortuous complexities of the law. They're not clear about what matters and things are forbidden; they do not understand how one thing is a serious crime and another thing is a light crime. And indeed there's no one who teaches them so that they will know."[5]

What little people did know tended to give the impression that the juridical system was corrupt and unfair. The crooked and unreliable nature of

3. AOM, Gouvernement général, 193, Rébellion de Poulo Condore—M. Quesnel, March 15, 1918.
4. The secondary literature on the history of nineteenth- and early twentieth-century French prisons reveals a remarkably thin body of evidence about revolts or collective violence. See, e.g., Patricia O'Brien, *The Promise of Punishment: Prisons in Nineteenth-Century France* (Princeton, N.J., 1982); Michel Foucault, *Discipline and Punish: The Birth of the Prison*, trans. Alan Sheridan (New York, 1979); Robert Badinter, *La Prison républicaine, 1871–1914* (Paris, 1992); and Pieter Spierenburg, *The Prison Experience: Disciplinary Institutions and Their Inmates in Early Modern Europe* (New Brunswick, N.J., 1991).
5. Cited in Alexander Woodside, *Community and Revolution in Modern Vietnam* (Boston, 1976), 25.

colonial justice was a common source of popular discontent and a central preoccupation of politically engaged Indochinese journalism.[6] In an essay published in *Tieng Dan* in 1928, Huynh Thuc Khang identified high taxes, poor schools, and "the unfair and erratic administration of penal law" as the three most prevalent grievances against the colonial state.[7] Stories of incompetent attorneys, bribed judges, witness tampering, or the perfidy of court interpreters were staples of colonial-era literature. The corruption of the justice system is a central theme in the work of Ngo Tat To, Nguyen Cong Hoan, and Nguyen Hong. Vu Trong Phung's *So Do* [Dumb Luck] includes a scathing parody of a local police court in which arrests are driven by monthly quotas and judicial decisions are based on the remarks of a devious fortune-teller.[8] Given the juridical system's poor reputation, it is not surprising that many inmates saw their prison sentences as unfair and illegitimate.

In addition to negative popular sentiments about the juridical system, certain structural features of colonial prisons may also have encouraged collective violence among inmates. The fact that prison directors in Indochina were subject to only sporadic and superficial checks on their institutional authority contributed to the brutal and erratic nature of prison conditions. Such brutality and unpredictability, in turn, provided the context for uprisings. Moreover, prison directors tended to remain in their posts for remarkably short periods of time, generating an explosive combination of authoritarianism and instability. Indeed, there is evidence that prison revolts in Indochina often followed abrupt changes in administrative personnel.

Another destabilizing structural factor was the organization of prison labor. As colonial officials were well aware, the employment of prison inmates on public works projects undermined security by disseminating dangerous and desperate prisoners throughout the neighboring countryside. Because indigenous guards were often prohibited from bearing arms, security at work sites was easily breached. Moreover, tools provided to laboring prisoners such as shovels, hoes, and spades could be used as deadly weapons and were often instrumental in the outbreak of revolts. For the colonial state, the contradiction inherent in prison labor—economically

6. Nguyen Thanh, *Lich Su Bao Tieng Dan* (Da Nang, 1992), 82.
7. Nguyen The Anh, "A Case of Confucian Survival in Twentieth-Century Vietnam: Huynh Thuc Khang and His Newspaper *Tieng Dan*," *Vietnam Forum* 8 (Summer–Fall 1986): 177.
8. Vu Trong Phung, *So Do* (1936; reprint, Hanoi, 1988), 16–24.

beneficial on the one hand but deeply complicit in outbreaks of prison violence on the other—was never adequately resolved.

Prisons were also subject to attacks by bandit gangs, secret societies, and anticolonial political parties seeking to free jailed comrades and swell their ranks. Civilian mobs sometimes broke into prisons to free inmates whom they believed to have been incarcerated unjustly. Numerous attacks of this nature occurred in response to the arrest of thousands of draft evaders during World War I.

This chapter examines a handful of the best-documented prison revolts in Indochina prior to 1930 to illustrate some of the reasons for the profound instability of the colonial prison system. A rebellion on Poulo Condore in 1890 demonstrates how grievances against the legal system played a catalytic role in revolts. Major uprisings on Poulo Condore in 1918 and Lai Chau in 1927 illustrate the explosive combination of autocratic management and the rapid turnover of prison directors. Episodes such as the Lao Bao revolt of 1915 reveal how forced labor facilitated collective violence. Finally, the reasons for external attacks on prisons are briefly considered.

ILLEGITIMATE JUSTICE: THE POULO CONDORE REVOLT OF 1890

On June 19, 1890, several dozen Tonkinese prisoners breaking rocks at a forced-labor work site on Poulo Condore turned their sledgehammers against their guards. Several *matas* were set upon and beaten, and one was stabbed to death with a homemade knife.[9] Disorder reigned for several minutes before the remaining surveillants opened fire, killing nine prisoners and wounding five. The following week, the governor of Cochin China ordered Daurand Forgues, a prosecutor from the Saigon Tribunal, to visit the island, carry out an investigation and prepare a report on the "root causes" of the uprising.[10] He concluded that prisoners rebelled not in response to poor treatment or conditions but because they did not view the circumstances of their incarcerations as fair or legitimate in the first place.

According to Forgues, the revolt of 1890 was not caused by poor living conditions. Prisoners enjoyed a diet "sufficient in quality and quantity,"

---

9. AOM, Gouvernement général, 22791 and 22773, Tentative de rébellion au pénitencier de Poulo Condore, 1890.

10. Ibid. Forgues's report, completed July 26, 1890, was entitled "Une Enquête sur les faits criminels commis au pénitencier de Poulo Condore le 19 Juin dernier," AOM, Gouvernement général, 22791. Cited below as "Forgues Report."

which included regular rations of vegetables and pork.[11] They were paid for their labor and disciplined in a way that "could not be considered excessively severe."[12] More important, although prisoners from all regions of Indochina were subjected to identical treatment on Poulo Condore, only those from Tonkin rose in revolt.[13] Thus, Forgues reasoned, the uprising must have been triggered by something other than the general conditions of the penitentiary.

After interviewing the surviving participants, Forgues discerned a clue to the origins of the uprising in the fact that few of the Tonkinese prisoners could state the duration of their sentences or the nature of their crimes.[14] Some even claimed to have been transferred directly from district jails to the island penitentiary without intervening legal proceedings. Upon requesting dossiers on the prisoners with whom he had spoken, Forgues was appalled to discover that many had arrived from Tonkin without accompanying paperwork. Others had in their files inconsistent or contradictory juridical records stipulating their legal status or the terms of their sentences. He cited the following example:

> Prisoner 932, Nguyen Van Phat, possesses two separate orders of imprisonment, neither of which is dated or signed, nor do they indicate the date of the trial or the case number. One records that he is twenty-eight, the other that he is thirty-two. Both identify his crime as banditry but one sentences him to hard labor for five years, the other to hard labor for life.[15]

Forgues's report prompted a follow-up investigation into the process by which prisoners from Tonkin were sentenced and transported to Poulo Condore.[16] It suggested that the military suppression of civil disorder in

11. Ibid., 2.

12. Ibid.

13. Ibid. 3. According to eyewitness accounts, prisoners from Cochin China dropped face down on the earth during the revolt so as to demonstrate their non-participation.

14. Ibid. Several prisoners told Forgues that they only discovered what their sentences were after being admitted to the prison infirmary where their "vital statistics" were posted above their beds. On the contrary prisoners who had been sent from the court system in Cochin China were reasonably well apprised of their legal status.

15. Ibid., 5.

16. This second report (no. 120), addressed to the governor-general, was completed on September 27, 1890, by an official of the judicial service. The signature of the investigating official is illegible. Cited below as "Report 120."

Tonkin after the French seizure of Hanoi in 1882 had created a confused and frenzied atmosphere in which miscarriages of justice were a common occurrence. During the 1880s, most sentences were issued by military tribunals that ignored normal legal procedures. Defendants suspected of supporting anti-French forces were tried in large groups without legal representation. Many prisoners were simple coolies who had been dragooned into carrying supplies for guerrilla leaders. Others were arrested by colonial troops in mass sweeps of villages suspected of supporting the resistance. Informants complained that French officers relied on corrupt interpreters and self-interested local elites to identify rebels and their supporters. Some described how rich families bribed jailers to release their imprisoned relatives and replace them surreptitiously with destitute local villagers.

For the inspector, the most tragic cases involved falsely accused prisoners who were mentally or physically disabled. Prisoner 1060, Le Kinh, described as "blind and infirm," was out in his family's rice field when he was seized by a French officer and thrown into a crowded jail with a group of captured guerrillas. The following day, the guerrillas were taken to a ship destined for Poulo Condore and, in the confusion that ensued, Le Kinh was mistakenly transported along with them. No transcript of any court proceeding for Le Kinh could be found in the registrar of the penitentiary. Likewise, no court records existed for prisoner 1679, Nguyen Van Ky, whom the inspector described as "a sixteen-year-old imbecile who knows nothing about the circumstances of his arrest."[17] In the absence of legal paperwork, the investigator failed to determine how prison authorities had attributed to Nguyen Van Ky a sentence of ten years' hard labor.

Of course, the inspector's conclusions might be interpreted as a partisan effort to displace responsibility for the revolt of 1890 from the justice department of Cochin China, for which he worked, to the legal system of Tonkin, with which he was only tenuously connected. We should also be skeptical of Forgues's assurances that living conditions on the island were good. After all, Poulo Condore during the 1890s was plagued by extremely high rates of malaria, cholera, beriberi, and dysentery, a considerable reputation for physical brutality, and annual mortality rates as high as 13 percent.[18]

17. Ibid., 5.
18. The figure of 13 percent is from 1892. *Annuaire de l'Indo-Chine française,* pt. 1: *Cochinchine et Cambodge,* 1892.

However, the numerous cases the inspector documented are compelling evidence that many inmates on Poulo Condore had no idea why they were there or how long they would be compelled to remain:

> Nguyen Van Tam from Gia Lam district, Bac Ninh province, was imprisoned for possessing the mischievousness of a child. At the time of his arrest, he was only fourteen by Vietnamese calculations, which means thirteen to us. It seems that army troops had entered his village while pursuing some rebels. At the sight of the soldiers, his whole village, including his parents, ran off, but he stayed behind to watch. He recalls his arrest but claims to have no idea about how he was condemned. He never met any authority nor was he ever questioned. Apparently no paperwork accompanied him to Poulo Condore.[19]

As the several dozen interviews conducted by Forgues make clear, many prisoners believed that they had been jailed unjustly because of the corruption of the infant juridical system in newly colonized Tonkin. It is not difficult to imagine how prisoners incarcerated under such circumstances might be overcome with feelings of hopelessness and desperation, which could, in turn, fuel participation in riots and uprisings.

Nineteenth-century Indochinese convicts left no accounts of their subjective experience of imprisonment, but Forgues used the interviews he conducted to piece together a speculative picture of the mind-set of a typical prisoner:

> Try to imagine the mental state of an inmate arriving here from Tonkin after a more or less unjust arrest. When he arrives, he is still under the impression that his detention is temporary or the result of a soon-to-be-discovered error. He immediately learns that he has been condemned *in perpetuity* by a judge whom he has never seen or heard. Suddenly, all hope of returning to his homeland vanishes (and we know how attached the Annamites are in general to their native soil). No chances of appeal are offered. He is then subjected to a regime of constant hard labor and humiliating discipline. In these circumstances, is there anything unusual if the prisoner, feeling he has nothing left to lose, embarks on the course of revolt?[20]

UNSTABLE AUTHORITARIANISM, I:
THE POULO CONDORE UPRISING OF 1918

Several factors converged to endow prison directors in Indochina with unbridled institutional power. In provincial prisons, the post was always as-

19. Report 120, 6.
20. Forgues Report, 8.

sumed by the provincial resident, the highest civil official in the province. Hence, local administrations lacked a category of official more powerful than the prison director who could monitor and assess his performance. Moreover, because most penitentiaries and provincial prisons were situated in remote locales, there was little effective supervision by outside officials.[21] When external inspections did occur, they were often announced in advance, giving directors ample time to cover up the kinds of abusive practices that tended to provoke revolts.

For inmates, the unchecked power of prison directors was made all the more unsettling by the frequency with which these autocratic functionaries replaced one another. Between 1862 and 1947, Poulo Condore was headed by thirty-nine different directors, roughly one every two years.[22] During the thirteen years he was confined on Poulo Condore, Huynh Thuc Khang experienced the regimes of eight different directors.[23] His prison memoir suggests that the high turnover rate kept prisoners off balance as they struggled to adjust to an ever-changing institutional environment. The Poulo Condore rebellion of 1918 reveals the potentially explosive effects of such frequent and dramatic changes in prison management.

On February 14, 1918, two hundred convicts breaking rocks in the main courtyard of Bagne I attacked their guards with sledgehammers and pickaxes.[24] After killing a French officer and two Vietnamese *matas*, the prisoners smashed their leg irons and broke into the kitchen, the basketry, and

21. Because outside inspections occurred intermittently and were announced in advance, prison directors could easily conceal the kinds of brutal conditions that, when left unchecked, tended to provoke revolts. The effectiveness of inspections was routinely questioned in prison memoirs and in the reports of the inspectors themselves. For example, an inspector from the Ministry of Colonies visiting Hai Phong Prison in 1931 discovered a circular that had floated throughout the prison months before that warned of his upcoming visit. AOM, Indochine, Affaires politiques 1728, mission d'inspection, 17. For a scathing attack on inspections by a political prisoner, see Nguyen Van Nguyen, "Con Lon Dia Nguc Tran Gian" [Con Lon: Hell on Earth], in *Tong Tap Van Hoc Viet Nam, Tap 35* [Anthology of Vietnamese Literature, vol. 35] (Hanoi, 1985), 640–66.

22. See "Tableau chronologique des directeurs des îles et du pénitencier de Poulo Condore," in *Poulo Condore* (Hanoi, 1947), 47.

23. Huynh Thuc Khang, *Thi Tu Tung Thoai* (Prison Verse) (1939; reprint, Saigon, 1951), 169.

24. The following account is based on a report on the rebellion authored by Quesnel, bearing the number 160 and completed on March 15, 1918. It is cited below as the "Quesnel Report." It can be found in AOM, Gouvernement générale, 193. Rébellion de Poulo Condore, 1918. Also useful are the accounts in Jean-Claude Demariaux, *Les Secrets des îles Poulo-Condore: Le Grand Bagne indochinois* (Paris, 1956), 71–76, Huynh Thuc Khang, *Thi Tu Tung Thoai*, 224–26, and Ban

the rice-husking room, where they tried to induce fellow prisoners to join them in revolt. Others ransacked the office of the chief warder in a desperate but unsuccessful search for arms and ammunition. The failure of this effort left the rebels defenseless when a contingent of colonial infantrymen arrived within the hour to retake the prison. Following the orders of the prison director, Lieutenant Andouard, the troops fired through the doors and windows of each room occupied by the rebels, killing seventy-two prisoners and wounding six. According to eyewitness accounts, the small number of survivors was explained by the fact that Andouard had ordered wounded prisoners to be executed summarily by revolver shots to the head.[25]

Two sources shed light on the origins of the 1918 revolt. The first is a 27-page report on the event submitted to the governor of Cochin China by Inspector of Political Affairs Quesnel on March 15, 1918. The second is the prison memoir of Huynh Thuc Khang. Both sources locate the origins of the event in the dramatic changes that occurred on Poulo Condore in 1917 when Prison Director Andouard replaced his controversial predecessor, M. O'Connell.[26]

While little is known of O'Connell's background, there is no question that he was a remarkably idiosyncratic official. Upon assuming the post of prison director in 1914, he immediately set about refashioning the basic elements of the penitentiary. His most radical reform was the introduction of a policy that allowed numerous categories of prisoners to live and work in relative freedom outside on the island. *Relégués*, for example, were released from the *bagne*, granted arable land, and encouraged to grow vegetables and raise livestock. Cambodian prisoners were moved to a special agricultural camp and entrusted with responsibility for their own livelihood. Political prisoners were granted permission to live in the island's bustling market town, where they ran a grocery store and a small distillery. Even prisoners considered dangerous or disruptive were now allowed to form their own labor teams and work outside on the island.[27]

Nghien Cuu Lich Su Dang Dac Khu Vung Tau—Con Dao, *Nha Tu Con Dao, 1862–1945*, 68–69. The future Ho Chi Minh referred briefly to the rebellion in his famous polemic "French Colonialism on Trial," in *Ho Chi Minh: Toan Tap II* [Ho Chi Minh: Collected Works, vol. 2] (Hanoi, 1981), 342.
    25. Demariaux, *Secrets des îles de Poulo-Condore*, 72.
    26. Valuable information on the O'Connell years can be found in AOM, Gouvernement général, 4260, Affaire d'O'Connell.
    27. The extraordinary relaxation of physical confinement during the O'Connell period is described in both Huynh Thuc Khang, *Thi Tu Tung Thoai*, 178–80, and Quesnel Report, 12–13.

In addition to providing opportunities for inmates to demonstrate economic initiative, O'Connell attempted to stimulate demand for what they produced. In 1915, for example, he recruited several hundred skilled laborers from the mainland to build a second *bagne*.[28] To the dismay of the island's Chinese shopkeepers, O'Connell encouraged prisoners to sell their produce directly to these civilian workers.[29] He also invited agents from several large Saigon trading firms to purchase the coral and tortoiseshell trinkets manufactured by prison work teams.

O'Connell liberalized other aspects of the regime as well. He augmented daily rice rations, raised monthly forced-labor salaries, and promoted a large number of inmates into the ranks of the *caplans*. On July 14 and at Tet, he provided bonuses to prisoners that were four to five times greater than what they had received under previous directors.[30] He also prohibited corporal punishment and issued unusually lenient penalties for disciplinary infractions.

The extraordinary scope of O'Connell's reforms illustrates the power of Indochinese prison directors to shape the institutions under their authority. It is remarkable that, in spite of literally turning the penitentiary inside out, O'Connell never sought approval for his policies from higher officials on the mainland. "[T]he penitentiary on Poulo Condore changed its very form based solely on the will of the director," Inspector Quesnel noted in his report. "It no longer executed the penalty of privation of liberty. Instead, the entire archipelago became an agricultural colony where everyone could do as they pleased; where one worked not for the penitentiary but for oneself on the condition that a portion was reserved for the director."[31]

Given the absence of sustained top-down supervision, it is not surprising that resistance to O'Connell's reforms originated not in Saigon, Hanoi, or Paris but from within his own staff and the island's small civilian community.[32] The former bemoaned a rise in gambling, theft, drunkenness, and insubordination among the inmate population.[33] The latter, mostly

28. Ban Nghien Cuu Lich Su Dang Dac Khu Vung Tau—Con Dao, *Nha Tu Con Dao, 1862–1945*, 34.

29. Huynh Thuc Khang remarked that because of O'Connell's policies regarding this matter, "Poulo Condore became my first business school" (*Thi Tu Tung Thoai*, 171).

30. Quesnel Report, 13

31. Ibid., 13–14.

32. Huynh Thuc Khang, *Thi Tu Tung Thoai*, 187.

33. According to Quesnel, guards complained that under O'Connell, prisoners showed them little respect, "keeping cigarettes in their mouth when speaking and spitting at their feet" (Quesnel Report, 14).

shopkeepers and fishermen, complained that O'Connell's economic policies generated competition that drove down prices for their goods.

Although the O'Connell era was derided bitterly by guards and islanders, inmates experienced it as something of a golden age. After his departure, many prisoners recalled O'Connell with affection and urged colonial inspectors to arrange for his prompt return.[34] Huynh Thuc Khang devoted a dozen pages of his prison memoir to O'Connell, praising the director's "supreme efficiency," "mastery of Vietnamese," and the way he "treated prisoners like members of his own household." Khang described the director's impact on prisoner morale in almost mythical terms: "Under O'Connell's rule, a humane atmosphere descended on the *bagne*. The whole village of prisoners sang and danced merrily as the dead when they live again. They admonished each other not to violate any rules, and their cruelty and villainy seemed to vanish."[35]

By 1916, a steady drumbeat of complaints from the penitentiary staff prompted the governor of Cochin China to send an inspector to the island. The O'Connell administration made a poor first impression when 900 of the penitentiary's 1,500 prisoners failed to show up for a morning roll call.[36] Coining the derisive oxymoron "detention in liberty" to refer to the regime, the inspector reported that "the hierarchy of punishments is no longer followed on Poulo Condore; in fact, punishment as a form of chastisement simply does not exist."[37] While admitting that O'Connell's economic reforms had enhanced levels of production, he protested that the extra income merely contributed to "all manner of vices" on the island and was "certain to encourage escape attempts."[38] Perhaps most damning were insinuations that the reforms had been driven by O'Connell's personal greed: "This regime, which has evolved little by little toward the kind favored by the Russians, can only accrue advantages to O'Connell," the inspector concluded. "It allows him to draw out profits, while proving extremely expensive to the administration."[39]

Following the investigation, O'Connell was recalled and replaced temporarily by an interim director. In May 1917, he was succeeded permanently by Lieutenant Andouard, a career military officer who had lost an

34. Ibid.
35. Huynh Thuc Khang, *Thi Tu Tung Thoai*, 180.
36. AOM, Gouvernement général, 4260, Affaire O'Connell.
37. Ibid.
38. Ibid.
39. Ibid.

arm and earned a cross of the Legion of Honor at the battle of Verdun.[40] Andouard's background as a soldier, no doubt, contributed to his disdain for the lax character of O'Connell's regime and shaped his efforts to reestablish a military-style discipline in the penitentiary.

According to Huynh Thuc Khang, prisoners experienced the replacement of O'Connell by Andouard as a change from a "liberal" (*khoi phong*) regime to one that was "tight and cruel" (*buoc cay nghiet*).[41] Consistent with his belief that the penitentiary's primary function was to "deprive prisoners of their liberty," Andouard ordered *relégués* and political prisoners back to their wards.[42] Likewise, so-called dangerous prisoners were once again forced to spend their days breaking rocks in the penitentiary's courtyard. In place of the economic incentives introduced by O'Connell, Andouard set new production quotas, twice as high, reportedly, as those in place under previous regimes.[43] Finally, he reduced rice rations to earlier levels and eliminated the generous holiday bonuses that prisoners had enjoyed under O'Connell.[44]

It is impossible to be certain that the change from O'Connell to Andouard served as the decisive trigger for the revolt of 1918, but Inspector Quesnel and Huynh Thuc Khang each highlight the transition as the critical catalytic element. Both suggest that the inmate population's discontent with Andouard's regime was heightened by their affection for O'Connell's. There is no doubt that hatred of Andouard was singularly intense. Eighteen months after the rebellion, he was assassinated by a prisoner who worked in his home as a domestic servant. According to one account, the prisoner finished the job by defecating on the prison director's corpse.[45]

Moreover, survivors reported that Andouard's new work quotas had been a major source of discontent among the leaders of the revolt. One complained that under Andouard, work teams were expected to crush twice as much rock as had been required during previous regimes.[46] This grievance

---

40. Demariaux, *Secrets des îles Poulo Condore*, 72.
41. Huynh Thuc Khang, *Thi Tu Tung Thoai*, 224.
42. Quesnel Report, 15.
43. According to Quesnel, prisoners claimed that Andouard would assign four prisoners production quotas that had been assigned to eight under O'Connell (ibid., 11).
44. Under O'Connell, the rice ration had been raised from 800 grams to one kilogram. Upon taking power, Andouard immediately reduced the ration to 900 and announced another reduction of 100 grams to be instituted in the near future (ibid., 21).
45. Demariaux, *Secrets des îles Poulo-Condore*, 75.
46. Quesnel Report, 11.

was doubtless exacerbated by the fact that O'Connell had allowed dangerous prisoners, typically assigned rock-breaking duties, to pursue a variety of less onerous tasks outside of the main prison buildings. It was perhaps for these reasons that the revolt originated among rock breakers. Another informant pointed out that the uprising occurred the day after the distribution of supplementary Tet bonuses that were several times smaller than the ones provided by O'Connell the previous year.[47]

These comments point to the significance of a sense of relative hardship and injustice among the inmate population arising from the extreme discrepancy between the regimes of O'Connell and Andouard. Although the contrast between the two regimes may have been unusually stark, there was nothing exceptional about the existence of the discrepancy itself. It was merely a function of a system in which prison directors turned over quickly and were subjected to few external checks on their institutional authority. Indeed, a similar dynamic led to a large-scale revolt at the Lai Chau penitentiary in 1927.

UNSTABLE AUTHORITARIANISM, II:
THE LAI CHAU REVOLT OF 1927

Like the Poulo Condore Revolt of 1918, the Lai Chau uprising of 1927 followed a sudden change in prison management. Inmates at the Lai Chau Penitentiary adapted poorly when the idiosyncratic regime of their chief warder, Sergeant Durupt, was replaced by a new administration headed by Commander Roux, the military resident of the province. As at Poulo Condore, the power of the prison director at Lai Chau was heightened by the remoteness of the penitentiary. Lai Chau was located in the inaccessible and mountainous western corner of Tonkin, over fifty miles north of Dien Bien Phu. Surveillance was entrusted to the provincial Garde indigène, roughly half of whom were ethnic Thais and Meos. On the last day of 1926, the penitentiary contained 426 prisoners, the majority of whom were ethnic Vietnamese sentenced to forced labor for five years or more.[48] The

---

47. Ibid.

48. This account of the revolt at Lai Chau is based on three extensive reports completed in its aftermath by French officials. The longest was completed by Inspector Servoise on April 5, 1927 (cited below as Servoise Report). A second was completed by Commandant Roux on July 20, 1927 (cited below as Roux Report). A third was completed by Juge d'instruction Forsans (cited below as Forsans Report). All three can be found in AOM, Indochine, Affaires politiques, 7F54, Révolte des prisonniers de Lai Chau.

fact that over 10 percent were serving life sentences made the inmate population among the most dangerous in Indochina. For colonial officials, the remoteness of the penitentiary and the ethnic composition of its staff were thought to offset the menacing nature of its inmate population.

On the morning of January 24, 1927, twenty-one prisoners working at a limestone kiln 1,500 meters from the center of Lai Chau Town overpowered their guards, seized their rifles, and fired a round of bullets into the air. Hearing the shots, convicts at four nearby work sites went into action. At the brickyard, thirty-eight prisoners attacked their guards with shovels and pickaxes. Ten inmates gathering firewood in a nearby grove jumped the sentry who was supervising them and stabbed him repeatedly in the chest with a makeshift knife. A dozen prisoners transporting limestone along the main road into town disarmed their guards and killed a Thai sentry who happened upon the attack. Even at the stone quarry, over twenty kilometers away and well out of earshot of the initial shootings, prisoners managed to turn the tables on their guards, tying them up and confiscating their weapons and clothes.

Moments later, groups of inmates converged on Lai Chau Town under the mock surveillance of fellow convicts disguised as guards.[49] Several prisoners used shovels and sledgehammers to break into the barracks of the Garde indigène. There, they seized thirty-five rifles and a large cache of ammunition. Others entered the police station, where they destroyed the telegraph machine and shot its operator.

Watching these events unfold from the roof of his residence, Province Chief Roux managed to assemble a force of provincial militiamen, which arrived on the scene and engaged the rebels in a protracted firefight. After several hours, seventy-two prisoners fled into the countryside, where they infiltrated a Thai village and kidnapped several inhabitants to serve as guides and hostages.[50] Tracked by Meo and Thai militiamen, they eventually divided into small groups and headed for the Chinese border. All but ten were eventually killed or recaptured. Two French officials and four native guards died in the initial attack and six members of the Garde indigène perished while pursuing the fugitives over the following week.

49. Roux reports that he realized that the guards were actually prisoners in disguise when he recognized that "the timber of their voice sounded Annamite and not Thai" (Roux Report, 1).

50. Twenty-two rifles were seized from guards on corvée, and nine from the barracks; four "old Remingtons" were taken from the police post (Forsans Report, 7).

Following the uprising, the resident superior of Tonkin ordered Inspector of Political Affairs Servoise to carry out an investigation into the causes of the event. As with the Poulo Condore Revolt of 1918, Servoise highlighted the significance of the abrupt transformation of prison conditions at Lai Chau that resulted when Commander Roux replaced the penitentiary's unconventional chief warder, Sergeant Durupt, in June 1926.[51] Like Andouard ten years earlier, Roux tried to standardize the institution's operations after years of Durupt's highly irregular administration. And just as inmates on Poulo Condore reacted violently to Andouard's efforts to reverse O'Connell's reforms, prisoners at Lai Chau rose in revolt in response to the changes introduced by Roux.

If O'Connell's regime on Poulo Condore was marked by a strangely zealous liberalism, Durupt's administration of Lai Chau was characterized by an almost Kurtzian despotic paternalism. Eschewing ordinary bureaucratic mechanisms of surveillance and control, Durupt governed through the force of his charismatic personality. Because of his long residence in Lai Chau, Durupt claimed to possess an intimate knowledge of the provincial terrain and a deep understanding of the customs of its inhabitants. Fellow colonial officials saw him as arrogant and self-dramatizing, but inmates came to believe that he possessed unusual, almost superhuman powers. According to several prisoners, rumors that Durupt was clairvoyant circulated widely among the inmate population. He cultivated this belief by periodically arranging breakouts from the prison that provided him the opportunity to stage "surprise" ambushes in which unsuspecting fugitives were killed or recaptured. According to an inmate who helped Durupt with such arrangements, the latter's "objective was to demonstrate to prisoners a supernatural aptitude for capturing fugitives—dead or alive."[52]

Instead of administering the prison through the guard corps, which was undermanned and overworked, Durupt created a special entourage of privileged prisoners, who acted as his personal enforcers within the institution. As Servoise explained, "under Durupt, prisoners were terrorized and managed by a gang of ruffians who, in exchange for certain favors, established an appearance of order and security inside."[53] "These prisoners," he continued, "were treated almost as functionaries, collecting a high monthly

51. "The main cause of the revolt is discontent generated by the suppression of the regime of favor that had flourished under Sergeant Durupt" (Servoise Report, 1).
52. Roux Report, 3.
53. Ibid., 4

salary and circulating freely outside the prison."[54] Inhabitants of Lai Chau claimed that Durupt's favored inmates were even permitted to roam the town at night, thieving, gambling, and attacking local women.

In addition to its antibureaucratic personalism, the Durupt regime was characterized by the chronic neglect of numerous minor regulations. According to Servoise, inmates were not provided with mats or nets, and neither guards nor prisoners were outfitted with standard uniforms. Rules regarding hairstyles and personal grooming were ignored, and inmates were allowed to keep their own lock boxes, which often contained "irregular items such as cash, opium, pipes, tools, knives, and matches." It was the eventual exposure of such conditions that led to Durupt's dismissal in June 1926.

Like Andouard a decade earlier, Roux moved quickly to roll back the unorthodox policies of his predecessor. He dismissed the powerful Thai warder Deo Van Mon, known to be Durupt's main henchman and dispenser of perks and largesse within the prison. He suppressed the special salaries received by Durupt's privileged prisoners. He abolished lock boxes, introduced regular body searches, and forbade prisoners to receive money from their families. Finally, he attempted to prevent inmates from leaving the penitentiary at night by forcing all hard-labor prisoners to wear chains. According to Servoise, "it was these measures that clearly provoked the agitation, because they contrasted too much with the absolutely special regime instituted by Durupt."[55]

Although there is significant evidence to support Servoise's version of events, it is important to note how the inspector's explanation served to deflect attention from the catalytic role of the penitentiary's horrible living conditions. The fact that 74 inmates passed away at Lai Chau in 1925 and 53 died in 1926 must be considered in any attempt to explain the willingness of prisoners to embark on a risky course of revolt. For prisoners who witnessed the death of at least one fellow inmate every week, the hazards of joining a revolt may have been tempered by the dangers of trying to serve out a lengthy sentence. Indeed, Commander Roux acknowledged that the "the climate of Lai Chau is so bad that even a short penalty is the equivalent of a death sentence, postponed perhaps by several joyless months or years in the penitentiary."[56]

54. Ibid.
55. Servoise Report, 5.
56. Roux Report, 1.

The uprising may also have been instigated by Durupt's impetuous actions upon learning of his dismissal. Furious at being replaced, he called an extraordinary evening meeting of the inmate population several days before leaving his post.[57] His remarks were translated simultaneously into Vietnamese and Thai by prisoners later identified as among the leaders of the revolt. Durupt's Vietnamese translator, Pham Van Voi, left the following verbatim record of his provocative parting words: "Act as wickedly as you like. Refuse the work you are forced to do. You are now completely free. Those who wish to escape, do it. Only I am capable of capturing you, and as I am now leaving, you have nothing left to fear. No one else knows how to retake you. Escape and you will let them know that I was once useful here."[58] According to other eyewitness accounts, Durupt encouraged inmates to "follow in the footsteps" of prisoner rebels years before at Thai Nguyen and Bac Kan.[59]

It is difficult to know their precise impact on the prisoners being addressed, but Durupt's remarks were followed by five mass escape attempts over the next six months. The largest and most successful occurred on December 23, 1926, during which twelve prisoners managed to slip out of the prison at night and cross over the Chinese border.[60] According to Pham Van Voi, prisoners who participated in the escape were supremely confident in the success of their venture because they believed that only Durupt "knew the province well enough to retake them."[61] French officials also believed that both the escapes and the revolt were the "inevitable consequence of Durupt's reckless exhortations."[62] As Commander Roux explained, "M. Durupt has clearly incited the prisoners to revolt. I consider this to have been established beyond a shadow of a doubt. Since M. Durupt's departure, we have all lived in an atmosphere of immanent rebellion. There is not a single European living here who has not had a presentiment of the thing."[63]

Although Durupt's administration was significantly different from O'Connell's, the idiosyncratic regime that each was able to establish illus-

---

57. Ibid.
58. Ibid.
59. In 1914, 130 convicts in the Bac Kan Provincial Prison seized the institution, infiltrated the barracks of the *Garde indigène*, and killed three prison guards.
60. Ibid., 4.
61. Ibid., 3.
62. Ibid.
63. Ibid., 6.

trates the tremendous latitude enjoyed by prison directors in Indochina. When combined with the rapid turnover of prison administrators, this latitude appears to have contributed significantly to the outbreak of prisoner revolts. In addition, the uprising at Lai Chau suggests that collective violence in prison was provoked, not only by the way inmates experienced the disorienting change from one administrative regime to another, but by the very disorderliness of the transition process itself.

PRISON REVOLTS AND PRISON LABOR

Not only does the uprising at Lai Chau confirm the link between prison revolts and sudden, disorderly changes in prison administration, it also highlights the role played by prison labor in facilitating collective violence. From its origins at the limestone kiln, the revolt at Lai Chau spread like a chain reaction to other work sites around the penitentiary. It was from these isolated locations, outside the main prison buildings, that prisoners gained the opportunity and secured the resources that enabled them to launch a coordinated attack on strategic points in Lai Chau Town.

During Inspector's Servoise's investigation, officials pointed to the "arrangement of corvée" as a prominent secondary cause of the revolt. The 346 prisoners at Lai Chau were dispersed among fifty work sites, twenty-nine of which were guarded by fewer than five men apiece.[64] "One of the factors that facilitated the revolt of January 24," Servoise argued, "is the establishment of work sites too far away and too widely dispersed. The problem is all the more difficult to resolve because we cannot give up the manufacturing of bricks and limestone, the principal use of penal labor."[65] Judging the abolition of corvée too costly, Servoise suggested that guards assigned to work sites should carry truncheons rather than guns, arguing that although this might well increase the number of escapes, it would decrease the intensity of violence associated with them.[66] Roux was less sanguine about the impact of limited reforms. "There is no doubt that the penitentiary at Lai Chau has been a model of poor organization," he wrote to

64. Fifty-four prisoners were semi-permanently stationed at a work camp in Dien Bien Phu (Servoise Report, 11).

65. Servoise also pointed out that penal labor had been used in the construction of nine new public buildings the previous year. The exploitation of penal labor at Lai Chau had proved so successful that in January 1926, Durupt requested that 150 new prisoners be transferred to the penitentiary (ibid., 60).

66. Ibid., 38. "I propose that Commandant Roux only arm the guards with a solid truncheon in order to avoid a situation where the arms and ammunition of the personnel of the surveillance can pass into the hands of the detainees such as

the resident superior four months after the revolt. "It should not only be refashioned, but entirely reconstructed on a new site. But when all is said and done, if prisoners continue to work outside the prison, the risks of escape and rebellion will remain basically the same."[67]

The archival record suggests that officials had long recognized the seriousness of the security concerns raised by prison labor. In 1906 and again in 1910, the resident superior of Tonkin requested that each provincial resident provide him with a detailed account of the measures in place to prevent escapes and revolts.[68] In their responses, residents tended to emphasize the myriad regulations they enforced to lower the risks of "incidents" during corvée. "Work gangs are composed in such manner as to avoid grouping and concentrating prisoners with heavy punishments," explained the resident of Thai Nguyen, "and in all cases, the number of guards corresponds to the number of prisoners at the work site."[69] The mayor of Hanoi wrote that "dangerous convicts at the Central Prison never leave the prison; only those sentenced to short terms are employed at external corvée."[70] Some residents elaborated on precautions taken when work gangs left and entered the prison and when tools were distributed and collected. Others described the variety of work-site inspections carried out daily and the positioning, training, and arming of surveillants.[71]

The measures undertaken by warders to secure work sites failed to discourage prisoners from taking advantage of the slackening of security during corvée. The majority of the prison revolts during the colonial era originated at work sites. In addition to the Lai Chau revolt, others included the 1883 rebellion by convicts building the lighthouse on Bai Canh Island, the 1894 insurrection among coral collectors on Poulo Condore, and the Poulo Condore revolts of 1910 and 1918, which were spearheaded by rock breakers.

---

occurred January 24. I consider the system preferable: it puts us, in case of a collective revolt, in a better position to remove from the prisoners all effective means of attack and if it produces several partial escapes, an armed detachment reinforced by a patrol, solidly equipped and armed, should be able to track them down."

67. Roux Report, 7.

68. TTLT, Résidence supérieure au Tonkin, 79540, Circulaire 58, January 30, 1906, and TTLT, Résidence supérieure au Tonkin, 3872, Circulaire 721c, August 30, 1910.

69. TTLT, Résidence supérieure au Tonkin, 79540.

70. TTLT, Résidence supérieure au Tonkin, 38722.

71. Ibid.

A revolt at the Lao Bao Penitentiary in 1915 illustrates the dangers of providing prisoner workers with sharp tools. On October 15, sixteen inmates in the prison yard used the short-handled knives that they had been issued to make cloth hats in order to launch a surprise attack on their warders. After stabbing three guards, one of whom they decapitated, the prisoners broke into the barracks of the Garde indigène, killed the handful of militiamen they found inside, seized several dozen rifles, and pillaged the treasury. After setting fire to the seventeen buildings in the penitentiary complex, forty-two prisoners fled across the border into Laos, leaving behind eight dead guards and the ashes of what had once been the largest penitentiary in Annam.[72]

PRISONS AS TARGETS FOR OUTSIDE ATTACKS

Not only did the internal workings of colonial prisons generate high levels of collective violence, prisons were also frequently targeted for attacks from the outside. Outlaw gangs and sectarian groups typically attacked prisons to free imprisoned comrades and recruit new followers. Attempts by secret societies and bandit gangs to forcibly free their followers from colonial jails date from as early as the 1890s. In March 1892, a monk calling himself the king of Tam Dao released forty-four of his followers from the Son Tay provincial prison in a daring midday assault.[73] In 1897, another renegade bonze, Tan Thuat, and his "soldiers of the sky" led simultaneous raids on the provincial prisons in Hai Phong, Hai Duong, and Thai Binh.[74] In 1909, a spectacular attack was launched on the Hoa Binh Provincial Prison by a Muong bandit leader known to the French as Kiem. When three of his clansmen were arrested and imprisoned for arms smuggling, Kiem led his men directly to the provincial prison, cut the throats of three sentries standing guard, and scaled the prison walls. Once inside, they forced their way into the prison storehouse where guns and ammunition

---

72. The Lao Bao revolt was led by Lieu Hanh, described in French reports as "a scholar, fluent French speaker and an agent of Prince Cuong De." The penitentiary was almost completely destroyed in the fire lit by the rebels. AOM, Gouvernement général, 176, Révolte de pénitencier de Lao Bao 1915. According to the British travel writer Harry Hervey, who visited the penitentiary in the 1920s: "Over the entrance-way of the prison was a plaque commemorating the bravery of prison guards during a mutiny of convicts in 1915" (Hervey, *Travels in French Indochina* [London, 1928], 259).

73. E. Daufès, *La Garde indigène de l'Indochine de sa création à nos jours* (Avignon, 1933), 131.

74. Ibid., 164.

were kept. They then burst into the adjoining barracks and opened fire on the militiamen sleeping there. Twenty members of the provincial Garde indigène and one French officer were killed or fatally wounded. After releasing his imprisoned clansmen, Kiem carried off a small fortune in arms, ammunition, and confiscated opium seized from a storehouse adjoining the prison.[75]

Coming on the heels of a similar attack on the provincial prison in Son La, the "Hoa Binh Affair" sent shock waves through Tonkin's prison system.[76] The resident superior ordered wardens throughout the protectorate to shore up their defenses and prepare reports detailing the measures currently in place to prevent similar episodes in the future. A perusal of these reports suggests that local officials considered external attacks on prisons to be a threat against which constant vigilance was required. In Phuc Yen, for example, the resident was so anxious about plots to scale the prison walls from the outside that he ordered an elaborate moat dug around the prison, "two meters deep and studded with wooden stakes."[77] The resident of Phu Tho noted that the main purpose of the jagged glass shards embedded atop the concrete walls of the prison in his province was to discourage "an attempt to break in at night and free the prisoners."[78]

While some attacks on prisons were intended to free old comrades, others were launched to recruit new ones. In 1926, Georges Coulet, the colonial state's most prolific researcher on anti-French sectarian movements pointed out that secret societies looked to the prison population as a significant "reservoir" of manpower. Coulet saw such logic at work in the Phan Xich Long Rebellion of 1916, during which hundreds of adherents of a millenarian Buddhist sect simultaneously stormed Saigon Central Prison and the Cho Lon Provincial Prison in a futile attempt to release their spiritual leader.[79] "The attack on Saigon Central Prison was not simply an attempt to release the pseudo-emperor, Phan Xich Long," Coulet cautioned, "but was intended to deliver all the prisoners."[80] According to Coulet, the at-

---

75. Ibid., 219.

76. No secondary source mentions the Son La raid, but it is referred to in the correspondence of the Tonkin resident superior following the attack on Hoa Binh. See TTLT, Résidence supérieure au Tonkin, 38722.

77. Ibid., Résident de Phuc Yen au Résident supérieur au Tonkin, November 18, 1910. In 1910, the resident of Phuc Yen was M. Darles, later to gain notoriety as the resident of Thai Nguyen during the 1917 rebellion.

78. Ibid. Résident de Phu Tho au Résident supérieur au Tonkin, October 22, 1910.

79. Georges Coulet, *Les Sociétés secrètes en terre d'Annam* (Saigon, 1926), 343.

80. Ibid.

tackers reasoned that the freed prisoners would be at their mercy and would thus have "little choice but to join with them against the government that had imprisoned them."[81]

There were also cases in which popular outrage over arrests that were deemed unjust led civilian mobs to storm colonial prisons. For example, crowds attacked prisons repeatedly during World War I in order to free inmates arrested for draft evasion. It is well known that around 50,000 Indochinese were sent to Europe as laborers between 1914 and 1918, but there were also a large number of conscripts who were incarcerated for refusing to take part in the war effort. During the war, crowds in at least twenty Indochinese provinces marched on prisons to protest the colonial state's conscription policy.[82] An especially dramatic episode of this nature occurred in Bien Hoa Province on January 25, 1916, during which a mob of peasants broke into the provincial prison, killed several guards, and released the entire inmate population.

CONCLUSION

Along with the catalytic ingredients highlighted in this chapter—popular antipathy to the colonial justice system, the unstable authoritarianism of prison administration, the security lapses caused by corvée labor, and the vulnerability of prisons to external attacks—other factors also help explain the high frequency of collective violence in colonial prisons. There is no question that communal architecture, a characteristic feature of colonial prisons, facilitated conspiratorial plotting among inmates. As has been mentioned, murderous health and living conditions induced feelings of desperation that provided a breeding ground for revolt. Moreover, the peculiar racial dynamics of the colonial prison heightened possibilities for collusion between guards and prisoners that could occasionally lead to episodes of collective violence. Some of these factors were certainly at work in the episodes discussed above, and chapter 6 examines them in greater detail by looking at colonial Indochina's greatest prison uprising, the Thai Nguyen rebellion of 1917.

81. Ibid.
82. Coulet recorded such attacks in thirteen of Cochin China's twenty provinces: Vinh Long, Sa Dec, Gia Dinh, My Tho, Cho Lon, Ba Ria, Tay Ninh, Can Tho, Tra Vinh, Chau Doc, Bien Hoa, Long Xuyen and Thu Dau Mot (ibid., 20).

6   The Thai Nguyen Rebellion

Between the pacification of Tonkin in the late 1880s and the Depression-era revolts of 1930–31, the Thai Nguyen rebellion was the largest and most destructive anticolonial uprising in French Indochina. On August 31, 1917, an eclectic band of political prisoners, common criminals, and mutinous prison guards seized the Thai Nguyen Penitentiary, the largest penal institution in northern Tonkin. From their base within the penitentiary, the rebels stormed the provincial arsenal and captured a large cache of weapons. They then seized a series of strategic buildings in the town and executed French officials and Vietnamese collaborators. In anticipation of a counterattack, the rebels fortified the perimeter of the town and issued a proclamation calling for a general uprising against the colonial state. French forces retook the town following five days of intense fighting, but mopping-up campaigns in the surrounding countryside stretched on for six months and led to hundreds of casualties on both sides.

Not only was the Thai Nguyen rebellion among the most dramatic and destructive uprisings of the colonial era but it marks a transition from traditional Vietnamese anticolonialism to the modern nationalist movements of the 1930s. During the late nineteenth century, anticolonial efforts were hampered by regionalism and traditional patterns of political authority.[1] As David Marr has argued, they were organized locally and led by scholar-gentry whose followings were limited to members of their own lineages

1. See, e.g., David Marr, *Vietnamese Anticolonialism, 1885–1925* (Berkeley and Los Angeles, 1971), 53; Truong Buu Lam, *Patterns of Vietnamese Response to Foreign Intervention, 1858–1900*, Yale Monograph Series, no. 11 (New Haven, Conn., 1967), 34; John T. McAlister Jr., *Vietnam: The Origins of Revolution* (New York, 1971), 12, 54, 58.

and villages. Such traditionalism made it difficult for the leaders of these movements to "maintain effective liaison with their counterparts in other provinces and regions and . . . to develop any overall political or military strategy."[2] Although reformist scholars such as Phan Boi Chau and Phan Chu Trinh tried to overcome these problems around the turn of the century, it was only the nationalist movements of the 1930s (including the communist movement) that succeeded in integrating anticolonial forces from different parts of Indochina and establishing new, more flexible patterns of command and authority.

Despite the fact that it occurred a decade before the appearance of organized nationalist parties, the Thai Nguyen rebellion also managed to transcend the regional and social limitations that characterized earlier movements. In stark contrast to virtually all the anticolonial risings that had preceded it, rebels came from over thirty provinces and were led by individuals from every stratum of Indochinese society. It was the extraordinary regional and social diversity of its forces that makes the Thai Nguyen rebellion a compelling overture to the modern nationalist movements of the 1930s. This chapter argues that the modern protonational orientation of the Thai Nguyen rebellion was a direct result of the structure and functioning of the Thai Nguyen Penitentiary. Like many colonial prisons, it brought a diverse array of individuals together within an enclosed institutional environment, endowed them with similar interests and commitments, and created conditions for them to forge new collective identities. In short, the penitentiary provided a discrete site where traditional class and regional divisions might be overcome and new ideas of fraternity and community could develop, flourish, and serve as a powerful foundation for collective resistance to the colonial state.

THE REBELLION

At 11:00 P.M. on August 30, 1917, in the town of Thai Nguyen, fifty miles north of Hanoi, two sergeants from the provincial brigade of the Garde indigène knocked on the door to the residence of M. Noel, the brigade commander, and announced the delivery of an urgent telegram.[3] When Noel

---

2. Marr, *Vietnamese Anticolonialism,* 53.
3. The following narrative is based on official letters, telegrams, and reports currently located in the Dépôt des Archives d'Outre-Mer in Aix-en-Provence and filed under the subseries 7F (Sûreté générale) in carton 51 (hereafter cited as AOM, 7F51). I have also consulted the following secondary sources: Tran Huy Lieu, *Loan Thai Nguyen* [The Thai Nguyen Uprising] (Hanoi, 1935); Dao Trinh Nhat, *Luong*

opened the door, Sergeant Pham Van Truong leapt across the verandah and attacked him with a knife.[4] A scuffle ensued, during which Truong drew a pistol and killed Noel with a shot in the back. After decapitating Noel's corpse, Truong carried the head back to his barracks, where he handed it over to Sergeant Trinh Van Can. Sergeant Can set it on an offering tray next to two more freshly severed heads and placed it beneath a five-star red and yellow flag that had been unfurled minutes beforehand in the barracks.[5]

The additional heads belonged to Sergeant Hanh and Deputy Supervisor Lap, two loyal Vietnamese officers who, like Noel, had been murdered and decapitated under orders from Sergeant Can. Standing astride the three severed heads, Sergeant Can addressed the roughly 150 *gardes* assembled in the barracks.[6] He denounced the brutality of Noel and the treachery of Provincial Resident Darles and implored the *gardes* to join him in rebellion against the French. Perhaps as an additional inducement,

---

Ngoc Quyen va Cuoc Khoi Nghia Thai Nguyen 1917 [Luong Ngoc Quyen and the Thai Nguyen Rebellion of 1917] (Saigon, 1957); Phuong Huu, *105 Ngay Khoi Nghia Thai Nguyen* [105 Days of the Thai Nguyen Rebellion] (Saigon, 1949); and Alfred Echinard, *Histoire politique et militaire de la province de Thai-Nguyên: Ses forces de police* (Hanoi: Trung-Bac Tan-Van, 1934). I have also made use of a *quoc ngu* version of the interrogation of the rebel Nguyen Van Nhieu, conducted by the Ha Dong province chief on October 10, 1917, originally written in *chu nom*. It was discovered and published in a Vietnamese historical journal in 1987: see "Ve Cuoc Khoi Nghia Thai Nguyen Nam 1917: Ban Khau Cung Nguyen Van Nhieu" [On the Thai Nguyen Rebellion, 1917: The Interrogation of Nguyen Van Nhieu], ed. Le Xuan Phong, *Nghien Cuu Lich Su* 237 (1987): 76–80 (hereafter cited as Nguyen Van Nhieu). I wish to thank Brian Ostrowski for bringing the latter source to my attention.

4. Most accounts name Sergeant Truong as Noel's assailant, but Nguyen Van Nhieu attributes the attack to "Sergeant Can, jailer Map and jailer 81." Given that Noel was killed before the destruction of the prison, however, it is unlikely that two jailers would have taken part. Nguyen Van Nhieu, 78.

5. In addition to interrogation reports of *gardes* found in AOM, 7F51, Dao Trinh Nhat and Tran Huy Lieu provide the clearest description of the events that transpired in the barracks. The severed heads were "an offering made to the flag," according to Dao Trinh Nhat, *Luong Ngoc Quyen va Cuoc Khoi Nghia Thai Nguyen 1917,* 72.

6. It is difficult to determine the exact number of *gardes* in the barracks at that time. Dao Trinh Nhat says 175, Tran Huy Lieu says 150, and Phuong Huu says 130. I have gone with 150, inasmuch as this figure is also given in an enquiry completed by the Garde indigène itself. See AOM, 751F, "Notes sommaires sur la rébellion de Thai Nguyen," Association professionelle des anciens de la Garde indigène de l'Indochine, *Bulletin semestriel* 4, no. 7 (December 31, 1917): 3.

the sergeant ordered the immediate execution of seven elderly *gardes* who objected to the plot.[7] Meanwhile, a group of *gardes* stole into the office of the resident, smashed the telegraph equipment to prevent communication with Hanoi, seized the arsenal, and emptied over 71,000 piasters from the provincial treasury.[8] Others began to ransack the houses of the town's European residents, many of whom had overheard the gunfire and taken refuge in the blockhouse of the colonial infantry. Those caught unaware, like the director of provincial public works and his wife, were killed and decapitated. The rebels broke into the home of Resident Darles but were disappointed to find him away. They then took up strategic positions in the courthouse, treasury, and post office and began digging trenches around the perimeter of the town.[9]

Led by another sergeant, Duong Van Gia, thirty mutineers left the barracks and headed for the Thai Nguyen Penitentiary. Because the night watch was entrusted to members of the Garde indigène, the rebels entered the prison without resistance.[10] Once inside, Sergeant Gia's men shot and killed the French warden and bludgeoned his Vietnamese wife to death with a hammer.[11] Sergeant Gia then ordered his men to release the prison's 220 inmates. "We are rebelling because we have suffered much cruelty from Resident Darles," Sergeant Gia announced to the prisoners. "We go now to liberate the countries of Annam and expel the French."[12] Moments later, Sergeant Can entered the prison yard. As *gardes* and prisoners looked

7. The killing of the seven *gardes* is mentioned in official reports and in Tran Huy Lieu, *Loan Thai Nguyen,* 10. It is interesting (but not surprising given the imperatives of DRV historiography) that Lieu does not mention the killings in any of the subsequent versions of the rebellion he produced after 1954. See, e.g., Tran Huy Lieu, *Lich Su Tam Muoi Nam Chong Phap* [History of Eighty Years Against the French] (Hanoi, 1956), 192–200.

8. The treasury contained 30,000 piasters in bills and 41,000 in coins (Echinard, *Histoire politique et militaire,* 205).

9. AOM, 7F51, Notes sommaires sur la rébellion de Thai Nguyen, December 31, 1917 (cited n. 6 above), and Rapport confidentiel 26-R.C., August 24, 1918.

10. The prison guards opened the door only after Sergeant Gia had uttered a secret password, according to Tran Huy Lieu, *Loan Thai Nguyen,* 11.

11. Again, there are different accounts of who killed the warden and his wife. Both murders were committed by Sergeant Nam and an unnamed prison guard, according to Nguyen Van Nhieu, 79. The warden's wife was killed by Gia, but not the warden himself, according to Tran Huy Lieu, *Loan Thai Nguyen,* 11. Gia is credited with the warden's murder in numerous French reports and interrogation transcripts and by Dao Trinh Nhat, *Luong Ngoc Quyen va Cuoc Khoi Nghia Thai Nguyen 1917,* 72.

12. AOM, 7F51, Rapport confidentiel 26-R.C., August 24, 1918, Interrogation of the prisoner Dieu Doan Cung.

on, Ba Chi, a bandit serving a twenty-five-year sentence, carried a disabled convict named Luong Ngoc Quyen from his solitary cell into the prison courtyard and placed him before Sergeant Can.[13] Witnesses reported that a lengthy conversation took place between the two men.[14]

Luong Ngoc Quyen was no ordinary prisoner. Born in 1890, Quyen was the eldest son of the reformist mandarin Luong Van Can, a principal bene-factor of the influential modernist educational experiment known as the Dong Kinh Free School.[15] Like many highborn boys of his generation, Quyen spent his youth preparing dutifully for the Confucian examina-tions. In 1905, however, he abruptly abandoned his studies. Setting off for Japan, Quyen became the first Vietnamese participant in the Eastern Travel Movement, a foreign-study program founded by the anticolonial activist Phan Boi Chau, whose purpose was to provide military and scientific train-ing to Vietnamese youth.[16] In his memoirs, Phan lauded Quyen's "irre-

13. "I saw the prisoner Ba Chi carrying Luong Ngoc Quyen on his back, because he had been kept locked up for many days; both his legs were lame, and he could not walk" (Nguyen Van Nhieu, 77).

14. All secondary sources describe the encounter. Interrogations of rebels pro-duced many eyewitness accounts of the meeting between Trinh Van Can and Luong Ngoc Quyen. See, e.g., the interrogations of Pham Van Phuc and Hoang Van Dau in AOM, 7F51, Rapport confidentiel 26-R.C., August 24, 1918, 33–34.

15. The best Western-language treatment of Luong Van Can's career is Vu Duc Bang, "The Dong Kinh Free School Movement, 1907–1908," in *Aspects of Viet-namese History*, ed. Walter Vella (Honolulu, 1973), 30–96. See also Marr, *Viet-namese Anticolonialism*, 156–85; Nguyen Hien Le, *Dong Kinh Nghia Thuc* (Saigon, 1968); and Chuong Thau, *Dong Kinh Nghia Thuc* (Hanoi, 1982).

16. Led by Phan Boi Chau between 1905 and 1909, the Eastern Travel movement was an attempt to bring Vietnamese activists to Japan for military and technical training. See *Phan Boi Chau and the Dong Du Movement*, ed. Vinh Sinh (New Haven, Conn., 1988). For an account of Luong Ngoc Quyen's trip to Japan, see the translation of Phan Boi Chau's 1914 memoir *Nguc Trung Thu* [Prison Notes], in *Reflections from Captivity: Phan Boi Chau's Prison Notes and Ho Chi Minh's Prison Diary*, ed. David Marr (Athens, Ohio, 1978), 35. Phan writes:

> In the 10th month of that year (1905) I arrived in Yokohama and went to the boarding house I stayed at before. There I saw a young Vietnamese student, Luong Lap Nham (Luong Ngoc Quyen), who had arrived before me. He appeared to be a man of enthusi-astic character, disheveled in appearance. After sounding him out I learned that he left Vietnam for Japan alone, arriving here with only three piasters in his pocket. Seeing him I was both overjoyed and dumbfounded. He was a young fellow countryman who alone had dared to risk his life to brave the wind and waves to come to a faraway coun-try that he had never seen or heard of before. Certainly Luong was the first one to do so. In fact it turned out that Luong had not yet spiritually prepared himself for such a venture. He had merely heard that I was in Tokyo and thus determined to abandon his home and country. How many young intelligent countrymen might there be after Luong?

pressible behavior, cheerful disposition, and large-hearted outlook" and praised him as "the most admirable" of all the Vietnamese students in Japan.[17] Quyen spent his first months in Japan working with a group of Chinese revolutionaries based in Tokyo. He then enrolled in the Shimbu (Gakko) Military Academy, from which he graduated in 1908.[18] The following year, he left Japan for China, where he pursued further military studies in Kwangsi and Peking.[19] Joining up with Phan Boi Chau again in 1912, Quyen helped him found the Viet Nam Quang Phuc Hoi (Vietnam Restoration Society), which became the leading Vietnamese anticolonial party of the early twentieth century. As head of the party's external relations committee, Quyen traveled widely, carrying out political work in Indochina, Siam, and Southern China.[20] In 1915, he was arrested in Hong Kong, extradited to Hanoi, and tried for his role in a 1913 bombing attack at Phu Tho.[21] He was convicted, sentenced to hard labor for life, and transferred to the Thai Nguyen Penitentiary in July 1916.[22] Fearful of the impact that the presence of this "notorious revolutionary" might have on the other prisoners, the warden kept Quyen locked in a solitary cell, where ill-fitting iron shackles cut off the flow of blood to his feet, leaving him an invalid.[23]

17. Phan recalled Quyen's spirited resourcefulness in the following episode:

Quyen once walked from Yokohama to Tokyo on an empty stomach. Arriving during the night, he fell asleep in the doorway of a police station. The police questioned him in Japanese and he responded with blank incomprehension. Finding his pockets empty, they suspected him of feeble-mindedness. When brush-conversation [written communication in Chinese characters] began, however, they discovered that he was a young man from our country. Astonished, they gave him train-fare back to Yokohama. With enough money now to eat for several days, Luong did not return but visited the lodgings of various Chinese students in Tokyo. By chance, he found the office of the *Minpao*, the newspaper of China's revolutionary party. Both the editor, Chang Tai-Yen, and the manager, Chang Chi, were founding members. Luong explained to them his current situation and they felt sorry for him. They hired him as a clerk and told him to return to Yokohama and bring back his friends who they would take on as well. Source: *Phan Boi Chau Nien Bieu* [Autobiography of Phan Boi Chau] (1925), in *Phan Boi Chau Toan Tap* [Collected Works], ed. Chuong Thau (Hue, 1990), 104.

18. Ibid., 104.
19. Dao Trinh Nhat, *Luong Ngoc Quyen Va Cuoc Khoi Nghia Thai Nguyen*, 29.
20. Ibid., 32–43.
21. Ibid., 44–54.
22. For an account of Luong Ngoc Quyen's arrest and trial, see Vu Van Tinh, "Mot Chut Tai Lieu Ve Luong Ngoc Quyen" [A Few Documents about Luong Ngoc Quyen], *Nghien Cuu Lich Su* 128 (November 1969). See also AOM, 7F51, Rapport confidentiel 811c, September 25, 1917.
23. AOM, 7F51, Rapport confidentiel 811c, September 25, 1917.

Following the conversation between Can and Quyen, a meeting was convened in the prison yard during which two courses of action were debated.[24] Quyen advised the rebels to dig in and attempt to hold the town until reinforcements arrived in the form of sympathetic colonial troops, Quang Phuc Hoi activists, and brigands from the gang of De Tham, a recently deceased anti-French bandit chief. In contrast, Ba Chi, Ba Quoc, and Hai Lam, lieutenants of De Tham's serving sentences for piracy, favored an offensive strategy that entailed abandoning the town and launching attacks on nearby French outposts. Whereas the static defensive approach Quyen advocated derived from his military training abroad, the mobile offensive strategy favored by the bandits reflected their familiarity with hit-and-run tactics and intimate knowledge of the local terrain. After intense deliberations, the matter was settled when Sergeant Can threw his support behind the plan outlined by Quyen.[25]

The collaboration between Trinh Van Can and Luong Ngoc Quyen was especially remarkable considering the vast social distance separating the two men. In ordinary circumstances, it would have been difficult to imagine someone of Quyen's patrician background entering into extended intercourse with Sergeant Can, the son of an impoverished rural laborer from mountainous Vinh-Yen Province.[26] Whereas Quyen had been a fixture in anticolonial political and intellectual circles in Japan, China, Hong Kong, and Siam since his late teens, Can had joined the Garde indigène as a youth and had served his entire adult life on the remote Tonkinese frontier guarding prisoners and fighting bandits for the French. Quyen composed excellent classical Chinese verse and followed an austere personal regimen inspired by the Chinese reformer Liang Ch'i-ch'ao. Can, a confirmed opium addict and heavy gambler, was rumored to be illiterate.

The following morning, the rebels released a proclamation appealing to the population for support.[27] It was read aloud in the streets of Thai

24. Tran Huy Lieu, *Loan Thai Nguyen*, 19–20, gives the most detailed account of the debate, which he characterizes as "heated" (*kich liet*). French accounts, on the other hand, provide little insight into the internal dynamics of the rebellion.

25. "Can followed the suggestion of Quyen because he believed that his military background endowed him with greater foresight than the others" (ibid., 19).

26. For biographical information on Trinh Van Can, see ibid., 6–7, 60. Luong Ngoc Quyen's life history is well documented in Dao Trinh Nhat, *Luong Ngoc Quyen va Cuoc Khoi Nghi Thai Nguyen*.

27. No original copies of the proclamations seem to have survived, but French-language translations can be found in AOM/AP, 7F51, and two *quoc ngu* versions are reproduced in Dao Trinh Nhat, *Luong Ngoc Quyen va Cuoc Khoi Nghi Thai Nguyen*, 76–86. My English translation is from the Dao Trinh Nhat version.

Nguyen, posted at intersections, and sent with accompanying letters to neighboring military outposts at Hoa Binh and Cho Chu.[28] In contrast to Can's address in the barracks, which emphasized the wickedness of Thai Nguyen's top French officials, the proclamation highlighted the historic injustice of the French colonial project as a whole.[29] It denounced the unfairness of colonial law, the violation of traditional burial customs, the disempowerment of the monarchy, the imposition of an onerous tax system, the impoverishment of the rural population, and the recruitment of Indochinese troops and workers for perilous service in the European war. In conclusion, the proclamation discussed the psychological predicament of native troops in the colonial military and described the gradual emergence of their determination to revolt:

> The moment has come. In the country, we now have loyal subjects who draw their swords to kill the enemy. Soon revolutionaries will come from outside to help us. We appeal to men animated by a spirit of liberty and independence. We are forming battalions of liberation soldiers, and we begin in Thai Nguyen province. The five-star flag has been raised; we have proclaimed independence. We are all brothers in the countries of Annam, intelligent men to whom education has been able to suggest some useful measures. Men of good health, aid us with your arms. Allow us to mobilize you, and you may join us to destroy our enemies. But a warning to those who prefer servitude, or become partisans

28. Tran Huy Lieu, *Loan Thai Nguyen,* 20.

29. The rebel denunciation of French colonial rule read in part:

The French do not hesitate to transgress their own laws in order to eliminate our race. They pronounce excessively severe penalties, commit the most detestable acts of barbarity, and cover everything up with lies. Compounding their tyranny, they have violated our dynastic tombs in search of treasure and dethroned and exiled our kings to a desert island. During the thirty years since they seized Hanoi, they have made and unmade kings three times without ever consulting the will of the people. Every day our taxes increase and our compatriots succumb under their weight. Each of us is strangled at the neck by a double noose which grows progressively tighter; nine of every ten families live in dire poverty. At this moment, our enemy is under attack in Europe. They requisition our men and use them like a high wall to protect them from bullets. They take our goods to provision their troops. Over there, our compatriots are overwhelmed with work and those who die are not given decent burials. Our widows and orphans cry in their homes; our old fathers cry along the road. The situation of our country is so deplorable it baffles the imagination; our sufferings are innumerable. We cannot tolerate this state of things any longer. Our country has become poor and powerless, like a broken thread. Suffering has taken away our final breath. This time we begin anew the struggle for independence and if we are not fated to succeed, we no longer desire to live. Source: Dao Trinh Nhat, *Luong Ngoc Quyen va Cuoc Khoi Nghia Thai Nguyen,* 78.

of the enemy, for we shall remove your heads. Thus in clear terms is the proclamation.[30]

By all accounts, the rebels found a receptive audience among the poorest residents of the town. Witnesses reported that coolies, miners, and itinerant boatmen quickly swelled the ranks of the rebellion.[31] According to informed estimates, 300 civilians were led to the barracks, where they joined roughly 200 ex-prisoners and 130 *gardes*.[32] Following orders issued by Luong Ngoc Quyen, Sergeant Can divided the rebels into two battalions. The first was composed of *gardes* and the second of prisoners and civilians under the command of Ba Chi.[33] Can passed out ammunition and the 92 muskets and 75 rifles that had been seized from the provincial arsenal.[34] Rebel troops fashioned military armbands for themselves and hung banners around the town.[35]

For the next five days, this motley assortment of common-law prisoners, political prisoners, *gardes*, and civilians defended Thai Nguyen against repeated attacks by colonial forces. The French mobilized local militiamen and transported heavy artillery and over 500 regular troops to the outskirts of Thai Nguyen.[36] On September 4, with French bombing threatening to completely raze the town, the rebels divided into four groups and beat a hasty and chaotic retreat into the neighboring countryside. Amid the confusion, hundreds of combatants on both sides were slain.[37] French officers discovered the body of Luong Ngoc Quyen among the dead but were unable to determine if he had been killed by incoming fire or by a self-inflicted bullet wound to the head.[38]

30. Ibid.
31. "Many poor people who lived in or were passing through Thai Nguyen more or less spontaneously offered their services to the leaders of the revolt" (AOM, 7F51, Rapport confidentiel 26-R.C., August 24, 1918, 8).
32. AOM AF, 7F51, Notes sommaires sur la rébellion de Thai Nguyen, December 31, 1917, 3.
33. Tran Huy Lieu, *Loan Thai Nguyen*, 14. An identical account of the division of rebel forces can be found in the interrogation transcript of Nguyen Van Nhieu.
34. Tran Huy Lieu, *Loan Thai Nguyen*, 15.
35. Ibid.
36. AOM, 7F51, Notes sommaires sur la répression de la rébellion de Thai Nguyen, December 18, 1917, 8.
37. According to Tran Huy Lieu, over 100 colonial troops and 50 rebels were killed in the assault on Thai Nguyen. Tran Huy Lieu, *Cach Mang Can Dai Viet Nam III* [Vietnam's Modern Revolution, vol. 3] (Hanoi, 1955), 111.
38. Ibid.

Sergeant Can's fate was even more mysterious. Fleeing westward from Thai Nguyen, Can led a handful of rebels on a desperate trek up the rugged slope of Tam Dao Mountain. Although his men were weakened by defections, disease, and attacks by colonial troops, they eventually eluded their pursuers and dispersed into the mountainous terrain. On January 7, 1918, a civilian calling himself Si appeared at a French military outpost and announced that he had accompanied Can to Tam Dao but had turned against the sergeant and murdered him. Si led French officers to a shallow, unmarked grave where they found Can's bullet-ridden corpse. A rifle, pipe, and opium tray had been arranged neatly on its chest. Officially, the French did not challenge Si's version of events. However, the careful way in which Can's corpse had been equipped for the afterlife—opium and all—raised questions about Si's account of the murder. Hence, rumors circulated that Can had been wounded during an earlier skirmish with French troops and had ordered his comrades, Si included, to kill and bury him so that he might avoid falling into French hands. According to this theory, Si had concocted the story of his betrayal and murder of Can in the hopes of garnering a pardon from the French for his role in the rebellion.[39]

Mopping-up campaigns stretched on until March 1918, at which time most rebels had been shot or recaptured.[40] A strategy to induce rebels to surrender by arresting their close relatives proved strikingly effective.[41] In early December and late May, hastily convened criminal commissions bypassed the "unreliable" Tonkin court system and sentenced recaptured rebels to capital punishment or to lengthy terms of hard labor on Poulo Condore.[42] An investigation was launched to determine the culpability of

39. The controversy over Can's death is discussed in Tran Huy Lieu, *Loan Thai Nguyen*, 51–56. For a French account of Si's story and the discovery of Can's body, see AOM, 7F51, L'Administrateur de 2ème classe Poulin, Résident de France à Thai-Nguyen, à M. le Résident supérieur au Tonkin à Hanoi, February 2, 1918.

40. See AOM, 7F51, Notes sommaires sur la répression de la rébellion de Thai Nguyen, April 4, 1918, and Tran Huy Lieu, *Loan Thai Nguyen*, 19–50, for detailed accounts of the suppression of the rebellion.

41. Tran Huy Lieu, *Loan Thai Nguyen*, 58.

42. Governor-General Sarraut explained that he did not want the rebels tried before either the Cour criminelle or the Cour d'assises because each court "functioned with the assistance of indigenous jurors" and he feared that in this extraordinary case, "the spirit of race might predominate over the spirit of justice" (AOM, 7F51, Rapport 37-S, December 9, 1918, 13). A complete account of the sentences passed down by the Criminal Commission can be found in the file Commission criminelle 1917–1918, Affaire de Thai Nguyen, December 18, 1918, in AOM, SLOTFOM, III, carton 55.

Resident Darles, but no action was taken against him. In a final report on the rebellion, Inspector Nicolas of the Tonkin Garde indigène acknowledged that, given its destructiveness and duration, the "affair of Thai Nguyen has been a drama without precedent in the history of Tonkin."[43]

INTERPRETING THE REBELLION

In its aftermath, conflicting interpretations emerged over the rebellion's origins and character. Conceived in terms of two mutually exclusive categories, the debate considered whether the rebellion ought to be identified as a "political" or merely a "local" event.[44] To qualify as "political," according to a particular colonial logic, a rebellion needed to manifest a determination to overthrow the colonial state, cultivate popular support, and exhibit evidence of clandestine preparation prior to the actual event. On the other hand, a "local" rebellion was everything a "political" rebellion was not. It did not challenge state authority or pursue mass backing, and it tended to take the form of a spontaneous and inarticulate explosion of violence rather than a deliberate execution of a well-prepared plot.

Because many of the protagonists in the debate over the rebellion had a personal stake in its outcome, self-interest tended to dictate who adopted which position. Hence, Darles clung to the conviction that the rebellion was a revolutionary movement because it drew attention away from his own role in the creation of the oppressive "local" context that had provoked it.[45] On the other hand, Commandant Nicolas of the Garde indigène downplayed the movement's "political" character because such an emphasis called into question the loyalty and trustworthiness of his beloved corps.[46] For captured rebels facing trial and certain punishment, to admit to "political" sympathies guaranteed a harsher penalty. As a result, they

---

43. AOM, 7F51, Rapport confidentiel 26-R.C., August 24, 1918, 6.

44. Ibid., 2. The narrow, instrumental character of the debate recalls Ranajit Guha's description of colonial discourse on anticolonial insurgency. See Ranajit Guha, "The Prose of Counter-Insurgency," in *Selected Subaltern Studies*, ed. id. and Gayatri Chakravorty Spivak (New York, 1988), 44–86.

45. AOM, 7F51, Rapport confidentiel 26-R.C., August 24, 1918.

46. "The Thai Nguyen rebellion was an isolated event, which is not to be seen as a reflection of the spirit of our corps. The motives were of a purely local order. They constituted a desire for collective vengeance against residential authority and had nothing in common with a revolutionary rising." AOM, 7F51, Procès-verbal de la réunion du 21 octobre 1917 à laquelle les comités des deux amicales du corps étaient conviés et ont pris part, 5.

tended to point to dissatisfaction with "local" conditions or to tactics of intimidation on the part of rebel leaders to explain their own participation.[47]

Slightly broader considerations shaped the efforts of high-level colonial officials to interpret the rebellion. On the one hand, it was important to counteract fears gaining ground in France that an inept and oppressive colonial administration was inflaming anti-French passions in Indochina. Officials also desired to dampen a pervasive anxiety about "native treachery" that had overcome the French colonial population during World War I.[48] Immediately after the rebellion, such concerns prompted Governor-General Sarraut to enforce draconian controls over Tonkin's typically unfettered French-language press.[49] They also served as a strong inducement for Sarraut to craft an explanation of the rebellion that emphasized its "local" character:

> I have examined all the reports pertaining to the affair of Thai Nguyen. When read together, they show very clearly that the events that bloodied the province at the end of last summer exhibited no political character, that they were purely local, and that they derived exclusively from the passionate discontent of the Garde indigène, who had been subjected to a heavy, severe, and often brutal regime of service.[50]

Ignoring the participation of hundreds of prisoners and civilians, the governor-general reassuringly underlined the rebellion's narrow base by pointing to its alleged failure to attract any popular support. "The appeals of the rebels found no echo in the countryside," he boasted disingenuously. "Two months after the event, the indifferent calm of the people and their cooperation with our troops confirms the absence of a widespread political conspiracy."[51]

The problem with Sarraut's exclusively "local" interpretation was the conspicuous accumulation of a mass of countervailing evidence—the leading role of political activists, the active support of hundreds of civilians, the patriotic flags and armbands that rebels displayed, and the proclamations they released demanding the annihilation of the colonial state. To finesse

---

47. AOM, 7F51, Rapport confidentiel 26-R.C., August 24, 1918, 14–35.

48. See Milton Osborne, "The Faithful Few: The Politics of Collaboration in Cochinchina in the 1920s," in *Aspects of Vietnamese History*, ed. Walter Vella (Honolulu, 1973), 163–67, on the "acute sense of fear" that dominated Indochina's French population during World War I.

49. AOM, 7F51, Télégramme officiel 3305, September 3, 1917.

50. AOM, 7F51, Rapport confidentiel 1060, July 12, 1918.

51. AOM, 7F51, Rapport confidentiel 37-S, September 12, 1918, 20–21.

the contradiction, Sarraut devised an intricate narrative of the rebellion in which political prisoners had hijacked what was, from its inception, a "local" movement led by disgruntled *gardes*. He explained that in his initial haste to make sense of the uprising, he had jumped to the mistaken conclusion that it was a "political" act:

> The words of the proclamation, the call for a general insurrection against the French, the dispersion of appeals throughout the province, and other tangible acts suggested a movement whose general character was clearly political. This is undeniable. But we must not be mesmerized by the hypothesis of a revolutionary plot and only consider as secondary the local causes that, based on information we have gathered, truly explain the rebellion.[52]

He continued that once a thorough investigation had been concluded, he was able to confirm that the rebellion's "political" trappings were no more than a superficial covering for its "local" roots: "The conclusion reached today is that the rebellion was born in the provincial corps of the Garde indigène and was the exclusive work of a small number of native officers who were determined to take vengeance for the humiliations and brutalities to which they had been subjected."[53]

In regard to political prisoners, Sarraut dismissed them as little more than tardy opportunists, who had been, in his words, "excluded completely from the preparation of the plot."[54] "It is also true that other participants in the rebellion, such as De Tham's old partisans and Luong Ngoc Quyen, immediately upon being released from the penitentiary used the circumstances to transform a revolt of mutinous soldiers against their immediate superiors into a kind of anti-French insurrection."[55] Here, the governor-general's language underlined the existence of cross-purposes and tensions between different groups taking part in the rebellion. By arguing that political prisoners attempted to appropriate an initiative conceived and launched by *gardes*, Sarraut downplayed the extent to which the rebellion might be conceived as a genuinely collaborative endeavor.

It was not enough, however, to assert that apolitical *gardes* rather than revolutionary activists had spearheaded the rebellion. To further neutralize the perception that the rebellion was only the most recent manifestation of a much broader subterranean culture of native conspiracy, Sarraut at-

---

52. Ibid., 7.
53. Ibid., 19–20.
54. Ibid., 21.
55. Ibid., 2.

tempted to soft-pedal the degree of premeditation on the part of the *gardes.* "The arbitrary acts of violence perpetrated by Resident Darles," he insisted, "provoked in the *gardes* an exasperated and fatigued state that brought them to their final excess."[56] Hence, the rebellion was figured as a desperate and impulsive act of self-preservation and not as the result of a calculated seditious intrigue.

Another dilemma for Sarraut concerned the depiction of Resident Darles. To be sure, the villainy of the resident was an essential catalytic element in a persuasive "local" interpretation. However, Sarraut also desired to protect the reputations of his officials and to nullify an impression that colonial administrators were brutal, incompetent, and widely hated by their native subjects. Hence, while acknowledging that Darles's behavior served as the primary impetus for the revolt, Sarraut also praised the resident's "ensemble of positive qualities"—"his decisiveness, productivity, initiative, and cultivated spirit."[57] The trick here was to place blame squarely on the resident's shoulders while simultaneously laying the groundwork for his eventual exoneration.

Riddled with inconsistencies and selective attention to evidence, Sarraut's version of events reveals more about the political imperatives of the colonial state than about the causes and character of the Thai Nguyen rebellion. While the chronic mistreatment of the provincial Garde was certainly part of the story, Sarraut's account failed adequately to examine the role and motivations of the several hundred civilians, political prisoners, and common criminals who had participated in the revolt. More important, Sarraut did not explore the conditions that led to the unprecedented dynamics of cooperation between the rebellion's remarkably heterogeneous forces.

Sarraut's account of the rebellion contrasts significantly with a reconstruction of the event put forward by Tran Huy Lieu, the Democratic Republic of Vietnam's preeminent historian during the 1950s and 1960s. Lieu began to research the rebellion during the 1930s, a transitional period in his revolutionary career, during which he gradually transferred his allegiance from the Vietnamese Nationalist Party (Viet Nam Quoc Dan Dang) to the Indochinese Communist Party (Dang Cong San Dong Duong).[58]

56. Ibid., 19.
57. Ibid., 24.
58. Lieu recounts this period of his life in his memoir "Phan Dau De Tro Nen Mot Dang Vien Cong San" [Striving to Become a Communist Party Member], in *Hoi Ky Tran Huy Lieu,* ed. Pham Nhu Thom (Hanoi, 1991), 155–66.

Imprisoned on the Poulo Condore Archipelago for political activity in 1930, Lieu developed an interest in the rebellion after he came into contact with Thai Nguyen rebels who had been recaptured and deported to the islands in 1918. In 1932, he was able to interview rebels during several months that they were confined together in a makeshift work camp on Hon Cau Island.[59] Following his release in 1934, Lieu produced the first historical account of the rebellion by combining the stories he had recorded on Hon Cau with data culled from French sources.[60] He submitted his manuscript to Hanoi's Bao Ngoc publishing house, which released the book the following year under the title *Loan Thai Nguyen* (The Thai Nguyen Uprising).[61]

As with Sarraut's account, Lieu's monograph was shaped by the political environment in which it was produced. To avoid drawing the attention of colonial censors, Lieu changed the name of the monograph from *Thai Nguyen Khoi Nghia* (The Righteous Rebellion of Thai Nguyen) to the more pejorative *Loan Thai Nguyen*, a title suggesting a riot or an illegitimate rising.[62] He also criticized the rebellion's more violent excesses, such as the murder of the prison warden's Vietnamese wife. He reported that when questioned about the crime before the Criminal Commission, Sergeant Gia admitted that he had killed the woman because "she had mothered Western [*tay*] not Annamese offspring." "Based on this statement," Lieu remarked, "we can see that Sergeant Gia's spirit was xenophobic, narrow, and extremely severe."[63]

The threat of censorship may also have prompted Lieu to erase from his account all evidence of Darles's abuses. The resident's leading role in Sarraut's version of events contrasts sharply with the bit part he plays in the

---

59. "On Hon Cau, in addition to ICP and VNQDD members, there were convicts arrested for participation in the Yen The and Thai Nguyen rebellions, in Nam Ky secret societies and in the Man uprising at Yen Bai. Through the stories they told, I began to gather material for *The Righteous Rising at Thai Nguyen* and *The Righteous Rising at Yen The.*" Tran Huy Lieu, "Tren Dao Hon Cau" [On Hon Cau Island], in *Hoi Ky Tran Huy Lieu*, ed. Pham Nhu Thom (Hanoi, 1991), 112.

60. Lieu relied extensively on the account of the rebellion provided by Alfred Echinard. In the introduction to the monograph, Lieu wrote: "We must thank all who helped us gather the documents used here, especially the resident of Thai Nguyen, M. Alfred Echinard, the author of *Histoire politique et militaire de la province de Thai-Nguyen.*" Tran Huy Lieu, *Loan Thai Nguyen*, 3.

61. Tran Huy Lieu, *Mat Tran Dan Chu Dong Duong* [The Popular Front in Indochina] (Hanoi, 1960), 7.

62. Lieu also used the pseudonym Hai Khanh rather than his real name.

63. Tran Huy Lieu, *Loan Thai Nguyen*, 12.

drama as outlined by Lieu; this is the most striking difference between the two accounts. Not only does Darles make few appearances in Lieu's narrative, but he is depicted as a marginal leader of the military forces that suppressed the rebellion, rather than as the individual most responsible for triggering its outbreak.

Whatever its reason, the absence of Darles from *Loan Thai Nguyen* eliminated the crucial motivational factor in the governor-general's interpretation. In its place, Lieu highlighted the profound anticolonial inclinations of Sergeant Can, a catalytic ingredient that the governor-general had been careful to dismiss. In a section of the text entitled the "The Background and Aspirations of Trinh Van Can," Lieu traced the sergeant's decision to rebel to the psychological effects of his participation in numerous failed campaigns against De Tham's bandit gang.[64] Based on the interviews he had conducted, Lieu concluded that Can's defiant proclivities had been stimulated and sustained during the many months he had spent tracking the crafty outlaw through the "high mountains and wild forests" (*nui cao rung ram*) of Tonkin.[65] Many rebels believed that the untamed wildness of De Tham's home territory had penetrated Can's mind, nurturing his rebellious impulses.

However, the fact that De Tham's exploits had inspired Can to rebel did not suggest to Lieu that the decision was "impulsive or eccentric." Rather, "it had brewed in Can's mind for a long time," and he was finally prompted to act only after becoming convinced "that the French had grown preoccupied with the war in Europe."[66] Lieu underlined the extent of Can's secret maneuvering by describing three alternate plots the sergeant had devised and aborted (for various reasons) prior to the actual event.[67] Here was an interpretation that colonial officials were especially loathe to reach. It was one thing to depict the sergeant striking out impetuously against brutal superiors but quite another to view him as a deliberate, calculating agent, biding his time, and plotting clandestinely against the colonial project as a whole.

Whether or not Sergeant Can played the singularly decisive role attributed to him in *Loan Thai Nguyen*, Lieu's account of the sergeant stands as a classic early example of a mode of nationalist hagiography that came to

64. Ibid., 6–9.
65. Ibid., 7.
66. Ibid.
67. Ibid., 8–9.

dominate Vietnamese historiography in the postcolonial era. Such ha-
giographies endeavored to establish virtuous pedigrees for putatively nationalist figures by linking them through blood or sentiment to various patriotic forbears. In this vein, Lieu not only underlined Can's admiration for
De Tham but reported rumors that the sergeant's father had participated in
the Save-the-King movement in the 1880s.[68] Within the distinctive idiom
of Vietnamese nationalist historiography, Can's relationship with his father and veneration of De Tham represented sufficient motivation for rebellion.

In addition, Lieu attributed to Can a handful of qualities that were to become emblematic of modern Vietnamese notions of revolutionary political
charisma. Most famously embodied in the image cultivated by Ho Chi
Minh, this cluster of attributes comprised three basic ingredients: strategic
prowess, compassion, and informality. Calling him "very courageous,"
Lieu portrayed Can as "a natural commander."[69] "In the heat of battle," he
reported, "when bullets fell like rain, Can stood out in that he never ducked
his head but remained erect and poised."[70] According to Lieu, the sergeant
cut a dashing figure in the field, with "binoculars in one hand, a loaded pistol in the other, and a loaded rifle slung over his shoulder." Although a
skilled fighter, Can was said to have disliked violence. In contrast to some
of his followers, who "killed people like frogs," Can was "merciful" and
"kind-hearted." Even during the desperate flight from Thai Nguyen, Can
prevented his men from "looting villages" and "raping local women."[71]
But perhaps the sergeant's most memorable and endearing quality was his
utter lack of pretension. Whereas his fellow noncoms were seen as "vain
and status conscience," the rebels "praised Can's good manners and even
temper."[72] As evidence of his "fondness for simplicity," they pointed to the
fact that he dressed plainly in the traditional garb worn by ethnic Tho villagers, an outfit that included coconut-shell sandals, an ordinary walking
stick, and a brown conical hat.[73]

In short, Lieu's account of the rebellion substituted an embryonic nationalist theory about the central role played by great Vietnamese men in

68. Ibid., 60.
69. Ibid.
70. Ibid., 61.
71. Ibid.
72. Ibid., 14.
73. Ibid., 60.

the nation's history for Sarraut's effort to portray the event as an aberrant episode provoked by an unusually brutal official. Despite their different agendas, the interpretive strategies Lieu and Sarraut adopted both stressed the catalytic role of a single individual. To absolve the colonial state of responsibility for the rebellion, Sarraut needed to focus attention on Darles's provocative behavior and character. Similarly, Lieu's desire to promote a Vietnamese tradition of national heroism induced him to depict the rebellion as little more than the work of Sergeant Can.

Explanations that highlight the decisive role of individuals overlook what was really unique about the Thai Nguyen rebellion: the way in which a remarkably diverse assortment of colonial subjects transcended regional, social, and political divisions to launch a coordinated action against the colonial state. It is the degree and intensity of the vertical and horizontal alliances within the rebel forces that most distinguish the Thai Nguyen rebellion from virtually all the anticolonial movements that preceded it. To understand the conditions that facilitated these alliances requires a consideration of the rebellion's institutional context rather than a narrow assessment of individual responsibility. No factor shaped the rebellion as fundamentally as the Thai Nguyen Penitentiary, an institution that brought hardened criminals, casual lawbreakers, political activists, and soldiers from far-flung regions of Indochina into prolonged proximity to one another, invested them with a set of common grievances, and prompted them to launch a violent attack against the colonial state.

LAWLESSNESS IN THE MIDDLE REGION

Both the Thai Nguyen Penitentiary and the rebellion to which it gave rise were shaped by the historical geography of crime and punishment in Tonkin. For the French, Tonkin comprised three distinct zones: the Delta region, the high region, and the middle region, which included Thai Nguyen.[74] Lying between the densely populated, wealth-producing Delta and the lightly peopled, mountainous high region, the middle region

---

74. The Delta region included the provinces of Kien An, Thai Binh, Nam Dinh, Ninh Binh, Hai Duong, Hung Yen, Bac Ninh, Vinh Yen, Son Tay, and Ha Dong; the high region included Lang Son, Bac Kan, Lao Kay, Lai Chau, and Son La; and the middle region included Quang Yen, Bac Giang, Tuyen Quang, Yen Bay, Phu Tho, Hoa Binh and Thai Nguyen. See Henri Brenier, *Essai d'atlas statistique de l'Indochine française: Indochine physique—population—administration—finances—agriculture—commerce—industrie* (Hanoi, 1914), 197.

served as a base and safe haven for all manner of predatory criminals. Also important was the middle region's vulnerability to frontier banditry, a condition that derived from its proximity to the poorly policed Sino-Vietnamese border.[75] For centuries, fugitives, smugglers, brigands, and military deserters from both sides of the border had sought refuge in the densely forested mountain ranges and upland plateaus that run northwest to southeast across the middle region. In addition to being situated only eighty miles south of the border, Thai Nguyen is ringed by four separate mountain ranges: Tam Dao to the west, Bac Son to the east, Dong Trieu to the southeast, and the limestone massifs of Kun Hi and Coc Xo to the north. Thai Nguyen's geographical position at the center of this lightly populated upland loop made it a prime target for the various outlaw groups who found shelter there.

Like its mountainous topography, the fact that much of the middle region was peopled by ethnic minority communities whose villages had never been fully integrated into the Vietnamese state heightened the potential for disorder.[76] During the precolonial era, friction among the Man (Dzao), Tho (Tay), and Nung, and between these upland groups and the lowland Vietnamese, frequently exploded into violence.[77] The opium-producing Man were especially prone to clash with dynastic officials, drug smugglers, and criminal bands.[78] Tension between the Man and the colonial state grew equally fierce after the latter tried to monopolize Tonkin's opium trade.[79] French hostility was compounded by reports that Man villages routinely harbored smugglers and assisted fugitives from justice.[80] In 1914, an uprising by 1,500 Man at Yen Bay was brutally put down by the

75. Kim Munholland, "The French Army and the Imperial Frontier in Tonkin, 1885–1897," in *Proceedings of Third Annual Meeting of the French Colonial Historical Society* (Montréal, 1977); John Laffey, "Land, Labor and Law in Colonial Tonkin Before 1914," *Historical Reflections* 2, no. 2 (Winter 1975): 223–63.

76. Non-Vietnamese ethnic minorities were estimated at roughly a quarter of the population of the middle region in 1901 (Echinard, *Histoire politique et militaire*, 130).

77. A revolt led by ethnic minority communities against Minh Mang's pants-wearing edict in the 1840s is mentioned, for example (ibid., 101).

78. John T. McAlister Jr. "Mountain Minorities and the Viet Minh: A Key to the Indochina War," in *Southeast Asian Tribes, Minorities, and Nations*, ed. Peter Kunstadter (Princeton, N.J., 1967), 820–21.

79. Chantal Descours-Gatin, *Quand l'opium finançait la colonisation en Indochine: L'Elaboration de la régie générale de l'opium, 1860 à 1914* (Paris, 1992), 142.

80. Patrice Morlat, *La Repression coloniale au Vietnam, 1908–1940* (Paris, 1990), 32.

French.[81] Sixty-seven participants were executed and several hundred jailed.[82]

Political disorder in China also contributed to lawlessness in the middle region. The suppression of the Taiping Rebellion in China in 1864 triggered a massive influx of uprooted rebels across the border, where they reconstituted themselves into heavily armed bands and terrorized local communities.[83] Vietnamese efforts to check the power of marauding Taiping bands suffered from the fact that Emperor Gia Long had relocated the royal court and imperial army several hundred kilometers to the south at the start of the nineteenth century. During the 1860s and 1870s, an eclectic band of ex-Taipings and local outlaws, known as the Yellow Flags, terrorized the middle region. In 1862 and again in 1874, they seized the citadel at Thai Nguyen and carried off its arsenal, treasury, and grain reserves.[84]

Between the suppression of the Taipings and the Republican Revolution, the decentralization of power in China compounded the anarchic conditions along the border. Following the Ch'ing defeat in the Sino-French War of 1885, political power in China's southern provinces devolved into the hands of local gentry.[85] Dissatisfied with the concessions the Manchu court had conceded to the French, southern Chinese provincial leaders refused to respect the border with Tonkin and actively aided members of the Vietnamese resistance. Between 1885 and 1895, anticolonial activists such as Ton That Thuyet and Nguyen Quang Bich received arms, supplies, and protection from local Chinese military leaders.[86] In 1907, Sun Yat-sen and his followers initiated a series of uprisings in Yunnan, Kwantung, and Kwangsi, generating additional French anxiety about the security of the border.[87]

Although the French chided Chinese officials for their inability or unwillingness to suppress criminal activity along the frontier, attempts to police the region had historically done more harm than good. When local

81. Marr, *Vietnamese Anticolonialism*, 230.
82. Ibid.
83. Echinard, *Histoire politique et militaire*, 56–58.
84. Ibid.
85. Lloyd E. Eastman, *Throne and Mandarins: China's Search for a Policy During the Sino-French Controversy, 1880–1885* (Cambridge, Mass., 1967).
86. Ella S. Laffey, "The Tonkin Frontier: The View from China, 1885–1914," in *Proceedings of Third Annual Meeting of the French Colonial Historical Society* (Montréal, 1977), 114.
87. Kim Munholland, "The French Response to the Vietnamese Nationalist Movement, 1905–1914," *Journal of Modern History* 47 (December 1975): 668.

Chinese militias forayed across the border in pursuit of fleeing bandits, they frequently came into conflict with Vietnamese troops and rarely missed an opportunity to pillage local communities.[88] Moreover, to maintain a semblance of order with a minimum of expenditure, Chinese and Vietnamese officials entered into collusive agreements with powerful bandit chiefs. Through such arrangements, leaders of large bands agreed to suppress the activities of smaller rivals and, in return, were allowed to pursue their predatory activities free from official harassment. Prior to the colonial conquest, the most powerful bandit to ally with local officials in Tonkin was Luu Vinh Phuc, whose notorious Black Flags led vigorous campaigns against French incursions in the 1870s and 1880s.[89]

The relationship between bandits and the state continued uninterrupted when the French assumed power in Tonkin in 1884. Unable to control the banditry that had long plagued the northern frontier, French officials in 1890 struck a deal with Luong Tam Ky, the charismatic Sino-Vietnamese leader of the Yellow Flags.[90] In return for his assistance tracking down smaller bands and enforcing civil order, the French ceded to Ky military, administrative, and tax-collecting powers over four districts in western Thai Nguyen.[91] For the following thirty-five years, Ky and his men received arms, ammunition, and a generous monthly salary from the colonial budget. One official described the colonial state's arrangement with Ky in the following manner: "It has been admitted publicly that we have ceded these regions (Cho Chu, Dai Tu, Pho Yen, and Binh Xuyen) to the pirate chief who is master there, collecting taxes, rendering justice, and carrying out all acts of administration. Moreover, the Protectorate pays him a regular tribute in order to purchase his friendship or, at least, his neutrality."[92]

In his memoirs, Phan Boi Chau offered a similar assessment of Luong Tam Ky's powerful position in the province and of his cozy alliance with the colonial state:

88. Echinard, *Histoire politique et militaire,* 56–58.
89. See Tran Huy Lieu, "Danh Gia Luu Vinh Phuc Va Quan Co-Den Trong Cuoc Khang Phap O Viet Nam" [Assessing Luu Vinh Phuc and the Black Flags in the Anti-French Resistance in Vietnam], *Nghien Cuu Lich Su* 42 (1961): 21–25, 38; Ella S. Laffey, "French Adventurers and Chinese Bandits in Tonkin: The Garnier Affair in Its Local Context," *Journal of Southeast Asian Studies* 6, no. 1 (1975): 8–51; and Henry McAleavy, *Black Flags in Vietnam: The Story of a Chinese Intervention* (New York, 1968).
90. Echinard, *Histoire politique et militaire,* 79–83.
91. Ibid.
92. Ibid., 106.

As I approached the border of Thai Nguyen Province, I realized that Luong Tam Ky held sway over the region. All the mountainous provinces were full of merciless bandits and notorious outlaws who frightened everyone passing through. . . . I heard that Luong Tam Ky had previously been the man who created so much disturbance in the Cao Bang and Thai Nguyen areas. The French, when they had just taken over Bac Ky, regarded Cao Bang and Thai Nguyen as dangerous and inaccessible, and, wishing to win over Luong Tam Ky, they appointed him to be their plenipotentiary for pacification. For this reason the local people called him the "grand official."[93]

Even with the assistance of the "grand official," the French failed to stem the tide of lawlessness in northern Tonkin. Luong Tam Ky's continued interests in the illicit opium trade and his tolerance of the extensive gun-running, smuggling, and extortion rackets run by his underlings were only part of the problem.[94] Despite French support, it took Ky twenty years to catch and kill De Tham, who had long spearheaded an array of criminal and politically subversive activities from his base in Yen The.[95] De Tham was of special concern to the French because of the moral and material support he provided to urban anticolonial activists, including Phan Boi Chau.[96] After Ky's men finally assassinated De Tham in 1912, the bandit's children and followers continued to attract support, collude with political dissidents, and extract rents from the rural population well into the 1920s. And because Yen The was situated only five kilometers from its southeastern border, Thai Nguyen remained a major zone for the activities of De Tham's partisans.

Given the significance of banditry in the history of the middle region, it is no surprise that the penal population of Thai Nguyen was dominated by gang members and rural brigands. At the outbreak of the rebellion, 82 convicts, out of a prison population of 211, were serving terms for "pillage" or "piracy," the criminal categories most commonly applied to acts of rural

93. Phan Boi Chau, *Phan Boi Chau Nien Bieu*, 129.

94. According to one historian, the French alliance with Luong Tam Ky "gave banditry a new lease on life from 1893 to 1895. The money so liberally given went into purchasing firearms superior to those used by the French Army itself" (Virginia Thompson, *French Indochina* [New York, 1968], 75).

95. Tran Huy Lieu, Nguyen Cong Binh, Van Tao, *Tai Lieu Tham Khao Lich Su Cach Mang Can Dai Viet Nam: Khoi Nghia Yen The, Khoi Nghia Cua Cac Dan Toc Mien Nui Tap II* [Documentary History of the Modern Vietnamese Revolution: The Uprisings of Yen The and of the Mountain People] (Hanoi, 1958), 5–62.

96. Borrowing Eric Hobsbawn's phrase, one historian has described De Tham as a "primitive rebel" (John Laffey, "Land, Labor and Law," 251).

banditry.[97] As a result of Luong Tam Ky's sluggish but ultimately effective campaign against De Tham during the decade prior to 1912, dozens of the bandit chief's partisans had been confined at Thai Nguyen, and at least twenty remained there in 1917.[98] Among these were Duong Van Ngoc (Bep Ngoc), Tran Van Ba (Ba Quoc), Nguyen Van Ba (Do Ba), Nguyen Van Lam (Ba Lam), and Nguyen Van Chi (Ba Chi), the latter playing an especially significant role in the rebellion.[99]

The proximity of Thai Nguyen to De Tham's home base shaped the rebellion in other ways as well. There are grounds to believe that rebel leaders fully expected De Tham's followers to rally to their aid. In an early statement he made to the jittery rebel troops, Luong Ngoc Quyen announced that reinforcements from De Tham's band would soon be on their way.[100] And in the written proclamation he likely produced hours after leaving his prison cell, Quyen linked the rebellion's objectives to those of De Tham and Phan Dinh Phung: "heroic men" who "despite small numbers, had nevertheless been able to retain control over remote corners of the country."[101] The rebels also sent a letter requesting the assistance of Luong Tam Ky, an overture that failed but that reflected a palpable belief that the region's distinctive legacy of warlordism and banditry could be mobilized in service to the rebellion.[102]

As with the lengthy tradition of frontier banditry, the more recent development of capitalist enterprise in the middle region also influenced the composition of the Thai Nguyen rebellion. During the first decade of the

97. AOM, 7F51, Liste des prisonniers évadés du pénitencier de Thai-Nguyen à la date du 30 août 1917.

98. On March 8, 1910, the Bac Giang *Tribunal mixte* had convicted twenty of De Tham's followers imprisoned at Thai Nguyen of piracy.

99. Tran Huy Lieu, *Loan Thai Nguyen*, 7–8; Dao Trinh Nhat, *Luong Ngoc Quyen va Cuoc Khoi Nghia Thai Nguyen*, 70; and the interrogation transcript of Nguyen Van Nhieu, 77, all highlight Ba Chi's pivotal role.

100. "It was announced that all the provinces of the Delta were in rebel hands and that reinforcements, including Chinese troops and partisans of De Tham would be arriving soon" (AOM, 7F51, Rapport confidentiel 26-R.C., August 24, 1918, interrogation of Nguyen Van Kinh).

101. Dao Trinh Nhat, *Luong Ngoc Quyen va Cuoc Khoi Nghia Thai Nguyen*, 78.

102. AOM, 7F51, Rapport confidentiel 26-R.C., August 24, 1918, interrogation of Hoang Van Dau. The Quang Phuc Hoi had reason to believe that Luong Tam Ky might be recruited to their side. During a meeting with Phan Boi Chau in 1907, Ky reportedly held out the possibility of an alliance once Phan's military forces had been sufficiently strengthened: "As soon as your army can defeat the Japanese," he told Phan, "then I will support you with two provinces of Thai Nguyen and Bac Kan" (*Nguc Trung Thu*, in *Reflections from Captivity*, ed. Marr, 41).

twentieth century, French capital began to exploit northern Tonkin's abundant mineral wealth.[103] The mining industry was centered at Hon Gai along the northeastern coast, but French companies discovered rich coal fields and zinc deposits in Thai Nguyen.[104] When attracting a local labor force proved difficult, companies recruited thousands of coolies from southern China and from the overpopulated provinces of Nam Dinh, Ninh Binh, and Thai Binh in the southeastern corner of the Red River Delta.[105] The number of workers employed in the Tonkin mines increased from 4,000 in 1904 to 9,000 in 1908 and 12,000 in 1913.[106] However, rather than forming settled communities, immigrant mine workers remained a transient and erratic labor force well into the 1930s: "The mines and coal yards of upper Tonkin and Laos have at their disposal only a floating labor supply which is basically unstable; mines and coal yards in other parts of Tonkin have been unable to settle more than a small minority of the labor force in permanent homes, in spite of considerable effort over a period of fifty years," Charles Robequain observed.[107]

By 1910, colonial officials noted uncommonly high rates of crime around mining areas.[108] Not only were the mines magnets for illegal opium traffic, prostitution, and gambling enterprises, but bandits found mining communities easy prey for extortion and looting. De Tham's gang became particularly adept at intercepting convoys transporting mine wages.[109] The growth in criminal activity was further linked to the tendency for coolies to drift from mining into banditry at the expiration of their contracts.[110]

It is difficult to determine the precise number of ex-mine workers among the provincial penal population, but the high proportion of Thai Nguyen prisoners who originated from the three provinces in which most miners were recruited is significant. In 1917, over twice as many prisoners

103. Martin Murray, *The Development of Capitalism in Colonial Indochina, 1870–1940* (Berkeley and Los Angeles, 1990), 315–74.

104. Coal was mined at Phan Me and zinc was mined at Lang Hit, Thanh Moi, Cho Dien, and Yen Linh. Charles Robequain, *The Economic Development of French Indo-China* (1939; trans., London, 1944), 257–58.

105. Virginia Thompson, *Labor Problems in Southeast Asia* (New Haven, Conn., 1947), 181.

106. Robequain, *L'Evolution économique de l'Indochine française* (1939), trans. as *Economic Development of French Indo-China*, 251.

107. Ibid., 77.

108. Echinard, *Histoire politique et militaire*, 185.

109. Ibid.

110. Ibid., 189.

(36) came from Nam Dinh, the undisputed center for the recruitment of mine workers, than from any other province.[111] If we include prisoners from important secondary recruitment zones in Thai Binh and Ninh Binh, roughly one-quarter of all prisoners at the penitentiary came from areas that provided the bulk of the labor force for Thai Nguyen's mining industry.[112] That most of these prisoners were sentenced for theft, assault, or homicide rather than pillage or piracy supports the hypothesis that many may have been arrested for the kind of criminal activity endemic in Tonkin's unstable mining communities.[113]

The development of mining in the middle region also sheds light on the nature of civilian support for the rebellion. Eyewitness accounts confirm that following the seizure of the town, roughly three hundred townspeople voluntarily joined with rebel forces. According to colonial investigators, civilian support derived primarily from the most destitute inhabitants of the province: petty criminals, river boatmen, and day laborers. Alfred Echinard remarked that "there are always in Thai Nguyen an important number of rogues in a state of semi-permanent vagabondage who come from the Delta. It seems that many such men joined the rebellion."[114] On the other hand, according to the interrogation transcript of the rebel Nguyen Van Nhieu, the first civilians to join the rebels were "approximately fifty coolies drawn from the coal and zinc mines."[115] Given that miners tended to work intermittently and to periodically drift back and forth between legal and illegal economic pursuits, it is likely that Echinard's "vagabonds" and Nhieu's "miners" were one and the same group.

While maintaining a tight surveillance over bandits and itinerant mineworkers, French security forces in Tonkin also paid close attention to the growth of secret societies. This development was linked to the rise of revolutionary forces in China prior to 1911 and to the efforts of republican and anti-Manchu activists to win support among overseas Chinese. "To seduce the Chinese miners of Cho Chu, bandits passing through the village showed photographs of Sun Yat-sen and the [Chinese] republican flag," Echinard noted. "They say that they are not pirates but that they have

111. AOM, 7F51, Liste des prisonniers évadés du pénitencier de Thai-Nguyen à la date du 30 août 1917.

112. Ibid.

113. It is instructive that roughly 70 percent of those prisoners convicted for homicide, as opposed to crimes related to bandit activity, originated from Nam Dinh, Thai Binh, and Ninh Binh.

114. Echinard, *Histoire politique et militaire*, 207.

115. Nguyen Van Nhieu, 79.

been sent by the 'Sun King' to learn about the country and that soon their king will send thousands of soldiers to help reconquer the empire of Annam."[116]

The character of Thai Nguyen's prison population was also shaped by the growth of the Restoration Society after its foundation by Phan Boi Chau in Canton in 1912. With Sun Yat-sen's Tongmenghui as a model, the Restoration Society raised funds, recruited members, and launched attacks against colonial targets from its base in southern China. Although Phan failed to secure support from Sun's nationalist government, the Restoration Society gained a loosely coordinated momentum on its own. In 1912, it founded the Restoration Army (Quang Phuc Quan) and formed a cabinet in exile. Later that year, it began printing its own currency and designed a national flag that displayed five red stars against a yellow backdrop. In 1913, its supporters carried out high-profile bombings in Thai Binh and at a luxury hotel in Hanoi. During 1914 and 1915, it attacked a handful of military outposts along the Sino-Tonkinese border.[117] And in 1916, scholar-gentry affiliated with Restoration Society elements in Annam instigated the Duy Tan plot, a failed attempt to spirit the teenage Vietnamese emperor out of the capital as the first step to a renewed monarchist insurgency.[118] Restoration Society activities during the early 1910s led to thousands of arrests and convictions, as well as to numerous executions and life sentences. For the bombing of the Hanoi Hotel alone, over 250 suspects were arrested and sixty imprisoned or executed.[119]

French repression of Restoration Society activities triggered an influx of political activists into the colonial prison system. Although the classification of convicts as political offenders was a notoriously slippery business, there are grounds to support the claim of the historian Vu Van Tinh that in August 1917 Thai Nguyen held forty-one political prisoners, nearly a fifth

---

116. Echinard, *Histoire politique et militaire*, 188. Echinard recorded another episode the previous year: "At the beginning of 1912, secret meetings were held under the pretext of the foundation of a new cult called Tam-Thanh and one edition of a seditious book was found at the village of Dong-Du. . . . The book was produced by a society called the Thieu Hoi, whose chief, known as Do Nam or Ba Chu, circulates continuously throughout the province" (ibid., 185).

117. See Marr, *Vietnamese Anticolonialism*, 216–21. Attacks were launched at Luc Nam on October 20, 1914; at Nho Quan, Phu Tho, and Mong Cay on January 7, 1915; at Cao Bang on March 13, 1915; and at Lao Cay on August 8, 1915. See Tran Huy Lieu, *Lich Su Tam Muoi Nam Chong Phap*, 176–77.

118. For an account of the Duy Tan Plot, see Hanh Son, *Cu Tran Cao Van* (Paris, 1952).

119. Marr, *Vietnamese Anticolonialism*, 220.

of its inmates.[120] A review of prison ledgers for August 1917 reveals that twenty prisoners had been convicted for offenses that were commonly classified as political crimes: conspiracy, espionage, rebellion, and crimes against state security.[121] Another dozen prisoners, all from the central Vietnamese province of Quang Ngai, had been subjected to the unambiguously political sentence of deportation.[122] Prison records confirm that several of the Quang Ngai deportees—Binh Thieu and Chau Dich, for example—had been arrested for their role in the Duy Tan plot.[123] In addition to Luong Ngoc Quyen, considered the most dangerous political criminal in the prison, Thai Nguyen also held Nguyen Gia Cau (Hoi Xuan), Vu Si Lap (Vu Chi), and Ba Con (Ba Nho), each of whom had played an important role in Restoration Society operations during the preceding decade.[124]

For some observers, the Thai Nguyen rebellion was little more than one instance of the expansion of Restoration Society operations in Tonkin after 1912. Such was the analysis of Resident Darles who argued forcefully before the Criminal Commission that the rebellion had been "clearly provoked by revolutionaries." Although this interpretation conveniently drew attention away from the resident's own responsibility for creating the institutional conditions that had instigated the rebellion, Darles's argument rested on evidence that could not be ignored. After all, Luong Ngoc Quyen, the first participant in the Eastern Travel Movement and a founding member of the Restoration Society, had played a crucial role in the rebellion. Not only did the rebels hoist the five-star red and yellow Restoration Society flag in the barracks but the banners they hung around town proclaimed: "Annamese Armies Will Reclaim the Country" (Nam Binh Phuc Quoc). Eyewitness accounts reported that some armbands worn by rebel combatants displayed the Chinese characters: "The Thai Nguyen Restoration Army" (Thai Nguyen Quang Phuc Quan).[125]

Anxiety about the growth of banditry, secret society activity, and Restoration Society operations in Tonkin grew more urgent during the

---

120. Vu Van Tinh, "Mot Chut Tai Lieu Ve Luong Ngoc Quyen," 61.

121. AOM, 7F51, Liste des prisonniers évadés du pénitencier de Thai-Nguyen à la date du 30 août 1917.

122. Ibid.

123. In June 1916, Tonkin received twenty-eight prisoners sentenced to hard labor for their participation in the Duy Tan Plot (AOM, 7F51, Rapport confidentiel 811c, September 25, 1917).

124. AOM, 7F51, Liste des prisonniers évadés du pénitencier de Thai-Nguyen à la date du 30 août 1917.

125. AOM, 7F51, Rapport confidentiel 26-R.C., August 24, 1918.

highly charged atmosphere of World War I. By the end of 1914, French newspapers frequently complained that the security of the colony had been compromised by the return of thousands of troops from Indochina to France.[126] Rumors about the activities of conspiratorial German agents circulated widely. A series of secret society attacks in the Mekong Delta, in particular the Phan Xich Long uprisings of 1913 and 1916, seemed to confirm a creeping premonition of impending doom.[127] In addition, heavy-handed efforts by the colonial state to recruit Indochinese soldiers and laborers for the war effort in Europe provoked an uncoordinated but widespread movement of resistance to forced conscription.[128] As a result, Indochina's prisons were glutted with draft evaders, and the penal system came to be seen as deeply involved in the unpopular conscription policy. Between 1914 and 1917, angry crowds in at least thirteen provinces marched on provincial prisons to demand the release of deserters and draft resisters.[129]

As we have seen, it was their extreme heterogeneity that distinguished the Thai Nguyen rebels from other early anticolonial movements. They amounted to a cross-section of French Indochinese society that was virtually without precedent: smugglers and secret society members, murderers and mineworkers, draft dodgers and day laborers, bandits and boatmen, urban anticolonial activists and rural vagabonds, along with 130 members of the Garde indigène. That the rebels came from over thirty provinces, including a significant number from central Vietnam, added a striking regional spread as well. To understand how such a diverse assortment of colonial subjects could band together into a single movement, we need to look at the structure and functioning of the Thai Nguyen Penitentiary.

THE THAI NGUYEN PENITENTIARY: THE CRADLE OF REVOLT

The eclectic composition of rebel forces at Thai Nguyen reflected the peculiar dynamics of colonial prison administration. As a penitentiary located in Indochina's northern tier, Thai Nguyen was authorized to receive political offenders and hardened criminals from every corner of Annam and

126. Osborne, "Faithful Few," 164–66.
127. Ralph Smith, "The Development of Opposition to French Rule in Southern Vietnam, 1880–1940," *Past and Present* 54 (December 1972): 107–11.
128. Hue-Tam Ho Tai, *Radicalism and the Origins of the Vietnamese Revolution* (Cambridge, Mass., 1992), 31.
129. Georges Coulet, *Les Sociétés secrets en terre d'Annam* (Saigon, 1926), 342–45.

Tonkin. Moreover, as at every other prison in Indochina, officials at Thai Nguyen disregarded regulations concerning the segregation of different categories of prisoners. Such neglect derived from the usual factors— administrative torpor, architectural shortcomings, and budgetary constraints— but was compounded by the unusual circumstance that the institution at Thai Nguyen functioned simultaneously as a provincial prison and a penitentiary.

During the first decade of civilian administration at Thai Nguyen (1892–1902), officials used a variety of makeshift buildings to incarcerate local lawbreakers. In 1903, a regular provincial prison was built, consisting of a rectangular cluster of buildings ringed by a circular path, patrolled day and night. The path was surrounded by a three-meter-high, rectangular concrete wall, in which jagged shards of glass were embedded. Additional security was provided by two towers at opposite corners of the wall.[130] The prison's main residential quarter was a single communal dormitory, unfurnished except for an elevated concrete platform along three of the inside walls. During the night, prisoners lay side by side atop the platform, their feet manacled to iron rings set into the concrete. Other than those confined for short periods to a handful of punitive cells, all prisoners were housed together in the main dormitory.[131]

Following an upsurge of anticolonial activity in 1908, the resident superior ordered the expansion of the prison at Thai Nguyen so that "it might receive, from each of the provinces in the protectorate, those convicts serving the longest and most severe sentences."[132] Thai Nguyen was chosen as the site for a more important penal institution because of its "remoteness from French population centers" and because the province badly needed penal labor for roadwork and construction projects.[133] Completing the renovation in 1910, the resident announced that "the newly refurbished institution is no longer, properly speaking, a provincial prison, but a penitentiary that contains, at present, around 200 prisoners chosen from among the most dangerous of the Delta and the object, on my part, of a completely special surveillance."[134]

130. Echinard, *Histoire politique et militaire*, 197.
131. TTLT, Fonds de la Résidence supérieure au Tonkin, 79540, L'Administrateur Résident de France à Thai-Nguyen à M. le Résident supérieur à Hanoi, January 31, 1906.
132. Ibid., 79552, March 7, 1908.
133. Ibid.
134. Ibid., 10929, September 6, 1910.

Although the prison at Thai Nguyen had been upgraded administratively to the status of a penitentiary, fiscal constraints prevented officials from constructing a new provincial prison as a replacement. As a result, Thai Nguyen continued to perform the functions of a provincial prison.[135] This meant that short-term convicts sentenced by local tribunals were incarcerated together with long-term convicts sent to Thai Nguyen from distant provinces. Despite some concern generated by its unorthodox, hybrid character, officials still considered Thai Nguyen the most important and secure island in Tonkin's penal archipelago:

> The establishment of Ile de la Table is in ruins. As for the so-called penitentiaries of Son La and Lai Chau, they are in reality simple prisons, not set up to receive and effectively guard dangerous convicts. With regard to Cao Bang, its proximity to the frontier presents serious inconveniences from the point of view of ever-possible escapes. There remains, therefore, the penitentiary of Thai Nguyen, being well situated in the heart of the middle region and providing secure buildings that truly serve their intended purpose. The administration has a strong interest in developing this establishment and endowing it with a special personnel and making it a *true*, strongly organized penitentiary that will serve in Tonkin as Poulo Condore does in Cochin China.[136]

Consistent with its mission, Thai Nguyen became a dumping ground for the most dangerous prisoners in Tonkin.[137] In August 1917, offenders sentenced to from ten to twenty-five years' forced labor were in the majority among the prison's population.[138] However, because the site continued to function as a provincial prison, it also held a large number of short-term convicts and defendants awaiting trial. At the outbreak of the rebellion, almost fifty prisoners, all from Thai Nguyen, were serving terms of simple imprisonment—a sentence that typically entailed a briefer (six months to a year) and milder punitive regime.[139] Most had been sentenced for misdemeanors: petty theft, small-time banditry, battery, or crimes against public order such as vagrancy or chronic drunkenness.

135. Ibid., 81781, Rapports sur le fonctionnement des établissements penitenciaires du Tonkin et du Service de l'identité, 1913–16.
136. Ibid.
137. These hardened prisoners originated from every province in Tonkin, with especially large contingents from Nam Dinh (36), Hung Yen (18), Hai Duong (17), Bac Giang (16), Ha Nam (15), Kien An (13), and Thai Nguyen (13). See AOM, 7F51, Liste des prisonniers évadés du pénitencier de Thai Nguyen à la date du 30 août 1917.
138. Ibid. Eleven were serving life sentences.
139. Ibid.

Although the prison's population grew increasingly complex, its basic layout remained a single communal dormitory—now enlarged—and a handful of individual cells. Indeed, the renovation of 1908 only augmented the scale of the prison without introducing any significant structural changes. In 1910, provincial officials acknowledged the dangers posed by the prison's crude configuration but took no measures to rectify the situation. According to a prophetic report on prison conditions from that year:

> A single modification that seems needed at Thai Nguyen concerns the interior setup of the prison for the purpose of stopping an ever-possible revolt. The prisoners are for the most part confined in a large building with no separation, such that in case of a concerted plot during which the detainees escape their bars, we would have to act against a mass of 175 individuals.[140]

Colonial officials were less inclined to highlight flaws in institutional design and inadequate mechanisms of segregation to help explain the catastrophic violence that erupted at Thai Nguyen in 1917. After all, such an analysis underscored their own failure to undertake the necessary modifications, particularly since they had recognized the problem years before. It is not surprising, therefore, that officials in France (rather than their colonial counterparts) took the lead in linking the outbreak of the rebellion with the distinctive procedures and conditions of colonial incarceration. In the Chamber of Deputies in Paris, M. Lacave Laplagne declared that the very structure of the prison had allowed "the political prisoners at Thai Nguyen to rise up, win over the Garde indigène and their comrade prisoners, seize the provincial capital and massacre the French population." Taking a shot at Governor-General Sarraut, Lacave Laplagne charged that "the rebellion resulted from the considerable imprudence of the colonial administration, which allows, in the prisons of the colony, a dangerous melange of political prisoners and common criminals."[141]

In a defensive response, Sarraut acknowledged the problem but said that, rather than being intrinsic to the Indochinese prison system, it had arisen because World War I prevented the deportation of political prisoners to Guyana and New Caledonia.[142] Moreover, the Phan Xich Long rebel-

---

140. TTLT, Fonds de la Résidence supérieure au Tonkin, 10929, Résident de Thai Nguyen au Résident superieur au Tonkin, September 6, 1910.

141. AOM, 7F51, Le Gouverneur général de L'Indochine à M. le Ministre des colonies, 37-S, December 9, 1918.

142. Ibid., 30.

lions of 1913 and 1916 and the simultaneous growth of Restoration Society activity had created a shortage of prison space throughout Indochina. In other words, Sarraut assured the deputy that the problem was a temporary one, and that in the future, a greater effort would be made to enforce what he called "a rigorous penal triage" so as to "prevent local movements in the penitentiary from taking on a political character."[143]

In contrast to Sarraut's efforts at political damage control, others in the colony admitted that the problem had more durable roots. During his interrogation, Hoang Dinh Deu (*sic*), a *garde*, maintained that "at Thai Nguyen, those condemned to light sentences (six months to a year) were *always* subjected to the same regime as those condemned to heavy sentences (ten to twenty years)."[144] And in a letter to the *procureur général*, the resident superior explained that "although the decree of October 26, 1914, states that prisons are to be arranged in such a way so as to permit certain *prescribed and imperative separations* among diverse categories of prisoners, the locales have *always* been poorly or insufficiently set up for this purpose."[145]

The resident's comments suggest that colonial officials were not unaware of the security problems generated by a situation in which a broad mix of prisoners were incarcerated together in communal wards. Indeed, the fact that prison officials kept Luong Ngoc Quyen confined in one of the penitentiary's solitary cells confirms that they did take measures to isolate especially dangerous convicts from the general population. Hence, the problem was less a conceptual blind spot than a structural shortcoming. With no more than a handful of individual cells, the prison lacked the fundamental capability to segregate a large number of political activists such as the several dozen who ended up at Thai Nguyen in 1917.

FORCED LABOR AND MORTALITY

As in most colonial prisons, all inmates at Thai Nguyen were subjected to the same brutal regime of forced labor, irrespective of sentence or juridical status. Since the turn of the century, prison labor from Thai Nguyen had been used to build roads linking the expanding mining and agricultural

143. Ibid., 31.
144. AOM, 7F51, Rapport confidentiel 26-R.C., August 24, 1918, interrogation of Hoang Dinh Deu, 54 (emphasis added).
145. TTLT, Fonds de la Résidence supérieure au Tonkin, 02571, November 22, 1917 (emphasis added).

concessions in the middle region to the urban centers in the Delta.[146] Although the colonial state could also requisition civilian labor, a series of reforms introduced between 1897 and 1916 restricted the state's ability to mobilize villagers for hazardous projects in remote areas.[147] Convict labor thus came to be used for the most dangerous work. According to a report in 1917: "In Thai Nguyen, those condemned to forced labor are used for the most laborious tasks of colonization, including road building and the construction of public works. This regime is particularly harsh in such an unsanitary country."[148]

Again, in violation of penal regulations, prison officials forced political criminals and convicts serving terms of simple imprisonment to work alongside prisoners sentenced to forced labor.[149] When questioned by investigators, officials maintained that pressing demands for manpower had prompted them to include all categories of prisoners in the forced labor regime.

Not only were convicts forced to undertake the most dangerous and onerous work but labor discipline was enforced through a host of brutal and coercive measures. According to an investigation of penal labor practices launched in 1918, a high proportion of disciplinary beatings at Thai Nguyen occurred at work sites. The investigation reported that "between 1915 and 1917 numerous beatings (often with truncheons) and other assorted acts of violence were directed at prisoners while they worked at quarries and road construction sites."[150] By way of illustration, it detailed a number of incidents from December 1916, including one in which *gardes*

146. "The extent of the road penetration into the mountains of the north is easily explained. Northern Tonkin is not only the gateway to that part of China of which the Red River is the natural outlet, but it has considerable economic riches of its own; it is comparatively populous, especially along the Chinese frontier in the group of fertile valleys running from Cao Bang to Lang Son. It is also a mining region. Transportation is relatively easy through deep valleys which encircle the granite and limestone mountains, in a setting that is varied and unusually picturesque." Robequain, *Economic Development of French Indo-China*, 101.

147. For a discussion of the forced labor system, see Murray, *Development of Capitalism in Colonial Indochina*, 80–85. For a treatment of labor reforms, see Jean Goudal, "Labour Problems in Indochina," *Asiatic Review* 24 (July 1928): 362–63.

148. AOM, 7F51, Rapport 960-c, December 18, 1917, 4.

149. "It is unfortunate that prisoners at Thai Nguyen condemned to light sentences are subjected to the same regime and treatment as those condemned to heavy sentences" (ibid., Rapport confidentiel 26-R.C., August 24, 1918, 54).

150. Ibid., Rapport confidentiel 2547, December 24, 1918, 8.

punished a prisoner for unsatisfactory work on a road detail by fracturing his wrists with a shovel.[151]

No doubt, the rigors of forced labor contributed to the penitentiary's extraordinarily high number of annual deaths. As prison records from this era do not report the number of convicts who entered and exited an institution during any given period, it is impossible to calculate mortality as a percentage of the total number of prisoners. However, a medical report comparing the absolute number of deaths in colonial penal institutions between 1908 and 1912 shows that more prisoners died at Thai Nguyen (332) during this five-year period than at any other prison in Indochina with the exception of Nam Dinh (355).[152] Another document reveals that 192 prisoners died at Thai Nguyen in 1915, 165 in 1916, and, remarkably, 162 in the first half of 1917.[153] A separate study undertaken by officers of the Garde indigène claimed that 670 prisoners ("roughly 250 per year") died at Thai Nguyen between January 1, 1915, and August 31, 1917.[154]

Just as all prisoners shared in the unnerving experience of forced labor, the penitentiary's murderous death toll must have encouraged a powerful sense of their shared predicament among different categories of prisoners. "The revolt was greeted with joy by all those who had long sentences," one prisoner, Dang Van Lu, explained to an interrogator, "because we believed that if we did not rebel, we would never leave the penitentiary alive."[155] His sentiments were echoed by Inspector Nicolas who concluded bluntly that the penitentiary was "less like a place of detention and more like a crematorium."[156]

RESIDENT DARLES AND THE GARDE INDIGÈNE

As with the prison uprisings at Poulo Condore in 1918 and Lai Chau in 1927, the capricious despotism of a local French official contributed to the outbreak of the Thai Nguyen rebellion. The official in this case, Provincial Resident

151. Ibid., 7.
152. AOM, Fonds du Gouvernement général, carton 274, 4251, Mortalité dans les prisons du Tonkin de 1908 à 1912.
153. AOM, 7F51, Rapport confidentiel 26-R.C.: 30.
154. Ibid., Procès-verbal de la réunion du 21 octobre à laquelle les comités des deux amicales du corps étaient conviés et ont pris part.
155. Ibid., Rapport confidentiel 26-R.C., August 24, 1918, interrogation of Dang Van Lu.
156. Ibid., Procès-verbal de la réunion du 21 octobre 1917 à laquelle les comités des deux amicales du corps étaient conviés et ont pris part.

Darles, had served in the province for three years, during which time he earned the appellation "the butcher of Thai Nguyen."[157] The hatred rebels harbored for Darles is reflected in the dissatisfaction that they expressed upon learning that the resident was not among the early casualties of the revolt. According to one eyewitness account: "When the severed head of M. Martini was brought before Sergeant Can at the Thai Nguyen Market, he expressed disappointment because it was not the head of M. Darles."[158]

In 1925, Nguyen Ai Quoc (the future Ho Chi Minh) provided a vivid description of the notorious resident in "French Colonialism on Trial," his well-known polemical indictment of France's colonial empire. "This M. Darles is a valuable administrator," he began sardonically:

> He acquired his political science in the Latin Quarter, where he was a restaurant keeper. Through the wishes of an influential politician, M. Darles, then without resources and loaded with debts, was made an administrator in Indochina. Comfortably installed at the head of a province of several thousand inhabitants, and invested with limitless power, he was mayor, judge, bailiff, and bailiff's man; in a word, he held all the offices. Justice, taxes, property, lives and property of the natives, rights of officials, elections of mayors and canton chiefs, that is to say, the fate of a whole province was entrusted to the hands of a former innkeeper. As he had not been able to get rich by extracting money from his clients in Paris, he got his own back in Tonkin by having Annamese arbitrarily arrested, imprisoned, and condemned to extort money from them.[159]

Ho's portrayal of Darles as a petty provincial autocrat is confirmed by official sources. According to a report prepared in the wake of the rebellion, Darles's unchecked power over prison administration derived from his successful efforts to wrest control of the Garde indigène from military officers:

> In a number of provinces, the residents have a more or less marked tendency to substitute themselves for the brigade commandant and to seize all power and authority over his men and his European subordi-

---

157. Hue-Tam Ho Tai, *Radicalism and the Origins of the Vietnamese Revolution*, 23.

158. AOM, 7F51, unlabeled report signed by Inspector Nicolas, November 2, 1917.

159. "French Colonialism on Trial" was written in French and published in Paris in 1925. A Vietnamese translation was not completed until 1960. This excerpt is taken from a subsection entitled "The Administrators," in Ho Chi Minh, *Selected Works* (Hanoi, 1978), 195.

nates. The commandant then becomes a sort of "corporal," incapable of supporting his personnel and garnering from them the appropriate respect and discipline. The Thai Nguyen brigade, in terms of the annihilation of the commandant, was a model of this genre.[160]

Indeed, Inspector Noel, the officer in charge of the Garde indigène at Thai Nguyen and the rebellion's first casualty, frequently complained that the constant meddling of the resident had undercut his authority. "I am nothing. I do nothing," Noel was quoted as saying. "The resident does everything. He names noncommissioned officers, orders promotions, demotions, and punishments, and corresponds with other posts without my knowledge."[161] Several eyewitnesses concurred that the almost complete usurpation of his authority by the resident had demoralized Noel.

Moreover, Darles was sadistically brutal toward prisoners, *gardes,* and native civil servants. The extent of his cruelty was documented in an enquiry commissioned by the governor-general in November 1917.[162] Beginning with his first posting at Son Tay Province in 1908, it chronicled twenty-seven documented instances of beatings, canings, whippings, and assorted "acts of violence" perpetrated by the resident. The following excerpt from the enquiry conveys something of its flavor:

1. Son Tay, 1909—breaking the fingers of the interpreter Pham Van Thanh with a metal rod. Witness: M. Tragan, administrator of the Civil Service.
2. Phuc Yen, 1911—acts of violence and beating of his domestic servants. Witness: M. Martin.
3. Phuc Yen, 1912—violent beating of a soldier engaged in guarding prisoners. Witness: M. Pierrard, inspector of the Garde indigène, M. Bonin, *garde principal.*
4. Phuc Yen, 1912—beating of Cai Boi, official of the Public Works Department. Witness: M. Marnac: engineer of Public Works Department.
5. Phuc Yen, 1912—bloody caning of a canton chief while he supervised coolies along a road work site. Witness: M. Marnac.
6. Phuc Yen, 1912—punching of an anonymous native, who was then thrown into a pond. Witness: M. Marnac.

160. AOM, 7F51, Supplément au bulletin 7, Révolte de Thai Nguyen, October 21, 1917, 5.
161. Ibid.
162. Ibid., Rapport confidentiel 2547, December 24, 1918.

7. Thai Nguyen, 1914—on the route from Dong Du to Cho-Chu, violent beating with a truncheon of an unidentified public works official. Witness: M. Herninet, administrator of the Civil Service.

8. Lang Hit, 1914—beating the soldier Hoang Van Chuc with a riding whip.

9. Thai Nguyen, 1914—grave acts of violence on three militiamen who had allowed a suspect to escape. Witness: M. Tustes, administrator, M. Bary, administrator.

In addition to the depressing litany of everyday physical abuse covered in the report, the administration gathered a number of more detailed accounts of the resident's violent behavior. Commonplace were cases in which Darles had struck *gardes* and prisoners in the face, stomach, and groin for insignificant or obscure reasons. He allegedly relished contriving creative disciplinary measures such as forcing *gardes* to carry sacks of sand and gravel while supervising *corvée* or making prisoners stand at attention or run in place for hours under the blazing afternoon sun. Among the most severe cases were an instance in which an abrupt baton blow by Darles put out the eye of a prisoner and another in which an impromptu beating shattered the collarbone of a hapless clerk.[163] According to another allegation, the resident was rumored to have raped the wife of a prominent native administrator.[164]

Perhaps the most striking conclusion demonstrated by the various investigations concerned the utterly indiscriminate nature of the resident's wrath. Just as convicts and coolies were subjected to regular thrashings, so, too, were interpreters, clerks, soldiers, and civil servants. *Gardes* frequently complained that the resident and his men treated them no better than prisoners. They charged that, like prisoners, they were continually subjected to verbal harassment, unfair punitive measures, and beatings. One reported: "I was beaten one time with three baton blows to my face because I did not understand the resident when he spoke to me in French."[165] Another stated: "The resident often punished the men for minor reasons such as smoking or speaking in the barracks after lights out."[166] And still another said: "Often the resident would arrive on a route where prisoners were

163. Ibid.
164. AOM, 751F, Rapport confidentiel 26-R.C., August 24, 1918, 49.
165. Ibid., interrogation of Dang Van Ngan.
166. Ibid., interrogation of Nguyen Van Nganh.

working and beat the files of prisoners and their *gardes* at the same time."[167] French eyewitnesses described similar episodes: "When M. Darles came to inspect the *corvée*, he typically beat the *gardes* and prisoners with a large stick if the work failed to meet his standards."[168] Within the confines of the penitentiary, this virtual democracy of abuse no doubt muddied the sense of division between the keepers and the kept.

Many *gardes* even described their military service as a form of captivity. The similarities were easy to discern, given the parallels of forced recruitment, physical brutalization, constant surveillance, and communal living. Moreover, *gardes* described being coerced to remain in the corps despite the termination of their initial contracts. "Some of us were especially discontented," explained Nguyen Van Hoa, "because we have been forced to continue in the service over six months after the expiration of our five-year terms."[169] Tran Van Phuong related a similar story: "I have been forcibly retained for over two months despite the end of my term and have received no back pay."[170]

Lines blurred further when French officials disciplined *gardes* by forcing them to work alongside convicts on forced labor details. Even more remarkable, *gardes* were sometimes punished with short periods of confinement within the penitentiary.[171] "Certain *gardes* actually serve punishments for disciplinary infractions within the prison," one report explained. "In such cases, *gardes* are placed in the company of the very prisoners whom they had previously been assigned to guard on *corvée* duty."[172] Appalled at the practice, one investigator argued that it laid at the root of the rebellion. "This in my opinion, sheds light on the real cause of the Thai Nguyen Revolt. Treated like prisoners, sometimes worse, the Garde indigène freed the convicts, who became willing auxiliaries. Maltreated by

---

167. Ibid., interrogation of Nguyen Van Thang. See also interrogation of Nguyen Van La: "*Gardes* and prisoners had equal complaints against the resident, who periodically beat them both."

168. Ibid., interrogation of Monsieur Viala, Conducteur des travaux publics.

169. Ibid., interrogation of Nguyen Van Hoa.

170. Ibid., interrogation of Tran Van Phuong.

171. This policy was not unique to Thai Nguyen. Inspector Roux observed it at Lai Chau as well. See AOM, 7F54, Révolte des prisonniers de Lai Chau, Roux Report: "Among the prisoners at Lai Chau are six *gardes* imprisoned for negligence in having allowed prisoners to escape. These *gardes* are therefore interned with the very prisoners they had been guarding. I have seen the same thing in Cao Bang."

172. AOM, 7F51, Supplément au bulletin 7, Révolte de Thai Nguyen le 30 août 1917, October 21, 1917, 7.

the resident, they united with the prisoners in their hatred for the administration that was supposed to protect them."[173]

CONCLUSION

If the record suggests that the structure and functioning of the Thai Nguyen Penitentiary fostered the unlikely alliances that animated the Thai Nguyen rebellion, it sheds less light on the internal dynamics of these alliances. Although there is no doubt that both Sergeant Can and Luong Ngoc Quyen assumed important roles within the rebel leadership, it is less clear who conceived and proposed the plot initially. Nor do we know much about the rebellion's interior chain of command or the way in which *gardes*, political prisoners, and criminals interacted and worked together. It is also difficult to determine the extent to which various rebel groups were in on the plot beforehand, or whether they were persuaded or intimidated into taking part only after the fact.

What little evidence exists, however, does indicate that the internal workings of the rebellion were marked by a broadly inclusive process of decision-making. Regardless of who made the initial overtures, there are numerous reports that Quyen and Can conferred extensively with each other through a clandestine communication network prior to the outbreak of the rebellion.[174] According to Tran Huy Lieu's reconstruction: "Because Can's colleagues guarded the solitary confinement cells, Quyen and Can could correspond regularly with each other. Quyen encouraged Can, and Can believed deeply that Quyen's military training would be of invaluable assistance in meeting the difficulties that lay ahead. He found Quyen's presence reassuring, and it prompted him to act."[175] Thus, although Lieu's account tends to highlight the preeminent role of Can in the conception and execution of the rebellion, it nonetheless portrays the sergeant's relationship with Quyen as a mutually beneficial partnership.

Once set in motion, the rebellion was apparently guided by a deliberative body made up of a diverse mix of *gardes*, political prisoners, and criminals. We have already seen how Quyen clashed over tactics with bandits connected to De Tham during a remarkably open meeting following the seizure of the town. The dispersion of power within the rebellion suggested

---

173. Ibid., 11.
174. Dao Trinh Nhat, *Luong Ngoc Quyen va Cuoc Khoi Nghia Thai Nguyen*, 55–66; Tran Huy Lieu, *Loan Thai Nguyen*, 8.
175. Tran Huy Lieu, *Loan Thai Nguyen*. 8.

by this episode is further apparent in the interrogation transcript of Nguyen Van Nhieu: "Among the prisoners, Luong Ngoc Quyen and Quan Hai Tau commanded the most respect. During the five days we held Thai Nguyen, these two often sat with the four sergeants doing paperwork. In addition, the prisoners Ba Chi and Do Ba, as well as jailer Co, consulted regularly with the sergeants."[176] Hence, according to Nhieu's account, two political prisoners, two bandits, four sergeants, and a civilian jailer all played some role in decision-making.

The significance of the collaborative alliances underpinning the Thai Nguyen rebellion goes beyond the fact that leaders of disparate social, regional, and occupational groups worked expediently together toward a common goal. There are grounds to believe that the rebellion gave rise to remarkable efforts by members of the urban anticolonial political elite to comprehend and empathize with the particular predicaments faced by the subaltern rural social orders. Communal imaginings of this nature had few precedents in Vietnamese political history and recall the "horizontal comradeship"—transcending class and regional origins—characteristic of modern political nationalism.[177] The clearest evidence of this development can be seen in the proclamation that the rebels released the morning after they secured the town.

Although it is unsigned, the proclamation is assumed to have been authored by a political prisoner, most likely Luong Ngoc Quyen or Tu Hoi Xuan. There is strong evidence to support this supposition. Many eyewitnesses, including Nguyen Van Nhieu, reported that Quyen and other political convicts were seen at work—writing—in the company of the sergeants soon after their release from prison.[178] Moreover, the proclamation employed a host of protonationalist imagery characteristic of the Restoration Society rhetoric of the era. It opened with a reference to a popular myth of national origins in which the Vietnamese nation "descended from a race of dragons and fairies." This was followed by an appeal to the beauty and abundance of the Vietnamese landscape, saying, "our land is fertile, several thousand miles long and covered with magnificent mountains." Next came allusions to the mythical Hong Bang kings and to 4,000 years of Vietnamese history, prominent nationalist fictions designed to place the antiquity of the Vietnamese nation on an equal footing with that of China. Finally, the

176. Nguyen Van Nhieu, 77.
177. Benedict Anderson, *Imagined Communities: Reflections on the Origins and Spread of Nationalism* (London, 1991), 7.
178. Nguyen Van Nhieu, 7.

passage listed a historical chronology of independent Vietnamese dynasties and alluded to a "national" tradition of resistance to foreign rule.[179]

Given its rhetorical and thematic sophistication, it is unlikely that the proclamation was composed by anyone other than a well-educated political prisoner. However, in its closing passage, the text abruptly adopts the collective voice of the provincial Garde indigène, thereby conveying the impression that it was written by an ordinary soldier:

> We, men of arms, have never stopped thinking of the misfortune of our people, even while living peacefully in our village. So many times we have had the intention to raise our swords and behead our enemies, but have instead been reduced to impotence because we failed to seize the proper moment. This is why we resigned ourselves to enter into the Garde indigène. Our mouths shut, we mingle with the robust men of our country for more than ten years, always nourishing in our hearts an unyielding hatred. Until now, we have not yet had sufficient force or outside support and have limited ourselves to a constant longing.[180]

Given the likelihood that the proclamation was, in fact, written by a political prisoner, it is instructive to reflect upon the remarkable act of imagination needed to produce it. In effect, an urbane, classically educated political dissident had to imagine and try to articulate convincingly the mental world of an uneducated provincial soldier. Little in the overtly elitist Sino-Vietnamese political tradition anticipated this sort of sociopolitical transference. Rather, the production of the proclamation foreshadowed the growth of a national style of communal imagining in which a modern political identity was determined by shared history, ethnicity, and race rather than native place or social station.[181]

179. Dao Trinh Nhat, *Luong Ngoc Quyen va Cuoc Khoi Nghia Thai Nguyen,* 77–78:

Our country Nam-Viet, which is now part of Indochina, was formerly named Tuong Quan. We descend from a race of dragons and fairies. Our land is fertile, several thousand miles in length and covered with magnificent mountains. Since the Hong Bang kings, our country has lived for more than 4,000 years, ruled successively by Kinh Duong Vuong, Dinh Tien Hoang, Le Dai Hanh, and the Ly, Tran, later Le, and Nguyen dynasties. Our ancestors expended much energy, intelligence, and many human lives in order to maintain possession of this land which they have bequeathed to us.

180. Ibid.

181. By the early 1930s, nationalist and communist activists had developed elaborate methods to transcend their own class and regional divisions by pursuing strategies to penetrate, comprehend, and represent the collective consciousness of segments of a national underclass. Such was the objective of the ICP's proletarian-

Although the Thai Nguyen rebellion has heretofore occupied a marginal place in the history of the Vietnamese revolution, the multifarious social and regional composition of its participants and its origins within the institutional matrix of the colonial state provide grounds for considering it among the earliest manifestations of modern anticolonial nationalism. It is possible that its neglect by historians derives from the fact that the institution in which it was contrived was a prison rather than a school or a political party. However, as this chapter has suggested, and as chapter 7 argues further, prisons were as significant as schools and political parties in creating a "consciousness of connectedness." This was especially the case with Tran Huy Lieu's political generation.

In his memoirs, Lieu explains how a sentence he had served on Poulo Condore placed him in close proximity with communist prisoners, thus facilitating his own conversion to the ICP.[182] Indeed, Lieu's contact with the Thai Nguyen rebels and his subsequent effort to promote them as national heroes was facilitated by the fact that Poulo Condore, like the Thai Nguyen Penitentiary, indiscriminately grouped diverse categories of prisoners together in communal settings, forging powerful bonds among them and investing them with common grievances, identities, and political commitments.

---

ization (*vo san hoa*) campaign, in which revolutionaries infiltrated the rural and urban proletariat in order to experience the rhythms of their lives. See Gareth Porter, "Proletariat and Peasantry in Early Vietnamese Communism," *Asian Thought and Society* 1, no. 3 (December 1976): 333–46.

182. Tran Huy Lieu, "Phan Dau De Tro Nen Mot Dang Vien Cong San" [Striving to Become a Communist Party Member], in *Hoi Ky Tran Huy Lieu*, ed. Pham Nhu Thom (Hanoi, 1991).

7 Prison Cells and Party Cells

*The Indochinese Communist Party
in Prison, 1930–1936*

The early 1930s marked a turning point in the history of the Indochinese prison. An upsurge of anticolonial activity at the start of the decade triggered a flood of communists, nationalists, secret-society members, and radicalized workers and peasants into the prison system. In addition to exacerbating a host of existing administrative problems, this influx of politicized prisoners transformed the nature of inmate opposition to the prison regime. In place of the everyday forms of resistance and sporadic outbursts of violence that inmates had initiated in the past, jailed activists formed mutual aid networks, organized political indoctrination campaigns, printed clandestine prison newspapers, and orchestrated protest demonstrations. For the first time, prisoners planned and carried out acts of resistance as part of long-term strategies to undermine the authority of the colonial state rather than as preludes to escape attempts or efforts to disrupt temporarily the functioning of the institutions in which they were held. In another unprecedented development, inmates held in different prisons coordinated resistance efforts with one another and with allies on the outside. For French officials, these changes signified the transformation of the prison system from a nagging administrative problem into a poisonous wellspring of deliberate anticolonial activism.

Although a broad array of political and common-law inmates participated in the prisoner resistance movements of the 1930s, the most elaborate and sustained efforts were carried out by members of the Indochinese Communist Party. Between 1930 and 1936, the ICP conducted extensive political work in prison—rebuilding its organizational apparatus, recruiting and training new members, spearheading demonstrations for improved prison conditions, and maintaining communication with communists forces still at large. To a significant extent, the reconstruction of the Party, following the devastation it suffered at the hands of French security forces at the start of the decade, occurred within the colonial prison. The ICP's re-birth in prison contrasts sharply with the fate of rival anticolonial groups that were subjected to the same devastating wave of colonial police repres-sion at the start of the 1930s. For example, the Vietnamese Nationalist Party, which boasted significant numerical strength and popular support during the late 1920s, never recovered following the destruction of its un-derground networks at the start of the decade. The fact that colonial offi-cials kept extraordinarily close tabs on the intricate structure and opera-tions of communist networks in prison but found little worth reporting about the activities of noncommunist political prisoners indicates that the origins of the ICP's ultimate ascendance over its rivals may be traced to its greater capacity to carry out political work behind bars during the period of mass imprisonment in the first half of the 1930s.

The remarkable vitality of communist political activity in prison was largely a function of the dramatic contrast between the ICP's intense fi-delity to Leninist principles of revolutionary action—centralization, hier-archy, functional specialization, secrecy, and strict internal discipline—and the characteristically disorganized, haphazard, and ill-disciplined character of the colonial prison.[1] The organizational structures and operational codes of Leninism had long appealed to Vietnamese communists, who, like the prerevolutionary Bolsheviks, worked within a political environment of il-legality and extreme persecution.[2] It is no coincidence that *Duong Kach Menh* (The Revolutionary Road), Ho Chi Minh's influential elementary text for Vietnamese professional revolutionaries, opens with a quotation from Lenin's most systematic account of the need for a clandestine politi-cal party, *What Is to Be Done?*[3] During the late 1920s, several hundred Vietnamese activists studied *Duong Kach Menh* under Ho's guidance in Siam and southern China and applied its blueprints for political mobiliza-tion, propaganda, and organization within the various institutions and

---

1. For a useful introduction to Leninism, see Neil Harding, *Leninism* (Durham, N.C., 1996).

2. Ho acknowledged the influence of Lenin on his political thinking in numer-ous essays. See, e.g., "The Path Which Lead Me to Leninism," "Lenin and the Colo-nial Peoples," "Lenin and the Peoples of the East," "Lenin and the East," and "Leninism and the Liberation of the Oppressed Peoples," in *Ho Chi Minh on Rev-olution: Selected Writings, 1920–66*, ed. Bernard Fall (New York, 1967).

3. Ho Chi Minh, *Duong Kach Menh* [The Revolutionary Road], in *Ho Chi Minh Toan Tap II, 1924–1930* [Complete Works of Ho Chi Minh, vol. 2: 1924–1930] (Hanoi, 1995), 258.

enterprises into which they were eventually infiltrated. These same organizational strategies and operational tactics proved stunningly effective when deployed behind the walls of the colonial prison and must be seen as a major reason for the ICP's unusual resilience in the repressive political environment of the 1930s.

THE GREAT CONFINEMENT

The mass incarceration of political activists during the early 1930s followed the rapid growth of new anticolonial parties during the preceding decade. In 1925, Ho Chi Minh founded the Vietnamese Revolutionary Youth League (Viet Nam Thanh Nien Kach Menh Hoi), a protocommunist organization that became the nucleus of the Indochinese Communist Party in 1930.[4] From its base in Canton, the Youth League provided practical and theoretical training to neophyte revolutionaries, who were then smuggled into Indochina to organize the masses and prepare for a general insurrection. Surveillance of the Youth League by the Sûreté (the French equivalent of the FBI) intensified in December 1928 after local activists in Saigon carried out an internal purge known as the Barbier Street Murders. In the wake of the killings, most leading members of the Cochin Chinese branch of the Youth League were arrested, put on trial, and incarcerated.[5]

Another important anticolonial group that emerged in the mid 1920s was the Nguyen An Ninh Secret Society (Hoi Kin Nguyen An Ninh).[6] Organized along the lines of a Chinese-style Heaven and Earth Society in 1926, the Nguyen An Ninh Secret Society disseminated anti-French propaganda and recruited hundreds of workers and peasants from the Saigon

4. William Duiker, "The Revolutionary Youth League: Cradle of Communism in Vietnam," *China Quarterly*, no. 53 (July–September 1972): 475–99; Huynh Kim Khanh, *Vietnamese Communism, 1925–1945* (Ithaca, N.Y., 1982), 63–88; Hue-Tam Ho Tai, *Radicalism and the Origins of the Vietnamese Revolution* (Cambridge, Mass., 1992), 176–78.

5. Among those arrested as a result of the murders were Pham Van Dong, Ton Duc Thang, Nguyen Duy Trinh, and Nguyen Kim Cuong. For brief accounts of the Barbier Street Murders, see Hue-Tam Ho Tai, *Radicalism and the Origins of the Vietnamese Revolution*, 214–17, and Ralph Smith, "The Development of Opposition to French Rule in Southern Vietnam, 1890–1940," *Past and Present* 54 (December 1972): 116.

6. The best Western-language account of the Nguyen An Ninh Secret Society is in Hue-Tam Ho Tai, *Radicalism and the Origins of the Vietnamese Revolution*, 187–94. For Vietnamese-language accounts, see Phuong Lan, *Nha Cach Mang Nguyen An Ninh* [Nguyen An Ninh, Revolutionary] (Saigon, 1970) and *Nguyen An Ninh*, ed. Nguyen An Tinh (Ho Chi Minh City, 1996).

suburbs. Its rapid growth, subversive rhetoric, and charismatic eponymous leader quickly drew the attention of the Sûreté. On September 28, 1928, a scuffle between Nguyen An Ninh and a railway patrolman precipitated a series of police sweeps against the society. In the following months, 500 members of the society were arrested and roughly 100 were tried and jailed.[7]

The rapid growth and sudden demise of the Vietnamese Nationalist Party ushered more political activists into the colonial prison system.[8] Founded by Nguyen Thai Hoc in 1927, the Nationalist Party emerged as the Youth League's greatest rival for the leadership of the anticolonial movement. While the communists devoted most of their energy to indoctrination and organization, the more quixotic Nationalists favored terrorist attacks and recruitment among native soldiers in the colonial army. The Nationalists' penchant for spectacular acts of political violence attracted many new members but made them an easy target for the police. In February 1929, a Nationalist assassination team killed Hervé Bazin, the director of the General Office of Indochinese Manpower.[9] In response, the Sûreté arrested several hundred members of the Nationalist Party, including most of the Central Committee. Seventy-three were sentenced to prison terms of between two and fifteen years.[10]

The arrests connected to the Barbier Street Murders, the Nguyen An Ninh Affair, and the assassination of Bazin anticipated the Sûreté's massive strike against communists and nationalists at the start of the 1930s. The crackdown was precipitated in February 1930 by the Yen Bay Mutiny, an aborted insurrection by colonial troops loyal to the Nationalist Party at a handful of military posts in northern Tonkin.[11] The reaction of the colonial state was swift and merciless. Thousands were arrested and air power was brought to bear against villages suspected of harboring Nationalist Party

7. Hue-Tam Ho Tai, *Radicalism and the Origins of the Vietnamese Revolution*, 193.

8. The most detailed accounts of the early history of the Nationalist Party are Hoang Van Dao, *Viet Nam Quoc-Dan Dang* (Saigon, 1970), and Nhuong Tong, *Nguyen Thai Hoc* (Saigon, 1949).

9. Truong Ngoc Phu, "Tu Vu Am Sat Bazin Nam 1929 Den Cuoc Khoi Nghia Yen Bay Nam 1930 Cua Viet Nam Quoc Dan Dang" [From the Assassination of Bazin in 1929 to the Yen Bay Rebellion in 1930 of the Vietnamese Nationalist Party], *Su Dia* [History and Geography] 9, no. 26 (January–March 1974): 98–118.

10. Hoang Van Dao, *Viet Nam Quoc-Dan Dang*, 69–70.

11. For an instructive account of the Yen Bay Mutiny, see Hy Van Luong, *Revolution in the Village: Tradition and Transformation in North Vietnam, 1925–1988* (Honolulu, 1992), 51–95.

rebels. By July 1930, at least 30 Nationalist party members had been executed and over 600 were issued prison sentences by the Tonkin Criminal
Commission.[12]

Following the Yen Bay Mutiny, police repression reached its most fever-
ish pitch in response to an explosion of political disorder at the outset of
the Depression.[13] Between mid 1930 and late 1931, hundreds of worker and
peasant demonstrations erupted throughout Tonkin, Annam, and Cochin
China. While many episodes were spontaneous expressions of popular discontent, others were spearheaded by local communist activists. According
to one scholar of the period, 129 urban strikes and 535 rural protests of
varying sizes took place between April 1930 and November 1931.[14] The
movement peaked in September 1930 when rebels dislodged the colonial
administrations from several districts in the provinces of Nghe An and Ha
Tinh and replaced them with peasant-led soviets. The colonial state responded with the full force of its power. Martial law was imposed in disorderly areas and a system of mandatory identity cards was put into place.
Foreign Legionnaires arrived in the summer of 1930 and initiated a reign
of indiscriminate terror.[15] Following May Day demonstrations in 1931, the
Legion carried out a series of massacres in which roughly 500 demonstra-
tors were killed.[16] According to one estimate, 1,300 men, women, and children died as a result of measures taken against the rebels by the colonial
state.[17]

The repression of the Depression-era rebellions entailed a huge number
of arrests and incarcerations. Precise police and juridical figures connected

12. Ibid., 155–73.

13. Ngo Vinh Long, "The Indochinese Communist Party and Peasant Rebellion
in Central Vietnam, 1930–1931," *Bulletin of Concerned Asian Scholars* 10, no. 4
(December 1978): 15–34; Hy Van Luong, "Agrarian Unrest from an Anthropological Perspective: The Case of Vietnam," *Comparative Politics* 17, no. 2 (January
1985): 53–175; William Duiker, "The Red Soviets of Nghe-Tinh: An Early Com-
munist Revolution in Vietnam," *Journal of Southeast Asian Studies* 4, no. 2
(September 1973): 186–98; Milton Osborne, "Continuity and Motivation in the
Vietnamese Revolution: New Light from the 1930s," *Pacific Affairs* 47, no. 1
(Spring 1974): 37–55; Martin Bernal, "The Nghe Tinh Soviet Movement,
1930–31," *Past and Present* 92 (August 1981): 149–68; James Scott, *The Moral
Economy of the Peasant: Rebellion and Subsistence in Southeast Asia* (New
Haven, Conn., 1976), 120–49.

14. Ngo Vinh Long, "Indochinese Communist Party and Peasant Rebellion," 17.

15. A vivid journalistic account of the role of the Foreign Legion in the repression of the rebellions may be found in Andrée Viollis, *Indochine S.O.S.*, 144–47.

16. Bernal, "Nghe Tinh Soviet Movement," 154.

17. Ibid., 161.

to the crackdown are unavailable, but annual penal statistics show an abrupt increase in the Indochinese prison population coinciding with official efforts to crush the rebellions. On December 31, 1929, immediately prior to the Yen Bay Mutiny, prisons in Annam, Tonkin, and Cochin China held 16,087 inmates.[18] One year later, the number had risen by 25 percent to 20,312. During the following two years, the inmate population grew by 3,401 and 4,384 respectively, so that by December 31, 1932, the total number of prisoners in the three territories had grown by 75 percent to 28,097.[19]

Prison statistics, however, convey only part of the story. The onset of the Depression in Indochina generated a crime wave in addition to political disorder, and it is therefore impossible to determine precisely the number incarcerated for political activity.[20] Moreover, among those jailed for participation in the rebellions, it is difficult to distinguish between professional activists who saw the rebellions as part of a broader revolutionary strategy, on the one hand, and workers and peasants who joined the movement because of local grievances, on the other. William Duiker's assertion that 400 communists were issued long-term prison sentences in 1930–1931 (in addition to 51,000 "militants" who were arrested and held for varying periods) would seem to account for most of the ICP's core membership—cadres who had undergone significant training and saw revolutionary work as a full-time vocation.[21] More difficult to interpret is Ho Chi Minh's contention, in a letter written to the Comintern in late January 1931, that "6,000 Indochinese revolutionaries are currently in prison."[22] In 1933, the

18. Gouvernement général de l'Indochine, *Annuaire statistique de l'Indochine* (Hanoi), 1929–32.

19. The years after 1932 witnessed gradual decreases in the prison population before sharp increases in the late 1930s drove the figure to a new all-time high of 29,871 in 1942.

20. Because the Depression triggered a huge crime wave, the growth of the prison population cannot be explained solely with reference to an upsurge of imprisoned political activists. "Over the past three years," wrote Governor-General Pasquier early in 1932, "the economic crisis has aggravated the misery of certain social classes and caused a sharp increase in criminality in Cochin China, Annam, and Tonkin" (AOM AF POL, 1728, Etude de l'organisation pénitentiaire de l'Indochine, Mission de M. Lacombe, December 1, 1932). See also SLOTFOM, 3d ser., carton 52, *AAPCI*, February–March 1932, for a discussion of the "general augmentation of criminality over the past two years."

21. William Duiker, *The Communist Road to Power in Vietnam* (Boulder, Colo., 1996), 42.

22. Ho Chi Minh, "Phong Trao Cach Mang O Dong Duong" [Revolutionary Movement in Indochina], in *Ho Chi Minh Toan Tap III, 1930–1945* (Hanoi: Chinh

French League for the Rights of Man placed the number of political prisoners in Indochina at around 10,000.[23] Whatever the exact figure, there is no doubt that virtually all leading members of the VNQDD, the Nguyen An Ninh Secret Society, and the ICP were killed, incarcerated, or forced into exile as a result of the repression. The damage to the Nationalist Party and the Nguyen An Ninh Secret Society was so severe that these groups ceased to function as significant independent political forces for the remainder of the colonial era. The resiliency of the ICP should not obscure the degree of devastation it suffered as well.[24] By 1932, all members of the Party Central Committee, the Northern (Bac Ky) Regional Committee, and the Southern (Nam Ky) Regional Committee were in jail, and every leader of the Central (Trung Ky) Regional Committee had been killed.[25] According to Huynh Kim Khanh: "By the end of 1932, there were few signs to indicate that the ICP was still functioning."[26]

THE SYSTEM IN CRISIS

Disturbed by the explosive growth of the Indochinese prison population, the minister of colonies ordered an investigation of the prison system in the summer of 1931.[27] Although ministerial inspections had surveyed prison conditions as part of general inquests in 1885 and 1913, the investigation of 1931 was the first to focus exclusively on the Indochinese prison. Arriving from Paris, Inspectors Le Gregam and Chastenet de Géry visited fifteen prisons over a three-month period. They toured dormitories, au-

---

Tri Quoc Gia, 1995), 59. The letter, dated January 24, 1934, is signed "Victo," one of Ho's aliases.

23. See the *Bulletin d'information* of the Committee for Amnesty in Indochina, April 1, 1933 (AOM, SLOTFOM, 3d ser., carton 43).

24. According to the Party historian Tran Van Giau, an important communist activist during the 1930s: "Ninety-nine per cent of our leaders were arrested during 1931 and 1932" (cited in Huynh Kim Khanh, *Vietnamese Communism*, 160).

25. Ibid.

26. Ibid.

27. The reports from the inspection can be found in AOM, Indochine, Affaires politiques, 1728, Rapport de la mission d'inspection des Colonies, 1932. There were three major reports: (1) Rapport fait par M. Chastenet de Géry, Inspecteur des Colonies, concernant l'organisation du régime pénitentiaire au Tonkin April 26, 1932; (2) Rapport fait par M. Le Gregam, Inspecteur des Colonies, concernant la Maison centrale de Saigon, January 30, 1932; and (3) Rapport fait par M. Le Gregam, Inspecteur des Colonies concernant les îles et le pénitencier de Poulo Condore, February 23, 1932. They are cited below as the Tonkin Report, the Saigon Report, and the Poulo Condore Report.

dited account books, inventoried warehouses, examined records, and conducted interviews. In January 1932, they forwarded a series of reports to the ministry in Paris detailing conditions in the Hanoi and Saigon Central Prisons, the penitentiaries of Poulo Condore and Thai Nguyen, the large civil prison at Haiphong, and a handful of provincial prisons. The picture of the colonial prison system conveyed in the reports was nothing short of catastrophic.

Acute overcrowding overshadowed a multitude of related problems. At Hanoi Central Prison, de Géry found a prison population in excess of 1,300 living in a space intended for 600.[28] He described 375 prisoners crammed "elbow to elbow" in a single ward, many sleeping on "filthy straw mats" that covered every inch of the concrete floor.[29] Le Gregam observed a similar situation at Saigon Central Prison. "Although the prison was constructed to receive a maximum of 800 detainees," he reported, "it currently holds 1,823."[30] Shortages of space were also noted at Haiphong, where 480 convicts were squeezed into a prison meant for 400, and at Thai Nguyen, where 283 occupied a single communal room designed for 200.[31]

Not surprisingly, congestion coincided with a dramatic deterioration of sanitary conditions. On Poulo Condore, Le Gregam pointed to outbreaks of typhoid, dysentery, tuberculosis, malaria, cholera, and scurvy to explain the penitentiary's 10 percent mortality rate during 1930.[32] A large number of deaths on the islands were attributed to cachexia, a diagnostic catchall that denoted the wasting away of the body due to inactivity or chronic disease.[33] As overcrowding forced wardens in Hanoi, Saigon, and Thai Nguyen to convert prison workshops into residential space, cachexia emerged as a major cause of death in mainland prisons as well.[34]

Conditions for female prisoners were no less cramped and squalid. Following a visit to the female dormitory at the Hanoi Maison centrale, de Géry wrote:

> The female quarter exhibits from a hygienic and moral point of view and from the standpoint of simple humanity, a truly revolting picture. In an area built for 100 prisoners maximum, 225 of these miserable

28. AOM Indochine, Affaires politiques, 1728, Tonkin Report, 6.
29. Ibid., 7.
30. AOM, Indochine, Affaires politiques, 1728. Saigon Report, 18.
31. AOM, Indochine, Affaires politiques, 1728, Tonkin Report, 16, 24.
32. AOM, Indochine, Affaires politiques, 1728, Poulo Condore Report, 68.
33. Ibid., 71.
34. AOM, Indochine, Affaires politiques, 1728, Saigon Report, 39; Tonkin Report, 12, 25.

creatures are locked up. Neither classed nor categorized, they form an indescribable mob; political prisoners, common-law prisoners, juvenile delinquents, and twelve mothers, together with their infants.[35]

De Géry's reference to juvenile delinquents pointed to another dimension of the crisis. In 1932, Indochina possessed only two reformatories for boys, one at Tri Cu, in northern Bac Giang Province, and the other at Thu Dau Mot, outside Saigon. Owing to overcrowding at both sites and the absence of a detention center for female juveniles, teenagers were held in the adult dormitories of every prison in Indochina. Eleven prisoners under fifteen years of age were reported in Haiphong, twenty-five in Hanoi, and thirty-five in Saigon.[36] Le Gregam detailed the case of "an eleven year old girl thief" in Saigon Central Prison, whom he described as "living in constant contact with adult prisoners."[37] In addition to concerns about their physical safety, inspectors worried that teenage inmates might be corrupted "morally and politically" by extended proximity to hardened convicts and revolutionaries. The issue was complicated further at Hanoi Central Prison, where a dozen boys and four girls in their early teens had been convicted for "plotting against state security" and categorized as political prisoners.[38] The resident superior refused to send these "political children" to the Juvenile Reformatory at Tri Cu because he feared "communist contamination of the other delinquents."[39]

Another series of problems concerned the quantity and the quality of the prison staff. Inspectors complained about a growing shortage of European warders. According to de Géry, "the static number of French guards at the Central Prison is out of all proportion to the very increased quantity of prisoners, who include many dangerous and turbulent elements."[40] This raised the disturbing prospect that the "vigilance of the guard corps may become dull through overwork."[41] The inspectors also underlined the hazards posed by overburdened medical officers, such as the doctor at Saigon Central Prison who was described as "incompetent, inert, and largely responsible for a horrible record of prison sanitation."[42] On Poulo Condore,

35. AOM, Indochine, Affaires politiques, 1728, Tonkin Report, 9.
36. AOM, Indochine, Affaires politiques, 1728, Tonkin Report, 10, 20; Saigon Report, 33.
37. AOM, Indochine, Affaires politiques, 1728, Saigon Report, 21.
38. AOM, Indochine, Affaires politiques, 1728, Tonkin Report, 10.
39. Ibid., 2.
40. Ibid., 6.
41. Ibid., 7.
42. AOM, Indochine, Affaires politiques, 1728, Saigon Report, 27.

the combined pressures of stress, overwork, and isolation from the mainland bred disharmony among the European staff. The prison director feuded openly with the infantry commander and was not even on speaking terms with the head of the island's office of public works, an official whom he derided to the inspectors as "chronically drunk and dissolute."[43]

A more serious concern for colonial officials was the alleged incompetence and disloyalty of native guards. "With regard to the native personnel, the value of 80 to 85 percent of them is doubtful," Le Gregam remarked. "Most are drunks, opium addicts, and gamblers who float between the prisoners and the administration. Neither punishment nor good council can succeed in reforming them. In a word, their mentality is not superior to that of most of the prisoners."[44] The inspector's low opinion was confirmed during an unannounced visit that he paid to a work camp for forced labor convicts on Poulo Condore. There, he discovered the wife of a guard overseeing several dozen prisoners while her husband took his regular afternoon nap. Le Gregam concluded that a recent rash of escapes from work camps on the islands must be owing "either to collusion or to the poor attitude of the indigenous guards."[45]

The prison conditions described in the inspection report are an important context for understanding the remarkable expansion of communist activity behind bars during the early 1930s. Congested communal dormitories were difficult to police and provided a perfect setting for organizational work and clandestine plotting. The failure of the colonial prison to segregate different categories of prisoners and subject them to qualitatively distinct penal regimes encouraged bonding and a sense of shared predicament among prisoners with diverse backgrounds and ideological inclinations. Moreover, communists could exploit the health hazards generated by overcrowding as a compelling rallying point to unify the inmate population. None of these points was lost on Inspector de Géry, who related the growth of communist propaganda behind bars directly to the peculiar organization of space in the colonial prison:

> The mass of detainees, poorly compartmentalized and living in close contact with one another, surrender to a constant exchange of ideas, both written and oral. This is not surprising when dealing with individuals imbued with a doctrine whose nature instills in its adepts a mental exaltation manifesting itself in a quasi-sick need to make propa-

43. AOM, Indochine, Affaires politiques, 1728, Poulo Condore Report, 10.
44. Ibid., 52.
45. Ibid., 54.

ganda. . . . The lack of available space permits them to plan together at leisure all inclinations at rebellion, which could easily produce a general uprising. The defective material installation thus constitutes both an aggravation of their penalty and a major source of their discontent.[46]

In addition, communist efforts in prison profited from the burdensome demands that overcrowding made on the Garde indigène. Since the mid nineteenth century, Vietnamese guards had exhibited a tendency to identify with inmates rather than French prison officials, who treated them with suspicion and disdain. It is not surprising, therefore, that certain guards came to sympathize and collude with communist prisoners and that some were even recruited into the Party. "Following the discovery of a communist cell in the Ha Tinh Prison," a colonial official reported in 1931, "a corporal and a member of the Garde indigène admitted their affiliation with a provincial communist cell."[47] A similar episode was reported in Saigon Central Prison: "The Saigon Municipal Police recently caught a guard in the Central Prison in the process of sending a letter from political detainees to members of extremist groups with whom they had been affiliated before their incarceration. An investigation has established collaboration between the ICP and other prison guards, notably in the provincial prisons of Bac Lieu and Ha Tien."[48]

Although the inspectors expressed dismay at the rapid deterioration of prison conditions, there was nothing qualitatively new about space shortages, poor sanitation, inadequate segregation, and unreliable guards. Indeed, such problems had plagued the colonial prison system since its inception in the mid nineteenth century. What had changed, however, was the degree and character of organized resistance to the prison regime—a transformation triggered by the influx into the system of thousands of political prisoners, several hundred of whom were experienced communist activists. "The propaganda that circulates at Hanoi Central Prison develops in a perfectly organized way," de Géry noted. "The individual action of leaders who agitate in a more or less dispersed fashion when they are at liberty has been transformed by us—by interning them in the way that has been demonstrated—into a sort of university of propaganda, collective formation, and mutual excitation, which radiates to the exterior."[49]

46. AOM, Indochine, Affaires politiques, 1728, Tonkin Report, 12.
47. AOM, SLOTFOM, 3d ser., carton 49, *AAPCI*, November–December 1931, 6.
48. AOM, SLOTFOM, 3d ser., carton 59, *AAPCI*, January 1939, 3.
49. AOM, Indochine, Affaires politiques, 1728, Tonkin Report, 14.

THE COMMUNISTS IN PRISON

The "perfectly organized" propaganda observed by de Géry prompted the colonial authorities to increase surveillance over political activity in prison and to record its growth in their confidential quarterly security report, *Les Associations anti-françaises et la propagande communiste en Indochine (AAPCI).*[50] Since the mid 1920s, *AAPCI* had been divided into chapters named for different categories of subversive activity: assassinations, plots, propaganda, protest demonstrations, labor agitation, mass meetings, and arms smuggling. In March 1931, two new chapters abruptly appeared: "demonstrations in prison" and "propaganda in prison."[51] During the following months, "demonstrations in prison" and "propaganda in prison" expanded with alacrity, and they eventually became among the largest components of the report.

The new chapters of *AAPCI* focused overwhelmingly on the structure and development of communist organization behind bars. As in society at large, communists in prison were organized into secret fraternal groupings known as cells (*chi bo*).[52] They were composed of three to ten members who worked together at specialized tasks and monitored one another's performance and political commitment.[53] In Indochina's largest penitentiaries and central prisons, it was not unusual to find numerous cells, honeycombed within different sections of the institution. Cells were also found in smaller provincial prisons. Between 1931 and 1936, *AAPCI* reported the discovery of communist cells in the provincial prisons of Ben Tre, My Tho, Bac Lieu, Cho Lon, Chau Doc, Hai Duong, Bac Giang, Can Tho, Vung Tau, Ha Tien, Nam Dinh, Thai Binh, Nha Trang, Ha Tinh, Quang Ngai, Hai Phong, and Vinh.

50. *AAPCI* may be found in the records of the Ministry of Colonies' Service de liaison des originaires des territoires français d'outre-mer (SLOTFOM), set up to monitor colonial troops in France during World War I. In the 1920s, SLOTFOM redeployed its formidable intelligence-gathering apparatus to focus on nationalist movements gaining strength in the colonies.

51. AOM, SLOTFOM, 3d ser., carton 55, *AAPCI*, March–April 1931.

52. Party historians claim that the first communist cell on Poulo Condore was set up in late 1931 by Nguyen Hoi. Early members included Ton Duc Thang, Ta Uyen, Tong Van Tran, Bay Cui, Ngo Gia Tu, Pham Hung, Le Van Luong, Le Quang Sung, and Nguyen Chi Dieu. See Vu Thuy, "Chi Bo Dac Biet, 1930–1945" [The Special Cell, 1930–1945], *Tap Chi Lich Su Dang* [Journal of Party History] 5, no. 33 (1990): 47.

53. For a discussion of the *chi bo* and its role in party organizational structure, see Huynh Kim Khanh, *Vietnamese Communism*, 136–37.

Consistent with basic principles of Leninist political organization, communist cells in prison were integrated into networks that were vertically ordered and functionally specialized: "Currently [in late 1934], each dormitory on Poulo Condore possesses at least one cell composed of four members. Each member assumes one of four positions: secretary, chief of propaganda, chief of self-defense, and chief of control. Through their secretaries, each cell maintains relations with a central bureau led by distinguished political prisoners who are currently being held in special quarters."[54] The cell network in Hanoi Central Prison exhibited analogous characteristics: "The most dangerous and intelligent revolutionaries are detained at Hanoi Central Prison. They have succeeded in forming a secret organization, which comprises several departments, each serving a distinct function. One organizes propaganda, another maintains lines of communication between different categories of prisoners and with the exterior, another looks after the prisoners' immediate needs, still another plans actions against the administration."[55]

Vietnamese historical accounts based on internal Party documents confirm the elaborate picture of communist cell networks described in colonial intelligence reporting. According to the Institute of Party History, the communist network formed in Hanoi Central Prison in 1932 had over twenty members, divided into four cells.[56] The first was responsible for propaganda and training, the second managed relations with common criminals, and the third dealt with the prison staff and provided general leadership. A special three-man cell published two clandestine newspapers (*The Proletarian* and *The Prisoner*) and hand-copied and circulated dozens of political tracts. Official communist histories describe equally intricate cell networks in the penitentiaries at Son La and Buon Ma Thuot.[57]

Another characteristically Leninist feature of communist cells in prison was their tendency to operate behind ostensibly apolitical mass organiza-

---

54. AOM, SLOTFOM, 3d ser., carton 52, *AAPCI*, 4th quarter, 1934, 5.

55. Ibid., February–March 1932, 11.

56. So Van Hoa Thong Tin Ha Noi and Vien Lich Su Dang, *Dau Tranh Cua Cac Chien Si Yeu Nuoc Va Cach Mang Tai Nha Tu Hoa Lo, 1899–1954* [The Struggle of Patriotic and Revolutionary Fighters in Hoa Lo Prison, 1899–1954] (Hanoi, 1994), 70.

57. Vien Mac-Lenin and Vien Lich Su Dang, *Nguc Son La, Truong Hoc Dau Tranh Cach Mang* [Son La Prison, The School of Revolutionary Struggle] (Hanoi, 1992), 35–41; Vien Lich Su Dang and Tinh Uy Dak Lak, *Lich Su Nha Day Buon Ma Thuot, 1930–1945* [History of Buon Ma Thuot Penitentiary, 1930–1945] (Hanoi, 1991), 37–62.

tions known as prisoners' associations (*lao tu hoi* or *tu nhan hoi*).[58] In *Duong Kach Menh,* Ho Chi Minh devoted considerable attention to the form and functions of mass organizations and provided detailed instructions for setting them up.[59] As in society at large, mass organizations in prison were intended to penetrate into and control noncommunist segments of the population.[60] According to the inaugural charter of a prisoners' association founded in Hanoi Central Prison, membership was available to all inmates "regardless of nationality, class, sex, sentence, or party affiliation."[61] Indeed, the charter drew special attention to the organization's ideological neutrality; "The *tu nhan hoi* is a society of prisoners and not a revolutionary party. Its purpose is to group together all prisoners to help them better resist disease, oppression, and abuse by the administration. It is also concerned with the intellectual and moral enlightenment of its members."[62] Prisoners' associations were, in fact, little more than communist front organizations. In 1933, colonial officials observed that "communist propaganda spreads more actively than ever under the auspices of so-called prisoners' associations."[63] Party historians confirm that prisoners' associations were set up and controlled by communist cells.[64] As the official history of the Buon Ma Thuot Penitentiary explains: "The Prisoners' Association, the first mass organization in Buon Ma Thuot, was secretly established by communist prisoners."[65]

Like communist cell networks, prisoners' associations were broken down into an array of functional bodies. The prisoners' association of Son La, for example, was divided into ten "boards" (*ban*), responsible for internal discipline, external discipline, propaganda and publications, education

58. For the importance of front organizations in Vietnamese communist strategy, see Jayne Werner, "New Light on Vietnamese Marxism," *Bulletin of Concerned Asian Scholars* 10, no. 4 (1978): 42–48; Douglas Pike, *Vietnam and the Soviet Union: Anatomy of an Alliance* (Boulder, Colo., 1987), 27.

59. Ho Chi Minh, *Duong Kach Menh,* 302–8.

60. Huynh Kim Khanh, *Vietnamese Communism,* 139.

61. So Van Hoa Thong Tin Ha Noi and Vien Lich Su Dang, *Dau Tranh Cua Cac Chien Si Yeu Nuoc Va Cach Mang Tai Nha Tu Hoa Lo,* 75.

62. AOM, SLOTFOM, 3d ser., carton 52, *AAPCI,* 4th quarter 1934.

63. Ibid., 1st quarter 1933.

64. See, e.g, Ban Nghien Cuu Lich Su Dang Trung Uong [Board of Historical Research on the Party Central Committee], *Nhung Su Kien Lich Su Dang, Tap I (1920–1945)* [Events in Party History, vol. 1: 1920–1945] (Hanoi, 1976), 290–91.

65. Tinh Uy Dak Lak and Vien Lich Su Dang, *Lich Su Nha Day Buon Ma Thuot, 1930–1945,* 46.

and training, medicine, economics, culture, foreign relations, commemorations, and mobilization.[66] In Hanoi Central Prison, the prisoners' association set up a communist youth league, a women's union, a Red Cross brigade, a relief board, a foreign relations committee, a culture and literature council, and even a laundry committee.[67]

Although imprisonment was intended to sever inmates from the outside world, the administrative reach of communist cells in prison frequently expanded beyond the walls of the institution and penetrated into the wider community. "The Hanoi *tu nhan hoi* does not limit its activities to the Central Prison," *AAPCI* concluded gloomily in 1934, "but by the constant circulation of prisoners, it has succeeded in expanding its influence throughout the provincial prisons of Tonkin, where it has organized secondary sections."[68] As early as 1931, evidence emerged that prisoner organizations regularly corresponded with cells on the outside. "Liaison between Saigon Central Prison's *tu nhan hoi* and the ICP's executive committee for Cochin China is perpetual," *AAPCI* reported, "and is assured by the constant flow of prisoners entering and leaving the prison."[69]

While it might be assumed that prison-based cells received guidance and support from party organs on the outside, advice and assistance could also flow in the opposite direction. Messages sent by jailed communists to comrades in the wider community and intercepted by prison authorities contain direct orders about revolutionary strategy and tactics. In a letter intercepted from the Haiphong Civil Prison in 1933, jailed party members tersely instructed the provincial Party committee to "recruit more poor peasants and workers" and avoid alliances with "rich cultivators or notables."[70] Based on other confiscated letters, *AAPCI* concluded that a communist cell in the Quang Ngai Provincial Prison had assumed responsibility for all political work in the province.[71] "We see here," the report

---

66. Vien Mac-Lenin and Vien Lich Su Dang, *Nguc Son La, Truong Hoc Dau Tranh Cach Mang,* 38.

67. So Van Hoa Thong Tin Ha Noi and Vien Lich Su Dang, *Dau Tranh Cua Cac Chien Si Yeu Nuoc Va Cach Mang Tai Nha Tu Hoa Lo,* 78–83.

68. AOM, SLOTFOM, 3d ser., carton 52, *AAPCI,* 4th quarter 1934, 5.

69. Ibid., carton 49, *AAPCI,* November–December 1931, 5.

70. Ibid., carton 52, *AAPCI* 1st quarter 1933, 3.

71. "Last January, communist cells were organized in the prison of Quang Ngai. Two months later, leaders had formed a provincial committee, functioning in the interior of this same prison. This committee has decided to reconstitute the Communist Party using individuals who have recently been freed after acquiring a good revolutionary education during their detention." AOM, SLOTFOM, 3d ser., carton 52, *AAPCI,* April–May 1932, 6.

concluded," the provincial committee of Quang Ngai, created by inmates, functioning in the interior of the prison and, from there, directing propaganda for the entire province."[72] Communist cells formed in the provincial prisons of Son La and Quang Nam represented the Party's earliest efforts at political organization in those provinces as well.[73]

In his prison memoir "I Must Live To Fight," the ICP member Nguyen Tao confirms that communist cells in prison assumed a leading role in the Party apparatus during the early 1930s. Tao's account opens in 1933, when he and several comrades escaped from Hanoi Central Prison and joined up with a local party cell in Nam Dinh. Although he had been confined for over a year, Tao apprised the Nam Dinh cadres of the movement's recent progress:

> The very night of our arrival, we held a meeting with five activists from neighboring hamlets. Transported with the delight of finding ourselves among friends, Dam and I spoke tirelessly until dawn. We talked about the world situation and the danger of war, the home situation and the forthcoming task of the revolution. Our friends' eagerness, it must be recalled, incited us to speak at length: deprived of news for a long time and cut off from the rest of the organization, they wanted to know everything and asked us question after question.[74]

It is instructive that Tao, a recently escaped convict, describes his hosts and not himself as "deprived of news for a long time" and "cut off from the rest of the organization." Also striking is the breath of information available to the fugitives—from changes in local revolutionary strategy to developments on the global geopolitical scene. Rather than marginalizing them, imprisonment seems to have thrust Tao and his fellow escapees into the very vortex of the revolutionary movement.

THE LAO BAO REPORT

In 1934, officials at the Lao Bao Penitentiary confiscated a sixteen-page document from a communist inmate that confirmed their worst fears

---

72. Ibid.

73. "Several political prisoners in Quang Nam have succeeded in setting up a provisional committee in the interior of this establishment. It maintains a constant liaison with the exterior through released prisoners." AOM, SLOTFOM, 3d ser., carton 52, *AAPCI*, 4th quarter 1933, 19. For Son La, see Vien Mac-Lenin and Vien Lich Su Dang, *Nguc Son La, Truong Hoc Dau Tranh Cach Mang*, 41.

74. Nguyen Tao, "I Must Live to Fight," in *In the Enemies' Net* (Hanoi, 1962), 64.

about the power and sophistication of communist organization in prison.[75] An opening chapter of the document entitled "political situation" provided a detailed evaluation of the prison staff and assessed the morale and political orientation of the inmate population. The warden was portrayed as "crafty" and possessing significant "political flair." The guards were described as "overworked, underpaid, harshly treated" and therefore "susceptible to proselytization and patriotic appeals."[76] Because common criminals were kept segregated from political prisoners, "as the sea from the sky," they suffered from a "spiritual malaise" and "lack of direction." While political prisoners were less despondent, they too were chided for exhibiting "a regrettable penchant for factionalism."[77]

In a second chapter entitled "plan of action," the report detailed the organizational structure and division of labor among Lao Bao's communist inmates. There were three communist cells, made up of three members apiece, in each of the penitentiary's five dormitories (*lao*). Every three months, the cell members in each dormitory would meet, forming a body known as an intercell (*to truong*) to elect three individuals to serve on a dormitory committee (*lao uy*). Every year, the five dormitory committees selected a five-man general committee (*tong uy*), led by a powerful general secretary (*le tong uy*) who spearheaded and monitored the activities of the entire network.[78] Positioned between the general committee and the dormitory committees were five liaison sections responsible in turn for education, propaganda, discipline, aid, and resistance. Each dormitory possessed five functional boards that paralleled the five liaison sections and were staffed with overlapping personnel. Education sections devised a curriculum that highlighted "revolutionary principles, tactics, and experiences," plus special courses for common-law prisoners on "general science and literacy." Propaganda sections developed three distinct "indoctrination programs" that targeted guards, common-law prisoners and political prisoners. For guards, propaganda was to focus on "class misery and revolutionary propaganda." For common criminals, it stressed "resistance to the warden's divisive maneuvers," and for political prisoners, it emphasized "opposition to false opinions, partisanship, and erroneous tendencies." Discipline and

---

75. AOM, SLOTFOM, 3d ser., carton 52, *AAPCI*, 1st quarter 1934. Subsequently cited as Lao Bao Report.
76. Ibid., 1.
77. Ibid., 2.
78. Ibid., 3.

aid sections identified prisoners deserving special assistance or punitive sanctions and carried out the "appropriate measures." Resistance sections monitored and punished collaboration and espionage, targeted abusive guards and agents provocateurs, and worked against hostile gangs and religious groupings.[79]

Chapter 3 of the report, entitled "Bylaws," announced the formation of a prisoner association and spelled out its objectives, the rights and responsibilities of its members, and a schedule of regular meetings. The association's dual purpose was to "ameliorate conditions for all detainees" and "realize work in the interest of the revolution." Membership was inclusively open to any prisoner endorsed by two current members. The chapter concluded by listing punishments for members who "violated the bylaws or resolutions passed by the association."[80]

The Lao Bao document underlines the commitment of jailed communists to Leninist political organization. The hierarchical orientation of the cell network in Lao Bao is evidenced by the five levels of graded authority that separated rank-and-file party cells at the bottom of the system from the powerful general secretary at the top. The formation of boards with fixed jurisdictional responsibilities points to a high level of functional specialization. The detailed assessment of the prison staff and the elaborate depiction of educational efforts reveal the high priority given to intelligence-gathering and theoretical and practical training—features closely associated with Leninist mechanisms of power.[81] Moreover, the very existence of the document, and many others like it, serves as a compelling testament to the modern, bureaucratic orientation of communist power, even in prison.[82] From Weber to Foucault, theorists of power have identified written documents—files, reports, dossiers—as a fundamental component of modern regimes of authority and control.[83] Not only do written documents ensure efficiency, predictability, and the normalization of vast

---

79. Ibid., 4–5.

80. Ibid., 6–7.

81. Harding, *Leninism*, 28–32.

82. It must have been a further source of anxiety to French officials that reports prepared by Communist Party cells in other penal institutions closely resembled the Lao Bao document in layout, language, and content. See, e.g., the party document seized at the Hanoi Maison centrale: AOM, SLOTFOM, 3d ser., carton 52, AAPCI, 4th quarter 1934.

83. For Weber's discussion of the relationship between bureaucratic power and "scribes," "documents," and "filing services," see *From Max Weber: Essays in Sociology*, ed. H. H. Gerth and C. Wright Mills (New York, 1946), 197–214. For Foucault's arguments about the power of the "small techniques of notation,

amounts of information but they facilitate the surveillance and supervision of people and their activities. The fact that jailed members of the ICP produced such lengthy internal documents, despite the considerable risks generated by their production and circulation, testifies to the remarkably modernist character of communist power.

EDUCATION AND TRAINING

As the Lao Bao document makes clear, communist cells in prison devoted much of their energy and resources to political training. Hence, it is not surprising that French officials came to routinely describe colonial prisons as revolutionary schools. In November 1931, prison authorities complained that "inmates at the Saigon Central Prison are receiving a comprehensive communist education."[84] Several months later, *AAPCI* again employed a scholastic metaphor, describing the Nha Trang Provincial Prison as a "permanent school of communism."[85]

For many Vietnamese communists, prison provided their first sustained exposure to Marxism-Leninism as an integrated body of knowledge. Up through the 1930s, police surveillance made it hazardous for the Comintern or the Youth League to organize revolutionary instruction within the borders of Indochina. As a result, with the exception of several hundred activists trained in the Soviet Union, Siam, or southern China, most early Vietnamese revolutionaries possessed only a superficial familiarity with Marxist-Leninist theory or the history of the communist movement. Because the establishment of the ICP in 1930 coincided with the colonial state's massive crackdown on anticolonial forces, many neophyte Party members found themselves jailed for communist activity before they had developed an even rudimentary understanding of communist ideology. Indeed, the Comintern blamed the failure of the Nghe-Tinh soviets on "infantile mistakes" committed by poorly trained Party activists. Prison, therefore, created opportunities for unschooled comrades and raw recruits to read Marxist-Leninist literature and embark on rigorous courses of study with fellow inmates who had been trained abroad.

---

of registration, of constituting files, of arranging facts in columns and tables," see *Discipline and Punish: The Birth of the Prison*, trans. Alan Sheridan (New York, 1979), 189–91.

84. AOM, SLOTFOM, 3d ser., carton 49, *AAPCI*, November–December 1931, 5.

85. Ibid., carton 55, *AAPCI*, March–April 1932, 7.

An instructive account of communist political education in prison can be found in "From the Dungeon," a revolutionary memoir by a future mid-level ICP official named Ha The Hanh.[86] Born in the central Vietnamese province of Binh Tri Thien in 1912, Hanh entered politics in 1926 while still a high-school student in Hue. Although he participated in "campus patriotic activities" from an early age, Hanh's grasp of Marxist theory was limited. "I was given a number of introductory books on Marxism," he wrote, "but my understanding was still very poor."[87] Eventually, Hanh was recruited by the Youth League and admitted into the ICP soon after its establishment in 1930. Almost immediately, he was sent to work in a factory as part of an ICP campaign to proletarianize its ranks. In his memoir, Hanh recalled that the drudgery of factory work left him with "little time to study theoretical problems."[88]

In July 1931, Hanh was arrested near Qui Nhon, and he was jailed subsequently at penitentiaries at Buon Ma Thuot and Lao Bao. It was through contact with foreign-trained communists in Lao Bao that he began to "learn something about Marxism-Leninism and the proletarian revolution in a systematic manner."[89] In June 1935, Hanh was transferred to Poulo Condore, where, for the first time, he "read the classic works of Marx, Engels, and Lenin":

> A number of Lenin's works were translated into Vietnamese by comrades who knew French and many manuscript copies of the translations were popular within the prison, such as *Leftist Infantile Diseases of Communism* (1920) and *Two Tactics of the Social-Democratic Party in the Democratic Revolution* (1905). What struck me most was that, for the first time, I developed a thorough knowledge of the October Revolution. At the start of my revolutionary consciousness, I knew about the Revolution of 1917 but had failed to understand its significance for the world revolutionary movement.[90]

Upon his release in 1936, Hanh's intellectual development in prison enabled him to secure an editorial position with the legal communist newspaper *Dan* (The People). "The knowledge that I had acquired during my

---

86. Ha The Hanh, "From the Dungeon," in *From the Russian October Revolution to the Vietnamese August Revolution* (Hanoi, 1987), 93–100.
87. Ibid., 93.
88. Ibid.
89. Ibid., 96.
90. Ibid.

prison terms," he wrote, "was of great help to me in my career as a journalist from 1938 to 1939."[91]

A similar narrative appears in the inelegantly titled prison memoir "Hoc Tap, Hoc Tap, Hoc Tap de Hoat Dong Tot cho Dang" (Study, Study, Study to Work Effectively for the Party) by Van Tan (Tran Duc Sac),[92] which relates the story of a communist labor organizer named Truc who was arrested in Laos and imprisoned in Hanoi Central Prison in 1935. Locked in a large dormitory with veteran political prisoners, Truc was introduced to communist theoretical texts, several of which he committed to memory. Following his release in 1937, the radical journalist Pham Van Hao encountered Truc organizing railway workers along the line between Vinh and Hoi An. Truc explained to Hao that it was prison that had endowed him with a basic knowledge of revolutionary theory:

> When I was in Laos, I agitated secretly but I had no idea what communism was. Only after I was imprisoned in Hoa Lo and had the opportunity to read books and study did I understand the correct way of communist struggle. When I think back to the months in Hoa Lo, the time seems so precious. It is only thanks to my months in Hoa Lo that I know something of revolutionary theory.[93]

The narratives of Hanh and Tan are not stories of political conversion in jail but of the role of incarceration in the cultivation of certain kinds of historical and theoretical knowledge. While the level of instruction was relatively rudimentary, it provided a basis for cadres to propagandize on behalf of the Party both in prison and following their release. Moreover, the teleological and scientific character of the Marxian theory and history that they studied endowed jailed communists with a powerful sense of the inevitability of the success of their enterprise.[94] Indeed, the remarkably high morale that communists were able to sustain in prison may be par-

---

91. Ibid., 98.

92. Van Tan, "Hoc Tap, Hoc Tap, Hoc Tap De Hoat Dong Tot Cho Dang," in *Truong Hoc Sau Song Sat: Hoi Ky Cach Mang* [School Behind the Iron Bars: Revolutionary Memoirs] (Hanoi, 1969), 21–51.

93. Ibid., 33.

94. "Communism seemed to promise the possibility of success. It provided a whole curriculum for the study of rebellion—Party schools, schooling in language theory and agit-prop tactics, and the possibility of higher training in Moscow. In the Soviet Union, a young Vietnamese could sense the international power of the movement, and feel that he had allies from China, Japan, Italy, Germany and elsewhere." Scott McConnell, *Leftward Journey: The Education of Vietnamese Students in France, 1919–1939* (New Brunswick, N.J., 1989), 120.

tially attributed to their protracted participation in such political study sessions.

Consistent with their predilection for functional specialization, communist cells created educational boards and committees to carry out political training in prison. These bodies crafted curricula, gathered material, and determined the timetables and methods of study.[95] In many prisons, introductory and advanced courses were offered to suit the varied needs and backgrounds of the inmate population. In Hanoi Central Prison, a formal screening process classified new prisoners and assigned them to courses according to their erudition, ability, and experience. "Upon arrival," reported *AAPCI*, "new prisoners are interrogated by cell members about their political opinions. Based on their knowledge, they are then assigned to one of several courses held nightly."[96]

Van Tan's prison memoir confirms that jailed communists set up a regular mechanism of educational assessment and placement for new inmates. Three nights after his arrival in Hanoi Central Prison, a political prisoner named Pham Quang Tham questioned Tan for several hours about his political experiences, sympathies, and knowledge. Owing to the sophistication of his answers, Tan was assigned to an advanced class on political theory, in which students read "classic texts of Marxism-Leninism" and participated in formal "discussions" (*thao luan*). On the other hand, a method known as "question and answer" (*van dap*) was employed to teach prisoners with less political sophistication. According to Tan, instructors in these introductory classes asked questions such as "What is Communism?" or "What is class struggle?" and provided answers in "simple, easy-to-understand language."[97]

Instruction in prison was often carried out by inmates who had undergone training in China and the Soviet Union.[98] During the 1920s and early 1930s, a significant number of Vietnamese revolutionaries enrolled in

95. AOM, SLOTFOM, ser. 3, carton 52, *AAPCI*, 1st quarter 1934, 3.

96. Ibid., 3–4. Huynh Kim Khanh describes a comparable setup on Poulo Condore: "There were two types of Marxist training courses [on Poulo Condore]. Long-term courses were for those sentenced to five-year or longer prison terms. This theoretical training involved a relatively systematic, thorough study of Marxism-Leninism and the policies of the ICP. Short-term courses were for prisoners with short sentences." Huynh Kim Khanh, *Vietnamese Communism*, 162.

97. Van Tan, "Hoc Tap, Hoc Tap, Hoc Tap De Hoat Dong Tot Cho Dang," 35.

98. For accounts of Vietnamese students in Moscow, see Jean Dorsenne, "Le Péril rouge en Indochine," *Revue des Deux Mondes*, April 1, 1932. Dorsenne claims that over 100 Vietnamese studied in Moscow during the late 1920s. See also Scott

Stalin's University for the Toilers of the East and the Kuomintang's military academy at Whampoa.[99] Several hundred more studied formally with Ho Chi Minh in Canton and Siam.[100] Late in 1931, *AAPCI* warned that "prisons have become centers of anti-French propaganda," where "communists and nationalists who have been shaped by long periods in China and Russia indoctrinate new adepts."[101] According to Ha The Hanh, classes on Poulo Condore were led by cadres such as Bui Cong Trung and Ha Huy Tap, who "had studied at the Oriental College in the Soviet Union . . . and had therefore seen for themselves the land of Lenin and the October Revolution."[102]

Tran Van Giau, a graduate of the Stalin School, acknowledged that the teaching methods he employed on Poulo Condore in the 1930s were shaped by pedagogic models he had observed in Moscow in the 1920s. For example, a "nine-unit class on Leninist theory" that Giau offered on Poulo Condore was based on a similar course that he had attended at the Stalin School.[103] "In terms of pedagogy," Giau explained, "I followed the model of the Eastern University." His teaching methods were especially influenced by a charismatic Italian professor with whom he had studied in the Soviet Union: "Professor Heluza would force us to read the classics completely. He would praise our good points and criticize our bad or biased ones but in a soft voice never dismissively. On Poulo Condore, I copied the methods of Professor Heluza but didn't dare to take on his professorial air."[104]

McConnell, *Leftward Journey*, 112, 120, and 128, and Huynh Kim Khanh, *Vietnamese Communism*, 175–77.

99. Pham Van Dong claims that "more than 200 cadres" were trained between 1925 and 1927 in the USSR and China. Pham Van Dong, *Le Président Ho Chi Minh* (Hanoi, 1961), 52. Graduates of the KUTV include Tran Phu, Le Hong Phong, Ngo Duc Tri, Tran Van Giau, Tran Ngoc Ranh, Ha Huy Tap, Bui Cong Trung, Nguyen Khanh Toan, Dang Dinh Tho, Nguyen Dinh Tu, Nguyen Huy Bon, Nguyen Thi Minh Khai, and Ho Chi Minh.

100. For firsthand accounts of the revolutionary training courses organized by Ho Chi Minh in Canton during the mid 1920s, see Le Manh Trinh, "In Canton and Siam," and Nguyen Luong Bang, "The Times I Met Him," in *Uncle Ho* (Hanoi, 1980), 98–167.

101. AOM, SLOTFOM, 3d ser., carton 49, *AAPCI*, November–December 1931, 5.

102. Ha The Hanh, "From the Dungeon," 96.

103. Tran Van Giau, "Lop Hoc Chu Nghia Mac-Lenin Va To Bao 'Y Kien Chung' O Banh I, Con Lon, 1935–36" [The Class of Marxism-Leninism and the Newspaper "Consensus" in Dormitory 1, Poulo Condore, 1935–36], *Tap Chi Lich Su Dang* 5, no. 33 (1990): 6.

104. Ibid.

Like Professor Heluza, Giau and fellow prison instructors emphasized the so-called "classics" of revolutionary political theory. Titles mentioned repeatedly in prison memoirs include *The Communist Manifesto, Capital, What Is to Be Done?, Basic Problems of Marxism, Historical Materialism: A System of Sociology, Political Economy, Principles of Leninism, The ABC of Communism,* and *Anti-Dühring.* Such books were smuggled into dormitories, hand-copied on scraps of paper and concealed in secret hiding places.[105] On Poulo Condore, new manuscripts were provided by politically sympathetic French sailors from ships that regularly stopped at the islands. The result, according to Ha The Hanh, was that "Poulo Condore received larger quantities of progressive literature than any other center of activity on the mainland."[106]

While communist educational efforts focused on political training, classes were also offered in basic literacy, math, science, history, geography, and foreign languages.[107] Hence, Tran Huy Lieu was able to claim that "in addition to their enhanced revolutionary knowledge, graduates of prison schools exhibited a heightened cultural level as well."[108] French was an especially popular subject. For teaching materials, inmates used French-language Bibles, dictionaries, and scraps of newsprint that had been used as wrapping paper for packages sent from the mainland. Prisoners with a greater degree of fluency read fiction by Hugo, Corneille, Daudet, Bourget, Maupassant, Molière, de Vigny, de Musset, and Zola. On Poulo Condore, Tran Huy Lieu obtained a copy of Anatole France's *The Crime of Sylvestre Bonnard,* which he claims to have reread ten times.[109] In the Hanoi Central Prison, Van Tan finished Flaubert's *Madame Bovary* and the future politburo member Pham Hung read *Les Misérables* and *The Three Musketeers.*[110]

In addition to providing formal instruction, communist prisoners promoted political education and indoctrination through songs and theatrical

---

105. For a description of the elaborate efforts of prisoners on Poulo Condore to secure secret reading material, see Tran Huy Lieu, "Tu Hoc Trong Tu" [Self-Study in Prison], in *Hoi Ky Tran Huy Lieu,* ed. Pham Nhu Thom (Hanoi, 1991), 152.
106. Ha The Hanh, "From the Dungeon," 95.
107. Ban Nghien Cuu Lich Su Dang Dac Khu Vung Tau—Con Dau, *Nha Tu Con Dao, 1862–1945* [Con Dao Penitentiary, 1862–1945] (Hanoi, 1987), 109–11.
108. Tran Huy Lieu, "Tu Hoc Trong Tu," 142.
109. Ibid., 154.
110. Pham Hung, "Never to Give Up Working As Long As One Lives," in *A Heroic People: Memoirs from the Revolution* (Hanoi, 1965), 74. Van Tan, "Hoc Tap, Hoc Tap, Hoc Tap, De Hoat Dong Tot Cho Dang," 43.

performances.[111] According to *AAPCI*, "copies of revolutionary songs" discovered in Hanoi Central Prison in 1932 were "intended to be sung to native guards in order to win them over to the cause."[112] In the Nha Trang Provincial Prison, a common-law inmate who was caught with revolutionary song lyrics explained to interrogators that he planned to "sing the song to other prisoners as the final step in his communist education."[113] In 1934, guards at the remote Lao Cai Penitentiary transcribed a revolutionary song that they had overheard and submitted it to the prison director. The lyrics, in French translation, eventually made their way into *AAPCI*:

> Prisoners, Prisoners!
> Prisoners are not all weak and stupid.
> How long has French tyranny provoked our indignation.
> In spite of our innocence
> They throw us in jail
> And beat us, oblivious to our cries.
> How long has French tyranny provoked our indignation.
> Free us from these unjust men.
> We'll exterminate them in self-defense.
> This should not be our final resting place.
> Forward, brothers who are locked up.
> In spite of those who watch over us in the courtyard
> Rise up! Rise up!
> Defy the dangers of this hell!
> Massacre these unjust men and liberty is ours.
> Let none of them be spared.[114]

Theater was also employed in prison as an educational instrument. While wardens occasionally forbade the production of theater by inmates, prison plays were more often tolerated but kept under strict surveillance. In the early 1930s, communist prisoners in Hanoi Central Prison put on a production of *The Bombs of Pham Hong Thai*—a biographical drama about the famous Vietnamese patriot who died trying to assassinate Governor-

---

111. After 1960, numerous collections of prison songs from the 1930s were published in North Vietnam, such as *Tieng Hat Trong Tu, Tap I* [Songs Sung in Prison], ed. Vo Van Truc (Hanoi, 1970); *Tieng Hat Trong Tu, Tap II* [Songs Sung in Prison, vol. 2] (Hanoi, 1974); and Ty Van Hoa Thong Tin Son La, *Tho Ca Cach Mang Nha Tu Son La, 1930–1945* [Revolutionary Songs from Son La Prison] (Son La, 1980).

112. AOM, SLOTFOM, 3d ser., carton 52, *AAPCI*, February–March 1932, 4.

113. Ibid.

114. Ibid., 1st quarter 1934, 10. The song lyrics appear in *AAPCI* in French translation from the Vietnamese, hence my translation is from the French.

General Merlin in 1924.[115] Inmates in Son La dramatized *Cement,* a socialist realist novel by the Soviet writer F. V. Gladkov, and an original play about the Vietnamese revolution entitled *Two Waves Against the Current.*[116] Political prisoners in Bagne II of Poulo Condore staged patriotic historical dramas about national heroes and heroines such as the Trung Sisters, Quang Trung, and Hoang Hoa Tham.[117] On Poulo Condore in 1933, the radical journalist Nguyen Van Nguyen wrote and directed *The Four Evils,* a play depicting the negative social consequences of prostitution, alcohol, gambling, and opium.[118] That same year, guards confiscated a handwritten playscript entitled *A Tragic Episode in the History of the Party* from the Saigon Central Prison that entailed a reenactment of the repression of the Nghe-Tinh soviets.[119]

Although colonial inmates had long used theater to relieve boredom and as an outlet for repressed sexual desire, Party historians contend that communist prisoners used it solely as a pedagogic device. Revolutionary plays taught political lessons and historical dramas inculcated patriotic values. While similar lessons might be conveyed through conventional study sessions, theater was seen as a more accessible and persuasive medium of instruction. In a letter written to Tran Huy Lieu from Poulo Condore in 1935, Nguyen Duc Chinh suggested that theater possessed greater propaganda value than literature: "Several of us want to research about the theater, Brother Lieu. Using plays to present ideology seems more profitable than using books or newspapers because a large audience is often easier to move emotionally than a person reading alone. Don't you think so?"[120]

Another reason political prisoners produced plays was to improve relations with their keepers. According to Party historians, European guards developed new respect for the "cultural level, humanity, and broad knowledge" of inmates after watching them perform in French plays.[121] In this vein, Ha Huy Giap claimed that a play produced on Poulo Condore about

115. So Van Hoa Thong Tin Ha Noi and Vien Lich Su Dang, *Dau Tranh Cua Cac Chien Si Yeu Nuoc va Cach Mang Tai Nha Tu Hoa Lo,* 82.

116. Dang Viet Chau, "Nguc Son La, 1935–1936" [Son La Prison, 1935–1936], in Bao Tang Cach Mang Viet Nam and Bao Tang Son La, *Suoi Reo Nam Ay: Hoi Ky Cach Mang* (Hanoi, 1993), 35.

117. Ban Nghien Cuu Lich Su Dang Dac Khu Vung Tau—Con Dao, *Nha Tu Con Dao, 1862–1945,* 100.

118. Ibid.

119. AOM, SLOTFOM, 3d ser., carton 52, *AAPCI,* 1st quarter 1933, 4.

120. Nguyen Duc Chinh, *Thu Con Lon,* 30.

121. Ibid.

the life of Napoleon was especially well received among Corsican jailers.[122] Likewise, Tran Huy Lieu was struck by the positive emotional response of French guards to the performance of a Molière play by Poulo Condore inmates on Bastille Day.[123]

NEWSPAPERS

The production of newspapers in prison may be seen as part of a more general Leninist organizational strategy on the part of the ICP. As Neil Harding has pointed out, Lenin believed that newspapers contributed to "the development of a party organization with a clearly defined functional division of labor and vertical patterns of accountability."[124] Newspapers required the distribution of reporter-agents throughout a strategic locality who could collect and provide information for a centralized editorial board staffed by Party leaders.[125] The structure of newspapers, in other words, facilitated grassroots intelligence gathering and processes of hierarchical communication that were fundamental to Party operations. The importance of journalism as an instrument of political organization was not lost on Ho Chi Minh, who edited *La Paria* and wrote for numerous left-wing publications in Paris during the early 1920s.[126] As part of their training with Ho in Canton during the late 1920s, neophyte Vietnamese revolutionaries learned the rudiments of newspaper work. Indeed, Ho established expatriate journals such as *Thanh Nien* (Revolutionary Youth), *Kong Nong* (Workers and Peasants), and *Linh Kach Menh* (Revolutionary Troops) to provide his students in Canton with practical experience that they could apply at the factories, mines, peasant associations, and plantations into which they were eventually infiltrated.[127]

Between 1930 and 1945, jailed communists produced dozens of clandestine newspapers. Titles from the period include *The Prisoner* (Poulo Con-

---

122. Ha Huy Giap, *Doi Toi, Nhung Dieu Nghe, Thay Va Song: Hoi Ky Cach Mang* [My Life—Things Heard, Seen, and Lived: Revolutionary Memoirs] (Ho Chi Minh City, 1994), 133.

123. Tran Huy Lieu, "Tinh Trong Nguc Toi" [Love in the Dark Prison] (1950), in *Hoi Ky Tran Huy Lieu*, ed. Pham Nhu Thom (Hanoi, 1991), 138.

124. Harding, *Leninism*, 31.

125. Lenin first posed and answered affirmatively the question: "Can a Newspaper be a Collective Organizer?" in *What Is to Be Done?* (in *The Lenin Anthology*, ed. Robert Tucker [New York, 1975], 99–107).

126. See Thu Trang-Gaspard, *Ho Chi Minh à Paris, 1917–1923* (Paris, 1992).

127. Nguyen Thanh, "The Revolutionary Press in Vietnam, 1925–1945," *Vietnamese Studies*, no. 15 (85) (1986): 39.

dore), *The Prison Journal* (Hanoi Central Prison), *Prison News* (Quang Nam), *The Red Prisoner* (Poulo Condore), *The Bolshevik* (Buon Ma Thuot), *The Path of Justice* (Hanoi Central Prison), *The Revolutionary Path* (Hanoi Central Prison), *Forward March* (Poulo Condore), and *The Trailblazer* (Hoa Binh).[128] Prison newspapers were typically handwritten at night on tiny sheets of tissue or cigarette paper. In some cases, inmates produced "oral newspapers" (*to bao mieng*), in which articles, essays, and editorials were committed to memory rather than paper and broadcast throughout the prison by word of mouth.[129]

In prison, as in civilian society, communist newspapers were less concerned with the news of the day than with the promotion of the Party line. Common features included announcements of changes in policy, lessons in communist history, and exemplary works of socialist cultural production. Special commemorative editions were put out to coincide with important days in communist history such as May 1 and October 17. One of the first issues of *Lao Tu Tap Chi* (The Prison Review)—a journal produced by communist inmates in Hanoi Central Prison—was devoted exclusively to a celebration of the anniversary of the Canton Commune.[130] In addition, prison newspapers contained practical advice about political struggle behind bars. "In our next issue," read a back-page announcement in a 1932 copy of *Lao Tu Tap Chi*, "we shall explain how to efficiently resist imperialists and guards and make skillful and prudent propaganda among the common-law prisoners."[131] While many papers came out intermittently and consisted of little more than a few slogan-filled pages, others appeared regularly and contained a wealth of material. During a visit to Poulo Condore in the mid 1930s, the journalist Jean-Claude Demariaux obtained a copy of the communist journal *Tien Len* (March Forward), in which he read about "events of the day, protests, hunger strikes, and criticism of certain guards."[132] Perhaps the most elaborate prison paper of the colonial era was *Suoi Reo* (Bubbling Spring), produced by communist prisoners in Son La. Edited by Xuan Thuy, a future member of the Central Committee, ambassador to

128. All references are from SLOTFOM.
129. Nguyen Duy Trinh, "Lam Bao Va Sang Tac Tieu Thuyet Trong Nha Lao Vinh" [Writing Newspapers and Novels in Vinh Prison], in *Truong Hoc Sau Song Sat: Hoi Ky Cach Mang* [School Behind Iron Bars: Revolutionary Memoirs] (Hanoi, 1969), 81.
130. AOM, SLOTFOM, 3d ser., carton 52, *AAPCI*, 4th quarter 1934, 8.
131. Ibid., 3d quarter 1932, appendix 9, 2.
132. Jean-Claude Demariaux, *Les Secrets des îles Poulo-Condore: Le Grand Bagne indochinois* (Paris, 1956), 63–66.

France, and Paris negotiator, *Suoi Reo* came out twice a month, ran several dozen pages in length, and contained a rich array of prose, poetry, reportage, essays, cartoons, and political theory.[133] The subversive significance of prison newspapers was not lost on colonial officials. "This January, communist writings have been discovered in the Quang Tri Provincial Prison," reported *AAPCI* in 1933. "Most important is *The Blue Shirt [Ao Xanh]*, a journal that attempts to promote a revolutionary spirit among the prisoners, to mobilize them and to aid them in their struggles."[134] Another installment of *AAPCI* summarized the troubling effects of a provocative article in a communist newspaper from Hanoi Central Prison: "The first edition of the journal *Prison Life* has made a great impression on the inmate population. After reading the article 'Live Long and Assume Power in the Village' ["Song Lau Len Lao Lang"], one inmate who had resigned from the Prisoners' Association was so impressed that he requested to be readmitted."[135]

Although the authorities tried to suppress prison newspapers, they also found them valuable sources of information. Officials analyzed handwriting samples to identify political ringleaders among the inmate population. Articles provided clues about the organization of communist cells and the timing of upcoming actions. Sometimes evidence about the disloyalty of prison guards could be found in prison newspapers. For example, in 1932, *AAPCI* included the following description of a newspaper seized in Hanoi Central Prison:

> Among documents recently seized at Hanoi Central Prison are issues number 2 and 3 of *The Prison Review [Lao Tu Tap Chi]*, an Annamite-language journal produced in miniature format (78 mm by 100 mm). Number 2 is 14 pages long; number 3 consists of 19 pages. Issue 3 is almost entirely devoted to the upcoming visit of the minister of colonies to Indochina. It also made allusion to the recent escape from Hai Phong Prison of the communist Nguyen The Long. According to an article in

133. For an early description of *Suoi Reo* by one of its editors, see Xuan Thuy, "Suoi Reo Nam Ay" [The Bubbling Spring That Year] in *Tap Chi Van Hoc* 1 (1960), reprinted in Bao Tang Cach Mang Viet Nam—Bao Tang Son La, *Suoi Reo Nam Ay: Hoi Ky Cach Mang* [The Bubbling Spring That Year: Revolutionary Memoirs] (Hanoi, 1993). For another treatment by a member of the editorial board, see Tran Huy Lieu, "Tu 'Tieng Suoi Reo,' den 'Dong Song Cong,' den 'Con Duong Nghia' " [From "Bubbling Spring" to "The Cong River" to "The Path of Justice"], in *Tran Huy Lieu: Hoi Ky*, ed. Pham Nhu Thom (Hanoi, 1991), 275–77.
134. AOM, SLOTFOM, 3d ser., carton 52. *AAPCI*, 1st quarter 1933, 5.
135. Ibid., 4th quarter 1934, appendix 3.

the journal, the escape was facilitated by the collaboration of a corporal and six guards who worked in the prison.[136]

POLITICAL CONVERSION

Evidence of political conversions was particularly disturbing to prison officials. "After a certain time in detention," *AAPCI* reported grimly in 1932, "prisoners ignorant of communism are well instructed in it and become perfectly capable of carrying out propaganda themselves."[137] According to *AAPCI*, young prisoners were especially vulnerable to communist appeals: "Propaganda is often aimed at young inmates who are easily won over and frequently leave prison committed to the communist cause."[138] In February 1932, *AAPCI* reported that a hunger strike at the Bac Lieu Provincial Prison was "led by a common-law inmate won over to communist ideas in prison."[139]

Conversion narratives are a prominent feature of revolutionary prison memoirs. In "Never to Give Up Working So Long as One Lives," the future politburo member Pham Hung converts and indoctrinates three criminals with whom he is incarcerated in the Saigon Central Prison.[140] He teaches them to read and drills them regarding the objectives and strategy of the Communist Party. "I have been acquainted with nonpolitical prisoners in different jails," Hung explains, "and usually, they follow the political prisoners."[141] At the close of the memoir, Hung's cellmates shout "Long Live the Communist Party!" as they are dragged off to face the executioner.

Prison memoirs also contain episodes in which noncommunist political prisoners transfer their allegiance to the ICP in jail. In "Brought to Political Maturity Thanks to the People and the Party," for example, Nguyen Luong Bang claims that three members of the Nationalist Party imprisoned with him in Son La "were won over to the ranks of communism."[142] Likewise, in "Our People, a Very Heroic People," Hoang Quoc Viet witnesses defections of Nationalist Party members to the communist camp in

136. Ibid., 1st quarter 1932, 4.
137. Ibid., 2.
138. Ibid.
139. Ibid.
140. Pham Hung, "Never to Give Up Working So Long As One Lives," 67–77.
141. Ibid., 70.
142. Nguyen Luong Bang, "Brought to Political Maturity Thanks to the People and the Party," in *A Heroic People: Memoirs from the Revolution* (Hanoi, 1965), 55.

prisons at Hai Phong, Hanoi and Poulo Condore.[143] During a visit to Poulo Condore in 1936, Demariaux interviewed a former nationalist prisoner named Mao Van Guang (*sic*) who admitted that he had "joined the Third International while in prison."[144] Other prominent nationalists who converted to communism in prison were Pham Tuan Tai, Nguyen Phuong Thao, and To Chan—each of whom eventually rose to important leadership positions within the ICP.

An instructive account of political conversion in prison can be found in Tran Huy Lieu's memoir "Phan Dau de Tro Nen Mot Dang Vien Cong San" (Striving to Become a Communist Party Member).[145] A Nationalist Party leader when he was sent to Poulo Condore in 1929, Lieu confirms the crucial role of seminars, plays, popular songs, and prison newspapers in triggering his ideological about-face. After growing disillusioned with the recklessness and theoretical incoherence of his fellow nationalist prisoners, Lieu joined the study sessions of the communist prisoners and fell under the influence of an ICP member, Bui Cong Trung. Shortly before his release, Lieu openly rejected the main planks of the Nationalist Party, making his views known in a short book entitled *Self-Criticism*. He entered the ICP formally upon his release in 1934.

STRUGGLE MOVEMENTS

In addition to their efforts at education and indoctrination, communist prison cells planned and carried out acts of collective protest. Between 1931 and 1936, twenty-six protest demonstrations in seventeen different prisons were recorded in *AAPCI*.[146] Numerous additional incidents were re-

---

143. Hoang Quoc Viet, "Our People, a Very Heroic People," in ibid., 162–67.

144. Demariaux, *Secrets des îles Poulo-Condore*, 171.

145. Tran Huy Lieu, "Phan Dau De Tro Nen Mot Dang Vien Cong San" [Striving to Become a Communist Party Member]. In *Hoi Ky Tran Huy Lieu*, ed. Pham Nhu Thom (Hanoi, 1991), 158–67.

146. See the following entries in AOM, SLOTFOM: Ben Tre, January 31, 1932; Kham Lon, November 20, 1931; Kon Tum, December 12, 1931; Hai Phong, December 22, 1931; My Tho, January 16, 1932; Quang Ngai, February 3, 1932; Bac Lieu, February 11, 1932; Cho Lon, February 15, 1932; Chau Doc, February 29, 1932; Hai Duong, November 17, 1932; Bac Giang, February 6, 1933; Hai Phong, February 19, 1933; Buon Ma Thuot, April 22, 1933; Chau Doc, March 28, 1933; Can Tho, October 17, 1933; Vung Tau, November 3, 1933; Hai Phong, February 14, 1934; Kham Lon, April 28, 1934; Ha Tien, May 4, 1934; Lao Bao, February 24, 1935; Kham Lon, July 28, 1935; Buon Ma Thuot, February 7 and 13, 1936; Kham Lon, February 29, 1936; Bac Lieu, April 15, 1936; and Con Dao, May 27, 1936.

ported in the colonial press.[147] They commonly took the form of hunger strikes and work stoppages. Also common were performative acts of symbolic resistance: the unfurling of a red banner, the collective chanting of radical and anticolonial slogans, or the singing of "L'Internationale." Although some incidents involved attacks on prison personnel, most demonstrations were nonviolent, tightly disciplined, and designed to accomplish limited objectives.

In what may have reflected their own efforts at morale-building, the authors of *AAPCI* insisted that protest demonstrations launched by political prisoners rarely spread among other segments of inmate population. Following a week-long hunger strike by 44 communist inmates at the Lao Bao Penitentiary in 1936, the report pointed out that "the remaining 200 common-law prisoners have remained perfectly calm."[148] On the contrary, however, because shortages of space prevented penal segregation and protests tended to target general prison conditions that affected all inmates equally, it was not unusual for demonstrations to involve a mix of political and nonpolitical prisoners. Some episodes, in fact, succeeded in mobilizing the entire inmate population. For example, on February 29, 1932, all 120 inmates at the Chau Doc Provincial Prison struck to protest against the brutality of the guard corps.[149]

Given the horrific prison conditions described in the ministerial inspection report of 1931, it is not surprising that protesters frequently targeted bad food and poor working conditions.[150] Demonstrations were also staged

147. Prisoner demonstrations were covered extensively in *La Lutte*, a French-language newspaper established by an alliance of French-educated Trotskyists, Stalinists, nationalists, and anarchists in Saigon. Another chronicle of important communist-led movements in prison between 1931 and 1936 can be found in *Nhung Su Kien Lich Su Dang, Tap I (1920–1945)* [Events in Party History, vol. 1: 1920–1945] (Hanoi, 1976), which deemed the following seven movements worthy of note: Hai Phong, January 1931 (p. 192); Kham Lon, November 1931 (p. 234); Kon Tum, December 1931 (p. 264); Hoa Lo, December 1931, and July 1932 (p. 266); Buon Ma Thuot, 1934 (p. 326); and Con Dao, 1936 (p. 365).

148. AOM, SLOTFOM, 3d ser., carton 53, *AAPCI*, 1st quarter 1936, 47.

149. Ibid., February–March 1932, 3.

150. See AOM, SLOTFOM, 3d ser., carton 52, *AAPCI*, for some examples. On February 3, 1932, twenty-six political prisoners at Quang Ngai refused to work until the quantity and quality of prison food were improved. On February 14, 1933, fifty inmates at Haiphong staged a sit-down strike to protest unsafe labor practices. Two weeks later, forty-eight political prisoners at Chau Doc refused to eat unless the warden shortened the length of their work day. On February 7, 1936, forty-two communist prisoners at Buon Ma Thuot began a hunger strike, citing the abysmal sanitary state of the penitentiary.

to express solidarity with fellow inmates who had been treated unjustly by the administration. On December 20, 1931, political prisoners in Saigon Central Prison chanted revolutionary slogans for hours in response to the execution of an ICP member, Ly Tu Trong.[151] On February 11, 1932, prisoners at Bac Lieu refused to work when one of the leaders of the Prisoners' Association was beaten by guards and placed in solitary confinement.[152] On April 28, 1934, thirty political prisoners in Saigon Central Prison began a hunger strike to protest the punitive isolation of their comrade Nguyen Van Nguyen.[153]

Finally, some demonstrations were planned as explicit acts of political provocation or as a means to "induce a spirit of struggle among the inmate population."[154] Such may have been the case with a work stoppage organized by political prisoners in My Tho in 1932 to protest against mandatory haircuts.[155] A Party document seized from the Vinh Provincial Prison in 1932 reveals an episode in which communist prisoners admitted that their grievance was merely a pretext to maintain pressure on the administration.

> The date of commencement of the struggle is fixed for Thursday. If we can persuade our comrades to refuse food, we should be able to launch the strike. We shall certainly be able to persuade them to refuse the rotten meat. However, if by chance, the meat they serve this Thursday is not rotten, a signal will be given to change the slogan from a demand for untainted meat to a demand for something else.[156]

A similar logic was probably at work with efforts to commemorate important days in revolutionary history. On October 17, 1931, communist inmates at Saigon Central Prison fasted to mark the fourteenth anniversary of the Russian Revolution.[157] In 1934, political prisoners in Lao Bao barricaded themselves in their dormitories on the occasion of the fifth anniversary of the death of Nguyen Si Sach, the first communist prisoner killed at the penitentiary.[158]

151. AOM, SLOTFOM, 3d ser., carton 49, *AAPCI*, November–December 1931, 2.
152. Ibid., carton 52, *AAPCI*, February–March 1932, 4.
153. Ibid., 2d quarter 1934, 4.
154. Ibid., carton 42, *AAPCI*, February 1936, 3.
155. Ibid., carton 52, *AAPCI* February–March 1932, 13.
156. AOM, SLOTFOM, 3d ser., carton 52, *AAPCI*, April–May 1932, 4.
157. Ibid., carton 49, *AAPCI*, November–December 1931, 5.
158. Ibid., carton 52, *AAPCI*, 4th quarter 1934, 7. Nguyen Si Sach was shot in the back during an escape attempt from Lao Bao in 1929. For more on Nguyen Si Sach's death, see ibid., carton 129, Mutinerie au pénitencier de Lao Bao, December 1929.

Unfortunately, few sources shed light on the internal dynamics of protest demonstrations among prisoners during the 1930s. In 1936, the governor-general complained that his understanding of the growth of communist resistance in prison was hampered by the "provocative exaggerations of the colonial press" and the tendency of skittish local prison officials to "minimize the facts."[159] Moreover, while accounts of protest demonstrations abound in officially sanctioned communist prison memoirs penned years after the fact, the propagandistic function of the genre undercuts their credibility. Not only do all hunger strikes and work stoppages in communist prison memoirs end victoriously but they tend to unfold precisely according to the plans of an omnipotent Party leadership.

One antidote to the equally unreliable reports of colonial officials and communist leaders is an unusual prison memoir published in 1939 and entitled *Nhat Ky Tuyet Thuc 9 Ngay Ruoi: Mot Cuoc Tranh Dau Cua Chinh Tri Con Lon* (Diary of a Nine-and-a-Half-Day Hunger Strike: A Struggle of Political Prisoners on Poulo Condore).[160] Written by a communist activist using the pseudonym San Ho, this provides a first-person narrative of a hunger strike carried out by communist prisoners on Poulo Condore in 1936. San Ho published it during the open atmosphere of the Popular Front, before the Party had succeeded in homogenizing the autobiographical writings of its members. Indeed, despite San Ho's apparent communist affiliation, his diary reads less like a revolutionary memoir (*hoi ky cach mang*) than like realist reportage (*phong su*)—the genre of nonfiction writing that became popular in Indochina during the 1930s.[161]

In its opening entry, San Ho's diary sets the scene: a courtyard in Bagne I, in which groups of political and common-law prisoners are confined together—bathing, reading, planting vegetables, lifting weights, running in place, studying Morse code, and practicing revolutionary songs. Suddenly, the chief warder appears and announces that the new prison director, M. Bouvier, has issued an order forbidding inmates to stage theatrical productions. Moments later, guards enter the yard and confiscate a handful of crates filled with costumes, props, and sets. The leaders of the

159. AOM, Indochine, Affaires politiques, 1728, Régime pénitencier de Poulo Condore, July 4, 1936.

160. San Ho, *Nhat Ky Tuyet-Thuc 9 Ngay Ruoi: Mot Cuoc Tranh Dau Cua Tu Chinh Tri Con Lon* (Nam Dinh, 1939).

161. San Ho's stated intention of providing "a torch to light up Poulo Condore" (ibid., 2) recalls a familiar convention of the realist reportage genre, as does his dual role as participant and witness.

Prisoners' Association immediately convene a meeting in the yard, at which inmates enumerate a litany of unpopular policy changes implemented in the three weeks since Bouvier assumed the directorship of the penitentiary. New restrictions on time allowed in the yard and additional labor requirements top their list of complaints. Following the meeting, the Struggle Committee of the Prisoners' Association issues a series of written demands calling for a reversal of the new policies and a return of the theatrical equipment. Not to be intimidated, Bouvier counters by canceling the evening meal and locking the prisoners in their dormitories, where they are shackled together in pairs. In response, the Struggle Committee announces that prisoners will not eat until their chains are removed and their original demands met. Upping the ante further, Bouvier announces that prisoners will not be permitted out of their dormitory until the hunger strike has been called off.

The strike begins in earnest on March 14. Based on experience gained from previous strikes, the Struggle Committee advises prisoners to conserve strength by drinking plenty of water, sleeping as much as possible and refraining from singing, chanting, and playing cards or chess. In addition, the committee solicits support from prisoners in other parts of the penitentiary and from the public at large through letters smuggled to the Cochin Chinese press. Bouvier, however, refuses to offer even minor concessions. After a week, the determination of the strikers begins to wane. Rather than run the risk of defections that would not only erode the strength of the movement but might leave a legacy of bitterness and internal recriminations, the Struggle Committee decides to call off the hunger strike nine and a half days after it began.

The strike's failure to wrest concessions serves as a counterpoint to the monotonous accounts of successful resistance detailed in communist prison memoirs. As San Ho suggests, the record of such efforts was probably mixed, because prison officials like Bouvier were often prepared to allow communist inmates to starve themselves to death. Otherwise, San Ho's diary points to the significance of certain forces that shaped communist resistance efforts in prison. For example, it shows how the communal setup of the prison facilitated the organization of large meetings, at which inmates could be mobilized for collective action. It confirms the crucial leadership role played by the Prisoners' Association through the instrument of the Struggle Committee. Finally, the catalytic role of the new prison director in triggering the strike recalls the enduring significance of the unstable authoritarianism of colonial prison administration in provoking protest movements among inmates and provides a reminder that communist inmates were, in fact, heirs to a tradition of prison resistance.

THE LIMITS OF COMMUNIST ORGANIZATION

The ultimate failure of the hunger strike documented by San Ho serves as a useful reminder about the limits of communist power behind bars. Although the political accomplishments of imprisoned party activists during the early 1930s were formidable, it would be a mistake to view their efforts as unvaryingly successful. Indeed, the huge amount of intelligence that prison authorities were able to accumulate about their activities attests to the vulnerability of jailed communists and the fragility of their organizational efforts. Sûreté reports reveal that prison dormitories were honeycombed with spies and informers and that inmates frequently named names and provided vital information under torture and interrogation. In 1991, an unusually forthright essay in the *Journal of Party History* called attention to the suppression of historical evidence about rivalry, cowardice, and betrayal among activists imprisoned during the colonial era.[162] Insisting that an examination of this checkered underside of the Party's prison experience might hold important historical lessons, the essay referred obliquely to the disruptive impact on Party organization and operations in prison caused by communist inmates who clung to unspecified "prejudices" (*thanh kien*) and "fixed ideas" (*dinh kien*).[163] Such attitudes, the essay continued, provoked tense relations and debilitating "psychological complexes" (*mac cam*) among imprisoned activists "both during their incarcerations and following their release."[164]

A less cryptic account of tensions and internal rivalries among communist political prisoners may be found in the (previously discussed) communist report confiscated at Lao Bao Penitentiary in 1934. According to the report's fourth and final chapter, entitled "Commentary on the Two Old Factions," political prisoners at Lao Bao had once aligned themselves with one or another of two rival groups: the Prisoners (*tu nhan*) and the No-Names (*vo danh*). Despite the fact that each group was led by a founding member of the protocommunist Vietnamese Youth League, they competed intensely with each other in what the authors of the report

162. Trinh Quang Canh, "Lich Su Nha Day Buon Ma Thuot, 1930–1945" [History of Buon Ma Thuot Penitentiary, 1930–1945], *Tap Chi Lich Su Dang* 5 (1991): 51–54.
163. Ibid., 53.
164. Ibid.

described as "a spirit of mutual critique and reciprocal destruction." Organized by Tran Van Cung (alias Quoc Anh) in October 1931, the No-Names resented the subsequent formation of the Prisoners by Cung's old Youth League comrade Vo Mai (alias Quoc Hoa) in February 1932.[165] The Prisoners alleged that Tran Van Cung had eaten secretly during a recent hunger strike; that one of his comrades, Tran Van Nhi, had given compromising information to the warden in return for a pardon; and that the No-Names had botched the planning of a recent May Day demonstration. The No-Names, on the other hand, charged the Prisoners with "collaboration, reformism, formalism, and espionage," and maintained that their attacks were without basis and recklessly divisive. The Prisoners, they claimed, were paranoid extremists and had even threatened several of them with decapitation.[166] In February 1932, a number of so-called general assemblies were convened by representatives of the two groups, and late in August a rapprochement was reached between them.[167] They agreed to put aside their differences and form a single organization known as the Political Prisoners (*tu chinh tri*). Even as it praised the rapprochement, the report acknowledged that a "vague partisan spirit" continued to divide the Political Prisoners and damage their capacity for unified and effective struggle.

As with internal tensions and factional struggles, conflict with rival anticolonial groupings distracted the attention of jailed communists, frequently diluting their capacity to oppose the prison administration. A dramatic example is the well-documented confrontation that erupted between

---

165. For biographical information on Tran Van Cung, see Huynh Kim Khanh, *Vietnamese Communism*, 112: "Tran Van Cung, alias Quoc Hoc, was born in Nghe-An province on May 5, 1906. One of the earliest members of Thanh Nien, he became secretary of the Bac Ky Regional Committee and one of seven members of its secret cell, working to transform the organization into a communist party. Following the August Revolution he became secretary of the Nghe An–Ha Tinh Joint Province, and then member of the Standing Committee of the National Assembly. He died October 31, 1977 in Hanoi." For more on Tran Van Cung, see his memoirs, "Chi Bo Cong San Dau Tien Va Dong Duong Cong San Dang" [The First Communist Cell and the Indochinese Communist Party], in *Buoc Ngoat Vi Dai Cua Lich Su Cach Mang Viet Nam* [A Glorious Turning Point in the History of the Vietnam Communist Party] (Hanoi, 1960).

166. Lao Bao Report, 8–16.

167. The first General Assembly was held on February 1932, the second was held in March, the third in April, the fourth in June, and the fifth on August 28 that year.

communists and nationalists in Poulo Condore's Bagne II in 1935. The episode is described in both official reports and communist prison narratives but receives its most detailed treatment in the memoir of Nguyen Hai Ham, a nationalist.[168] According to Ham, animosity between communists and nationalists in Bagne II was initially provoked by ideological differences. The communists chided the nationalists for their adventurism, strategic myopia, and "veneration of Confucius," while the nationalists countered that the communists were unpatriotic (*vo to quoc*), unreligious (*vo ton giao*), and obsessed with foreign political theories. This verbal sparring escalated as nationalists accused the communists of attempting to win converts from among the younger and more impressionable members of their party. Early in 1935, Doi Lang, the leader of an "extremist faction" within the Nationalist Party observed his fellow nationalist Tuong Dan Bao fraternizing with a group of communists. Overcome with rage, Lang confronted Bao and stabbed him repeatedly in the chest with a homemade knife. Standing over his wounded ex-comrade, Lang is reported to have yelled, "Tuong Dan Bao is a traitor! I have killed him to protect us from danger! Long live the Vietnamese Nationalist Party!" He then plunged the knife into his own neck. Lang died almost immediately from his self-inflicted wounds, but Bao recovered from the attack and soon after joined the ICP. In the recriminations that followed the attack, communists and nationalists brawled repeatedly and were finally segregated in different dormitories by the administration.

It is instructive that communist, nationalist, and colonial accounts each explain the episode with regard to Tuong Dan Bao's planned defection to the communist side in the context of a general erosion of political commitment among jailed nationalists.[169] This interpretation supports the argument put forth in this chapter about the unique capacity of communists in prison to expand their base of support through Leninist strategies of education, agitation, and indoctrination. On the other hand, the episode also reveals how communist political tactics could lead to violent infighting within the population of political inmates as a whole, a situation that doubtless served the greater interests of the prison administration.

168. Nguyen Hai Ham, *Tu Yen Bay Den Con Lon, 1930–1945* [From Yen Bay to Con Lon, 1930–1945] (Saigon, 1970).

169. For the colonial administration's account of the 1935 hostilities, see AOM, SLOTFOM, 3d ser., carton 54, *AAPCI*, 1st quarter 1935, 7. For an ICP account, see Ha Huy Giap, *Doi Toi: Nhung Dieu Nghe, Thay va Song*, 120–22.

CONCLUSION

As the detailed record of confiscated documents and inside information presented in *AAPCI* makes clear, prison officials were able to monitor and suppress much of the secret political activity carried out by jailed communists during the first half of the 1930s. And yet their efforts could not prevent a fundamental shift in the balance of power from taking place in colonial prisons. During the late nineteenth and early twentieth centuries, the explosive but sporadic nature of inmate resistance left open an ever-present possibility of revolt but did not challenge day-to-day operations. In the early 1930s, however, the tightly disciplined organizational efforts and resistance tactics spearheaded by communist prisoners began to shift control over life in colonial prisons from the regime to the inmates themselves. Lacking adequate means of surveillance and coercion, the resident superior of Tonkin acknowledged in 1932,

> Prison authorities are obliged to *negotiate* in certain ways with the detainees. The lack of available space permits them to plan together at leisure all inclinations to rebellion, which could easily produce a general rising. The defective material installation, which constitutes a veritable aggravation of their penalty, has already been one cause of discontent. This inconvenience is dealt with by *conceding a maximum of tolerance*, compatible with security, but regrettable nonetheless.[170]

While the resident superior emphasized insufficient surveillance, weak means of coercion, and defective material conditions to explain the new balance of power within the colonial prison, these administrative shortcomings were only part of the story. Of equal importance was the administrative and operational sophistication exhibited by jailed communist inmates. In short, the insertion of a centralized, hierarchical, and highly disciplined political organization into an ethnically divided, administratively haphazard, and chronically ill-disciplined colonial prison system resulted in the former's virtual colonization of the latter.

Just as communists changed the colonial prison system, imprisonment shaped the character of the ICP. During the period of mass incarceration in the early 1930s, Vietnamese communists made significant progress rebuilding the organization, studying Marxist-Leninist theory, and indoctrinating new adepts. Moreover, for neophyte revolutionaries, the colonial prison provided a perfect training ground for mastering the Leninist arts of

---

170. AOM, Indochine, Affaires politiques, 1728, Tonkin Report, 13. Emphasis added.

underground organization. Since the consequences of negligence, recklessness, or disloyalty in prison might entail torture, solitary confinement, or death, political agitation behind bars reinforced the importance of the Leninist principles of secrecy, centralization, obedience, and discipline. Indeed, if the Party's emergence in the repressive political environment of colonial Indochina encouraged its commitment to Leninist revolutionary strategy, its rebirth within the coercive institutional atmosphere of the Indochinese prison served to radically intensify this tendency.

8 Prisons and the Colonial Press, 1934–1939

During the second half of the 1930s, colonial prisons came under constant scrutiny in the Indochinese press. Between 1934 and 1939, newspapers featured thousands of stories about overcrowded dormitories, wretched food, filthy living conditions, and the physical brutalization of prison inmates. To amplify the voices of the inmates themselves, editors printed their letters, excerpted their diaries, and commissioned them to write memoirs upon release. Not only did the vast proliferation of prison coverage provoke public outrage at the colonial administration but it checked the power of prison officials and provided a measure of protection for the inmate population. It also put forward an agenda for prison reform against which official efforts to improve the system were measured. In view of its capacity to express and channel public opinion while simultaneously restraining the power of the colonial state, media coverage of the prison system may be seen as among the earliest and most significant manifestations of civil society in colonial Indochina.

Although colonial officials saw press coverage of the prison system as part of an orchestrated communist plot, the evolution of the media's preoccupation with the topic was considerably more complex. It was nurtured by the explosive growth of publishing in interwar Indochina, stimulated by metropolitan investigative journalism and shaped by the development of complex personal networks linking prison dormitories and pressrooms. Indeed, a major reason journalists wrote so much about the colonial prison was that many were ex-prisoners themselves. Also important was the development of a movement of legal opposition to the colonial state, which expanded rapidly in Indochina when Léon Blum's Popular Front assumed power in France in 1936. Although members of the ICP participated in this movement of legal opposition, they did not dominate it. Rather, it was spearheaded by an eclectic array of anticolonial journalists—Trotskyists, anarchists, and nationalists—many of whom were openly hostile to the explicitly Stalinist orientation of the ICP. Following the mass amnesty of hundreds of communist prisoners in late 1936, the ICP's role in the legal opposition and campaign for prison reform expanded considerably. However, it remained only one among several anticolonial groups, many cohering around specific newspaper offices, that struggled, sometimes together and sometimes at cross-purposes, against the deprivations of the colonial prison.

This media campaign for prison reform led to real improvements in the way political prisoners were treated during the late 1930s, but its impact on popular attitudes to the colonial state was even more significant historically. Unlike other pressing social issues, such as inequality, poverty, and crime, blame for the wretched state of the colonial prison could not be pinned on abstract economic forces. On the contrary, inhuman prison conditions pointed inescapably to the corruption, negligence, and brutality of the colonial administration—an administration that press coverage embodied in sadistic guards, venal contractors, incompetent doctors, and autocratic wardens. Although there were many reasons for Indochinese subjects to despise the colonial state, few were as easily dramatized as the horrendous conditions of colonial imprisonment.

In addition to discussing the causes and immediate effects of the colonial media's preoccupation with the prison system during the late 1930s, this chapter examines the broader impact of prison coverage on the history of the modern Vietnamese nation. Like the prison system itself, representations of it in the colonial press contributed to the development of Vietnamese nationalism. By depicting abusive regimes and resistant inmates in prisons throughout Indochina's three Vietnamese territories, the press encouraged its readers in Tonkin, Annam, and Cochin China to view themselves and one another as part of the same wretched, yet defiant, collectivity. For the ICP, a focus on prison conditions provided a means to champion and identify itself with an issue that was truly national in its ability to transcend both regional and political divisions. Hence the movement contributed to the conflation of the communist and nationalist projects within the popular imagination. In addition, the capacity of the press coverage of the 1930s to transform political prisoners into public celebrities shaped how revolutionary leaders came to define their claims to political power in the postcolonial era.

COMMERCIAL INCENTIVES, POLITICAL MOTIVES, AND METROPOLITAN MODELS

The rapid development of publishing in interwar Indochina furnished commercial incentives for coverage of the colonial prison.[1] During the 1920s and 1930s, the growth of cities and the emergence of a new urban elite educated in Franco-Vietnamese schools generated demand for reading material in French and the romanized Vietnamese script (*quoc ngu*). As a result, the period witnessed both the proliferation of French-language "scandal sheets" and the unprecedented growth of the *quoc ngu* press.[2] Whereas fewer than 30 *quoc ngu* periodicals had appeared in Indochina prior to 1925, at least 40 were founded between 1926 and 1930, and another 400 came out during the 1930s.[3] The growth in publishing accelerated further between 1936 and 1939 as the Popular Front relaxed censorship in the colonies. As competition for market share increased, editors attempted to attract readers with coverage of sensational topics such as corruption, prostitution, underworld gangs, gambling, drug addiction, and crime and punishment in general. Since all of these elements were present in the Indochinese prison, it is not surprising that the topic came to preoccupy the colonial media.

The public appetite for coverage of the prison system transcended the topic's voyeuristic appeal. In 1935, Tran Huy Lieu pointed out that demand for reporting about Poulo Condore was generated by "thousands of families with imprisoned members who wait for news every day."[4] Since little information was available from official sources, reporters and editors came to see the relatives of colonial captives as something of a captive audience. Even for those fortunate enough to avoid imprisonment or the ordeal that accompanied the incarceration of a friend, relative, or loved one, rumors of inhuman prison conditions were verified by the high frequency of prison

---

1. For accounts of the rise of publishing in Indochina, see Huynh Van Tong, *Lich Su Bao Chi Viet Nam tu Khoi Thuy den 1930* (Saigon, 1973); Nguyen Thanh, *Bao Chi Cach Mang Viet Nam, 1925–1945* (Hanoi, 1984); David Marr, *Vietnamese Tradition on Trial, 1920–1945* (Berkeley and Los Angeles, 1981), 44–53; and Hue-Tam Ho Tai, *Radicalism and the Origins of the Vietnamese Revolution* (Cambridge, Mass., 1992), 114–46.

2. The term "scandal sheets" is from Hue-Tam Ho Tai, *Radicalism and the Origins of the Vietnamese Revolution*, 146.

3. John De Francis, *Colonialism and Language Policy in Viet-Nam* (The Hague, 1977), 213–17.

4. Tran Huy Lieu, "Con Lon Ky Su" [Con Lon Memoir], in *Hoi Ky Tran Huy Lieu*, ed. Pham Nhu Thom (Hanoi, 1991), 419.

uprisings. The commercial appeal of the press campaign was, therefore, heightened by its capacity to document and confirm an extensive body of lurid stories that had been circulating informally for decades.

Commercial considerations, however, were only part of the story. The growth of prison coverage was also linked with the development of a powerful movement of legal political opposition in Indochina.[5] This movement was spearheaded initially by young Cochin Chinese radicals who returned to Indochina after studying in France during the late 1920s.[6] Although they were divided ideologically into rival anticolonial factions, the returnees shared a faith in the efficacy of forms of aboveground political activity that they had observed and participated in during their years in France. From their base in Saigon, the returnees set up publishing houses, formed Marxist study groups, organized trade unions, and ran successfully in local elections for seats on the Colonial Council.[7] With most members of the ICP still in jail, the returnees rose rapidly within the anticolonial movement and made open political activity a significant part of its cutting edge.

The legal opposition achieved its greatest success by using the power of the press to poison public opinion about the colonial state. In 1933, a handful of returnees, including the Stalinists Nguyen Van Tao and Duong Bach Mai, the Trotskyists Ta Thu Thau and Phan Van Hum, the anarchist Trinh Hung Ngau, and the radical nationalist Nguyen An Ninh, founded a French-language weekly in Saigon called *La Lutte*.[8] Taking advantage of Indochina's loose censorship laws for French-language publications in Cochin China, *La Lutte* launched a barrage of blistering attacks against the administration. Its provocative critiques of racism, economic inequality, and official abuse of power incited widespread support for the anticolonial movement and introduced a new style of radical political discourse into Indochina. It was in the context of this wide-ranging media campaign that the abysmal state of colonial prisons emerged as an important public issue.

As ICP members were gradually released from prison during the mid 1930s, they swelled the ranks of the legal opposition. Their newfound

5. Huynh Kim Khanh, *Vietnamese Communism, 1925–1945* (Ithaca, N.Y., 1982), 189–231.

6. Scott McConnell, *Leftward Journey: The Education of Vietnamese Students in France, 1919–1939* (New Brunswick, N.J., 1989), 131–53.

7. Huynh Kim Khanh, *Vietnamese Communism*, 211–16.

8. The most detailed account of *La Lutte* and its activities is Daniel Hémery, *Révolutionnaires vietnamiens et pouvoir colonial en Indochine: Communistes, trotskystes, nationalistes à Saïgon de 1932 à 1937* (Paris, 1975).

enthusiasm for legal political activity followed a shift in Comintern policy in 1935 that encouraged communist parties to ally with antifascist forces and agitate for peace and democratic freedoms rather than social revolution.[9] Following the model of *La Lutte*, they founded their own opposition newspapers, participated in the electoral process and entered the labor movement. Not only did they cooperate periodically with the more cosmopolitan returnees but they sometimes joined forces with conservative anticolonial activists from the older generations. Hence, by 1936, the legal opposition included a range of anticolonial forces representing a broad array of backgrounds and ideological orientations.

The growth of prison coverage in Indochina was also influenced by the development of the prison exposé as an independent journalistic genre in metropolitan France.[10] The genre emerged in 1924 with the publication in Paris of *Au Bagne*, an exposé of the French penal colony on Devil's Island by the investigative reporter Albert Londres.[11] Not only was *Au Bagne* successful commercially but it prompted the minister of justice to send a Salvation Army officer named Charles Péan to conduct a formal investigation of the penal colony.[12] In 1934, he published *Terre de bagne*, which confirmed and expanded the dismal picture painted by Londres. "Never has the *bagne* rehabilitated a single man," Péan wrote; "its inmates emerge brutalized, disoriented, desocialized, rootless, and devoid of purpose."[13] A follow-up investigation by Péan entitled *Le Salut des parias* led the Chamber of Deputies to consider a proposal to close the South American *bagnes* permanently, but it was narrowly defeated.[14]

Encouraged by the success of *Au Bagne*, Londres made plans for an Indochinese sequel. In 1932, he set off for Poulo Condore, but he died en

---

9. William Duiker, *The Rise of Nationalism in Vietnam, 1900–1941* (Ithaca, N.Y., 1976), 239–40; Huynh Kim Khanh, *Vietnamese Communism*, 205–7.

10. See, e.g., Antoine Mesclon, *Comment j'ai subi quinze ans de bagne* (Paris, 1924); Jacques Dhur, *Visions de bagne* (Paris, 1925); Louis Merlat, *Au bout du monde* (Paris, 1928); L. Le Boucher, *Ce qu'il faut connaître du bagne* (Paris, 1930); Géo London, *Aux portes du bagne* (Paris, 1930); Dr. Louis Rousseau, *Un Médicin au bagne* (Paris, 1930); Georges Ferré, *Bagnards, colons et canaques* (Paris, 1932); Henri Huchon, *Quand j'étais au bagne* (Bordeaux, 1933); Marius Larique, *Dans la brousse* (Paris, 1933); and Paul Roussenq, *Vingt-cinq ans au bagne* (Paris, 1934).

11. Paul Musset, *Albert Londres; ou, L'Aventure du grand reportage* (Paris, 1972).

12. Gordon Wright, *Between the Guillotine and Liberty: Two Centuries of the Crime Problem in France* (New York, 1983), 186–87.

13. Ibid.

14. Ibid.

route when his ship sank in the Gulf of Aden.[15] Londres's death inspired the journalist Jean-Claude Demariaux, who visited Poulo Condore five times during the 1930s and published a series of reports about it in the French press. "Larique, Danant, Roubaud, Georges Lefevre, and Danjou have all gone to Guiana," he wrote, boasting of his newfound professional niche, "but none of these watchdogs of journalism have had the idea or the opportunity to visit the great Asian *bagne*."[16] When he finally collated his articles into a single volume, *Les Secrets des îles Poulo-Condore: Le Grand Bagne indochinois*, Demariaux dedicated the book to Londres, whom he praised for "understanding the great place occupied by the *bagne* in the thoughts of the Annamite world."[17]

An even more compelling model for Indochinese activists was provided by the leftist writer Andrée Viollis (Andrée d'Ardenne de Tizac), whose exposés of prison conditions and police brutality in Annam and Cochin China appeared in *Esprit* and *Le Petit Parisien* during the early 1930s. In 1935, Viollis published *Indochine S.O.S.*, a diary of a 1931 visit to Indochina that included grim descriptions of prison conditions and interviews with famous political prisoners such as Phan Boi Chau and Huynh Thuc Khang. In a preface to *Indochine S.O.S.*, André Malraux praised Viollis's work, comparing it to Londres's socially committed journalism.[18] Concluding with a lengthy appendix of letters by political prisoners and their families, *Indochine S.O.S.* established Viollis as a major metropolitan spokesperson for their plight.[19]

French prison exposés were certainly familiar to the Indochinese reading public and shaped early Vietnamese efforts to call attention to the brutality of the colonial system. "Should Poulo Condore Be Closed?" asked an essay that appeared in July 1937, citing Albert Londres, Jacques Dhur, Georges Le Favre, Marina Larrique, and E. Danjou to buttress its case.[20] Viollis gained a large following in Indochina after excerpts from *Indochine S.O.S.* were published in colonial newspapers such as *Tieng Dan, Duoc Nha Nam, Hon Tre*

15. Jean-Claude Demariaux, *Les Secrets des îles Poulo-Condore: Le Grand Bagne indochinois* (Paris, 1956), 7.

16. Ibid., 12.

17. Ibid., 7.

18. Andrée Viollis, *Indochine S.O.S.* (1935; reprint, Paris, 1949), viii.

19. Ibid., 215–27.

20. T.D., "Co Nen Bo Nguc Con-Lon Khong?" *Dong Duong Tap Chi* 10 (July 17, 1937).

Tap Moi, and *La Lutte.*[21] That the appeal of the genre translated into increased circulation and revenue was not lost on Vietnamese journalists struggling to keep their newspapers afloat in the highly competitive Indochinese publishing market of the 1930s. Moreover, the genre's impact on popular opinion and influence within the French Chamber of Deputies demonstrated that sensational prison exposés possessed the potential to shape public discourse and government policy at the highest levels.

Finally, as an important forerunner to the legal opposition's campaign for prison reform, mention should be made of the movement to secure an amnesty for Phan Boi Chau. Following his arrest and spectacular trial in Hanoi in 1925, the French High Criminal Commission sentenced the great Vietnamese patriot to life in prison at hard labor.[22] In response, activists flooded Indochina's infant publishing market with articles, editorials, and pamphlets that praised Phan's lifelong devotion to the anticolonial cause and denounced the severity of his sentence. They also employed nonviolent political tactics—letter-writing campaigns, petition drives, and peaceful demonstrations—to protest the court's decision. In late December, the movement attained a limited victory when Governor-General Varenne overturned the sentence and ordered Phan placed under permanent house arrest at his home in Hue.[23]

The campaign for an amnesty for Phan Boi Chau foreshadowed and shaped the legal opposition's preoccupation with the prison system a decade later. For many leaders of the legal opposition (especially those who had not studied in France), the amnesty campaign was their earliest experience with open anticolonial politics.[24] Varenne's capitulation encouraged them to believe that the colonial juridical system could be modified through the mobilization of public opinion. Moreover, their success contrasted with the failure of the rebellions of 1930–31 and promoted faith in the value of nonviolent protest and the media as instruments of political

21. Nguyen Thanh, *Lich Su Bao Tieng Dan* [The History of the Newspaper *Tieng Dan*] (Da Nang, 1992), 167.

22. Marr, *Vietnamese Tradition on Trial,* 15–19.

23. Varenne's decision is discussed in William Frederick, "Alexandre Varenne and Politics in Indochina, 1925–26," in *Aspects of Vietnamese History,* ed. Walter Vella, Asian Studies at Hawaii, no. 8 (Honolulu 1973), 118–20.

24. Among those whose first foray into political activity occurred in response to the conviction of Phan Boi Chau were at least three leading members of the ICP Politburo: Pham Van Dong, Vo Nguyen Giap, and Truong Chinh. Christine White, "The Vietnamese Revolutionary Alliance: Intellectuals, Workers and Peasants," in *Peasant Rebellion and Communist Revolution in Asia,* ed. John Lewis (Stanford, Calif., 1974), 85.

struggle. The amnesty movement also demonstrated the potential of political imprisonment, as a public issue, to highlight the cruelty of the colonial state, while at the same time elevating the reputations of political prisoners. That the movement transformed Phan into something of a nationalist celebrity was not lost on future activists, whose efforts during the 1930s enhanced the authority and prestige of numerous political prisoners.

JOURNALISTS IN JAIL

The media's fixation with the prison system was also driven by the fact that released political prisoners frequently found work at opposition newspapers. During the 1920s, journalism emerged as one of the only professions open to educated and ambitious Vietnamese men who were committed to social and political change.[25] A career in law was barely an option, because discrimination prevented all but a tiny handful of Vietnamese from entering the bar. Traditional prejudices against commerce and the domination of the colonial economy by the Chinese and French communities discouraged members of the Vietnamese elite from pursuing careers in business. Moreover, unlike the civil service and the colonial military, which set aside their highest posts for Frenchmen, journalism offered the possibility of rapid career advancement.

For political prisoners who had written for newspapers before being arrested, a return to journalism was a natural move. It offered an opportunity to engage in political struggle without the risks that accompanied underground activity. Others sought newspaper positions in order to put into practice the propaganda skills they had learned writing for prison journals. As more ex-prisoners gravitated toward journalism, newspapers came to function as extensions of the mutual aid associations that inmates had set up to look after one another behind bars. Not only did they furnish regular salaries for activists whose police records limited their employment opportunities, but they offered a site where old prison comrades could meet, reminisce, exchange information, and provide one another with emotional support.

A brief examination of the interwar careers of the leading figures within the legal opposition suggests that prisons and newspaper offices were part of an integrated network through which anticolonial activists circulated during the 1920s and 1930s. In 1937, the Sûreté identified three regional

25. Cedric Sampson, "Nationalism and Communism in Vietnam, 1925–1931" (Ph.D. diss., University of California, Los Angeles, 1975), 88–89.

centers of what it called "legal communist propaganda," each of which re-volved around an opposition newspaper:

> The agitators in charge of legal communist propaganda in Indochina fall into three groups: in Hanoi, the editors of the journal *Le Travail,* led by Tran Huy Lieu; in Hue, the ex-political prisoners who frequent *L'Épi de Riz* [*Nhanh Lua*], edited by Nguyen Khoa Van; and in Cochin China, the editors associated with the journal *La Lutte*—Nguyen Van Tao, Ta Thu Thau, Duong Bach Mai, Phan Van Hum, Nguyen Van Nguyen, and Nguyen An Ninh.[26]

Tran Huy Lieu, putative leader of the legal opposition in Hanoi, spent much of the 1920s and 1930s drifting between journalism and jail. During the mid 1920s, he worked as a writer and editor for newspapers in Saigon including *Nong Co Min Dam* (Agricultural Digest), *Dong Phap Thoi Bao* (The French Indochina Times), and *Phap Viet Nhat Gia* (The Franco-Vietnamese Family).[27] In June 1927, he was arrested for expressing anti-French views in print and jailed for six months in Saigon Central Prison.[28] Upon his release he joined the Nationalist Party and wrote *Nguc Trung Ky Su* (Prison Diary), the first prison memoir published in Indochina.[29] In 1929, he was arrested again and deported to Poulo Condore, where he served a five-year sentence.[30] It was on Poulo Condore that Lieu came under the influence of communist prisoners and transferred his allegiance to the ICP.[31]

Following his release in 1934, Lieu was forced to reside in rural Nam Dinh, but his prison experiences continued to dominate his activities. He wrote a second prison memoir, entitled *Con Lon Ky Su* (Poulo Condore Diary), and a history of the Thai Nguyen Rebellion, based on interviews with ex-rebels whom he had encountered on the islands. He also main-tained a lively correspondence with comrades left behind on Poulo Con-dore, such as Nguyen Duc Chinh, a leader of the Nationalist Party.[32] In 1935, Chinh's younger brother Nguyen Duc Kinh offered Lieu a job with

---

26. AOM, SLOTFOM, 3d ser., carton 59, July 1937.

27. Van Tan [Tran Duc Sac], "Journalist Tran Huy Lieu," *Vietnamese Studies,* no. 15 (85) (1986): 90–92.

28. Ibid.

29. Tran Huy Lieu, *Hoi Ky Tran Huy Lieu,* 417. The memoir is listed in the bib-liography but has never been republished.

30. Van Tan, "Journalist Tran Huy Lieu," 92.

31. He describes his political conversion in prison in Tran Huy Lieu, "Phan Dau De Tro Nen Mot Dang Vien Cong San" [Striving to Become a Communist Party Member], in *Hoi Ky Tran Huy Lieu,* 155–67.

32. Tran Huy Lieu, "Mat Tran Dan Chu Dong Duong" [The Indochinese Demo-cratic Front], in *Hoi Ky Tran Huy Lieu,* 169.

Doi Moi, an opposition newspaper that he had founded in Hanoi.[33] Not only had Lieu shared a dormitory with Kinh's older brother, but his prison background appealed to Kinh, who had recently completed his own hard-labor sentence in Son La Penitentiary.[34]

When *Doi Moi* was closed by colonial authorities, Lieu turned to his prison connections for work and financial assistance. Toward the end of 1935, he sent his eldest son to live with Nguyen Dan, an "old prison comrade" residing in Phu Ly.[35] In 1936, another companion from Poulo Condore, Nguyen Khoa Van, invited Lieu to join the staff of the opposition newspaper *Hon Tre*. From its editorial office, Lieu helped Van recruit former political prisoners to write for the paper. "We wanted to work alongside like-minded comrades," he explained years later in his memoirs, "hence, we always sought out people who had recently been released from prison."[36]

In 1937, Lieu took advantage of a large network of prison comrades in Hanoi to launch the newspaper *Le Travail,* perhaps his most important journalistic endeavor. Through Gianh Duc Cuong—yet another ex-political prisoner—Lieu was introduced to Vo Nguyen Giap, Dang Thai Mai, and Huynh Van Phuong, who eventually came to form *Le Travail*'s editorial board.[37] During the following six months, *Le Travail* attracted more former political prisoners to its staff, including Khuat Duy Tien, Truong Chinh, Hoang Quoc Viet, Dang Chau Tue, and Tong Phuc Chieu.[38] After *Le Travail* was closed by the authorities, Lieu wrote for *Thoi The, Thoi Bao,* and *Ban Dan*.[39] In 1939, he was arrested again and deported to Son La.[40] He was released near the end of World War II and went on to play a leading role in the August Revolution.

As with Tran Huy Lieu, Nguyen Khoa Van's participation in the legal opposition was shaped by periods in jail and a complex web of relations with fellow ex-prisoners who worked as journalists during the interwar years. In 1925, Van was expelled from the Quoc Hoc High School in Hue

33. Ibid., 173.
34. Ibid., 170.
35. Ibid., 176.
36. Ibid., 180.
37. Ibid., 189.
38. Ibid.
39. Van Tan, "Journalist Tran Huy Lieu," 93.
40. Lieu wrote a number of memoirs about Son La, including "Xuan No Trong Tu," "Duoi Ham Son La," and "Tu 'Tieng Suoi Reo,' Den 'Dong Song Cong,' Den 'Con Duong Nghia'" [From "Bubbling Spring" to "The Cong River" to "The Path of Justice"], in *Hoi Ky Tran Huy Lieu,* 222–78.

for participating in the amnesty movement for Phan Boi Chau.[41] In 1927, he joined the Tan Viet Cach Mang Dang, an anticolonial political party founded by Confucian scholars such as Le Huan, Ngo Duc Ke, and Tran Dinh Thanh, who had been incarcerated together on Poulo Condore in 1908.[42] In 1928, he began writing for *Tieng Dan*, a newspaper run by the famous ex-prisoner Huynh Thuc Khang and staffed by many of his prison comrades. After being jailed briefly in Hue during 1930, Van transferred his allegiance to the ICP and moved south to agitate on behalf of the Party.[43] In March 1931, he was arrested for a second time, transferred to Hue to stand trial, and sentenced to nine years' hard labor for illegal political activity.

Van was amnestied the following year and resumed writing for papers associated with the legal opposition.[44] Using the pseudonym Hai Trieu, he intervened in a series of literary debates and emerged as an influential advocate of art-for-life's-sake.[45] He also published a number of intensely personal ruminations on his prison experiences including "Cai Than Tu" (Prison Life) and "Su Thuc Trong Tu" (Truth in Prison).[46] In 1937, he returned to his native Hue and founded *Nhanh Lua* (The Ear of Rice), an opposition newspaper suspected by the Sûreté of "providing work for unemployed former political prisoners" and "attempting to call attention to their plight."[47] In 1940, Van was arrested again and placed in the Phong Huyen Concentration Camp, where he remained until the end of the war. After being released in 1945, he returned immediately to revolutionary work and participated in the August Revolution in Hue.

The editors of *La Lutte* also spent much of the 1920s and 1930s shuttling between prison and the press. Nguyen An Ninh was jailed five times between 1923, when he founded the influential newspaper *La Cloche fêlée*

41. See *Hai Trieu Toan Tap* [The Complete Works of Hai Trieu], ed. Pham Hong Toan (Hanoi, 1996), 12.

42. Hong Chuong, "Journalist Hai Trieu," in *Vietnamese Studies*, no. 15 (85) (1986): 81.

43. See Nguyen Khoa Van's "Canh Tu" [Prison Atmosphere], a poem he wrote in Hue in 1930, in *Hai Trieu Toan Tap*, 83.

44. Nguyen Khoa Van wrote for *Dan* [The People], *Doi Moi* [New Life], *Kien Van* [Things Seen and Heard], *Tieng Van* [Echo], *Hon Tre* [Spirit of Youth], *Tin Tuc* [News], and *Tin Moi* [New News]. Hong Chuong, "Journalist Hai Trieu," 82.

45. For Nguyen Khoa Van's role in these debates, see Hue-Tam Ho Tai, "Literature for the People: From Soviet Policies to Vietnamese Polemics," in *Borrowings and Adaptations in Vietnamese Culture* (Honolulu, 1987), 63–83.

46. "Su Thuc Trong Tu," *Doi Moi*, March 24, 1935, 4, and "Cai Than Tu," ibid., April 14, 1935.

47. AOM, SLOTFOM, 3d ser., carton 54, *AAPCI*, May 1936.

(The Cracked Bell), and 1941, when he died on Poulo Condore.[48] The Trotskyist writer Ta Thu Thau endured imprisonment on six separate occasions between his return from France in 1932 and his execution by the Viet Minh at the end of World War II.[49] Nguyen Van Nguyen and Phan Van Hum each served time in Poulo Condore and Saigon Central Prison and wrote widely read accounts of their experiences there.[50] Nguyen Van Tao, Ho Huu Tuong, and Duong Bach Mai were also jailed on multiple occasions during the interwar years. According to Huynh Kim Khanh, the editorial office of *La Lutte* served as "a mail drop and rendezvous where released political prisoners could quickly get their bearings upon release."[51]

In view of the amount of time that the leaders of the legal opposition spent behind bars, it is not surprising that the conditions of colonial imprisonment loomed large in their journalistic efforts. After all, they were familiar with a hidden world that had long been a source of curiosity for the reading public. Not only did they know the mysterious inner workings of this world intimately, but it may have been the only topic about which they possessed expertise following extended periods of isolation from the wider community. The compulsion to write about imprisonment may have also derived from the sheer intensity of the experience, as well as from feelings of guilt for abandoning comrades who had died in jail or been left behind.

PRISONS IN THE PRESS

Between late 1934 and early 1937, almost every issue of *La Lutte* featured reports on the colonial prison. Coverage peaked in 1936, when front-page articles and editorials about the prison system appeared in 41 of the 50 editions published that year. Prison stories were also a fixture of *Le Travail*, appearing in 95 percent of all issues during 1936 and 1937. Likewise, a recent study by Nguyen Thanh demonstrates that the prison system was one of only seven domestic topics that received consistent attention in *Tieng*

48. *Nguyen An Ninh*, ed. Nguyen An Tinh (Ho Chi Minh City, 1996), 25–72.

49. Ngo Van, "Quelques biographies des révolutionnaires vietnamiens," *Cahiers Léon Trotsky*, no. 41 (December 1989): 64–71. See also Phuong Lan, *Nha Cach Mang Ta Thu Thau, 1906–1945* [The Revolutionary Ta Thu Thau, 1906–1945] (Saigon, 1973), and David Marr, *Vietnam 1945: The Quest for Power* (Berkeley and Los Angeles, 1995), 136–37, 434–35.

50. Huynh Van Tieng, "Journalist Nguyen Van Nguyen," in *Vietnamese Studies*, no. 15 (85) (1986): 84–88; Ngo Van, "Quelques biographies," 75–77.

51. Huynh Kim Khanh, *Vietnamese Communism*, 204.

Dan during the 1930s.[52] It is instructive that *La Lutte* was published in Saigon, *Le Travail* in Hanoi, and *Tieng Dan* in Hue—the three most important cities in Cochin China, Tonkin, and Annam. In terms of political orientation, *Le Travail* was loosely aligned with the ICP, *Tieng Dan* expressed a moderate reformism hostile to the anticolonial left, and *La Lutte* pursued a complex radical agenda reflecting the uneasy collaboration between the Stalinists, Trotskyists, anarchists, and nationalists who formed its editorial board. The fact that prison coverage so dramatically transcended the regional and political boundaries that divided Indochina during the 1930s points to the emergence of the prison system as an issue of broad national significance.

Not only were prison stories ubiquitous in the colonial press but they were sensationalized in ways that made them difficult to ignore. Most appeared on the front page under eye-catching headlines such as "The Hell of Poulo Condore," "Bloody Struggle in the Lao Bao Penitentiary," or "Terror Reigns in the *Bagne* of Son La."[53] They typically featured graphic descriptions of inhuman prison conditions and atrocities committed against inmates by the prison staff. Accounts of beatings, torture, and food deprivation exhibited a degree of attention to detail that verged on the pornographic. A typical memoir in *Le Travail* described guards at the Kontum penitentiary forcing prisoners to eat their own excrement.[54] An article in *La Lutte* entitled "How They Are Killed on Poulo Condore," offered a macabre litany of unnatural death, including elaborate disquisitions on wrist-slitting, hanging, and self-starvation.[55]

Prison stories also attracted attention by featuring remarkably personal attacks on colonial officials. In 1935, *La Lutte* accused Poulo Condore's Director Crémazy of approving tainted beef for prison meals, while he and his deputies "made champagne toasts to the new year."[56] Another article— "When Monsieur Crémazy Gets Angry"—related an episode in which the thin-skinned director punished a prisoner for an impolite remark with a two-year extension of his sentence. "Considering Crémazy's recent behavior in Phnom Penh," the article concluded, "his gambling at Hotel Manol-

52. Nguyen Thanh, *Lich Su Bao Tieng Dan*, 167–206.
53. "Un Episode de lutte sanglante au bagne de Lao Bao," *La Lutte*, December 20, 1934; "L'Enfer de Poulo Condore," *La Lutte*, July 13, 1935; "La Terreur règne dans le bagne de Sonla," *Le Travail*, March 19, 1937.
54. "La Vie au pénitencier de Kontum," *Le Travail*, January 29, 1937.
55. "Comment ils meurent à Poulo Condore," *La Lutte*, April 13, 1935.
56. "A la porte, Crémazy," *La Lutte*, February 23, 1935.

lis, his relations with chronic opium smokers, and his so-called 'Chinese Affair,' we are not surprised by his recent conduct."[57] Weeks later, another story denounced the governor-general "for abandoning the prisoners of Poulo Condore to the privations and tortures of Director Crémazy and Chief Warder Cristiani, two individuals who barely qualify as human beings."[58]

To lure readers back on a weekly basis, prison exposés were often presented in serial format. One of the earliest serializations was Nguyen Van Nguyen's "Views on Poulo Condore," which ran in *La Lutte* for eight consecutive weeks in late 1934.[59] Given its length, "Views on Poulo Condore" conveys something of the range of issues raised in prison coverage more generally. Since the relatives of inmates were seen as a core audience for the series, they were addressed directly in its opening installment:

> Poulo Condore! Con Non! These sinister names echo heavily in the hearts of many Indochinese families. You, parents and friends, spouses, sisters, and mothers, who have had those whom you cherish most taken from you—we report to you the atrocious conditions to which the prisoners of Poulo Condore are currently subjected.[60]

The second installment portrayed the prison's cramped and poorly ventilated living quarters, comparing them to "monkey cages in a zoo":

> The dormitories—twelve meters by eight—were built to house forty prisoners at a time, but they typically hold over eighty. The single door and the four small windows are insufficient to ventilate these bloated tanks. The air reeks from the stench of latrines and sweat from dozens of naked bodies.[61]

Moving to prison food, the author described a typical meal of filthy rice served with fish that was so "rotten, stinking, and full of maggots" that "even a dog wouldn't eat it." The third installment argued that prison officials were "criminally negligent" for the deaths of 100 prisoners crushed to death when a typhoon toppled their ramshackle living quarters in 1931.[62] The following week, the author denounced the classification of certain political prisoners as common criminals—a policy that subjected them to a

---

57. "Quand Monsieur Crémazy se fâche," *La Lutte,* June 15, 1935.
58. "L'Enfer de Poulo-Condore," *La Lutte,* July 13, 1935.
59. "Regards sur Poulo Condore," *La Lutte,* October 11–December 13, 1934.
60. Ibid., October 11, 1934.
61. Ibid., October 18, 1934.
62. Ibid., October 25, 1934.

brutal regime of hard labor and forced them to live side by side with "common murderers and highway robbers."[63] The fifth installment detailed the sadistic cruelty of prison guards such as Sergeant Chay, a "ferocious brute," who had once beaten a prisoner to death with his bare hands.[64] Sections 6 and 7 discussed the high rates of malaria, dysentery, and tuberculosis among the prison population, as well as the murderous incompetence of the prison medical staff.[65] The series ended with a list of demands for improved conditions and a plea for the creation of a special regime for political prisoners.[66]

"Views on Poulo Condore" created a sensation with the reading public and spawned numerous imitations. The longest was Tran Huy Lieu's "Poulo Condore Memoirs," published in *Anh Sang* (Ray of Light) over a seven-month period in 1935.[67] Another was Le Van Hien's "Life in Kontum Penitentiary," which appeared in *Le Travail* for fifteen weeks starting in late 1936 and was eventually published as a book in *quoc ngu* translation under the title *Nguc Kontum* (Kontum Prison).[68] Other examples of the genre include "For the Application of a Political Regime," which ran for eight weeks in *La Lutte* during 1935; Nguyen Van Nguyen's two-part prison memoir entitled "Poulo Condore, Land of the Damned," featured in *Le Travail* in 1936; Hoc Phi's "Days of Manacles and Leg Irons," printed in *Tuong Lai* throughout April and May of 1937; and Pham Binh Ry's "Five Years on Noumea," published in *Tieng Dan* over a seven-week period in 1939.[69]

Editors also highlighted coverage of the prison system through special issues devoted almost exclusively to the topic. For example, on April 6, 1935, *La Lutte* printed a brief denunciation of the prison system in bold type directly under its masthead, followed by three front-page prison stories. "Hundreds of Lives Are in Danger" exposed a recent scandal in which the prison doctor on Poulo Condore had rejected a shipment of rotten fish

63. Ibid., November 1, 1934.
64. Ibid., November 22, 1934.
65. Ibid., November 29 and December 6, 1934.
66. Ibid., December 12, 1934.
67. "Con Lon Ky Su," *Anh Sang*, May 4–October 26, 1935.
68. "La Vie de pénitencier de Kontum," *Le Travail*, November 27, 1936–March 19, 1937.
69. "Pour l'application du régime politique," *La Lutte*, August 24–October 26, 1935; "Poulo condore: La Terre des damnés," *Le Travail*, November 13–20, 1936; "Nhung Ngay Cum Xich," *Tuong Lai*, April 15–May 15, 1937; and "Nam Nam O Noumea," *Tieng Dan*, May 5–27, 1939.

sent from the mainland, only to be overruled by the warden.[70] "Why the Prisoners Have Gone on a Hunger Strike" excerpted a chapter from J. Barthel's *Regards sur l'Indochine* that linked Poulo Condore's "fearful mortality rate" to regular outbreaks of dysentery and tuberculosis.[71] "A Beautiful Struggle" explained that a recent hunger strike by prisoners at the Rach Gia Provincial Prison had been launched to protest against sadistic beatings and bad food.[72] Finally, the entire second page of the issue was taken up by "Corrupt Wardens and Murderous Guards," a lengthy description of official efforts to cover up evidence of mismanagement, corruption, and abuse on Poulo Condore from a team of outside inspectors.[73]

Newspapers also published numerous letters and petitions from political prisoners.[74] "Today we publish a letter from political prisoners on Poulo-Condore," the editors of *La Lutte* explained on November 8, 1934. "The facts are recent but they represent more than an isolated case."[75] The letter related the ordeal of a convict named Nguyen Tri Dzieu, who had been beaten and placed in solitary confinement for resting during a work break. In 1935, *Tieng Dan* published a letter from prisoners in Buon Ma Thuot who complained about the warden's practice of punishing inmates for disciplinary infractions by extending their sentences. Among the specific cases it raised was that of Phan Dang Luu, who was issued a five-year extension for smuggling a letter to *Tieng Dan*.[76]

In a further effort to stimulate public outrage, journalists frequently contrasted the squalor of the prison system with the lofty rhetoric of France's civilizing mission. Among the first to employ this approach was Ho Chi Minh, who once pointed out the irony of the fact that the motto "Liberty, Equality, Fraternity" frequently adorned the gates of prisons in Indochina.[77] By the mid 1930s, journalists were regularly exploiting the same contradiction to demand amnesty for political prisoners. For example, an editorial in *Notre Voix* opened as follows:

70. "Des centaines de vies humaines sont en danger," *La Lutte,* April 6, 1935.
71. "Voilà pourquoi les prisonniers font la grève de la faim," *La Lutte,* April 6, 1935.
72. "Une Belle Lutte," *La Lutte,* April 6, 1935.
73. "Fonctionnaires cupides, gardiens assassins," *La Lutte,* April 6, 1935.
74. See, e.g., *Le Travail,* November 13 and 27, 1936; *Notre Voix,* March 19 and 26, 1939; and *La Lutte,* June 10 and September 16, 1936, and June 3, 1937.
75. "Lettre de Poulo-Condore," *La Lutte,* November 8, 1934.
76. The letter is summarized in Nguyen Thanh, *Lich Su Bao Tieng Dan,* 140–43.
77. The passage appeared in "French Colonization on Trial." See *Ho Chi Minh on Revolution,* ed. Bernard Fall (New York, 1967), 106.

In the name of the great revolution of 1789, the mother of republican government, whose prestige brightens the universe, and whose motto was Liberty, equality, and fraternity . . . in the name of the intolerable sufferings of men whose only crime is to possess the courage to declare their passion for liberty: the people of Indochina appeal to both the French and Indochinese authorities for the immediate liberation of 1,500 political convicts. They are the sons of the people; they are militants devoted to liberty.[78]

Of course, the fact that the French National Day celebrated the destruction of a notorious prison provided journalists with an absurdly easy target. By the mid 1930s, they regularly referred to prisons in Indochina as "colonial Bastilles," a move that cleverly identified the colonial state with the corrupt and decadent ancien régime of eighteenth-century France. In a letter published in *Le Travail* in 1936, a group of former political prisoners wrote: "Six years behind us. Six years locked in the colonial Bastille. Six years during which we have had to endure the notorious atrocities of a hateful and terrible regime."[79] An editorial in *La Lutte* was more emphatic: "This hellish regime is unbearable!! Down with the *bagne* and its regime of death! Down with all colonial Bastilles!"[80]

While typically more reserved, Vietnamese-language newspapers also utilized the image of the Bastille in their coverage of the colonial prison system. Under the guise of educating their readers about French national history, *Tieng Dan* fed local revolutionary fantasies by running annual descriptions of the famous "storming."[81] As the 150th anniversary of the Revolution approached in 1939, journalists relentlessly exploited the metaphorical power of the Bastille in articles and editorials. For instance, the editors of *Ngay Moi* [New Day] wrote:

Throughout France, the masses commemorate the 150th anniversary of the great revolution of 1789. It was there that the chains of human slavery were destroyed, the seeds of freedom planted, and humanity offered an ideal of untold beauty. One month from now, in rallies, speeches, and newspapers, people will honor the great revolution and

---

78. "Vers une action commune pour l'Amnistie," *Notre Voix*, June 23, 1939.
79. "Une lettre ouverte des libérés politiques à M. la Ministre des colonies," *Le Travail*, November 13, 1936.
80. "Appel des condamnés politiques de Poulo-Condore à M. le Président du Conseil, Chef du Gouvernement du Front Populaire et à Monsieur le Ministre des colonies pour l'amnistie immédiate et intégrale de tous les condamnés politques indochinois," *La Lutte*, June 10, 1936.
81. See, "14–7–1789, Pha Nguc Basti" [Destroying the Bastille], *Tieng Dan*, July 14, 1937.

the immortal spirit of those who fought for freedom. And standing most prominently among the fighters are the men who on July 14, 1789, destroyed the Bastille, the stronghold of despotism, oppression, exploitation, and slavery. . . . Today, there are 1,500 fighters who wait for death in Poulo Condore, Innini, Buon Ma Thuot, and other prisons because they too love freedom and desire to destroy the Bastilles of Indochina. In France, people praise the fighters who destroyed the Bastille. Here, people remain fettered, chained, slowly murdered, like those valiant fighters of old. What a bitter irony.[82]

A somewhat less attractive method of highlighting the abuse of political prisoners involved the racist denigration of ethnic minority guards who supervised inmates in upland penitentiaries. According to *Le Travail,* the misery of political prisoners in Annam was compounded by the "savagery" of the ethnic minority militiamen who supervised corvée: "The Moi militiamen, idiotic and ferocious by nature, are encouraged by their white masters to regard the Annamites with utter contempt."[83] Another article claimed that "surveillance in Buon Ma Thuot is entrusted to Rhadé militiamen, well known for their primitive cruelty and deep hatred and ferocity toward members of the Annamite race."[84]

PRISON REFORM AND APPEALS FOR A POLITICAL REGIME

Critical portrayals of prison conditions not only exposed the brutality, injustice, and hypocrisy of the colonial state but backed demands for reform. These included calls for improved food and medical care, relief from overcrowding and dangerous forced labor, the termination of corporal punishment and extrajudicial sentence extensions, and enhanced visitation rights and mail privileges. It is significant, however, that such appeals were nearly always raised in the context of a more general demand for the reestablishment of a special regime for political prisoners.[85] A political regime had existed in Indochinese prisons since 1910, but political prisoners lost many of their privileges around 1930 as a result of overcrowding and the growth of

82. "Doi Tu Do Cho 1,500 Chinh-Tri-Pham" [We Demand Freedom For 1,500 Political Prisoners], *Ngay Moi,* July 4, 1939.
83. "La Vie des condamnés politiques dans les pénitenciers," *Le Travail,* October 14, 1936. "Moi" referred to members of any ethnic minority and carried clear racist undertones.
84. "Pour la réforme des bagnes politiques," *Le Travail,* October 7, 1936.
85. "Pour l'application du régime politique," *La Lutte,* August 24–October 26, 1935, first made an extended case for the reestablishment of a political regime.

a new hard-line attitude among prison officials toward so-called communist subversives.[86] While inmates classified as political prisoners were still exempt from hard labor and segregated, more or less, from the criminal population, they no longer enjoyed special food, access to reading material, or the right to receive mail, newspapers, and an unlimited number of family visits. They also suffered the same effects of overcrowding as the rest of the inmate population.

Connected to demands for a political regime were calls for an end to the classification of political activists as common-law prisoners. This problem was most serious in Annam, where all Vietnamese defendants were tried according to the Gia Long code. As journalists pointed out repeatedly, the code did not include the sentences of deportation and detention and thus was incapable of triggering the classification of convicts as political prisoners. The only sentences available to courts in Annam for serious crimes were forced labor, imprisonment, or death, none of which conferred political prisoner status. Indeed, the vast majority of those convicted in Annam for nonviolent political offenses—leafleting, demonstrating, or joining a revolutionary party—received hard-labor sentences.[87]

Journalists also complained that activists who committed criminal acts for political reasons deserved to be classed as political prisoners. This argument was based on a circular from the Ministry of Colonies that allowed Indochinese courts to issue sentences of deportation and detention for ordinary crimes committed with demonstrably political motives.[88] The press noted that in practice, however, politically motivated criminals were always sentenced to hard labor. Such was the case with the nationalist and communist activists jailed in connection with the Yen Bay uprising and the Nghe-Tinh soviets, who were held together with common criminals and forced to work. Moreover, as hard-labor convicts, they were ineligible for the amnesties and sentence reductions offered to select political prisoners at Tet and on Bastille Day.[89] As a result, while scores of political prisoners were pardoned every February and July, prominent communists sentenced to hard-labor sentences such as Ton Duc Thang, Pham Hung, Le Van Luong,

86. Tran Huy Lieu discusses these changes in "Tren Dao Hon Cau" [On Hon Cau Island], in *Hoi Ky Tran Huy Lieu*, 100.

87. "La Vie des condamnés politiques dans les pénitenciers," *Le Travail*, October 14, 1936.

88. "Qui sont les détenus politiques?" *L'Echo Annamite*, June 7, 1927.

89. "Pas de distinction dans l'Amnistie," *La Lutte*, August 12, 1936.

and Nguyen Duy Trinh remained on Poulo Condore without interruption from the early 1930s until the Viet Minh liberated the islands in 1945.

The legal opposition's preoccupation with the treatment and status of political prisoners was not accompanied by an equivalent concern for the plight of common-law offenders. Despite making up the vast majority of the inmate population, ordinary criminals barely appear in the press coverage of the era. In essence, the legal opposition agitated tirelessly for special treatment for political prisoners (including its own jailed members) but betrayed little concern for the rights of the inmate population more generally. Furthermore, the logic of the arguments put forward in favor of the creation of a special regime for political prisoners encouraged the denigration of ordinary inmates in the press. In 1935, *La Lutte* wrote: "They are called political prisoners, but the regime imposed upon them differs little from the one for common-law detainees. If you rape a young girl, commit armed robbery, organize a labor union, or write a subversive tract, you are dealt with in exactly the same way. Identical food, identical treatment."[90]

The passage represents an attempt to strengthen the case for the reestablishment of a political regime by emphasizing the unfairness of the fact that political prisoners were treated no better than common criminals. To magnify the injustice of treating the two groups equally, the journalist characterized nonpolitical prisoners as negatively as possible—referring to them, in the abstract, as bandits and child rapists. This echoes the complaint in "Views on Poulo Condore" that the prison system failed to distinguish political prisoners from "common murderers and highway robbers." Not only did this misrepresent the nature of the criminal population, most of whom were jailed for petty theft, vagrancy, and smuggling, but it came close to sanctioning their mistreatment by the prison system. By demonizing ordinary lawbreakers, the legal opposition discouraged public support for more general and inclusive programs of prison reform. And to the extent that officials absorbed and responded to criticisms raised in the press, the legal opposition's disregard for ordinary criminals made it even easier for the colonial state to ignore them as well.[91]

90. "Pour l'application du régime politique," *La Lutte*, August 24, 1935.
91. The legal opposition's lack of interest in the rights of common-law inmates highlights a significant continuity between the position taken by the revolutionary anticolonial movement and the policies adopted by the postcolonial communist state. While the DRV's failure to establish a body of rights for convicts and criminal defendants might be construed as a betrayal of ideals expressed during the 1930s, the fact is that such rights were never a preoccupation of the revolutionary movement.

THE IMPACT OF THE PRESS COVERAGE

Colonial officials paid close attention to depictions of the Indochinese prison system in the press. In addition to shedding light on the strategies of the legal opposition, newspaper coverage provided concrete data about the seamy underside of prison administration. According to one governor of Cochin China, such information was not always forthcoming from prison officials, "who too frequently minimize the facts."[92] Information about Indochinese prison conditions in the colonial press was also of interest to officials in France who were worried about the political situation in Indochina. On April 26, 1935, Deputy Ernest Lafont requested information about prison conditions from the minister of colonies after reading troubling reports in the colonial press: "Certain newspapers have published unsettling information on the state of Poulo Condore. I request that you provide me with information on the events that have recently unfolded there and on the criticisms launched in the press against the dietary and disciplinary regime imposed on the prisoners."[93]

The value of the press as a source of information was heightened by the fact that journalists consulted and cited a variety of sources, including prison guards. "This morning we spoke with M. Durocher, a retired guard from the Penitentiary Service," the editors of *La Lutte* wrote in early 1935. "He has been kind enough to provide us with the following information."[94] In another article, editors claimed that their "principal method" entailed "discarding facts not confirmed by three or four recent returnees, each of whom is questioned individually in our offices."[95] The fact that mortality statistics for prisoners published in *La Lutte* and *Le Travail* mirrored official figures suggests that journalists may have consulted documentary records as well.[96]

92. AOM, Indochine, Affaires politiques, 1728, Régime pénitencier de Poulo Condore, July 4, 1936.

93. Ibid., April 26, 1935.

94. "A la porte, Crémazy," *La Lutte*, February 23, 1935.

95. "A Poulo-Condor," *La Lutte*, September 28, 1935.

96. "Fonctionnaires cupides, gardiens assassins," *La Lutte*, June 5, 1935, gives Poulo Condore's mortality rate as 1930, 305; 1931, 204; 1932, 105; 1933, 85; and 1934, 84, whereas the Gouvernement général's *Annuaire statistique de l'Indochine* gives 1930, 304; 1931, 197; 1932, 100; 1933, 78; and 1934, 76. Death statistics, dates, and main events in Le Van Hien's "La Vie au pénitencier de Kontum" mirror those in the official report on the Kontum Revolt prepared by M. Chastenet de Gery in February 1932.

Not only were press reports read by colonial officials but they occasionally prompted investigations into allegations of abuse. On June 10, 1936, *La Lutte* published "Un Episode de lutte dans l'enfer des vivants" (An Episode of Struggle in the Living Hell), a description of the brutal measures undertaken to crush a work strike on Poulo Condore.[97] It contended that a team of guards had entered the striking prisoners' dormitory after dark and attacked them with truncheons and gun butts. Dozens of prisoners were bloodied or knocked unconscious, and fifty-four ended up in the hospital. More troubling still, the article reported that a French guard had entered the dormitory hours after the attack and sadistically ordered the bruised and battered prisoners to stand up and sing "La Marseillaise."

The power of the article derived less from the brutality of the events themselves than from the meticulous way in which they were reported. The story came out only several days after the episodes it described, identified specific prisoners and guards by name and number, and presented verbal exchanges in direct quotation marks. The following week, the governor-general dispatched an envoy to the island to investigate the story. His report was eventually forwarded to the minister of colonies, along with the following introduction added by the governor-general himself:

> I submit a report completed July 1, by Inspector of Political Affairs Striedter, charged on my order with a mission to inspect the penitentiary of Poulo Condore following the publication of an article in the communist Saigon daily *La Lutte* (6/10) concerning violence inflicted on certain political prisoners. . . . I estimate that M. Bouvier has committed a serious mistake in not reporting the incident immediately, and that a simple rebuke will not suffice to punish his error. I ask therefore if you would be willing to postpone the promotion that Warden Bouvier is soon due, and I add that if you decide to relieve this functionary of his position, I have no objections.[98]

In the end, Bouvier managed to keep his job, but he was issued a formal reprimand and denied a promotion.

It is difficult to determine whether this episode reflected a larger pattern in which the press functioned as a watchdog for administrative abuse. However, even if such media-driven investigations were relatively rare, the reprimand of a top administrator like Bouvier must have represented a powerful warning to prison officials throughout the system and may have

97. "Un Episode de lutte dans l'enfer des vivants," *La Lutte*, June 10, 1936.
98. AOM, Indochine, Affaires politiques, 1728, Régime pénitencier, Pénitencier de Poulo Condore, Saigon, July 4, 1936.

encouraged them to abandon, tone down, or perhaps conceal especially brutal and abusive practices. Indeed, there is evidence that Bouvier himself emerged from the reprimand as a more circumspect administrator. When the *quoc ngu* weekly *Mai* (Tomorrow) published a devastating exposé of the treatment of incorrigibles on Poulo Condore the following year, Bouvier immediately forwarded an elaborate defense of his policies to the governor-general and urged him to visit the prison.[99] While the warden's self-possessed invitation to the governor-general was intended to convey an impression that the newspaper had exaggerated the charges of abuse, it raises the more likely possibility that *Mai's* reporting induced Bouvier to hastily improve the way in which incorrigibles on Poulo Condore were treated.

Official anxiety about media coverage may have also been behind an initiative introduced by the governor of Cochin China in November 1934 to improve living conditions for political prisoners on Poulo Condore. It is instructive that the governor announced the initiative within a month of the first wave of prison reporting and identified issues that mirrored complaints raised in the press.[100] He offered to increase rations for political prisoners, schedule more time in the yard, and allow them to receive packages of food and medicine from their families. He also announced plans to construct a separate medical facility for inmates suffering from malaria and tuberculosis. Perhaps most important, he gave permission for political prisoners to read certain approved works in French and *quoc ngu*. Acknowledging these changes late in 1934, Nguyen Duc Chinh wrote to his brother from Poulo Condore that "conditions for us here have recently improved":

> They have agreed to provide us with 100 grams of meat per week, to allow us to go out into the yard from 6:00 A.M. to 10:00 A.M. and from 2:00 P.M. to 5:00 P.M., and to permit us to receive packages of small household items. On the question of access to newspapers, they are seriously considering our request. For our spirits, newspapers are perhaps the most important thing.[101]

By 1935, Chinh could write that he was regularly receiving books, literary magazines, and newspapers, including *Dong Phap, Doi Moi,* and *Le Monde.*[102]

---

99. Ibid., August 17, 1937. The article in *Mai* appeared on July 3, 1936.
100. AOM, Indochine, Affaires politiques, 1728, Détenus politiques, November 28, 1934.
101. Nguyen Duc Chinh, *Thu Con Lon* [Con Lon Letters] (Hanoi, 1937), 21–22.
102. Ibid., 24.

Likewise, press coverage was probably instrumental in the creation of a new institutional category for common-law offenders whose crimes had been politically motivated. In 1935, almost immediately after the issue was first raised in the press, the warden of Poulo Condore announced that such prisoners were to be labeled "semi-politicals and segregated from the general population.[103] "Semi-politicals" continued to work, but they were assigned lighter tasks and treated with greater tolerance. In the late 1930s, Demariaux reported from Poulo Condore that the dormitories of the "semi-politicals" were "spacious and clean" compared to the living quarters of common-law inmates, and that their walls were covered with "portraits of Lenin and Stalin and maps of the Soviet Union."[104]

In addition to shaping public attitudes to the colonial state and providing a measure of protection for political prisoners during the 1930s, the media's preoccupation with the prison system contributed to the development of Vietnamese nationalism. As has been suggested, the high profile of prison coverage in newspapers as regionally and politically diverse as *La Lutte, Le Travail,* and *Tieng Dan* facilitated the emergence of an integrated national reading public. Not only were audiences in Annam, Tonkin, and Cochin China fixated simultaneously on the same provocative issue, but the transregional nature of the coverage encouraged readers to sympathize and identify with the plight of inmates outside of their home territories. Moreover, the themes dramatized in coverage of the prison system—suffering, endurance, and protracted resistance against overwhelming odds—prefigured what were to become characteristic features of an official Vietnamese national identity promoted by the postcolonial state.

For the ICP, participation in the campaign against the colonial prison strengthened its nationalist credentials. Unlike many of the issues that it championed, prison reform emphasized the injustices of colonialism rather than class domination and therefore appealed to elements of the middle and upper classes. Although the campaign for prison reform had been launched and dominated initially by *La Lutte,* the ICP assumed a greater role in it as more of its members were released from jail during the second half of the decade. Moreover, the colonial state's dismissive characterization of the

103. Tran Van Giau, "Lop Hoc Chu Nghia Mac-Lenin Va To Bao *Y Kien Chung* O Banh I, Con Lon, 1935–1936" [The Class of Marxism-Leninism and the Newspaper "Consensus" in Dormitory 1, Con Lon, 1935–1936], *Tap Chi Lich Su Dang* 5, no. 33 (1990): 4.

104. Demariaux, *Secrets des îles Poulo-Condore,* 95.

media's preoccupation with the prison system as a communist plot served to link the issue with the Party in the public imagination.

Finally, the media's idealization of political prisoners established a connection between nationalist heroism and political imprisonment, which, in turn, shaped how revolutionary leaders legitimized their claims to power in the postcolonial era. To bring the cruelty of the colonial prison into bold relief, the media highlighted the dignity and courage of its victims. An example of this tactic may be seen in *La Lutte's* re-creation of a dramatic courtroom speech delivered by an inmate who had been accused of beating to death a guard on Poulo Condore:

> The life we lead on Poulo Condore is unbearable. The work is subhuman, the food rotten, the medical care inadequate. The brutalities of the guards are inconceivable, their punishments inhumane. I am driven to ask if I am not a man, if my guards are not men. The baton blows rain down upon us, but there is no one to hear our cries. It was in such conditions that I decided to kill the most brutal guard of them all. You have brought me here to Saigon to stand trial and I stand before you to decry the infernal life of those damned to live on Poulo Condore. And because of this, I die content.[105]

During the late 1930s, media coverage of the arrest and incarceration of the leaders of *La Lutte* had the effect of enhancing their celebrity status. In 1936, Ta Thu Thau, Nguyen An Ninh, and Nguyen Van Tao became widely known and admired figures after they launched a highly publicized hunger strike in the Saigon Central Prison. "Ta Thu Thau, Nguyen An Ninh, and Nguyen Van Tao have become almost legendary heroes," the Sûreté reported, "because of the hunger strike they launched during their incarceration."[106] "By refusing food . . . , these three individuals have succeeded in generating sympathy for their situation and for the [Communist] Party in general. They have garnered support from the noncommunist press in French and *quoc ngu*, the urban population of Saigon and Cho Lon, several members of the colonial council, and a part of French public opinion."[107] This comment reveals that authorities were especially troubled by the range of support enjoyed by high-profile political prisoners. When two of *Le Travail's* editors initiated a hunger strike in the Hanoi Central Prison the following year, an extraordinarily diverse array of jour-

105. "Qui a menti? Poulo Condor," *La Lutte*, January 17, 1935.
106. AOM, SLOTFOM, 3d ser., carton 59, *AAPCI*, April 1937.
107. Ibid., November 1936.

nalists, including the communist Tran Huy Lieu, the conservative nationalist Nhat Linh, and the politically independent anticolonial publisher Vu Dinh Long, signed a petition on their behalf.[108]

Between 1937 and 1939, coverage of the imprisonment of Duong Bach Mai, Nguyen Van So, Ha Huy Tap, Nguyen Van Nguyen, and Phan Van Hum also enhanced their public reputations.[109] Newspapers provided sympathetic updates on Phan Van Hum's ten-day hunger strike in the Saigon Central Prison.[110] A report that Ta Thu Thau had become partially paralyzed as a result of inadequate medical attention provoked widespread public outrage.[111] His unexpected release, along with Nguyen Van Tao and Duong Bach Mai, during Tet in 1939 was front-page news.[112] Most lionized were the authors of serialized memoirs whose accounts of the horrors of prison life magnified an impression of their own bravery, resourcefulness, and endurance. Tran Huy Lieu, Phan Van Hum, Le Van Hien, Nguyen Van Nguyen, Huynh Thuc Khang, and Nguyen Khoa Van became household names following the publication of their prison memoirs. Tran Huy Lieu's multiple accounts of his own imprisonment enhanced his reputation to such an extent that the writer Vu Trong Phung produced a fictionalized account of his incarceration on Poulo Condore entitled "Nguoi Tu Duoc Tha" (The Prisoner Released).[113]

Although jailed members of the ICP received far less attention than inmates connected to the legal opposition during the 1930s, communists were keenly aware of the capacity of the colonial prison to make heroic figures out of political prisoners. Upon taking power in 1954, the Party attempted to amplify the prison credentials of its leaders by encouraging

108. "Tuyet Thuc" [Strike], *Dong Duong Tap Chi*, September 14, 1937.

109. "Pour Thau et Tao: Le Ligue des droits de l'homme est intervenue," *La Lutte*, October 10, 1937.

110. "Ong Phan Van Hum Tuyet Thuc" [Phan Van Hum Goes on Hunger Strike], *Tieng Dan*, July 25, 1939; "Ong Phan Van Hum Da An Lai" [Phan Van Hum Eats Again], ibid., August 3, 1939.

111. "Contre les mauvais traitements: Le Régime politique pour les condamnés politiques," *La Lutte*, February 13, 1938.

112. See, e.g., *Notre Voix*, March 5, 1939.

113. Vu Trong Phung, "Nguoi Tu Duoc Tha" [The Prisoner Released], in *Tuyen Tap Vu Trong Phung, I* [Collected Works of Vu Trong Phung, vol. 1], ed. Nguyen Dang Manh and Tran Huy Ta (Hanoi, 1996). The novella was written in 1938 but remained unpublished until 1986. See Hoai Anh, "Vu Trong Phung, Nha Hoa Hoc Cua Nhung Tinh Cach" [Vu Trong Phung, the Chemist of Characters], in Hoai Anh, *Chan Dung Van Hoc* [Literary Portraits] (Ho Chi Minh City, 1995), 45–55.

them to produce accounts of their own experiences behind bars during the colonial era. The result was the publication of a huge body of communist prison memoirs, poems, and songs and their widespread dissemination in school textbooks, literary anthologies, and museum displays. In this way, the legal opposition's celebration of political prisoners during the 1930s left an enduring mark on the official political culture of the postcolonial state.

9 The Prisoner Released

The period from 1936 to 1939 witnessed a dramatic expansion of anticolonial politics in Indochina. It was reflected in the rise of labor activism, the flowering of the radical press, the growth of the Communist Party, the formation of hundreds of popular Action Committees, and a campaign to establish an Indochinese Congress. While this explosion of political activity was facilitated by the electoral victory of the Popular Front, it was carried out by thousands of former political prisoners, many of whom were released collectively from Indochinese prisons during the second half of 1936. These liberations were the result of a widespread amnesty policy implemented by the new government in France several months after it assumed power.

It is often assumed that the amnesty was a manifestation of the Popular Front's enlightened colonial policy—a policy epitomized by the appointment of an outspoken critic of French colonial policy, Marius Moutet, to the post of minister of colonies in 1936. However, while the amnesty was consistent with the somewhat more liberal orientation of the Popular Front toward colonial questions, good intentions alone did not ensure that it would be carried out. Indeed, many of the new government's plans for colonial reforms failed to generate enough support at home or abroad to translate into policy. The Popular Front's commitment to the Indochinese amnesty, however, followed years of vigorous agitation both in France and in Indochina. Hence, it should not be seen as merely a top-down initiative, but also as a response to political pressures from below.

In addition to discussing the various political forces giving rise to the amnesty, this chapter examines why so many released political prisoners returned to the anticolonial struggle. As suggested earlier, the experience of communal incarceration, coupled with the efficacy of revolutionary training behind bars, served to deepen the political commitments of many jailed activists. Also important was a postinstitutional mechanism of control, known as administrative surveillance, that discouraged the reintegration of ex-prisoners into the wider community by undermining their financial prospects and leaving them open to harassment by local officials. In response to the hardships of administrative surveillance, ex-prisoners congregated together to form mutual aid associations and collective households. Coupled with widespread public sympathy and admiration for former political prisoners, these communal environments induced many of them to resume political activity.

THE AMNESTY AND THE FRENCH LEFT

Whereas the movement to reform colonial prisons was led from newspaper offices in Hanoi, Hue, and Saigon, support for a general amnesty for Indochinese political prisoners originated in France. The issue was first raised by the French League for the Rights of Man in 1908, after dozens of patriotic scholar-gentry were jailed for allegedly leading antitax revolts in Annam.[1] In 1911, pressure from the league prompted the Ministry of Colonies to amnesty a number of the jailed scholars, including Phan Chu Trinh.[2] During the 1920s, the league kept the issue alive through subsidiaries such as the Committee Against Colonial Oppression and Imperialism and the Committee for the Defense of Political Prisoners. These groups launched letter-writing campaigns, published anticolonial writing in the metropolitan press, and organized public forums to agitate on behalf of political prisoners in the colonies. On October 17, 1927, the Committee Against Colonial Oppression and Imperialism sponsored a forum in Paris entitled "A Meeting Against the Terror in Indochina," during which a speaker billed as a "student from Cochin China" described the persecution of journalists, the violation of civil liberties, and the torture of political prisoners in Indochina.[3] It was attended by over four hundred people, including several police spies.

1. The League for the Rights of Man emerged with the Dreyfus Affair and brought together an array of leftist intellectuals ranging from members of the republican Left to the Socialist Party. See François Furet, *The Passing of an Illusion: The Idea of Communism in the Twentieth Century* (Chicago, 1999).

2. David Marr, *Vietnamese Anticolonialism: 1885–1925* (Berkeley and Los Angeles, 1971), 241.

3. AOM, SLOTFOM, 3d ser., carton 17, Ligue des droits de l'homme, October 17, 1927.

Following the disorder of 1930–31, the League for the Rights of Man and its auxiliaries launched attacks against the criminal commissions that had been hastily set up to punish participants in the Yen Bay mutiny and the Nghe-Tinh soviets. At a meeting in Paris sponsored by the Committee for the Defense of Political Prisoners in 1930, the socialist legislator Marius Moutet chastised the Criminal Commission of Saigon for issuing 83 forced labor sentences and 34 death sentences over a single eighteen-hour period.[4] The following month, Moutet lamented the fate of those convicted before the criminal commissions from the floor of the Chamber of Deputies: "Everyone knows that in Indochina one leaves the *bagnes* more frequently through the door of death than the door of liberty. . . . I have been provided information from an ex-judge on the Criminal Commission that suggests that a sentence of three years at hard labor is the equivalent of capital punishment with a three-year delay."[5] The committees also attempted to secure the release of inmates whom they claimed had been falsely convicted or sentenced too severely. For example, in March 1930, the Committee for the Defense of Political Prisoners received an amnesty request from the parents of thirty inmates who claimed that their children had been convicted unjustly by the Criminal Commission in Vinh.[6] It forwarded the letter to the Ministry of Colonies and demanded an official enquiry.[7]

In March 1933, a series of mass trials of political activists in Indochina prompted the formation in Paris of the Committee for Amnesty in Indochina.[8] Loosely connected to the League for the Rights of Man, it was led by Vietnamese students studying in France and a handful of pacifist and

4. Ibid., May 27, 1930.

5. AOM, SLOTFOM, 3d ser., carton 129, which contains excerpts from the *Journal officiel de la République française: Débats parlementaires,* June 14, 1930.

6. A leader of the Committee was Jeanne Challaye, a well-known, feminist, pacifist, Soviet sympathizer, and the wife of Félicien Challaye. Other members included Agathe Thevenin, Rose Meymann, Noémie Lequiller, Elisabeth Brochart, and Albert Billaz.

7. AOM, SLOTFOM, 3d ser., carton 112, Comité de défense des prisonniers politiques, March 12, 1930.

8. Ibid., carton 46, Comité pour l'amnistie en faveur des Indochinois, March 14, 1933. People in France were especially outraged by a mass trial held from May 2 to May 7, 1933, before the Saigon Criminal Commission, in which 120 activists received sentences totaling 970 years' imprisonment: 19 got life sentences; 8 were condemned to terms of over 30 years' hard labor; and 6 were condemned to death. Most of the defendants had languished in Kham Lon for up to three years before being brought to trial. See Andrée Viollis, *Indochine S.O.S.* (1935; reprint, Paris, 1949), 201–2.

left-oriented French intellectuals, including Romain Rolland, Victor Basch, Louis Roubaud, Andrée Viollis, Madeleine Paz, Henri Barbusse, Francis Jourdain, René Maran, Félicien Challaye, and André Malraux. Its objective was to "obtain an amnesty for prisoners convicted of political crimes and for offenses committed during the course of the recent political demonstrations."[9] During the mid 1930s, it organized dozens of rallies and public meetings where demands for a general amnesty were raised.[10] Drawn by provocative titles such as "The Political Prisoners of Poulo Condore" and "The Hell of Indochinese Prisons," security agents in Paris attended nine public forums in 1933 and at least six in 1934. Attendance typically ranged from 50 to 200, but a meeting held at the Hôtel des Sociétiés savantes on May 16, 1933, drew an audience of over 600.[11]

Under the editorship of André Malraux, the committee published an information bulletin to amplify its case against the colonial juridical system and articulate a series of demands. Its first issue, published on May 1, 1933, contained chapters entitled "Torture and the Deportation of Innocents," "The Horrors of the Repression," and "The Prisons of Indochina Are Hells Where Innocents and Children Are Murdered."[12] It promoted what became a widely held but unsubstantiated claim, that there were 10,000 political prisoners in Indochina during the 1930s.[13] In a final chapter entitled "What to Do?" Malraux detailed the committee's strategy for the remainder of the decade. "We must organize protests," he wrote, "increase our in-

9. AOM, SLOTFOM, 3d ser., carton 112, Comité de défense des prisonniers politiques, March 12, 1930.

10. Viollis and Roubaud, both executive committee members, pledged to place articles in *Esprit* and *Le Petite Parisien*. René Maran and Madeleine Paz offered to approach editorial contacts at *Le Monde* and *Le Canard enchaîné*.

11. Sûreté coverage of the forums can be found in AOM, SLOTFOM, 3d ser., carton 43, Comité d'amnistie en Indochine.

12. A copy of the bulletin's first issue can be found in ibid., Comité pour l'amnistie des Indochinois. Most of the information contained in the bulletin was culled from the books on the reading list. They included Nguyen An Ninh's *La France en Indochine* (1925), Roland Dorgelès's *Sur la route mandarine* (1926), Nguyen Ai Quoc's *Le Procès de la colonisation française* (1926), Léon Werth's *Cochinchine* (1926), Camille Drevet's *Les Annamites chez eux* (1928), Luc Durtain's *Dieux blancs, hommes jaunes* (1930), Paul Monet's *Les Jauniers* (1930), and Louis Roubaud's *Viet Nam* (1931).

13. AOM, SLOTFOM, 3d ser., carton 43, Comité pour l'amnistie des Indochinois: "Since 1929, a pitiless repression has battered Indochina. Roughly 10,000 have been condemned to the *bagne* or to prison or to deportation. Dozens have been sentenced to death."

terventions with the authorities, and use the press to keep the French population abreast of the appalling atrocities committed in Indochina."[14]

As with other offshoots of the League for the Rights of Man, the Committee for Amnesty brought amnesty requests to the attention of the authorities. During the first eight months of its existence, it received over 1,000 letters from the relatives of colonial inmates.[15] After translating them into French, the committee mailed the requests to newspapers, parliamentary deputies, and the minister of colonies, and published the letters in its information bulletin.[16] For example, the committee published the following letter on May 11, 1933:

> I am Tran Van Nguon from Nhu-Long village outside of Can Tho. My son Tran Van Diep is political prisoner 4535 at the Saigon Central Prison. He was accused of neither murder, arson, or assault but simply of listening to others and participating in a single demonstration. The court ordered him held from September 15, 1931, until May 6, 1933, that is to say, for more than twenty months, before it gave him the excessively heavy sentence of five years at hard labor. My family is extremely poor and I have only one son of majority age. He is married and has his own three-year-old son. His wife is an orphan. My family is so poor that I cannot support his wife and child. I am currently taking care of four children, all of whom are too small to work. My situation is desperate. Therefore, I respectfully request the Committee of Amnesty to intervene to secure the liberation of my son.[17]

Hundreds of political prisoners and their relatives appealed to the committee for help, but many appear to have misunderstood the extent of its powers. "Unfortunately, our committee does not have an official character nor does it possess any real authority," Francis Jourdain wrote to the mother of a political prisoner in early 1936. "It is composed of individuals who are aware of the inexcusable procedures victimizing Indochinese prisoners and who attempt to publicize their plight and make appeals for their

---

14. Ibid.

15. At a well-attended public forum in November 1933, only eight months after the body was founded, committee spokesmen announced that they had already received over 1,000 letters from relatives of political prisoners. Ibid., Comité d'amnistie des Indochinois, November 13, 1933.

16. Ibid., Comité d'amnistie et de défense des Indochinois et des peuples colonisés, March 28, 1936.

17. The letter and six others from the families of political prisoners are published in the appendix to the 1949 edition of Viollis, *Indochine S.O.S.*, 24–25.

amnesty. We have therefore transmitted your letter to the minister of colonies, as we do with all the requests we receive from Indochina."[18]

Agitation in favor of an amnesty for political prisoners developed more slowly in Indochina than in France. During 1934 and 1935, the legal opposition virtually ignored the issue, dwelling instead on the quality of prison conditions and the absence of a special regime for political prisoners.[19] It was only after the Popular Front announced an amnesty for French political prisoners as part of its campaign platform in early 1936 that the legal opposition took up the issue. On February 4, *La Lutte* printed a passionate appeal for a "complete and total amnesty" by Andrée Viollis and Félicien Challaye:

> There are currently in the prisons and *bagnes* of different colonies and particularly in Indochina, thousands of political prisoners. These men, the greater part of whom have been formed in our schools and who represent the most French elements of the population, have only committed the crime of believing that the ideals of liberty, equality, and fraternity, which are fundamental to our democracy, are applicable to the colony. They have been judged in conditions that most Frenchmen consider inadequate, if not revolting. They have been condemned to punishments disproportionate to their crimes, most of which entail only political or union activity. We demand, M. Minister, that these unfortunates be made the beneficiaries of a large amnesty.[20]

Thereafter, the proposed amnesty attracted regular attention in the colonial press. The following month, *La Lutte* republished an editorial from the Paris journal *Paix et Liberté* that argued that the amnesty should not be like the "arbitrary" and "parsimonious" amnesties of the past that occurred following elections and holidays. Rather, it insisted, it should be applied systematically to four categories of offenders: war resisters, traitors, illegal strikers, and colonial peoples.[21]

The announcement of the Popular Front's electoral victory in early June, along with the appointment of Marius Moutet as minister of colonies, trig-

---

18. AOM, SLOTFOM, 3d ser., carton 43, Comité d'Amnistie et defense des Indochinois et des peuples colonisés, March 28, 1936.

19. See in *La Lutte*, "Grève générale de la faim à Poulo Condore," April 6, 1935; "A la Maison centrale de Saigon: Histoire d'une grève," August 31, 1935; and "Une Grève récente à Poulo-Condore," September 21, 1935. In the lists of prisoners' demands published in each article, a general amnesty does not appear, but all include a request for the introduction of a political regime.

20. See also "Amnistie et régime politique!" *La Lutte*, February 11, 1936.

21. "Nous voulons l'amnistie," *La Lutte*, March 4, 1936.

gered an outbreak of amnesty fever in Indochina. In a front-page editorial on June 4 entitled "An Xa! An Xa!" (Amnesty! Amnesty!), the editors of *Tieng Dan* wrote that "no story has provoked such ebullience [*soi noi*] as the news of the upcoming amnesty."[22] On June 10, *La Lutte* printed "AMNESTY!!" in bold lettering under the masthead and advertised page 2 as a "Special Page on Poulo-Condore." The issue printed a letter from prisoners on Poulo Condore welcoming the amnesty and provided further speculative details about the Popular Front's proposed policy. Even the normally restrained *La Tribune indochinoise*, the mouthpiece of the moderate Constitutionalist Party, led with an editorial lauding the decision: "We and our Annamite brothers have identified the opportunity, in fact, the necessity, of a measure of grace for political convicts. On the occasion of the victory of the Popular Front, our appeals have been heard."[23]

Among colonial officials in Indochina, attitudes toward the amnesty were decidedly more mixed. The policy was vigorously opposed by administrators directly responsible for civil order. It was rumored that Moutet's dismissal of Governor-General Robin in May, 1936 was because of his hard-line opposition to the new policy. Likewise, Sûreté reporting from the era betrays considerable skepticism about the wisdom of the amnesty. Prison officials may, however, have seen the amnesty as a partial solution to problems that had dogged the colonial prison system since the mass arrests at the start of the decade. In fact, these officials had long viewed amnesties as instruments to relieve overcrowding and inducements to persuade troublesome prisoners to improve their behavior.

The amnesty was announced officially by Minister of Justice Maurice Viollette in a speech on June 12, 1936:

> The purpose of this policy is to permit, by way of individual decrees, the granting of a measure of clemency and pardons to the authors of certain infractions presenting a political character or that have been committed with a political motive. The amnesty will benefit the perpetrators of so-called political crimes, crimes of the press, crimes of anarchist propaganda, or crimes connected with public demonstrations.[24]

22. The editorial concluded, "We've waited anxiously for this rain, after so many years of drought." "An Xa! An Xa!" *Tieng Dan*, June 4, 1936.

23. "L'Amnistie générale des condamnés politiques," *La Tribune indochinoise*, June 17, 1936.

24. "La Grâce amnistiante en faveur des condamnés: Ses effets seront ceux reconnus par les dernières lois," *La Tribune indochinoise*, June 29, 1936.

While the wide range of offenses covered by the amnesty pleased the legal opposition in Indochina and its allies in France, the minister's decision to grant clemencies "by way of individual degrees" was a source of disappointment. In effect, the policy stopped short of issuing a general amnesty for all political prisoners, offering instead to facilitate the release of specific prisoners on a case-by-case basis. The examination of individual cases would prove a complex and contentious process in which the colonial state, the Ministry of Colonies, metropolitan human rights groups, the legal opposition, and the prisoners themselves all played important roles.

Following Viollette's speech, Moutet ordered the governor-general of Indochina to submit to the Ministry of Colonies dossiers of prisoners eligible for amnesties or sentence reductions under the new law.[25] Before reaching the governor-general's office, dossiers were vetted by a complex bureaucratic approval process.[26] Based on a variety of factors including "conduct in prison and health status," prison directors identified eligible inmates and forwarded their files to the provincial resident. After a brief review, they were passed on to newly formed Amnesty Councils attached to the offices of the residents superior of Tonkin and Annam and the governor of Cochin China.[27] They were then sent to the Indochinese Department of Justice for a penultimate assessment. Finally, the files of prisoners tried before indigenous courts were forwarded to the governor-general for official approval, while those of inmates convicted in French courts were flown to Paris to receive ministerial signature.

Determined to announce the names of the beneficiaries of the amnesty on July 14, the Ministry of Colonies urged the Amnesty Councils to act with alacrity. Despite the complexity of the approval process, it ordered that final lists should be compiled within three weeks, with top priority going to "women, minors, and the very ill."[28] In the weeks following the minister's announcement, the press provided regular updates about the quantity of cases under examination at each stage of the process. On June 18, *Dong*

25. "1,500 Quoc Su Pham Sap Duoc An Xa Hoac An Giam," [1,500 Political Prisoners Soon to Have Amnesty or Sentence Reduction], *Dong Phap*, June 25, 1936.

26. "Mot Chinh Sach Khoan Hong Cua Chinh Phu" [A Merciful Government Policy], *Dong Phap*, June 18, 1936.

27. In Annam, the cases of prisoners sentenced by French and indigenous courts were handled by separate subcommittees. "Hoi Dong Xet Viec An Xa Va An Giam Chanh Tri Pham O Trung Ky" [Councils to Arrange Amnesties and Sentence Reductions in Central Vietnam], *Tieng Dan*, July 9, 1935.

28. "Mong Chinh Phu Chu Y: Hoi Nhan Quyen Voi Viec An Xa, An-Giam" [We Hope That the Government Pays Attention: The League for the Rights of Man and the Amnesty], *Dong Phap*, June 22, 1936.

Phap reported that wardens and provincial residents in Tonkin had selected over 500 cases for consideration, and that the Amnesty Council was reviewing 100 dossiers every day.[29] The following week, it disclosed that 1,500 cases were currently being processed and half-jokingly advised the government of Indochina to "rent an airplane to forward the dossiers to Paris."[30] On June 29, it announced that reviews of 850 cases had been completed.[31]

Unwilling to leave the initiation of amnesty cases to the same colonial officials that they had been attacking for years, the legal opposition and their metropolitan allies set up an alternative nomination process. On June 13, the League for the Rights of Man, in conjunction with the Cochin Chinese Branch of the Radical Socialist Party, announced the formation of an Indochinese wing of the Committee for Amnesty in Indochina.[32] Reflecting the broad political support enjoyed by the policy, the committee was headed by a team of left-leaning French lawyers, as well as Nguyen An Ninh and several members of the Cochin Chinese Constitutionalist Party.[33] In an early press release, the committee laid out its objectives:

> Among the prisoners serving sentences in the jails of Indochina, there are many who were condemned because of their general political opinions or because they were labeled communists, plotters, or subversives at the time of their prosecution. It is only fair that a measure of clemency be accorded to these prisoners, and that, in a spirit of tolerance, their convictions be overturned. Only a total amnesty will bring about the desired result.[34]

Unlike the Councils connected to the administration, the Indochinese branch of the Committee for Amnesty solicited amnesty requests directly from the families of political prisoners. It forwarded these requests to the appropriate Amnesty Council or to its headquarters in Paris, which then submitted them formally to the Ministry of Colonies.[35] To gather requests,

---

29. *Dong Phap*, June 18, 1936.

30. "1,500 Quoc Su Pham Sap Duoc An Xa Hoac An Giam," *Dong Phap*, June 25, 1936.

31. *Dong Phap*, June 29, 1936.

32. "Comité Indochinois d'Amnistie," *La Lutte*, June 17, 1936.

33. Ibid.

34. "L'Amnistie générale des condamnés politiques: Elle a recueilli tant ici qu'au Tonkin quantité d'adhésions," *La Tribune Indochinoise*, June 17, 36.

35. On June 27, 1936, Minister of Colonies Marius Moutet met with M. Vittori of the Committee for Amnesty and encouraged him to forward such requests. "The minister assured M. Vittori that the amnesty law about to be voted on was conceived to liberate the largest proportion of Indochinese political prisoners as possible." "Pour l'amnistie des prisoniers politiques," *La Lutte*, July 22, 1936.

the committee published notices in colonial newspapers in the form of coupons addressed "to the families of political prisoners."[36] They provided a standard form on which family members could write their jailed relative's full name, date of arrest, crime, sentence, and the court in which they had been tried.[37] "The body that rules on amnesty cases in France contains communist and socialist delegates," the committee wrote encouragingly in *Tieng Dan* on August 25, 1936. "Our committee approves most of the applications sent to us. We urge you to tell your neighbors with jailed relatives that an unusual opportunity has arisen. Just fill out this application in *quoc ngu* and send it to our offices in Paris or Saigon. Nothing else is required."[38]

Although the amnesty of 1936 is typically portrayed as a dramatically simultaneous liberation of political prisoners, it occurred in piecemeal fashion. Many inmates were approved for sentence reductions rather than amnesties and remained in prison well past July 14. The three Amnesty Councils worked at their own rates and judged cases based upon different standards. In Cochin China, foot-dragging on the part of colonial officials unhappy with the new policy caused the Amnesty Council there to miss the deadline altogether. As a result, no prisoners were released from Poulo Condore until the end of July. Moreover, Emperor Bao Dai stole some of the new regime's thunder by issuing 200 imperial amnesties and sentence reductions for prisoners in Annam in late June, on the occasion of his son's birthday.[39]

36. For examples of such notices, see *La Lutte*, July 22 and September 24, 1936, and January 14, 1937; *La Tribune Indochinoise*, October 10, 1936; *Tieng Dan*, June 30, 1936; *Le Travail*, October 21, 1936.

37. By late September, the Committee for Amnesty claimed to have received hundreds of letters concerning requests for amnesty. For every letter that came in, the committee created a dossier and submitted it to the appropriate body. In cases where adequate information was not provided, the committee corresponded with the letter writer in an attempt to retrieve the relevant data. "Aux Parents des emprisonés politiques d'Indochine," *La Lutte*, September 24, 1936.

38. "Mot Buc Thu ve Viec Xin An Xa" [A Letter about the Process for Requesting Amnesty], *Tieng Dan*, August 25, 1936.

39. The 200 measures included 11 amnesties and 31 sentence reductions for political prisoners and 69 amnesties and 91 sentence reductions for common-law prisoners. "O Trung Ky Cung Co Nhieu Chinh Tri Pham Va Thuong Pham Duoc Tha Cung Duoc Giam Toi" [In Central Vietnam, Many Political Prisoners and Common-Law Prisoners Benefit from an Amnesty or Sentence Reduction], *Dong Phap*, June 19, 1936.

Table 8.   Amnesties and Sentence Reductions in Indochina,
1930–1939

Year	No. of Reductions
1930	347
1931	936
1932	2,771
1933	5,394
1934	3,495
1935	1,745
1936	4,056
1937	1,414
1938	1,462
1939	1,077

SOURCE: Gouvernement général de l'Indochine, *Annuaire statistique de l'Indochine,* various years.

On July 14, the governor-general announced amnesties for roughly 700 prisoners: 269 from Tonkin, 399 from Annam, and 23 from Cochin China.[40] The Cochin Chinese administration finally released 293 political prisoners from Poulo Condore in late July, and another 263 in September.[41] In mid August, *Tieng Dan* reported an additional 556 amnesties and sentence reductions from Tonkin.[42] By mid October, *La Lutte* put the total number of amnesties issued since July at around 1,500. It is instructive that this figure represented well under half of the 4,056 political and common-law prisoners who were offered conditional liberation or sentence reductions during 1936 (see table 8).[43] Many inmates had been freed months earlier during Tet or at different points throughout the year as a reward for good behavior. It is also worth noting that the number of amnesties in 1936 did not surpass

40. "668 Chinh Tri Pham Duoc Tha" [668 Political Prisoners Are Released], *Tieng Dan,* July 21, 1936.
41. See "L'Amnistie doit être complète et totale: Des centaines de détenus politiques gémissent encore dans l'enfer des bagnes," *Le Travail,* November 20, 1936; "La Liberté entière aux libérés politiques," *Le Travail,* December 11, 1936.
42. "556 Thuong Pham O Bac Ky Da Duoc An Xa," *Tieng Dan,* August 11, 1936.
43. AOM, Indochine, Affaires politiques, 1728, Statistiques des effectifs pénitentiaires, 1936.

the 5,394 that were issued in 1933, primarily in an attempt to relieve over-crowding following the massive arrests at the start of the decade.[44]

Still, the 1936 amnesty was significant because of the high number of hardened political activists that it released into civilian life. Over six times the number of officially designated political prisoners (those sentenced to deportation and detention) were freed during July, August, and September 1936 (523) than during all of 1937 (84).[45] Most sources agree that many of the roughly 1,500 political prisoners liberated in 1936 were ICP members.[46] According to communist estimates, over half of the 556 prisoners released from Poulo Condore in July and August were ICP members.[47] They included four future communist party secretaries-general: Nguyen Van Cu, Truong Chinh, Le Duan, and Nguyen Van Linh. Other influential ICP members liberated in 1936 included Le Duc Tho, Pham Van Dong, Hoang Quoc Viet, Nguyen Chi Dieu, Ung Van Khiem, Le Thanh Nghi, Ha Huy Giap, Tran Cung, Phan Dang Luu, Tran Van Cung, Tran Thi Lien, Le Boi, Vo Cung, Dao Xuan Mai, and Nguyen Kim Cuong.[48]

THE PRESS AND THE AMNESTY

If officials expected the amnesty to dampen the intensity of attacks against the prison system in the colonial press, they were to be disappointed. As early as July 22, the editors of *La Lutte* warned their readers that the new

44. Gouvernement général de l'Indochine, *Annuaire statistique de l'Indochine* (Hanoi). In February 1936, just four months before the Popular Front came to power, the Ministry of Colonies issued total and partial amnesties for forty political prisoners. See "Larges mesures de clémence: 40 annamites condamnés politiques bénéficient de l'amnistie ou de réduction de peine," *La Tribune Indochinoise*, February 21, 1936.

45. AOM, Indochine, Affaires politiques, 1728, Statistiques des effectifs pénitentiaires, 1936.

46. Tinh Uy Dak Lak and Vien Lich Su Dang, *Lich Su Nha Day Buon Ma Thuot, 1930–1945* [History of Buon Ma Thuot Penitentiary, 1930–1945] (Hanoi, 1991), 66; Vien Mac-Lenin and Vien Lich Su Dang, *Nguc Son La, Truong Hoc Dau Tranh Cach Mang* [Son La Prison, the School of Revolutionary Struggle] (Hanoi, 1992), 29. It is unfortunate that figures for October, November, and December 1936 were missing from the archival files I was able to consult.

47. Ban Nghien Cuu Lich Su Dang Dac Khu Vung Tau—Con Dao, *Nha Tu Con Dao, 1862–1945* [Con Dao Penitentiary, 1862–1945] (Hanoi, 1987), 133.

48. In addition, approximately 100 members of the VNQDD were amnestied in 1936, including Pham Tuan Tai, Ho Van Mich, Nguyen The Nghiep, and Nguyen Ngoc Son. Hoang Van Dao, *Viet Nam Quoc Dan Dang: Lich Su Tranh Dau Can Dai (1927–1954)* [The Vietnam Quoc Dan Dang: A History of Modern Struggle] (Saigon, 1965), 226.

policy should not influence public opinion about the regime and urged their writers to expand their coverage of the prison system to include critiques of the implementation of the policy itself.[49] A major complaint about the amnesty was its limited scope. Some observers charged that it favored high-profile prisoners whose names had appeared in the colonial press but ignored the revolutionary rank-and-file.[50] In 1939, estimates of the number of political activists still in jail ranged from several hundred to 7,000 (depending on how political prisoners were defined).[51] *La Lutte* argued that an unintended consequence of the liberations was to weaken, both numerically and spiritually, political prisoners who remained behind.[52] Hence, it continued to publish atrocity stories, demands for reform, and requests for additional pardons.[53]

A related grievance was the fact that political activists serving common-law sentences remained ineligible for the amnesty. "To continue to consider political activists as common criminals," *La Lutte* wrote on August 12, "and therefore to exclude them from the amnesty is clear evidence of the administration's bad faith."[54] The predicament of activists sentenced for common-law crimes was taken up by *Le Travail*, which pointed out that

49. "Pour les prisonniers politiques de l'Annam-Tonkin," *La Lutte*, July 22, 1936.

50. Jean-Claude Demariaux, *Les Secrets des îles Poulo-Condore: Le Grand Bagne indochinois* (Paris, 1956), 176.

51. "Les Trotskystes réclament l'amnistie par le mensonge et la mauvaise foi," *Notre Voix*, June 4, 1939. The article attacked the Trotskyist journal *Dan Moi* for using the 7,000 figure.

52. "Pour une amnistie pleine et entière: Le Sort misérable des détenus politiques à Poulo Condore," *La Lutte*, February 23, 1937.

53. For examples of *La Lutte*'s continued coverage in 1937 and 1938, see "Sauvage répression au bagne de Banméthuot" and "A Poulo Condore rien ne change," January 14, 1937; "Les Indochinois, le Marseille et les bagnards d'Inini," February 21, 1937; "Une Lettre ouverte: Les Prisonniers politiques de Poulo-Condore à Monsieur le Gouverneur général de l'Indochine" and "Pour une amnistie pleine et entière: Le Sort misérable des détenus politiques à Poulo Condore," February 23, 1937; "500 déportés resteront à Innini!" February 28, 1937; "Encore des provocations à Poulo Condore," April 11, 1937; "Poulo Condore reste tel qu'il était: L'Enfer des vivants," April 13, 1937; "Les Tortures au pénitencier de Banméthuot," April 22, 1937; "Pour le régime politique dans les prisons! Abolition du régime d'interdiction de séjour et de résidence forcée," April 29, 1937; "Grève de la faim des détenus politiques à la Prison de Quang Ngai" and "Grève de la faim des prisonniers à Rach Gia," May 20, 1937; "Contre les mauvais Traitements: Le Régime politique pour les condamnés politiques," February 13, 1938; "La Bastille a été prise il y a un siècle et demi, eh bien! Elle reste à prendre," July 10, 1938; and "Un Contribuable défaillant exécuté en prison!" July 31, 1938.

54. "Pas de distinction dans l'amnistie," *La Lutte*, August 12, 1936.

"despite the recent amnesty, hundreds of our compatriots still suffer in the *bagnes*, some for protesting against heavy taxes or forming illegal organizations and others simply for expressing opinions that the administration prefers not to hear."[55]

The legal opposition blamed the shortcomings of the policy on the subversive efforts of conservative colonial officials who opposed the new government and its policy. Francis Jourdain remarked that the "partial and incomplete nature of the amnesty shows how a reactionary colonial bureaucracy can deform the good intentions of a ministry."[56] In *La Lutte*, a group of prisoners writing from Poulo Condore made a point to distinguish between the minister's "goodwill" and the "hostility and cruelty" of the colonial state. "In regard to the amnesty," they concluded, "it has been reduced to a partial measure, carried out in a confused and inequitable way. Thousands of political prisoners remain in *bagnes*."[57]

Another common complaint was that the hoopla surrounding the amnesties obscured the unjust nature of the original convictions in the first place. Writing in *La Lutte*, Andrée Viollis recalled the indiscriminate severity that marked the repression of 1929–32.[58] *Le Travail* revisited the conviction of Bui Cong Trung, an ICP member who had been sentenced to fifteen years' detention for visiting the Soviet Union.[59] Another article raised the case of a recently amnestied prisoner who had been sentenced to twenty years' hard labor for possessing a banned book: "This example confirms that the liberation of certain convicts should not be considered as a grace or an amnesty but as fair reparations for the crimes perpetrated by the extraordinary tribunals of Annam and Tonkin."[60]

With the closing of *La Lutte* in 1938, coverage of the abuses of the prison system and the shortcomings of the amnesty continued in newspapers such as *Mai, Dan Quyen, Duoc Nha Nam, Dan Chung, Tin Tuc, Song*

55. "L'Amnestie doit être complète et total: Des centaines de détenus politiques gémissent encore dans des bagnes," *Le Travail*, November 20, 1936.

56. "Francis Jourdain nous écrit," *Le Travail*, October 21, 1936.

57. "Une Lettre ouverte: Les Prisonniers politiques de Poulo Condore à Monsieur le Gouverneur général de l'Indochine," *La Lutte*, February 20, 1937.

58. Viollis recounted the 1933 trial of French legionnaires who openly admitted that they had tortured suspected communists and massacred Annamese captives to relieve overcrowding in makeshift prison camps in 1931. "Ce qu'attend l'Indochine," *La Lutte*, July 8, 1936.

59. "L'Amnistie doit être complète et totale," *Le Travail*, November 20, 1936.

60. "Pour une large amnistie," *La Lutte*, September 16, 36.

Huong, L'Avant-Garde, Le Travail, Le Peuple, En Avant, and *Notre Voix.*[61] In mid 1939, thirty editors and publishers signed a public petition demanding improved conditions and more pardons for political prisoners.[62] On July 14, the petition appeared simultaneously on the front pages of every one of their newspapers. Far from placating the legal opposition, the amnesty seemed to have intensified its efforts to denounce and discredit the colonial prison.

ADMINISTRATIVE SURVEILLANCE

For the beneficiaries of the amnesty, liberation did not translate into unfettered freedom. As we have seen, many ex-prisoners were subjected to a form of postinstitutional control known as administrative surveillance.[63] First introduced into France through the Napoleonic code of 1810, this supplemental penalty was tagged onto the original punishment during sentencing and varied in duration based on the severity of the crime. It had two basic components: the forbidden place and the restricted residence. The state made it a crime for ex-prisoners to reside in or visit certain localities by declaring them "forbidden places." Since the penalty was originally devised to counter public anxiety about collusion between the "dangerous classes" and the "laboring classes," the sites most frequently placed off limits were cities or large towns.[64] The concept of restricted residence compelled ex-prisoners to live in designated villages or districts, where they

61. Nguyen Thanh, *Bao Chi Cach Mang Viet Nam, 1925–1945* [Vietnamese Revolutionary Newspapers, 1925–1945] (Hanoi, 1984), 131–222.

62. "Une Pétition en faveur des condamnés politiques Indochinois" in *Notre Voix,* July 14, 1939, 1. The petition was signed by editors of the following newspapers: *L'Effort, Doi Nay, Bac Ky Dan Bao, Thoi Vu, Nam Cuong, Thoi Bao Tan Van, Ngay Nay, Notre Voix, Dong Tay, Tieu Thuyet Nhat Bao, Phu Nu, Dong Phap, Con Ong, Ngay Moi, Vit Duc, Tan Viet Nam, Le Monôme, Hanoi Soir, Tieu Thuyet Thu Nam, Tao Dan, Nguoi Moi, Chinh Tri, Viet Bao, Dan Ba, Tieu Thuyet Thu Bay, Demain, Quoc Gia, L'Annam nouveau,* and *Nuoc Nam.*

63. Administrative surveillance represented an official admission that prisons "failed to rehabilitate the criminal," Patricia O'Brien argues in *The Promise of Punishment: Prisons in Nineteenth-Century France* (Princeton, N.J., 1982), 226.

64. Hanoi, Haiphong, Nam Dinh, Ha Dong, and Bac Ninh were off-limits to ex-prisoners from Tonkin, while those from Cochin China were barred from Saigon, My Tho, Can Tho, and Bien Hoa (*Le Travail,* February 17, 1937). In France, urban sites were typically designated forbidden places because of fears of collusion between the so-called laboring and the dangerous classes. See Louis Chevalier, *Laboring Classes and Dangerous Classes in Paris During the First Half of the Nineteenth Century* (Princeton, N.J., 1973).

were to report weekly to the local office of the Sûreté. While some ex-prisoners were remanded to their native villages, most were sent to unfamiliar areas, far from protective networks of families and friends.[65] Those who desired to travel outside of their restricted residence or to a forbidden place, to attend a funeral or visit a sick relative, for example, were required to request permission, not only from the Sûreté, but from village and district officials as well.[66]

The implementation of administrative surveillance in Indochina gave rise to numerous opportunities for extortion and corruption. Critics charged that officials and police agents harassed ex-prisoners under their jurisdiction and demanded protection money and bribes. The worst feature of the policy, according to *La Lutte,* was that it made ex-prisoners "completely vulnerable to the caprice of local mandarins."[67] It cited the case of a mandarin in Phu Ly who was widely reviled for charging exorbitant fees for travel permits and requiring ex-prisoners to kowtow in his presence.[68] In Quang Ngai, it was reported that a mandarin arrested and tortured all ex-prisoners serving administrative surveillance under his authority after a politically provocative editorial appeared anonymously in a local newspaper.[69]

Another common complaint was that restricted residence to rural areas rendered superfluous years of education and training and led to serious financial problems. In an editorial discussing the issue in December 1936, *Le Travail* asked rhetorically: "How can intellectuals or electricians hope to find work in the countryside?"[70] The ICP member Ung Van Khiem made a similar point following his release from Poulo Condore in 1936: "Most occupations are now forbidden to me, and I remain the target of harassment by local notables and surveillance by the police."[71] Even those who attempted to secure employment within their designated localities were fre-

65. While scattered evidence suggests that prisoners were more often than not restricted to their native villages, many Tonkinese prisoners incarcerated on Poulo Condore for their participation in the movements of 1930–31 were remanded to Saigon. See "Pour le régime politique dans les prisons: Abolition de régime d'interdiction de séjour et de résidence de force," *La Lutte,* April 29, 1937.

66. *Le Travail,* April 11, 1937.

67. "Les Autorités rendant la vie impossible aux anciens détenus politiques," *La Lutte,* August 5, 36.

68. "La Voix des libérés politiques," *Le Travail,* November 27, 1936.

69. "Amnistie," *Le Travail,* February 17, 1937.

70. *Le Travail,* December 11, 1936.

71. Demariaux, *Secrets des îles Poulo-Condore,* 282.

quently thwarted by local officials. For example, in 1937 an ex-prisoner remanded to Hai Duong requested permission to open a small private school:

> Since the Popular Front released me, I have faced many hardships. Ruined by the economic crisis, my family can no longer nourish me. Thus, permit me to request your permission to open in the village of Phao Son a small private school for approximately fifteen students who wish to study *quoc ngu* and French. It is the only means at my disposal to earn a living.[72]

The request denied, he attempted to modify his plan by organizing an informal evening class for his brothers, nephews, and cousins. On March 27, Sûreté agents raided his house, confiscated his books, made out police reports on his students, and forced the class to disband.[73]

As the coverage of this story suggests, administrative surveillance provided the legal opposition with yet another contentious issue with which to assail the colonial state. During the Popular Front era, newspaper stories on the plight of ex-prisoners under administrative surveillance were as numerous and aggressively critical as exposés of the prison system. The issue also attracted the attention of French human rights groups. For example, on April 4, 1938, the Secours populaire raised it with the Ministry of Colonies in the following way:

> Ex-prisoners subjected to administrative surveillance, often in unfamiliar locales, find themselves in a pitiful material and moral situation. Employers dare not hire them. The administrative authorities refuse to help them. The police subject them to all manner of harassments, trying, on the one hand, to discredit them in the eyes of their entourage, and on the other, to subvert their attempts to find work.[74]

Not only did administrative surveillance tend to exacerbate the colonial state's negative public image but it contributed to the strength of the anticolonial movement by inducing ex-political prisoners to reenter the revolutionary struggle. For those already predisposed to return to political activity, the injustices of administrative surveillance fortified their resolve. For ex-prisoners who were reticent about risking their freedom so soon after release, administrative surveillance helped erode their resistance by demonstrating the futility of attempting to lead peaceful and productive

72. *Le Travail,* April 16, 1937.
73. Ibid.
74. AOM, Indochine, Affaires politiques, 1728, Situation faite aux libérés politiques indochinois, Interventions du Secours populaire.

lives as long as the colonial state held power in Indochina. Moreover, by severing them from family networks and restricting their employment opportunities, administrative surveillance encouraged ex-prisoners to seek each other out for emotional and financial support. As a result, the policy contributed to the formation of enclave communities of ex-political prisoners that nurtured and advanced anticolonial political activism throughout the Popular Front era.

Since at least the start of the 1930s, French officials observed that political prisoners tended to congregate together following liberation. These groupings frequently took the explicit form of social welfare associations designed to alleviate the financial burdens of administrative surveillance. In 1933, it was reported that "recently released ex-political prisoners in Annam are secretly forming corporative associations and mutual-aid societies."[75] In 1935, the Sûreté discovered a "clandestine organization of ex-prisoners" in Ben Tre whose main purpose was to "provide aid for destitute ex-prisoners and sanctuary for escapees."[76] Following the amnesties of 1936, the Sûreté observed the formation of many similar groups such as "a clique of ex-political prisoners in Hanoi who have opened a small shop that permits released political prisoners without means to purchase items at reduced prices."[77]

Perhaps the best-known community of ex-political prisoners in Indochina was based at the household of Phan Boi Chau. Although he was formally under house arrest in Hue, the local office of the Sûreté permitted Phan to receive guests and to travel around the city. According to numerous sources, dozens of former political prisoners frequented Phan's compound, including Huynh Thuc Khang, Le Boi, Nguyen Khoa Van, Bui Cong Trung, Nguyen Chi Dieu, and Bui San.[78] In August 1936, Phan Dang Luu, an ICP member, was released from Buon Ma Thuot and remanded to Hue, where he soon became a permanent member of Phan's household.[79] Ton Quang Phiet recalls that Phan also provided food and lodging for "seven children of political prisoners" whose fathers remained on Poulo

75. AOM, SLOTFOM, 3d ser., carton 52, *AAPCI*, 2d quarter 1933.

76. Ibid., carton 54, *AAPCI*, 1st quarter 1935.

77. Ibid., August 1936.

78. Among the ex-prisoners providing temporary assistance were Le Boi, Hai Trieu, Bui Cong Trung, Nguyen Chi Dieu, and Bui San. See Ton Quang Phiet, "Ve Dong Chi Phan Dang Luu: Mot Dong Chi Tri Thuc Cach Mang Kien Cuong" [Comrade Phan Dang Luu: A Steadfast Revolutionary Intellectual], *Nghien Cuu Lich Su* 147 (November–December 1972): 16.

79. Ibid., 17.

Condore.[80] When Lam Hong Phan stayed briefly at Phan's house late in 1936, he was struck by the presence there of numerous "silver-haired, thoughtful-looking old men" who had "returned from Poulo Condore and moved in more or less permanently with him."[81]

> Among them was Hoang Xuan Hanh, the younger brother of Hoang Xuan Duong, the uncle of dear Uncle Ho, who had been imprisoned on Poulo Condore following the Tax Movement of 1908. Released in 1926, he served as a sort of steward in Phan's house. Also living there were Tran Quan Cuu Cac (Tran Hoanh) from Quang Tri, famous for escaping from Poulo Condore . . . and Phan Nghi De, Phan's son who had only recently been released from Lao Bao.[82]

Remarking on the familial atmosphere of the household, Lam Hong Phan noted that Phan spent his mornings, evenings, and every meal in the company of his prison comrades. Tran Huy Lieu's account of a visit to Phan's compound in 1935 confirms Lam Hong Phan's description of Phan as a benevolent patriarch presiding over an extended brood of former political prisoners and their relatives:

> Uncle Phan's family at that time was composed of former political prisoners from different regions. Many long-term prisoners who had returned to find that their families had dispersed came to live with Uncle. Among them was Ky Nam, who had been arrested in Thailand and had served time with me on Poulo Condore. After [his] release, Phan had taken him in. In addition to other former political prisoners, there was also Mrs. Pham Than from Ha Tinh. Pham Than was the younger brother of Pham Duc Ngon. Both had been sent to Poulo Condore the previous year. Mrs. Phan Than came to live on Poulo Condore, but returned to the mainland after becoming pregnant. Sadly, her baby son died soon after he was born. Afterward Pham Than and his brother Ngon both died on Poulo Condore. The story of Mrs. Pham Than crossing the ocean to follow her husband became a favorite among prisoners on Poulo Condore and generated many singing poems. In Saigon's Kham Lon, Nguyen Dinh Kien loved to tell stories about "Aunt Pham." So, when Phan introduced us, I said, "So this is Aunt Pham?"[83]

---

80. Ton Quang Phiet, "Mot Vai Ky Niem Ve Phan Boi Chau," [Some Memories of Phan Boi Chau], in *Ong Gia Ben Ngu: Hoi Ky* [The Old Man from Ben Ngu: Memoirs] (Hue, 1982), 63.

81. Lam Hong Phan, "Lop Vo Long Tai Nha Phan Boi Chau" [The Pre-School Class in Phan Boi Chau's Household], in ibid., 157–58.

82. Ibid.

83. After Aunt Phan's departure, the two men were joined for lunch by Mai Lao Bang, imprisoned on Con Dao during the 1910s, about whom Lieu had also heard many stories during his own incarceration. Tran Huy Lieu, "Nho Lai 'Ong Gia Ben Ngu'" [Recalling the Old Man of Ben Ngu], in ibid., 456–57.

The depictions provided by Tran Huy Lieu and Lam Hong Phan suggest that the subcultural social formations that developed among political prisoners behind bars extended into civil society. It is instructive that the unorthodox, male-dominated residential arrangements observed at the household of Phan Boi Chau simulated the conditions of group living characteristic of prison society. Phan's home was both a forum for discussions of revolutionary strategy and a classroom where practical and theoretical knowledge was disseminated. It also functioned as a pilgrimage site to which activists such as Tran Huy Lieu periodically sojourned for information, political comradeship, and emotional support. Just as the communal nature of prison life generated social pressures that reinforced revolutionary commitments among inmates, the collective households formed by ex-prisoners sustained their continued political engagement.

EX-PRISONERS AND ANTICOLONIAL POLITICS

The years between 1936 and 1939 were among the most exuberant periods of anticolonial activism in the history of French Indochina. The electoral victory of the French Popular Front in May 1936 raised expectations of colonial reforms and generated a flurry of political activity. The easing of censorship, particularly in Cochin China, intensified the legal opposition's public relations campaign against the colonial state. A wave of militant labor activism overwhelmed the colonial economy, involving tens of thousands of workers in a wide array of industries. Under orders from the Comintern, the ICP aggressively pursued alliances with democratic, anti-imperialist, and antifascist forces and launched a massive recruiting drive that expanded the Party's membership to its highest levels ever. Although relations between the ICP and the Trotskyists broke down during this period, both groups worked to establish a national representative body known as the Indochinese Congress. In view of the scope and vitality of these developments, the historian Huynh Kim Khanh has characterized the Popular Front era as a qualitatively "new phase in communist-sponsored politics in Indochina," dominated by the eruption of a "boisterous mass movement."

Among the most significant factors contributing to this upsurge of political agitation was the amnesty of political prisoners. Occurring at the outset of the Popular Front era, the liberations helped create a public impression that radical changes in Indochina's political climate were afoot. This sentiment is apparent in the media's breathless coverage of the announcement of the amnesty in early June. It also comes across in the memoir of the celebrated novelist Nguyen Hong, which describes the extraordinary public jubilation provoked by news of the policy. Hong recounts that a student informed him of the proposed amnesty in the middle of a class he was teaching at a Haiphong high school. Overjoyed at the news, he immediately dismissed his students and rushed out into the street, shouting: "The political prisoners of Poulo Condore have returned! The political offenders of Poulo Condore have returned! The communists from Poulo Condore are home! The communist prisoners are back in Haiphong!" Rumors of the amnesty were spreading rapidly "from rickshaw drivers to bricklayers to coolies to miners to sailors to market women." "The news excited me in a strange way," he wrote. "'Where should I go now?' I asked myself. Where can I greet the political prisoners who are returning from Poulo Condore?"[84]

In another writerly memoir of the interwar years, the novelist Nguyen Cong Hoan described how the amnesty of 1936 transformed his own political consciousness: "During the Popular Front era, many political detainees were released and fanned out to different areas to conduct political activities. I had many opportunities to contact them and began to feel the influence of the Indochinese Communist Party."[85] Hoan linked his eventual conversion to communism to the influence of returnees during the Popular Front era: "The closer my contacts with former political detainees, especially Le Duc Tho, who often came to my house, the more I understood that communism is humanist and that class struggle is a struggle for the national liberation of the broad masses."[86]

In addition to its exhilarating impact on the popular mood, the amnesty invigorated the anticolonial movement's civilian leadership. Since radical press coverage of the prison system had long served to endow political prisoners with something of a heroic aura, anticolonial groups welcomed them immediately into positions of power and authority. For the ICP, the rapid reintegration of former political prisoners into leadership positions had been going on for years. "Every day, militant prisoners are liberated after serving their penalty," the Sûreté noted in 1932, "but far from being

84. Nguyen Hong, *Buoc Duong Viet Van* [On the Road to Writing] (Hanoi, 1970), 121.

85. Nguyen Cong Hoan, "My Life as a Writer: Reminiscences," in *Vietnamese Intellectuals at a Historic Turning Point in the Twentieth Century* (Hanoi, 1989), 72.

86. Ibid., 74. In addition to Le Duc Tho, Hoan points to the influence on his thinking of another returnee, Le Van Phuc. "Since Le Van Phuc, a released political prisoner explained to me such concepts as surplus value, exploitation, class, and class struggle. . . . I began to love the working people."

reformed, they tend immediately to reenter the violent struggle."[87] The following year, the Sûreté reported once again that "the leaders of the revolutionary reorganization movement in Tonkin are former political prisoners. They seek to mobilize freed prisoners in order to endow their renewed organizations with experienced leaders."[88] Following the first wave of amnesties in July, 1936, the Sûreté anticipated an intensification of this pattern: "The ICP hopes to find, among the recently amnestied political prisoners, a number of capable and tested militants who will inject new vitality into the operation of the party. Already a certain number have made contact with their leaders and have demonstrated enthusiasm for continued anti-French agitation."[89]

The activities of ex-prisoners observed by the Sûreté support the notion that administrative surveillance failed to discourage them from returning to the anticolonial movement. While some escaped the physical restraints of the policy by bribing local officials, others fled surreptitiously and were never pursued or recovered. According to Hoang Quoc Viet, local officials often found the presence of ex-prisoners in their localities "undesirable" and were relieved when they simply disappeared.[90] In August, the Sûreté again noted that returnees were rapidly taking up influential posts within the Party's chain of command: "The Central Committee of the ICP has published a letter to all party members that contains instructions for the reorganization of the party's apparatus. Information from various sources suggests that this reorganization has already begun, and that it has been greatly facilitated by the appointment of recently freed political prisoners to important positions."[91] Years later, the Institute of Party History confirmed this conjecture, arguing that "many communist prisoners released after the 1936 amnesty went on to assume leadership posts in the party during the Popular Front period."[92] It cited the examples of Nguyen Van Cu, Hoang Quoc Viet, Le Duan, Nguyen Chi Dieu, Ung Van Khiem, Le Thanh Nghi, Nguyen Van Linh, and Ha Huy Giap, each of whom eventually rose to a position within the Central Committee or the Politburo.

87. AOM, SLOTFOM, 3d ser., carton 52, *AAPCI,* April–May 1932, 2.
88. Ibid., 4th quarter 1933.
89. Ibid., carton 54, *AAPCI,* July 1936, 1.
90. Hoang Quoc Viet, "Our People, a Very Heroic People," in *A Heroic People: Memoirs from the Revolution* (Hanoi, 1965), 176.
91. AOM, SLOTFOM, 3d ser., carton 54, *AAPCI,* August 1936, 4.
92. Ban Nghien Cuu Lich Su Dang Dac Khu Vung Tau—Con Dao, *Nha Tu Con Dao, 1862–1945,* 134.

Released political prisoners were also at the forefront of efforts to energize the anticolonial movement at the grassroots level. "Suspicious meetings have been observed in the villages of Quang Ngai, Binh Son, Son Tinh, Tu Nghia, and Mo Duc," the Sûreté reported less than a month after the first wave of amnesties in 1936. "It appears that secret village groups with explicit communist tendencies are being formed, under the leadership of former political prisoners."[93] The Sûreté also reported that "released political prisoners are organizing themselves into mobile theatrical troupes that circulate throughout Annam," noting: "Outside of the possibilities for propaganda provided by their continual movements, it must be remarked that the repertoire of these groups comprise works exalting patriotic sentiments. Such is the case with a recent performance of 'The Two Sisters,' a historic amplification of the exploits of Trung Trac and Trung Nhi."[94] The Party historian Tran Van Giau, who was himself released from Poulo Condore in 1936, has also characterized liberated political prisoners as anticolonial shock troops during the Popular Front era:

> Almost all of our imprisoned brothers continued to struggle after release. They assumed "struggle positions" within villages, in factories, on the streets, and in progressive newspapers. They served as the core for hundreds and thousands of organizations which grew in both urban and rural areas. Without this large influx of ex-prisoners in 1936 and 1937, the mass movement would never have developed so relentlessly and so systematically.[95]

Notwithstanding that Giau alludes to the penetration of factories by former political prisoners, their contribution to the rise of militant labor activism during the era has yet to be fully documented. Still, it is suggestive that the amnesties were followed immediately by an unprecedented wave of strikes, over 300 of which occurred in Indochina between August 1936 and February 1937, involving roughly 150,000 workers.[96] Preliminary research suggests that former political prisoners helped trigger a series of work stoppages by railway workers late in 1936.[97] The connection between released political prisoners and trade union activism was also

93. AOM, SLOTFOM, 3d ser., carton 54, *AAPCI*, August 1936, 3.
94. Ibid.
95. Tran Van Giau, *Giai Cap Cong Nhan Viet Nam Tu Dang Cong San Thanh Lap Den Cach Mang Thanh Cong, Tap II: 1936–1939* [The Vietnamese Working Class from the Founding of the Communist Party to the Victory of the Revolution, vol. 2: 1936–1939] (Hanoi, 1962), 34–35.
96. Thomas Hodgkin, *Vietnam: The Revolutionary Path* (New York, 1981), 280.
97. Personal communication from David Del Testa, November 11, 1998.

made in the pages of *La Lutte:* "When a country has produced a contingent of 10,000 political prisoners who have struggled illegally for trade union rights, and when the country continues to struggle in the face of ferocious repression, can one really say that it is lacking in trade union leaders?"[98]

On the other hand, there is strong evidence that former political prisoners contributed decisively to the effort to set up an Indochinese Congress, a movement one historian has characterized as "the most spectacular organized legal movement in the history of Colonial Vietnam."[99] First proposed by Nguyen An Ninh in the pages of *La Lutte* on July 29, 1936, the Congress movement was an attempt to form a popular representative body for Indochina, the ostensible purpose of which was to prepare a list of grievances to present to an upcoming fact-finding mission from the Ministry of Colonies. Under the leadership of Communists, Trotskyists, and the editors of *La Lutte,* the movement endeavored to build popular support for the Congress by setting up so-called action committees at the grassroots level. By March 1937, between 600 and 1,000 action committees had been established in villages, neighborhoods, schools, and factories throughout Cochin China. Not only did they select delegates for the Congress but they constituted a vast forum for public discussion about the political future of Indochina.[100] As roughly half of the action committees were established clandestinely, they also provided an opening through which ICP and Trotskyist activists could penetrate and expand their influence over the populace.[101] Indeed, it was the formation of action committees that enabled the ICP to quintuple its southern membership between August 1936 and August 1937.[102]

According to Sûreté estimates, former political prisoners made up a remarkable 25 percent of those who joined action committees.[103] In October 1936, a local official in Rach Gia Province explained that the rapid growth of action committees in his district was because of the presence there of so

98. Cited in Hodgkin, *Vietnam:The Revolutionary Path,* 281.

99. Ibid., 276.

100. Daniel Hémery, *Révolutionaires vietnamiens et pouvoir colonial en Indochine: Communistes, trotskystes, nationalistes à Saïgon de 1932 à 1937* (Paris, 1975), 44–63.

101. Ibid., 318–20. "By the end of 1936, over 10,000 people had participated in public meetings connected with the action committee movement in Cochinchina alone" (Huynh Kim Khanh, *Vietnamese Communism, 1925–1945* [Ithaca, N.Y., 1982], 213–14).

102. Huynh Kim Khanh, *Vietnamese Communism, 1925–1945,* 396.

103. AOM, SLOTFOM, 3d ser., carton 59, May 8, 1937, Propagande révolutionaire en Indochine.

many former political prisoners: "This district is situated in an out-of-the-way region far from the capital and lacking in roads; it is an area of recent rice-fields, where the population is extremely uncouth and is composed in large part of undesirable elements who have come from the central and eastern provinces of Cochin China: former prisoners, common criminals, escapees from penal prison."[104] At rallies organized to drum up support for the Congress and attract recruits into action committees, one eyewitness reported that crowds "roared with approval" and "applauded with great enthusiasm" when speakers were introduced as former political prisoners.[105] The Sûreté observed that earlier generations of former political prisoners who had long been politically inactive were now being recruited into action committees by recently released prisoners. For example, it noted a growing interest in the movement among activists who had been arrested during the antitax riots of 1908 and the Phan Xich Long uprisings in 1916.[106]

Inasmuch as the Ministry of Colonies eventually canceled its plans for a fact-finding mission and permitted the colonial state to ban the Congress, the movement's most enduring legacy was the establishment of hundreds of local institutions through which the ICP (and the Trotskyists to a lesser extent) could penetrate the masses.[107] Official fears that the proliferation of action committees served to "swell in the ranks" of the ICP were expressed in the following report:

> The Indochinese Communist Party (also known as the Stalinist Party or the party of the Third International) has derived, from its recent agitation, a numerical increase in membership well beyond the wildest hopes of its most optimistic leaders. The freed political prisoners and the members of the Committees of Action have come in enormous numbers to swell the ranks of the party.[108]

As alluded to earlier, it is likely that the formidable organization and recruiting skills exhibited by former political prisoners during the campaign

---

104. Cited in Hue-Tam Ho Tai, *Millenarianism and Peasant Politics in Vietnam* (Cambridge, Mass.: Harvard University Press, 1983), 106.

105. AOM, SLOTFOM, 3d ser., carton 52, *AAPCI*, December 1936, 38.

106. Huynh Kim Khanh, *Vietnamese Communism*, 218.

107. See Tran Cung, "Tu Con Dao Tro Ve: Hoi Ky" [Returning from Con Dao: A Memoir], *Tap Chi Nghien Cuu Lich Su* 134 (September–October 1970): 18–26, for a useful account of political activity among returnees and the author's role in peasant associations and action committees in Thai Binh between 1936 and 1939.

108. Huynh Kim Khanh, *Vietnamese Communism*, 218.

to establish action committees were products of their training and experiences behind bars. This was especially the case after the minister of colonies banned the Congress movement and ordered colonial security agents to infiltrate and disband amnesty committees in late September. In this new environment of illegality, ex-prisoners employed techniques of underground agitation that they had mastered during their years in jail. The ICP member Nguyen Tao boasted to this effect in an account of his political activities following his release from Hanoi Central Prison: "Our writings were issued in small pamphlets, the size of three fingers, as was done in the prisons, making it easy to hide and circulate them."[109] The formation of mobile theatrical troupes, which functioned as organs for anticolonial propaganda, also recalls a common method of mobilization refined in colonial jails. Such similarities were not lost on the Sûreté. In April 1936, one of its undercover agents reported that a communist cell meeting in Hue "has been organized secretly according to the methods currently in use among political detainees in prison."[110]

THE PRESTIGE OF IMPRISONMENT

Of course, the tendency of imprisonment to reinforce political commitments and the structural obstacles to reintegration into civilian life created by administrative surveillance do not fully explain the huge influx of former political prisoners into the anticolonial movement after 1936. Also important were a variety of psychological factors, which carried more or less weight depending on the individual involved. In 1937, the influential anticolonial scholar Phan Khoi offered a penetrating analysis of these factors in an essay entitled "Cai Tam Ly Cua Nguoi Tu Chinh Tri Duoc Tha" (The Psychology of Released Political Prisoners). Published in *Dong Duong Tap Chi*, Phan Khoi's essay suggested several reasons why incarceration failed to depoliticize political prisoners and indeed predisposed them to resume revolutionary activity.[111] First, political activists tended to be well educated and to have arrived at their political beliefs through a deliberate process of intellectual enquiry. Phan Khoi argued that physical penalties such as imprisonment were inappropriate instruments to counteract commitments that were intellectually rooted. While allowing that Indochina's cerebral

109. Nguyen Tao, "I Must Live to Fight," in *In The Enemy's Net: Memoirs from the Revolution* (Hanoi, 1962), 66.

110. AOM, SLOTFOM, 3d ser., carton 54, *AAPCI*, April 1936, 7.

111. Phan Khoi, "Cai Tam Ly Cua Nguoi Tu Chinh Tri Duoc Tha," *Dong Duong Tap Chi*, April 3, 1937, 13–15.

revolutionaries might be seduced by the prospect of "fame and wealth," Phan Khoi insisted that they could not be intimidated by "chains and manacles."

A second reason jail failed to divert activists from the political arena was the injustice of the judicial process that led to their imprisonment in the first place. To illustrate the point, Phan Khoi described his own arrest, conviction, and deportation to Poulo Condore in 1908 as a result of trumped-up sedition charges. An even worse fate befell his comrade Tran Qui Cap, who was summarily executed the same year after an equally unfair judicial proceeding. According to Phan Khoi, the injustice and corruption of the colonial juridical system provoked anger, hatred, and a certain nihilistic recklessness in political prisoners rather then feelings of repentance or regret. It was owing to the power of such feelings, he explained, that inmates who were granted amnesties rarely expressed gratitude or contrition.

Moreover, the feelings of bitterness and alienation harbored by political prisoners overwhelmed their fear of returning to jail after their release. He observed that ex-prisoners who had been unfairly jailed tended to respond even more viscerally to episodes of injustice that they observed in the civilian world. The burdens and humiliation of administrative surveillance were frequently the trigger for a return to politics. To underline the failure of incarceration to deter activists from political activity in the future, he pointed out that most of the prisoners released from Poulo Condore with him in 1911 were rearrested for planning the Duy Tan uprising five years later. In more recent times, there were even cases in which incarceration had proved completely counterproductive, instead transforming moderate nationalist agitators into hardened communist activists.

Finally, and most significantly, Phan Khoi noted that since the turn of the century, political prisoners had emerged as among "the most respected category of men" in Indochinese society, "even more so than officials and scholars in the past." As evidence, he recalled an anecdote about a group of admiring vandals who erased "Doctorate Holder" (*tien si*) from the tombstone of the famous scholar and political prisoner Ngo Duc Ke and scrawled "Man of Ideals" (*chi si*) in its place. He also noted that the celebrated "rock breaker of Poulo Condore," Phan Chu Trinh, was so highly esteemed that even powerful French officials such as Marius Moutet expressed veneration and affection for him. According to Phan Khoi, there existed a positive relationship between the level of hardship that an activist endured in prison and the degree of public respect that he or she enjoyed.

Based overwhelmingly on his own experiences and firsthand observations, most of Phan Khoi's claims about the psychology of former political prisoners do not lend themselves to external verification. There is, however, significant impressionistic evidence to support his contention that they enjoyed widespread public sympathy and admiration. Numerous prison memoirs describe episodes in which ordinary people show extraordinary kindness and respect to recently released political prisoners. Strangers on a train offer Nhuong Tong money and fruit after he informs them of his recent prison experience.[112] In *Thi Tu Tung Thoai*, Huynh Thuc Khang recalls receiving a free suit from a tailor who surmised that he had recently returned from Poulo Condore. "Phan Chu Trinh used to come to my store after he left Poulo Condore," the tailor told him. "I do not know you, but since you are his friend, I offer you this small gift as a keepsake."[113]

Although Huynh Thuc Khang conveys a sense of gratitude for the deference paid to him by total strangers following his release, he does not express surprise. This subtle sense of entitlement helps explain the proliferation of urban panhandlers during the late 1930s who posed as destitute former political prisoners. This phenomenon was recorded in a curious story published in the *quoc ngu* weekly *Dong Phap* on February 2, 1937. According to the story, on the morning of February 19, 1937, a shabbily dressed beggar named Tran Van Thao entered a small shop across from Hanoi's Dong Xuan market. Addressing the assembled customers and salesclerks, Thao identified himself as a recently amnestied political prisoner and proceeded to recount his tragic life story. He described his unjust arrest and grueling imprisonment on Poulo Condore. He related how he had returned to his native village in 1936 only to find that his family had fled at the start of the Depression. Being without work or blood relations, he claimed, the charity of strangers represented his only means of subsistence. At the end of his story, Thao extended a tattered cap. After listening to Thao's appeal, the uncle of the shopkeeper, Nguyen Cong Nghi, stepped forward and denounced him as an imposter. As everyone present except Thao was aware, Nghi had recently completed his own seven-year sentence for political crimes on Poulo Condore. Not only did Nghi expose factual inaccuracies in Thao's story but he questioned why the two had never met during the lengthy overlapping period that they were allegedly confined together. Based on Nghi's charges, Thao was hauled down to the police station, where he confessed to being a day laborer from Haiphong. He

---

112. Nhuong Tong, *Doi Trong Nguc* [Life in Prison] (Hanoi, 1935), 14.
113. Huynh Thuc Khang, *Thi Tu Tung Thoai* [Prison Verse] (1939; reprint, Saigon, 1951), 252.

admitted that since losing his job the previous year, he had moved to Hanoi, where he earned a living pretending to be a former political prisoner and soliciting public donations.[114]

In a concluding comment, *Dong Phap* pointed out that Tran Van Thao's failed ruse was far from an isolated occurrence: "Since political prisoners have been amnestied from Poulo Condore in 1936, a category of men has appeared who take advantage of their plight in order to falsely gain sympathy for themselves. Because this damages the reputations of former political prisoners, many of them have grown determined to expose and eliminate these swindlers."[115]

While the story calls attention to the severe financial difficulties experienced by former political prisoners in Indochina, it also points to the high regard in which they were held. It is instructive that Tran Van Thao believed that his earning potential would be enhanced by impersonating a political prisoner. That he successfully carried out this subterfuge for over a year and was, as the article mentions, part of a broader "category" (*mot hang*) of impersonators testifies to the validity of the belief.

It would be an overstatement, of course, to claim that political activists went so far as to seek incarceration to boost their power and prestige. However, knowledge that imprisonment had its benefits may have figured in calculations about the risks accompanying a career in the anticolonial movement. When Ton Quang Phiet was hauled off to jail for political subversion in 1926, his friend Lam Cuong consoled him with the assurance that his fame would soon rival that of the anticolonial scholars who were imprisoned on Poulo Condore following antitax riots in 1908, such as Ngo Duc Ke and Le Huan.[116] It would not be surprising if such considerations played a role in the thinking of those former political prisoners who placed their newly acquired freedom at risk by agitating against the authority of the colonial state during the closing years of the 1930s.

114. *Dong Phap*, February 20, 1937.
115. Ibid.
116. Ton Quang Phiet, *Mot Ngay Ngan Thu (Lan Thu Nhat O Nha Nguc)* [The Eternal Day (My First Time in Prison)] (Hue, 1935), 11.

Epilogue

During World War II, the colonial prison resumed its role as a focal point of anticolonial activism. At the start of the war, an aborted communist rising in Cochin China precipitated a police crackdown on political activists even more extensive than the one that devastated the anticolonial movement during the early 1930s.[1] As a result, the colonial prison population soared to its highest levels ever. Whereas the system held an average of 21,000 prisoners between 1936 and 1939, the number jumped to over 26,000 in 1940 and peaked at just under 30,000 in 1942.[2] This figure surpassed the previous high of 28,000 in 1932. Moreover, the war years witnessed the incarceration of roughly 3,000 Communist Party members, a figure five times what it had been following the repression of the Nghe-Tinh soviets.[3]

Because the colonial authorities collaborated with the Japanese forces that occupied Indochina during the war, the prison system continued to be run by French officials and their underlings.[4] This arrangement was only

1. David Marr, *Vietnam 1945: The Quest for Power* (Berkeley and Los Angeles, 1995), 155–64.
2. Gouvernement général de l'Indochine, *Annuaire statistique de l'Indochine* (Hanoi), 1940–44.
3. Marr, *Vietnam 1945*, 193.
4. There is a substantial English-language literature on the Japanese occupation of Indochina. In addition to his magisterial *Vietnam 1945*, see David Marr, "Vietnam 1945: Some Questions," *Vietnam Forum*, no. 6 (Summer–Fall 1985): 155–93; id., "World War II and the Vietnamese Revolution," in *Southeast Asia under Japanese Occupation*, ed. Alfred McCoy (New Haven, Conn., 1980), 125–58; Stein Tønnesson, *The Vietnamese Revolution of 1945: Roosevelt, Ho Chi Minh, and De Gaulle in a World at War* (Newbury Park, Calif., 1991); Truong Buu Lam, "Japan and the Disruption of the Vietnamese Nationalist Movement,"

terminated in March 1945 when the Japanese launched a preemptive coup against the French administration and replaced it with an "independent" Vietnamese government led by the pro-Japanese politician Tran Trong Kim. Under the supervision of the Japanese, Kim's government assumed control over the prison system, which it managed until the end of the war.[5]

As during the early 1930s, the incarceration of thousands of political activists at the start of the war led to overcrowding and an abrupt deterioration in prison conditions. On Poulo Condore, the annual mortality rate increased from 48 in 1940 to 203 in 1941 and to 1,050 in 1942.[6] Prison officials rolled back many of the reforms that had been implemented during the second half of the 1930s. Between 1940 and 1942, colonial wardens cut rations, revoked reading privileges, restricted visitation rights, censored mail, and forced political prisoners to take part in forced labor. In response, political prisoners resumed the organizational and political work that had proved so effective during the first half of the 1930s.[7] With communist inmates taking the lead, they formed clandestine cells, established mutual aid associations, printed secret newspapers, spearheaded hunger strikes and work stoppages, recruited new followers, and organized elaborate programs of education and training. As in the past, they wrested a measure of control over the institutions in which they were held from their captors and succeeded in coordinating their activities with comrades in the wider commu-

in *Aspects of Vietnamese History,* ed. Walter Vella (Honolulu, 1973); Kyoto Kurusu Nitz, "Independence Without Nationalists? The Japanese and Vietnamese Nationalism During the Japanese Period, 1940–45," *Journal of Southeast Asian Studies* 14, no. 2 (September 1983): 108–33; Kyoto Kurusu Nitz, "Japanese Military Power Towards French Indochina During the Second World War: The Road to the Meigo Sakusen (9 March 1945)," *Journal of Southeast Asian Studies* 14, no. 2 (September 1983): 328–53.

5. For a treatment of the Tran Trong Kim regime, see Vu Ngu Chieu, "The Other Side of the 1945 Vietnamese Revolution: The Empire of Viet-Nam (March–August 1945)," *Journal of Asian Studies* 45, no. 2 (February 1986): 293–328.

6. Gouvernement général, *Annuaire statistique de L'Indochine,* 1940–42.

7. See Ban Nghien Cuu Lich Su Dang Dac Khu Vung Tau—Con Dao, *Nha Tu Con Dao, 1862–1945* [Con Dao Penitentiary, 1862–1945] (Hanoi, 1987), 139–84; So Van Hoa Thong Tin Ha Noi and Vien Lich Su Dang, *Dau Tranh Cua Cac Chien Si Yeu Nuoc Va Cach Mang Tai Nha Tu Hoa Lo, 1899–1954* [The Struggle of Patriotic and Revolutionary Fighters in Hoa Lo Prison, 1899–1954] (Hanoi, 1994), 52–196; Tinh Uy Dak Lak and Vien Lich Su Dang, *Lich Su Nha Day Buon Ma Thuot, 1930–1945* [History of Buon Ma Thuot Penitentiary, 1930–1945] (Hanoi, 1991), 86–125; and Vien Mac-Lenin and Vien Lich Su Dang, *Nguc Son La Truong Hoc Dau Tranh Cach Mang* [Son La Prison, the School of Revolutionary Struggle] (Hanoi, 1992), 32–119.

nity. The fact that many communists had been jailed at least once before during the early 1930s no doubt enhanced their capacity to operate effectively in prison during the first half of the 1940s.

Although neither the Japanese nor the Tran Trong Kim government issued a formal amnesty for political prisoners along the lines of the general amnesty of 1936, many inmates escaped or were released as a result of administrative instability during the war years. A large number were let go by local officials immediately after the Japanese coup, and hundreds more escaped in the chaotic months that followed.[8] During the heady days of August, Viet Minh partisans broke into dozens of provincial jails and freed thousands of political prisoners.[9] As during the Popular Front era, former political prisoners injected vitality into anti-French and anti-Japanese resistance efforts and played a major role in the August Revolution of 1945.

THE POSTCOLONIAL POLITICS OF COLONIAL IMPRISONMENT

The significance of the colonial prison in the political history of modern Vietnam transcends its role in the development of communism, nationalism, and anticolonialism during the 1930s and 1940s. During the postcolonial era, prison credentials became essential for promotion into the ICP's highest echelons.[10] According to Bui Tin, the political power of high-ranking Central Committee members such as Pham Hung, Le Duc Tho, Nguyen Chi Thanh, and To Huu was a function of their prison backgrounds. Following the dismissal of Truong Chinh during a campaign to rectify land-reform errors in the late 1950s, Le Duan's extensive prison record was instrumental in his elevation over Vo Nguyen Giap to the post of secretary-general of the ICP. As Bui Tin explains:

> Still the question remained who would replace Truong Chinh as Party General Secretary. Several cadres close to Ho Chi Minh at the time said that he had two people in mind. They were Vo Nguyen Giap and Le Duan, but Ho was inclined to favor the former with whom he had worked closely for many years. However, Le Duan was appointed because of the criteria then prevailing. He had spent two long periods in prison amounting to almost ten years in all. This was a significant

8. Marr, *Vietnam 1945*, 141–43, 148, 158, 195, 221–22.
9. Ibid., 414, 427, 431, 461, 470.
10. "The number of years in Poulo Condore and other French prisons was one of the most important elements in the curricula vitae of VCP leaders; it was an important qualification for advancement in the party hierarchy," Huynh Kim Khanh writes in *Vietnamese Communism, 1925–1945* (Ithaca, N.Y., 1992), 235.

qualification for rising to the top of the party, since it was considered that the more one had been put to the test, the more trustworthy one was. In fact, imprisonment was regarded as the university of politics and here General Giap did not qualify because his degree in law resulted from a conventional education.[11]

Bui Tin's analysis is supported by the fact that up until the early 1990s, prolonged imprisonment during the colonial era was an experience shared by virtually every Party secretary-general. The first four, Tran Phu, Le Hong Phong, Ha Huy Tap, and Nguyen Van Cu, each died in penal confinement prior to the end of World War II.[12] Truong Chinh, who served as the fifth and eighth secretary-general, spent seven years (1930–36) in Tonkin's Son La Penitentiary. Le Duan, the seventh secretary-general, endured two prison terms (1931–36 and 1940–45) on Poulo Condore. The next man to hold the post, the acclaimed reformer Nguyen Van Linh, was likewise imprisoned twice on Poulo Condore (1930–35 and 1940–45), for an approximate total of ten years. The ninth secretary-general, Do Muoi, spent five years in Hanoi Central Prison before escaping in 1945.[13]

The lone secretary-general never incarcerated by the French was, oddly enough, Ho Chi Minh himself, a fact obscured by his highly touted bouts of imprisonment in Hong Kong and southern China.[14] During the 1920s and 1930s, when his future colleagues in the Politburo were earning revolutionary credentials in French jails, Ho was abroad carrying out Comintern directives. The fact that Ho did not possess the same colonial prison record as virtually all of his colleagues was neatly effaced by the public appearance of his *Nhat Ky Trong Tu,* or *Prison Diary,* which he is said to have penned while incarcerated in 1942 by a warlord in southern China. Released almost twenty years after it was written and at the outset of a campaign to spread the prison memoirs of ICP leaders, the *Prison Diary,* which is easily Vietnam's most widely published and translated literary work, as

11. Bui Tin, *Following Ho Chi Minh: Memoirs of a North Vietnamese Colonel* (Honolulu, 1995), 32.

12. David Elliot, "Revolutionary Re-Integration: A Comparison of the Foundation of Post-Liberation Political Systems in North Vietnam and China" (Ph.D. diss., Cornell University, 1976), 69.

13. For brief biographical summaries, see Nguyen Q. Thang and Nguyen Ba The, *Tu Dien Nhan Vat Lich Su Vietnam* [Dictionary of Vietnamese Historical Figures] (Hanoi, 1991).

14. For accounts of Ho's imprisonments, see Jean Lacouture, *Ho Chi Minh: A Political Biography* (New York, 1968), 61–65, 71–85, and King Chen, *Vietnam and China, 1938–1954* (Princeton, N.J., 1969), 55–60.

well as a core secondary-school text, suggests an explicit attempt to bring Ho's revolutionary credentials into line with those of his comrades.

In addition, discursive representations of colonial-era imprisonment have played an important role in the efforts of the ICP to construct and convey an heroic public image of itself.[15] Official narratives of communist prison resistance highlight the endurance, courage, and resourcefulness of Party leaders and, in the absence of democratic elections or fundamental economic reforms, underline the validity of their claims to power. Depictions of the physical and emotional ordeals endured by jailed communists help justify the seemingly interminable sacrifices that the Party has demanded of the Vietnamese population throughout the postcolonial era.

The value of prison narratives to the Party has been enhanced by their alleged capacity to motivate and inspire during wartime. For example, in the early 1970s, at the height of America's Vietnam War, the Institute of Party History and the Youth Publishing House in Hanoi annotated a large body of colonial-era prison verse for a two-volume collection entitled *Tieng Hat Trong Tu* (Songs Sung in Prison). The editors of the anthology justified their efforts on didactic grounds: "The poetry of revolutionary fighters created in the prisons of the French imperialists, from the foundation of our Party to 1945, holds excellent educational value for the younger generations who grew up after the August Revolution."[16] During Vietnam's war with China in the late 1970s and early 1980s, the Culture and Information Committee of Son La Province published a collection of prison writings entitled *Tho Ca Cach Mang Nha Tu Son La, 1930–1945* (Revolutionary Poetry from Son La Prison, 1930–1945). In the introduction, the editor, Nguyen Anh Tuan, linked the timing of the anthology's publication to the national mobilization effort then under way to resist "Beijing's hegemonic expansionism." "Today, we reread prison stories from a period of 'blood and chains,' Tuan wrote, "and we find the precious souls of imprisoned communist fighters in the pages. Each of us must use this opportunity to reexamine ourselves, to cleanse and purify our souls in order to fortify our courage and expand our love for the entire nation."[17] The Party's successful manipulation of images of

15. Peter Zinoman, "Beyond the Revolutionary Prison Memoir," *Vietnam Review* 1 (Autumn–Winter 1996): 256–72.

16. Vo Van Truc, ed., *Tieng Hat Trong Tu, Tap I* [Songs Sung in Prisons, vol. 1] (Hanoi, 1972), 193.

17. Ty Van Hoa Thong Tin Son La, *Tho Ca Cach Mang Nha Tu Son La, 1930–1945* (Son La, 1980), 7.

the colonial prison during the postcolonial era represents another irony in the history of that institution. Not only did the colonial prison inadvertently facilitate the growth of forces exquisitely antithetical to the purposes for which it was created, but its image has continued to buttress the power and authority of the Vietnamese communist movement decades after the elimination of French power from the region.

A final historical legacy left by the colonial prison may be the way in which it has served as a kind of implicit negative example for communist institutional development in postcolonial Vietnam. If the colonial state deployed disciplinary technologies only haltingly and sporadically, its postcolonial successor has utilized them with great enthusiasm. Memoirs of those who have served time in Vietnamese reeducation camps after 1975 confirm the centrality of techniques of behavioral modification, physical segregation, reformative labor, and moral education within communist penology. As Huynh Sanh Thong explains: "The term 'reeducation' with its pedagogical overtones, does not quite convey the quasi-mystical resonance of *cai-tao* in Vietnamese. *Cai* [to transform] and *tao* [to create] combine to literally mean an attempt at 'recreation,' at 'making over' sinful or incomplete individuals."[18] Moreover, as Charles Armstrong has pointed out, communist institutional innovations such as rituals of public criticism and self-criticism embody modern disciplinary technologies more perfectly "than anything Foucault writes about in Western history."[19] Perhaps it is no surprise that the scope and intensity of the disciplinary power deployed by the colonial state pales beside that of the movement that eventually dislodged and replaced it.

18. Huynh Sanh Thong, ed. and trans., *To Be Made Over: Tales of Socialist Reeducation in Vietnam* (New Haven, Conn., and Boston, Mass., 1988).
19. Charles Armstrong, "Surveillance and Punishment in Postliberation North Korea," *Positions: East Asia Cultures Critique* 3, no. 3 (Winter 1995): 174.

Glossary

Ân
ân xá
anh
anh chị
Ánh Sáng
Ba Chỉ
Ba Con
Ba Lâm
Ba Nhỏ
Ba Quốc
Bà Rịa
Bắc Giang
Bắc Kạn
Bắc Kỳ
Bạc Liêu
Bắc Ninh
Bắc Sơn
bài ngà
ban
Ban Ma Thuột
Bánh chưng
Bảo Đại
Bến Tre
Bếp
Bếp Ngọc
Biên Hòa
Bình Sơn
Binh Thiều
bộ

bồi
bọn quan to
Bùi Công Trừng
Bùi Đình Nam
Bùi Quang Chiêu
Bùi San
Bùi Tín
Buôn Ma Thuột
Buôn Mê Thuột
cai
cải lương
Cần Thơ
Cần Vương
canh xe máy
Cao Bá Quát
Cao Bằng
cầu tiên
Châu Địch
Châu Đốc
chế độ bó buộc cay nghiệt
chi bộ
chí sĩ
chỉ tin
chính sách khai phóng
Chợ Chu
Chợ Diễn
Chợ Lớn
Chợ phiên
chú

chữ nôm
Chương Thâu
con công
Côn Đảo
Côn Lôn
Côn Nôn
Côn Sơn
công tử
cuộc chơi
Cường Để
Dân Mới
Diệp Văn Vang
Dương Bạch Mai
Dương Văn Giá
Dương Văn Ngọc
Duy Tân
Duy Tân Hội
Đà Nẵng
Đại Việt Sử Ký Toàn Thư
Đặng Châu Tuệ
Đảng Cộng Sản Đông Dương
Đặng Đình Thọ
Dăng Hỏa Tiền
Đặng Ngọc Kiêm
Đặng Nguyên Can
Đặng Thai Mai
Đặng Văn Ngân
Đặng Việt Châu
Đào Duy Anh
Đào Gia Lưu
Đào Trinh Nhất
Đào Xuân Mai
đấu tranh bất khuất
Đề Thám
Điện Biên Phủ
đinh bài
Đinh Tiên Hoàng
đỗ
Đồ Ba
Đỗ Mười
đội
Đội Lăng
Đời Mới
Đông Dương Tạp Chí
Đông Kinh

Đông Kinh Nghĩa Thục
Đông Pháp
Đông Triều
Đồng Xuân
Ê-Đê
em nuôi
em út
gia đình
Gia Định
Gia Lâm
Gia Long
Gianh Đức Cường
Giao Chỉ
gông cùm
Hà Đông
Hà Giang
Hà Huy Giáp
Hà Huy Tập
Hà Nam
Hà Nội
Hà Phú Hương
Hà Thế Hạnh
Hà Tiên
Hà Tĩnh
Hải Dương
Hải Khanh
Hai Lãm
Hải Phòng
Hải Triều
Hàm Nghi
Hàn Song Thanh
Hành
Hạnh Sơn
hát tuồng
Hình Bộ
Hồ Chí Minh
Hồ Hữu Tường
Hồ Văn Mịch
Hòa Bình
Hỏa Lò
Hoài Anh
Hoàng
Hoàng Đạo
Hoàng Hoa Thám
Hoàng Minh Đẩu

Hoàng Quốc Việt
Hoàng Văn Đào
Hoàng Xuân Đường
Hoàng Xuân Hành
Hội An
hồi ký
hồi ký cách mạng
Hồi Xuân
Hồng Bàng
Hồng Chương
Hồng Đức
Huế
Huệ-Tâm Hồ-Tài
Hưng Hóa
Hưng Yên
Hữu Ngọc
huyện
Huỳnh Kim Khánh
Huỳnh Sanh Thông
Huỳnh Thúc Kháng
Huỳnh Văn Phương
Huỳnh Văn Tiếng
Huỳnh Văn Tống
Kẻ Bảo
Khám Đường
Khám Lớn
khảo của
Khởi Nghĩa Nam Kỳ
Khuất Duy Tiên
kịch liệt
Kiến An
Kinh Dương Vương
Kỳ Nam
Lã Xuân Oai
Lai Châu
Lai Kỳ
Lam Cuồng
Lâm Hồng Phấn
Lang Hít
Lãnh Đạt
lao
Lào
Lao Bảo
Lào Cai
Lào Kay

Lao tù hội
Lao ủy
Lạp
lấy chiếu
Lê
Lê Anh Trà
Lê Bội
Lê Đại Hành
Lê Duẩn
Lê Đức Thọ
Lê Hồng Phong
Lê Huân
Lê Hữu Mục
Lê Hữu Phước
Lê Khanh
Lê Kim Quế
Lê Kính
Lê Ngọc Thiệu
Lê Quang Sung
Lê Thanh Nghị
Lê Tông Úy
Lê Trung Khánh
Lê Văn Hiến
Lê Văn Lương
Lê Xuân Phương
lính
Long Xuyên
Lục Nam
Lương Lập Nham
Lương Ngọc Quyến
Lương Tam Kỳ
Lương Văn Can
lưu
Lý
Lý Thánh Tông
Lý Thị Chung
Lý Tử Trọng
mã tà
Mai
Mai Lão Bạng
Mai Chí Thọ
Mán
mật cật
Mặt Trận Dân Chủ Đông Dương
mày

Mê Kông
Mèo
miếng phụng hoàng
mợ
Mộ Đức
mọi
Móng Cáy
một hạng
Mường
Mỹ Tho
Nam Binh Phục Quốc
Nam Định
Nam Kỳ
Nam Sách
Nam Việt
Ngày Mới
Nghệ An
Nghệ Tĩnh
Nghĩa Lộ
Nghiêm Xuân Toản
Ngô Đức Kế
Ngô Đức Trị
Ngô Gia Tự
Ngô Sĩ Liên
Ngô Tất Tố
Ngô Thị Thanh
Ngô Văn
Ngô Vĩnh Long
ngục
ngục thất
người tù
Nguyễn
Nguyễn Ái Quốc
Nguyễn An Nguyên
Nguyễn An Ninh
Nguyễn An Tịnh
Nguyễn Anh Tuấn
Nguyễn Bá Thế
Nguyễn Chí Điểu
Nguyễn Chí Thanh
Nguyễn Công Bình
Nguyễn Công Hoan
Nguyễn Công Nghị
Nguyễn Dân
Nguyễn Du

Nguyễn Đăng Mạnh
Nguyễn Đình Kiên
Nguyễn Đình Tứ
Nguyễn Đức Chính
Nguyễn Đức Kính
Nguyễn Duy Trinh
Nguyễn Gia Cầu
Nguyễn Hải Hàm
Nguyễn Hiến Lê
Nguyễn Hới
Nguyên Hồng
Nguyễn Huệ Chi
Nguyễn Huy Bổn
Nguyễn Khắc Viện
Nguyễn Khanh Toản
Nguyễn Khoa Văn
Nguyễn Kim Cương
Nguyễn Lương Bằng
Nguyễn Mỹ Lợi
Nguyễn Ngọc Huy
Nguyễn Ngọc Sơn
Nguyễn Phạm Tứ
Nguyễn Phan Quang
Nguyễn Phương Thảo
Nguyễn Q. Thắng
Nguyễn Quang Bích
Nguyễn Sĩ Sách
Nguyễn Tạo
Nguyễn Thái Học
Nguyễn Thành
Nguyễn Thế Anh
Nguyễn Thế Long
Nguyễn Thế Nghiệp
Nguyễn Thiện Kế
Nguyễn Thị Minh Khai
Nguyễn Trãi
Nguyễn Trí Dziểu
Nguyễn Văn Ba
Nguyễn Văn Bổng
Nguyễn Văn Chỉ
Nguyễn Văn Cừ
Nguyễn Văn Hòa
Nguyễn Văn Ký
Nguyễn Văn La
Nguyễn Văn Lâm

Nguyễn Văn Linh
Nguyễn Văn Nghành
Nguyễn Văn Nguyễn
Nguyễn Văn Nhiêu
Nguyễn Văn Phát
Nguyễn Văn Sở
Nguyễn Văn Tâm
Nguyễn Văn Tạo
Nguyễn Văn Thắng
Nguyễn Văn Truyền
Nguyễn Văn Tứ
Nguyễn Văn Tường
Nha Trang
Nhân Dân
Nhất Linh
Nho Quan
Như Long
Nhượng Tống
Ninh Bình
Ninh Hòa
núi cao rừng rậm
Nùng
ông
Ông Lớn
Ông Yêm
Phạm Đình Ry
Phạm Đức Ngôn
Phạm Hồng Toàn
Phạm Hùng
Phạm Huy Du
Phạm Như Thơm
Phạm Quang Tham
Phạm Thản
Phạm Thận Duật
Phạm Tuấn Tài
Phạm Văn Báo
Phạm Văn Đồng
Phạm Văn Hào
Phạm Văn Thu
Phạm Văn Trường
Phan Bội Châu
Phan Châu Trinh
Phan Đăng Lưu
Phan Đình Phùng
Phan Khôi

Phấn Mễ
Phan Nghi Đệ
Phan Văn Các
Phan Văn Huệ
Phan Văn Hùm
Phan Xích Long
Phổ Yên
Phong Huyền
phóng sự
Phong trào Cần Vương
Phong trào Văn Thân
phủ
Phú Khánh
Phủ Lạng Thương
Phủ Lý
Phú Quốc
Phú Thọ
Phục Long
Phúc Yên
Phương Hữu
Phương Lan
quan
quan án
quan Hai Tàu
Quảng Nam
Quảng Ngãi
Quang Phục Quân
Quảng Trị
Quang Trung
Quảng Yên
Qui Nhân
Qui Nhơn
Quốc Anh
Quốc Hoa
Quốc Học
quốc ngữ
Rạch Giá
Sa Đéc
Sài Gòn
San Hô
Sóc Trăng
Sơn La
Sơn Tây
sống lâu lên lão làng
sử học

Tạ Thu Thâu
Tạ Uyên
Tạ Văn Tài
Tam Đảo
Tam Lang
Tân Việt
táng gia bại sản
Tày
Tây Ninh
tay trơn
tên
Tết
Thái
Thái Bình
Thái Nguyên
Thái Nguyên Quang Phục Quân
Thái Sơn
thằng
Thanh Hóa
Thanh Niên
Thành Thái
thảo luận
thầy
thẻ bài
thi đàn
Thổ
thơ ký
thơ ngâm vịnh
Thọ Xương
Thuận Hóa
Thuận Thành
Thủ Dầu Một
tiến sĩ
Tiếng Dân
tiếng tây
tỉnh
tình địch
tờ báo miệng
Tô Chân
Tố Hữu
tổ trưởng
Tôn Đức Thắng
Tôn Quang Phiệt
Tôn Thất Định
Tôn Thất Thuyết

Tống Phục Chiêu
tổng ủy
Tống Văn Trân
Trà Vinh
trại lá
Trần
Trần Cung
Trần Đăng Ninh
Trần Đình Thanh
Trần Đức Sắc
Trần Hoành
Trần Huy Liệu
Trần Ngọc Danh
Trần Phú
Trần Quân Cửu Các
Trần Qúi Cáp
Trần Thanh Phương
Trần Thị Liên
Trần Thiên Tính
Trần Trọng Cung
Trần Trọng Kim
Trần Văn Ba
Trần Văn Cung
Trần Văn Diệp
Trần Văn Giàu
Trần Văn Nguôn
Trần Văn Nhị
Trần Văn Phương
Trần Văn Quê
Trần Văn Thảo
trợ y tá
Trí Cụ
Trịnh Đức Phạm
Trịnh Hưng Ngẫu
Trịnh Văn Cấn
Trực
Trưng
Trung Kỳ
Trưng Nhị
Trưng Trắc
trượng
Trương Bửu Lâm
Trường Chinh
Trương Định
Trương Ngọc Phú

Trương Văn Thủy
Truyện Kiều
tù
tù chính trị
Tú Hồi Xuân
Từ Nghĩa
tù nhân
Tù nhân Hội
Tưởng Dân Bảo
Tương Lai
Tưởng Quan
tùy phái
Tuyên Quang
Ung Văn Khiêm
vấn đáp
Văn Tân
Văn Tạo
Văn Tiến Dũng
Việt Minh
Việt Nam
Việt Nam Quang Phục Hội
Việt Nam Quốc Dân Đảng
Việt Nam Thanh Niên Kách
    Mệnh Hội
Vinh
Vĩnh Long

Vĩnh Yên
Võ Cung
vô danh
Võ Mai
Võ Nguyên Giáp
vô sản hóa
vô tổ quốc
vô tôn giáo
Võ Văn Trực
Vũ Chí
Vũ Đức Bằng
Vũ Đình Long
Vũ Ngự Chiêu
Vũ Sĩ Lập
Vũ Thúy
Vũ Trọng Phụng
Vũ Văn Tình
Vũng Tàu
Vương Trí Nhàn
Xạ Thư
Xuân Thủy
xưởng
Yên Báy
Yên Lĩnh
Yên Thế

Select Bibliography

ARCHIVES

Archival material used in this study is drawn from two archives: the Centre des Archives d'Outre-Mer, Aix-en-Provence (AOM) and the Trung Tam Luu Tru Quoc Gia–1 [National Archives Center, No. 1], Hanoi (TTLT). The following four *fonds* from the Centre des Archives d'Outre-Mer were consulted: (1) Fonds des Amiraux et du Gouvernement général; (2) Sous-série 7F, Sûreté général; (3) Fonds de la Direction des Affaires politiques du Gouvernement général; and (4) Fonds du Service de liaison avec les originaires des territoires français d'Outre-Mer (SLOTFOM). The following three *fonds* in the Trung Tam Luu Tru Quoc Gia–1 were consulted: (1) Fonds du Gouvernement général; (2) Fonds de la Résidence supérieure du Tonkin; and (3) Fonds de la municipalité de Hanoi.

SERIAL RUNS CONSULTED

Anh Sang
Cua Viet
Dan Moi
Doi Moi
Dong Duong Tap Chi
Dong Phap
La Lutte
La Tribune Indochinoise
L'Echo Annamite
Le Travail
Mai
Ngay Moi

Nhan Dan
Notre Voix
Tap Chi Lich Su Dang
Tap Chi Nghien Cuu Lich Su
Tieng Dan
Tuong Lai
Van Su Dia

ARTICLES AND BOOKS

Aldrich, Robert. *The French Presence in the South Pacific, 1842–1940.* Honolulu: University of Hawaii Press, 1990.
Anderson, Benedict. *Imagined Communities: Reflections on the Origins and Spread of Nationalism.* London: New Left Press, 1991.
Annuaire de la Cochinchine française. 1865–88. Saigon.
Annuaire de l'Indo-Chine française. Part 1: *Cochinchine et Cambodge.* 1889–97. Saigon.
Anonymous. "The Catfish and the Toad." Translated by Huynh Sanh Thong. In *The Heritage of Vietnamese Poetry: An Anthology,* ed. Huynh Sanh Thong. New Haven, Conn.: Yale University Press, 1979.
Armstrong, Charles. "Surveillance and Punishment in Postliberation North Korea." *Positions: East Asia Cultures Critique* 3, no. 3 (Winter 1995): 174.
Arnold, David. "Touching the Body: Perspectives on the Indian Plague, 1896–1900." In *Selected Subaltern Studies,* ed. Ranajit Guha and Gayatri Chakravorty Spivak. New York: Oxford University Press, 1988.
Badinter, Robert. *La Prison républicaine, 1871–1914.* Paris: Fayard, 1992.
Ballof, Daniel. "La Déportation des Indochinois en Guyane et les établissements pénitentiaires spéciaux, 1931–1945." *Revue guyanaise d' histoire et de géographie* 10 (April–May–June 1979): 1–25.
Ban Lien Lac Tu Chinh Tri So Van Hoa Thong Tin. *Con Dao Ky Su va Tu Lieu* [Con Dao: Reports and Documents]. Ho Chi Minh City: Tre, 1996.
Ban Nghien Cuu Lich Su Dang Dac Khu Vung Tau—Con Dao. *Nha Tu Con Dao, 1862–1945* [Con Dao Penitentiary, 1862–1945]. Hanoi: Su That, 1987.
Ban Nghien Cuu Lich Su Dang Son La. *Nha Tu Son La, 1908–1945* [Son La Prison: 1908–1945]. Son La: Son La, 1982.
Ban Nghien Cuu Lich Su Dang Trung Uong. *Nhung Su Kien Lich Su Dang, Tap I (1920–1945)* [Events in Party History, vol. 1: 1920–1945]. Hanoi: Su That, 1976.
Bender, John. *Imagining the Penitentiary: Fiction and Architecture of the Mind in Eighteenth-Century England.* Chicago: University of Chicago Press, 1987.
Bernal, Martin. "The Nghe Tinh Soviet Movement." *Past and Present* 92 (August 1981): 148–68.
Bonhomme, Albert. "Annam." In *La Justice en Indochine,* ed. H. Morché. Hanoi: Imprimerie d'Extrême-Orient, 1931.

Brenier, Henri. *Essai d'atlas statistique de l'Indochine française: Indochine physique—population—administration—finances—agriculture—commerce—industrie.* Hanoi: Imprimerie d'Extrême-Orient, 1914.

Brocheux, Pierre, and Daniel Hémery. *Indochine: La Colonisation ambiguë, 1858–1954.* Paris: Découverte, 1995.

Brown, Edward. *Cochin-China, and my experience of it; a seaman's narrative of his adventures and sufferings during a captivity among Chinese pirates on the coast of Cochin-China, and afterwards during a journey on foot across that country, in the years 1857–8, by Edward Brown.* 1861. Reprint, Taipei: Ch'eng Wen, 1971.

Bruinink-Darlang, and Anne Marie Christien. *Het penitentiair stelsel in Nederlands-Indie van 1905 tot 1940.* Alblasserdam: Kanters, 1986.

Bui Cong Trung. *O Con Dao* [In Con Dao]. In Chanh Thi et al., *Len Duong Thang Loi* [On The Road to Victory]. Hanoi: Van Hoc, 1960.

Bui Tin. *Following Ho Chi Minh: Memoirs of a North Vietnamese Colonel.* Honolulu: University of Hawaii Press, 1995.

Buttinger, Joseph. *Vietnam: A Dragon Embattled*, vol. 1: *From Colonialism to the Vietminh.* London: Pall Mall Press, 1967.

Cady, John. *The Roots of French Imperialism in Eastern Asia.* Ithaca, N.Y.: Cornell University Press, 1954.

Chatterjee, Partha. "More on Modes of Power and the Peasantry." In *Selected Subaltern Studies,* ed. Ranajit Guha and Gayatri Chakravorty Spivak. New York: Oxford University Press, 1988.

Chautemps, Maurice. *Le Vagabondage en pays annamite.* Thèse pour le doctorat, Université de Paris, Faculté de droit. Texte imprimé. Paris: A. Rousseau, 1908.

Chen, King C. *Vietnam and China, 1938–1954.* Princeton, N.J.: Princeton University Press, 1969.

Chevalier, Louis. *Laboring Classes and Dangerous Classes in Paris during the First Half of the Nineteenth Century.* Translated by Frank Jellinek. Princeton, N.J.: Princeton University Press, 1973. Originally published as *Classes laborieuses et classes dangereuses à Paris pendant la première moitié du XIXᵉ siècle* (Paris: Plon, 1958).

Chuong Thau. *Dong Kinh Nghia Thuc* [The Eastern Capital Free School]. Hanoi: Ha Noi, 1982.

Cohen, Stanley. *Vision of Social Control: Crime, Punishment and Classification.* Oxford: Polity Press, 1985.

Coldham, E. "Crime and Punishment in British Colonial Africa." In *Punishment: Transactions of the Jean Bodin Society for Comparative Institutional History,* LVIII. Brussels: De Boeke Université, 1989.

Conklin, Alice L. *A Mission to Civilize: The Republican Idea of Empire in France and West Africa, 1895–1930.* Stanford, Calif.: Stanford University Press, 1997.

Conley, John A. "Prisons, Production and Profit: Reconsidering the Importance of Prison Industries." *Journal of Social History* 14, no. 2 (1980): 257–76.

Conseil de gouvernement de l'Indo-Chine. *Session ordinaire de 1923: Discours prononcé par M. Martial Merlin*. Hanoi: Imprimerie d'Extrême-Orient, 1923.

Cooke, Nola. "The Composition of the Nineteenth-Century Political Elite of Pre-Colonial Nguyen Vietnam (1802–1883)." *Modern Asian Studies* 29, no. 4 (1995): 741–61.

———. "Nineteenth-Century Vietnamese Confucianism in Historical Perspective: Evidence from the Palace Examinations (1463–1883)." *Journal of Southeast Asian Studies* 25, no. 2 (September 1994): 270–312.

———. "Regionalism and the Nature of Nguyen Rule in Seventeenth-Century Dang Trong (Cochinchina)." *Journal of Southeast Asian Studies* 29, no. 1 (March 1998): 122–61.

Cooper, Frederick, and Ann Laura Stoler, eds.*Tensions of Empire: Colonial Cultures in a Bourgeois World*. Berkeley and Los Angeles: University of California Press, 1997.

Corre, Armand. *L'Ethnographie criminelle*. Paris: C. Reinwald, 1894.

Coulet, Georges. *Les Sociétés secrètes en terre d'Annam*. Saigon: C. Ardin, 1926.

Couzinet, Paul. "La Structure juridique de l'Union Indochinoise." *Revue Indochinoise Juridique et Economique* (Hanoi, 1939). Cited in Alexander B. Woodside, *Community and Revolution in Modern Vietnam* (Boston: Houghton Mifflin, 1976).

Dampier, William. *Voyages and Discoveries*. 1699. Edited by Clennell Wilkinson. London: Argonaut Press, 1931.

Dang Thai Mai, ed. *Van Tho Cach Mang Viet Nam Dau The Ky XX (1900–1925)* [Vietnamese Revolutionary Prose and Poetry from the Early Twentieth Century, 1900–1925]. Hanoi: Van Hoc, 1974.

Dang Viet Chau. "Nguc Son La, 1935–1936" [Son La Prison, 1935–1936]. In Bao Tang Cach Mang Viet Nam and Bao Tang Son La, *Suoi Reo Nam Ay: Hoi Ky Cach Mang* [The Bubbling Spring That Year: Revolutionary Memoirs]. Hanoi: Van Hoa–Thong Tin, 1993.

Dao Duy Anh. *Han Viet Tu Dien* [Sino-Vietnamese Dictionary]. Ho Chi Minh City: Thanh Pho Ho Chi Minh, 1994.

Dao Trinh Nhat. *Luong Ngoc Quyen Va Cuoc Khoi Nghia Thai Nguyen 1917* [Luong Ngoc Quyen and the Thai Nguyen Uprising of 1917]. Saigon: Tan Viet, 1957.

Daufès, E. *La Garde indigène de l'Indochine de sa création à nos jours*. Avignon: D. Seguin, 1933.

De Francis, John. *Colonialism and Language Policy in Viet-Nam*. The Hague: Mouton, 1977.

Demariaux, Jean-Claude. *Les Secrets des îles Poulo-Condore: Le Grand Bagne indochinois*. Paris: J. Peyronnet, 1956.

Descours-Gatin, Chantal. *Quand l'opium finançait la colonisation en Indochine: L'Elaboration de la régie générale de l'opium, 1860 à 1914*. Paris: L'Harmattan, 1992.

Dhur, Jacques. *Visions de bagne*. Paris: Ferenczi, 1925.

Dorgelès, Roland. *On the Mandarin Road*. Translated from the French by Gertrude Emerson. New York: Century Co., 1926. Originally published as *Sur la route mandarine* (Paris: A. Michel, 1925).

Dorsenne, Jean. "Le Péril rouge en Indochine." *Revue des Deux Mondes*, April 1, 1932.

Duiker, William. *The Communist Road to Power in Vietnam*. Boulder, Colo.: Westview Press, 1996.

————. "The Red Soviets of Nghe-Tinh: An Early Communist Revolution in Vietnam." *Journal of Southeast Asian Studies* 4, no. 2 (September 1973): 186–98.

————. "The Revolutionary Youth League: Cradle of Communism in Vietnam." *China Quarterly* no. 53 (July–September 1972): 475–69.

————. *The Rise of Nationalism in Vietnam, 1900–1941*. Ithaca, N.Y.: Cornell University Press, 1976.

Dutton, Michael R. *Policing and Punishment in China: From Patriarchy to the People*. Cambridge: Cambridge University Press, 1992.

Eastman, Lloyd E. *Throne and Mandarins: China's Search for a Policy During the Sino-French Controversy, 1880–1885*. Cambridge, Mass.: Harvard University Press, 1967.

Echinard, Alfred. *Histoire politique et militaire de la province de Thai-Nguyên: Ses forces de police*. Hanoi: Trung-Bac Tan-Van, 1934.

Elliot, David. "Revolutionary Re-Integration: A Comparison of the Foundation of Post Liberation Political Systems in North Vietnam and China." Ph.D. diss., Cornell University, 1976.

Evans, Robin. *The Fabrication of Virtue: English Prison Architecture, 1750–1840*. Cambridge: Cambridge University Press, 1982.

Ferré, Georges. *Bagnards, colons et canaques*. Paris: Jouve, 1932.

Foucault, Michel. *Discipline and Punish: The Birth of the Prison*. Translated by Alan Sheridan. New York: Random House, Vintage Books, 1979. Originally published as *Surveillir et punir: Naissance de la prison* (Paris: Gallimard, 1975).

————. "Prison Talk." In *Power/Knowledge: Selected Interviews and Other Writings 1972–1977*, trans. Colin Gordon, Leo Marshall, John Mepham, and Kate Soper; ed. Colin Gordon. New York: Pantheon Books, 1980.

Fourniau, Charles. *Annam-Tonkin (1885–1896): Lettrés et paysans vietnamiens face à la conquêt coloniale*. Paris: L'Harmattan, 1989.

Franke, Herman. "The Rise and Decline of Solitary Confinement: Socio-Historical Explanations of Long-Term Penal Changes." *British Journal of Criminology* 32, no. 2 (Spring 1992): 125–43.

Frederick, William. "Alexandre Varenne and Politics in Indochina, 1925–26." In *Aspects of Vietnamese History*, ed. Walter Vella. Honolulu: University of Hawaii Press, 1973.

Furnivall, J. S. *Colonial Policy and Practice: A Comparative Study of Burma and Netherlands India*. Cambridge: Cambridge University Press, 1948.

Galembert, J. de. *Les Administrations et les services publics indochinois.* Hanoi: Imprimerie Mac Dinh Tu, 1931.

Garland, David. *Punishment and Welfare: A History of Penal Strategies.* Aldershot, Hants: Gower, 1985.

Garner, Reuben. "The French in Indochina: Some Impressions of the Colonial Inspectors, 1867–1913." *Southeast Asia: An International Quarterly* 2 (1969): 831–40.

Garrigues, E. A. F. "Cochinchine." In *La Justice en Indochine*, ed. H. Morché. Hanoi: Imprimerie d'Extrême-Orient, 1931.

Gaspard, Thu Trang. *Ho Chi Minh à Paris, 1917–1923.* Paris: L'Harmattan, 1992.

Gerth, H. H., and C. Wright Mills, eds. *From Max Weber: Essays in Sociology.* New York: Oxford University Press, 1946.

Goscha, Christopher E. *Vietnam or Indochina? Contesting Conceptions of Space in Vietnamese Nationalism, 1887–1954.* Nordic Institute of Asian Studies Report Series, no. 28. Copenhagen: NAIS, 1995.

Goudal, Jean. "Labor Legislation in Indo-China." *Asiatic Review* 30 (January 1934): 136–45.

———. "Labor Problems in Indochina." *Asiatic Review* 24 (July 1928): 361–68.

Gouvernement général de l'Indochine. *Annuaire statistique de l'Indochine.* Hanoi: Imprimerie d'Extrême-Orient, 1913–42.

Guha, Ranajit. "The Prose of Counter-Insurgency." In *Selected Subaltern Studies*, ed. Ranajit Guha and Gayatri Chakravorty Spivak. New York: Oxford University Press, 1988.

Ha Huy Giap. *Doi Toi, Nhung Dieu Nghe, Thay Va Song: Hoi Ky Cach Mang* [My Life—Things Heard, Seen, and Lived: Revolutionary Memoirs]. Ho Chi Minh City: Thanh Pho Ho Chi Minh, 1994.

Ha Phu Huong. "O Nha Tu Lao Bao" [In Lao Bao Prison]. *Tap Chi Cua Viet* 3 (1990): 34–37.

Ha The Hanh. "From the Dungeon." In *From the Russian October Revolution to the Vietnamese August Revolution.* Hanoi: Foreign Languages Publishing House, 1987.

Habert, L. A. "Le Tonkin." In *La Justice en Indochine*, ed. H. Morché. Hanoi: Imprimerie d'Extrême-Orient, 1931.

Hacking, Ian. *The Taming of Chance.* Cambridge: Cambridge University Press, 1990.

Hai Trieu. *Hai Trieu Toan Tap* [The Complete Works of Hai Trieu]. Edited by Pham Hong Toan. Hanoi: Van Hoc, 1996.

Han Song Thanh. *Nhung Ngay Tu Nguc* [Prison Days]. Ho Chi Minh City: So Van Hoa Thong Tin Thanh Pho Ho Chi Minh, 1995.

Hanh Son. *Cu Tran Cao Van* [Old Tran Cao Van]. Paris: Minh Tan, 1952.

Harding, Neil. *Leninism.* Durham, N.C.: Duke University Press, 1996.

Hémery, Daniel. *Révolutionnaires vietnamiens et pouvoir colonial en Indochine: Communistes, trotskystes, nationalistes à Saïgon de 1932 à 1937.* Paris: Maspéro, 1975.

Henriques, U. R. Q. "The Rise and Decline of a Separate System of Prison Discipline." *Past and Present* 54 (1972): 61–93.

Hervey, Harry. *Travels in French Indochina.* London: Thornton Butterworth, 1928.

Hirshman, Charles. "Population and Society in Twentieth-Century Southeast Asia." *Journal of Southeast Asian Studies* 25, no. 2 (September 1994): 381–416.

Ho Chi Minh. "French Colonialism on Trial." 1925. In *Ho Chi Minh: Selected Works.* Hanoi: Foreign Languages Publishing House, 1978.

———. *Ho Chi Minh on Revolution: Selected Writings, 1920–66.* Edited by Bernard Fall. New York: Praeger, 1967.

———. *Ho Chi Minh Toan Tap II, 1924–1930* [Complete Works of Ho Chi Minh, vol. 2: 1924–1930]. Hanoi: Chinh Tri Quoc Gia, 1995.

——— *Ho Chi Minh Toan Tap III, 1930–1945* [Complete Works of Ho Chi Minh, vol. 3: 1930–1945]. Hanoi: Chinh Tri Quoc Gia, 1995.

———. "Khai Mac Le Ky Niem 30 Nam Ngay Thanh Lap Dang Toi Tai Ha Noi" [Commemoration of the Thirtieth Anniversary of the Establishment of My Party in Hanoi]. *Nhan Dan,* May 1, 1960. Reprinted in the introduction to *Nhung Nguoi Cong San* [The Communists]. Ho Chi Minh City: Thanh Nien, 1977.

———. *Nhat Ky Trong Tu* [Prison Diary]. Hanoi: Van Hoa, 1960. For a translation, see *Reflections from Captivity: Phan Boi Chau's Prison Notes and Ho Chi Minh's Prison Diary,* ed. David G. Marr (Athens: Ohio University Press, 1978).

Hoai Anh. "Vu Trong Phung, Nha Hoa Hoc Cua Nhung Tinh Cach" [Vu Trong Phung, the Chemist of Characters]. In Hoai Anh, *Chan Dung Van Hoc* [Literary Portraits]. Ho Chi Minh City: Van Nghe Thanh Pho Ho Chi Minh, 1995.

Hoang Dao. "Truoc Vanh Mong Ngua" [Before the Court of Justice]. In *Phong Su Chon Loc* [Selected Reportage], ed. Vuong Tri Nhan. Hanoi: Hoi Nha Van, 1994.

Hoang Dung, ed. *Tho Van Cach Mang, 1930–1945* [Revolutionary Poetry and Literature, 1930–1945]. Hanoi: Van Hoc, 1980.

Hoang Minh Dau. *Cai Than Tu Toi* [My Life as a Prisoner]. Saigon: Xua Nay, 1933.

Hoang Quoc Viet. "Our People, a Very Heroic People." In *A Heroic People: Memoirs from the Revolution.* 2d ed. Hanoi: Foreign Languages Publishing House, 1965.

Hoang Van Dao. *Viet-Nam Quoc-Dan Dang: Lich Su Tranh Dau Can Dai (1927–1954)* [The Vietnam Nationalist Party: A History of Modern Struggle, 1927–1954]. Saigon: Nguyen Hoa Hiep, 1965.

Hodgkin, Thomas. *Vietnam: The Revolutionary Path.* New York: St. Martin's Press, 1981.

Hong Chuong. "Journalist Hai Trieu." *Vietnamese Studies,* no. 15 (85) (1986): 80–84.

Hooker, M. B. *A Concise Legal History of South-East Asia.* Oxford: Clarendon Press: 1978.

Huchon, Henri. *Quand j'étais au bagne.* Bordeaux: Delmas, 1933.

Hue-Tam Ho Tai. "Literature for the People: From Soviet Policies to Vietnamese Polemics." In *Borrowings and Adaptations in Vietnamese Culture,* ed. Truong Buu Lam. Honolulu: University of Hawaii Press, 1987.

———. *Millenarianism and Peasant Politics in Vietnam.* Cambridge, Mass.: Harvard University Press, 1983.

———. *Radicalism and the Origins of the Vietnamese Revolution.* Cambridge, Mass.: Harvard University Press, 1992.

Huynh Kim Khanh. *Vietnamese Communism, 1925–1945.* Ithaca, N.Y.: Cornell University Press, 1982.

Huynh Sanh Thông, ed. and trans. *To Be Made Over: Tales of Socialist Reeducation in Vietnam.* Lac-Viêt series, no. 5. New Haven, Conn.: Council on Southeast Asia Studies, Yale Center for International and Area Studies; Boston, Mass.: William Joiner Center, 1988.

Huynh Thuc Khang. *Thi Tu Tung Thoai* [Prison Verse]. Tieng Dan, 1939. Reprint, Saigon: Nam Cuong, 1951.

Huynh Van Tieng. "Journalist Nguyen Van Nguyen." *Vietnamese Studies,* no. 15 (85) (1986): 84–88.

Huynh Van Tong. *Lich Su Bao Chi Viet Nam tu Khoi Thuy den 1930* [The History of Vietnamese Press from Its Beginnings to 1930]. Sai Gon: Tri Dang, 1973.

Hy Van Luong. "Agrarian Unrest from an Anthropological Perspective: The Case of Vietnam." *Comparative Politics* 17, no. 2 (January 1985): 153–74.

———. *Revolution in the Village: Tradition and Transformation in North Vietnam, 1925–1988.* Honolulu: University of Hawaii Press, 1992.

Ignatieff, Michael. *A Just Measure of Pain: The Penitentiary in the Industrial Revolution, 1750–1850.* New York: Pantheon Books, 1978.

Jamieson, Neil. *Understanding Vietnam.* Berkeley and Los Angeles: University of California Press, 1993.

Johnson, Elmer. *Japanese Corrections: Managing Convicted Offenders in an Orderly Society.* Carbondale: Southern Illinois University Press, 1996.

Katsiaficas, George, ed. *Vietnam Documents: American and Vietnamese Views of the War.* New York: M. E. Sharpe, 1992.

Kelly, Gail. "Franco-Vietnamese Schools, 1918–1938." Ph.D. diss., University of Wisconsin, 1975.

Kelly, Sean, and Colin Mackerras. "The Application of Marxism-Leninism to Vietnam." In *Marxism in Asia,* ed. Colin Mackerras and Nick Knight. New York: St. Martin's Press, 1985.

Lacouture, Jean. *Ho Chi Minh: A Political Biography.* New York: Random House, 1968.

Laffey, Ella S. "French Adventurers and Chinese Bandits in Tonkin: The Garnier Affair in Its Local Context." *Journal of Southeast Asian Studies* 6, no. 1 (1975): 38–51.

―――. "The Tonkin Frontier: The View from China, 1885–1914." In *Proceedings of Third Annual Meeting of the French Colonial Historical Society*, 108–18. Montréal, 1977.

Laffey, John. "Land, Labor and Law in Colonial Tonkin before 1914." *Historical Reflections* 2, no. 2 (Winter 1975): 223–63.

Lam Hong Phan. "Lop Vo Long Tai Nha Cu Phan Boi Chau" [The Preschool Class in Phan Boi Chau's Household]. In *Ong Gia Ben Ngu: Hoi Ky* [The Old Man from Ben Ngu: Memoirs]. Hue: Thuan Hoa, 1982.

Larique, Marius. *Dans la brousse*. Paris: Gallimard, 1933.

Le Boucher, L. *Ce qu'il faut connaître du bagne*. Paris: Boivin, 1930.

Le Huu Phuoc. "Lich Su Nha Tu Con Dao, 1862–1930" [History of Con Dao Prison, 1862–1930]. Master's thesis, Ho Chi Minh City Institute of Social Science, 1992.

Le Kim Que. "Tim Hieu Ve Nha Tu Lao Bao" [Understanding Lao Bao Prison]. *Tap Chi Lich Su Dang* 10 (1985): 71–74.

Le Manh Trinh. "In Canton and Siam." In Nguyen Luong Bang et al., *Uncle Ho*. Hanoi: Foreign Languages Publishing House, 1980.

Le Trong Khanh and Le Anh Tra, eds. *Xo Viet Nghe-Tinh Qua Mot So Tho Van* [The Nghe-Tinh Soviet Through Prose and Poetry]. Hanoi: Su That, 1959.

Le Van Hien. *Nguc Kontum* [Kontum Prison]. 1938. Hanoi: Hoi Nha Van, 1958.

Le Xuan Phuong, ed. "Ve Cuoc Khoi Nghia Thai Nguyen Nam 1917: Ban Khau Cung Nguyen Van Nhieu" [On the Thai Nguyen Uprising of 1917: The Interrogation of Nguyen Van Nhieu]. *Nghien Cuu Lich Su* 237 (1987): 76–80.

Lockhart, Bruce. *The End of the Vietnamese Monarchy*. New Haven, Conn.: Council on Southeast Asian Studies, 1993.

Lockhart, Greg. *Nation in Arms: The Origins of the People's Army of Vietnam*. Boston: Asian Studies Association of Australia in association with Allen & Unwin, 1989.

―――, ed. *The Light of the Capital: Three Modern Vietnamese Classics*. Kuala Lumpur: Oxford in Asia, 1996.

London, Géo. *Aux portes du bagne*. Paris: Portiques, 1930.

Londres, Albert. *Au Bagne*. Paris: Albin Michel, 1924.

Lorion, Louis. *Criminalité et médecine judiciare en Cochinchine*. Lyon: A. Storck, 1887.

Ly Thi Chung. "Nguoi tu phu nu cong san dau tien o Hoa Lo" [The First Female Communist Prisoner in Hoa Lo]. In *Mua Thu Cach Mang: Hoi Ky* [Revolutionary Autumn: Memoirs], ed. Nguyen Bau. Hanoi: Ha Noi, 1985.

Marr, David G. *Vietnamese Anticolonialism, 1885–1925*. Berkeley and Los Angeles: University of California Press, 1971.

―――. "Vietnam 1945: Some Questions." *Vietnam Forum*, no. 6 (Summer–Fall 1985): 155–93.

―――. *Vietnam 1945: The Quest for Power*. Berkeley and Los Angeles: University of California Press, 1995.

―――. *Vietnamese Tradition on Trial, 1920–1945*. Berkeley and Los Angeles: University of California Press, 1981.

————. "World War II and the Vietnamese Revolution." In *Southeast Asia under Japanese Occupation*, ed. Alfred W. McCoy, 125–58. Southeast Asia Studies Monograph Series, no. 22. New Haven, Conn.: Yale University, 1980.

————, ed. *Reflections from Captivity: Phan Boi Chau's Prison Notes and Ho Chi Minh's Prison Diary.* Translated by Christopher Jenkins, Tran Khanh Tuyet, and Huynh Sanh-Thong. Athens: Ohio University Press, 1978.

Martin, Benjamin F. *Crime and Criminal Justice under the Third Republic: The Shame of Marianne.* Baton Rouge: Louisiana State University Press, 1990.

McAleavy, Henry. *Black Flags in Vietnam: The Story of a Chinese Intervention.* New York: Macmillan, 1968.

McAlister, John T., Jr. "Mountain Minorities and the Viet Minh: A Key to the Indochina War." In *Southeast Asian Tribes, Minorities, and Nations*, ed. Peter Kunstadter. Princeton, N.J.: Princeton University Press, 1967.

————. *Vietnam: The Origins of Revolution, 1885–1946.* Washington, D.C.: Center for Research in Social Systems, 1968. Reprint, New York, 1971.

McConnell, Scott. *Leftward Journey: The Education of Vietnamese Students in France, 1919–1939.* New Brunswick, N.J.: Transaction Publishers, 1989.

McKnight, Brian. *The Quality of Mercy: Amnesties and Traditional Chinese Justice.* Honolulu: University of Hawaii Press, 1981.

McLeod, Mark W. "Truong Dinh and Vietnamese Anticolonialism (1859–1864): A Reappraisal." *Journal of Southeast Asian Studies* 24, no. 1 (March 1993): 88–105.

————. *The Vietnamese Response to French Intervention, 1862–1874.* New York: Praeger, 1991.

Melossi, Dario, and Massimo Pavarini. *The Prison and the Factory: Origins of the Penitentiary System.* Translated by Glynis Cousin. Totowa, N.J.: Barnes & Noble, 1981. Originally published as *Carcere e fabbrica: Alle origini del sistema penitenziario (XVI–XIX secolo)* (Bologna: Il mulino, 1977).

Merlat, Louis. *Au bout du monde.* Paris: Depeuch, 1928.

Mesclon, Antoine. *Comment j'ai subi quinze ans de bagne.* Paris: L'Auteur, 1924.

Mitchell, Timothy. *Colonising Egypt.* 1988. Berkeley and Los Angeles: University of California Press, 1991.

Morlat, Patrice. *La Répression coloniale au Vietnam, 1908–1940.* Paris: L'Harmattan, 1990.

Mossy, Léon. *Principes d'administration générale de l'Indochine.* Saigon: Imprimerie de l'Union, 1918.

Munholland, Kim. "The French Army and the Imperial Frontier, 1885–1897." In *Proceedings of Third Annual Meeting of the French Colonial Historical Society.* Montréal, 1977.

————. "The French Response to the Vietnamese Nationalist Movement, 1905–1914." *Journal of Modern History* 47 (December 1975): 655–75.

Murray, Martin. *The Development of Capitalism in Colonial Indochina, 1870–1940.* Berkeley and Los Angeles: University of California Press, 1990.

Musset, Paul. *Albert Londres; ou, L'Aventure du grand reportage*. Paris: Grasset, 1972.

Ngo Si Lien, comp. *Dai Viet Su Ky Toan Thu, Tap I* [The Complete Book of the Historical Records of Great Viet, vol. 1]. Hanoi: Khoa Hoc Xa Hoi, 1972.

Ngo Thi Thanh. "Hoat Dong Cua Nhung Tu Nhan Cong San Trong Nha Tu Hai Phong, 1930–1945" [Activities of Communist Prisoners in Haiphong Prison, 1930–1945]. Undergraduate honors thesis, 1987, History Department, Vietnam National University, Hanoi.

Ngo Van. "Quelques biographies des révolutionnaires vietnamiens." *Cahiers Léon Trotsky*, no. 41 (December 1989): 64–84.

Ngo Vinh Long. *Before the Revolution: The Vietnamese Peasants under the French*. New York: Columbia University Press, 1991.

———. "The Indochinese Communist Party and Peasant Rebellion in Central Vietnam, 1930–1931." *Bulletin of Concerned Asian Scholars* 10, no. 4 (October–December 1978): 15–36.

Nguyen An Tinh, ed. *Nguyen An Ninh*. Ho Chi Minh City: Tre, 1996.

Nguyen Cong Hoan. *Nguoi Cap Rang Cua Ham Xay Lua* [The Caplan of the Rice-Mill Stockade]. Hanoi: Kim Dong, 1978.

———. "The Stage in My Career as a Writer." In *Vietnamese Intellectuals at a Historic Turning-Point in the Twentieth Century*. Hanoi: Foreign Languages Publishing House, 1989.

Nguyen Duc Chinh. *Thu Con Lon* [Con Lon Letters]. Hanoi: Trinh Van Bich, 1937.

Nguyen Duy Trinh. "Lam Bao Va Sang Tac Tieu Thuyet Trong Nha Lao Vinh" [Writing Newspapers and Novels in Vinh Prison]. In *Truong Hoc Sau Song Sat: Hoi Ky Cach Mang* [School Behind Iron Bars: Revolutionary Memoirs]. Hanoi: Thanh Nien, 1969.

Nguyen Hai Ham. *Tu Yen Bay Den Con Lon, 1930–1945* [From Yen Bay to Con Lon, 1930–1945]. Saigon: Sai Gon, 1970.

Nguyen Hien Le. *Dong Kinh Nghia Thuc* [The Eastern Capital Free School]. Saigon: La Boi, 1968.

Nguyen Hong. *Buoc Duong Viet Van* [On the Road to Writing]. Hanoi: Van Hoc, 1970.

———. "Tet Cua Tu Dan Ba" [Tet for Female Prisoners]. *Tieu Thuyet Thu Bay* [Saturday Novel] 246 (Spring 1939). Reprinted in *Tuyen Tap Nguyen Hong, Tap I* [Collected Works of Nguyen Hong, vol. 1], ed. Le Khanh (Hanoi: Van Hoc, 1995).

Nguyen Khac Vien and Huu Ngoc, eds. *Vietnamese Literature: Historical Background and Texts*. Hanoi: Foreign Languages Publishing House, 1988.

Nguyen Luong Bang. "Brought to Political Maturity Thanks to the People and the Party." In *A Heroic People: Memoirs from the Revolution*. Hanoi: Foreign Languages Publishing House, 1965.

———. "The Times I Met Him." In Nguyen Luong Bang et al., *Uncle Ho*. Hanoi: Foreign Languages Publishing House, 1980.

Nguyen Ngoc Huy and Ta Van Tai. *The Lê Code: Law in Traditional Vietnam: A Comparative Sino-Vietnamese Legal Study with Historical-Juridical Analysis and Annotations.* Vol. 1. Athens: Ohio University Press, 1987.

Nguyen Phan Quang and Le Huu Phuoc. "Cuoc Noi Day Cua Tu Nhan Con Dao Tai Hon Bay Canh, 8/1883" [The Uprising of Con Dao Prisoners on Bay Canh Island, August 1883]. *Nghien Cuu Lich Su* 2, no. 261 (March–April 1992): 72–79.

Nguyen Q. Thang and Nguyen Ba The. *Tu Dien Nhan Vat Lich Su Viet Nam* [Dictionary of Vietnamese Historical Figures]. Hanoi: Khoa Hoc Xa Hoi, 1991.

Nguyen Tao. "I Must Live To Fight." In *In The Enemy's Net: Memoirs from the Revolution.* Hanoi: Foreign Languages Publishing House, 1962.

———. *Trong Nguc Toi Hoa Lo* [In The Dark Prison, Hoa Lo]. Hanoi: Van Hoc, 1959.

———. *Vuot Nguc Dark-Mil* [Escape From Dark-Mil Prison]. Hanoi: Thanh Nien, 1976.

Nguyen Thanh. *Bao Chi Cach Mang Viet Nam, 1925–1945* [Vietnamese Revolutionary Newspapers, 1925–1945]. Hanoi: Khoa Hoc Xa Hoi, 1984.

———. *Lich Su Bao Tieng Dan* [The History of the Newspaper *Tieng Dan*]. Da Nang: Da Nang, 1992.

———. "The Revolutionary Press in Vietnam, 1925–1945." *Vietnamese Studies,* no. 15 (85) (1986): 37–59.

Nguyen The Anh. "A Case of Confucian Survival in Twentieth-Century Vietnam: Huynh Thuc Khang and His Newspaper *Tieng Dan.*" *Vietnam Forum* 8 (Summer–Fall 1986): 173–203.

Nguyen Van Nguyen. "Poulo Condore: La Terre des damnés." *Le Travail,* November 13–20, 1936.

Nguyen Van Tu. "Toi Lam Cau Doi Tet O Nha Tu Son La" [I Made Rhyming Couplets for Tet in Son La Prison]. In Bao Tang Cach Mang Viet Nam and Bao Tang Son La, *Suoi Reo Nam Ay: Hoi Ky Cach Mang* [The Bubbling Spring That Year: Revolutionary Memoirs]. Hanoi: Van Hoa–Thong Tin, 1993.

Nhuong Tong. *Doi Trong Nguc* [Life in Prison]. Hanoi: Van Hoa Moi, 1935.

———. *Nguyen Thai Hoc.* Saigon: Tan Viet, 1956.

Nitz, Kyoto Kurusu. "Independence Without Nationalists? The Japanese and Vietnamese Nationalism During the Japanese Period, 1940–45." *Journal of Southeast Asian Studies* 15, no. 1 (March 1984): 108–33.

———. "Japanese Military Policy Towards French Indochina During the Second World War: The Road to the Meigo Sakusen (9 March 1945)." *Journal of Southeast Asian Studies* 14, no. 2 (September 1983): 328–53.

Nye, Robert A. *Crime, Madness, and Politics in Modern France: The Medical Concept of National Decline.* Princeton, N.J.: Princeton University Press, 1984.

O'Brien, Patricia. "The Prison on the Continent, 1865–1965." In *The Oxford History of the Prison: The Practice of Punishment in Western Society,* ed. Norval Morris and David Rothmand. New York: Oxford University Press, 1995.

———. *The Promise of Punishment: Prisons in Nineteenth-Century France.* Princeton, N.J.: Princeton University Press, 1982.

Osborne, Milton. "Continuity and Motivation in the Vietnamese Revolution: New Light from the 1930s." *Pacific Affairs* 47, no.1 (Spring 1974): 37–55.

———. "The Debate on the Legal Code for Colonial Cochin China." *Journal of Southeast Asian History* 10, no. 2 (1969): 224–35.

———. "The Faithful Few: The Politics of Collaboration in Cochinchina in the 1920s." In *Aspects of Vietnamese History,* ed. Walter Vella. Asian Studies at Hawaii, no. 8. Honolulu: University Press of Hawaii, 1973.

———. *The French Presence in Cochinchina and Cambodia: Rule and Response, 1859–1905.* Ithaca, N.Y.: Cornell University Press, 1969.

Péan, Charles. *Le Salut des parias.* 5th ed. Paris: Gallimard, 1935.

———. *Terre de bagne.* Paris: La Renaissance moderne, 1933.

Perrot, Michelle. "Delinquency and the Penitentiary System in Nineteenth-Century France." In *Deviants and the Abandoned in French Society: Selections from the « Annales, économies, sociétés, civilisations »,* Volume IV, ed. Robert Forster and Orest Ranum. Translated by Elborg Forster and Patricia M. Ranum. Baltimore: Johns Hopkins University Press, 1978.

Peters, Edward M. "Prisons Before the Prison: The Ancient and Medieval Worlds." In *The Oxford History of the Prison: The Practice of Punishment in Western Society,* ed. Norval Morris and David Rothmand. New York: Oxford University Press, 1995.

Petit, Jacques-Guy. *Ces peines obscures: La Prison pénale en France, 1780–1875.* Paris: Fayard, 1990.

Pham Cao Duong. *Vietnamese Peasants under French Domination: 1861–1945.* Berkeley, Calif.: Center for South and Southeast Asian Studies, 1985.

Pham Hung. "Never to Give Up Working So Long As One Lives." In *A Heroic People: Memoirs from the Revolution.* 2d ed. Hanoi: Foreign Languages Publishing House, 1965.

Pham Nhu Thom, ed. *Hoi Ky Tran Huy Lieu* [Memoirs of Tran Huy Lieu]. Hanoi: Khoa Hoc Xa Hoi, 1991.

Pham Van Dong. *Le Président Ho Chi Minh.* Hanoi: Foreign Languages Publishing House, 1961.

Phan Boi Chau. "Phan Boi Chau Nien Bieu." [Autobiography of Phan Boi Chau]. In *Phan Boi Chau Toan Tap* [Complete Works of Phan Boi Chau], ed. Chuong Thau. Hue: Thuan Hoa, 1990.

Phan Khoi. "Cai Tam Ly Cua Nguoi Tu Chinh Tri Duoc Tha" [The Psychology of Released Political Prisoners]. *Dong Duong Tap Chi,* April 3, 1937, 13–15.

Phan Van Cac. "Tu Ban Dich Nam 1960 Den Ban Dich Bo Sung Va Chinh Ly Nam 1983" [From the 1960 Translation to the Supplemented and Corrected Translation of 1983]. In *Suy Nghi Moi Ve Nhat Ky Trong Tu* [New Reflections on the Prison Diary], ed. Nguyen Hue Chi. Hanoi: Khoa Hoc Xa Hoi, 1990.

Phan Van Hum. *Ngoi Tu Kham Lon* [Sitting in the Big Jail]. *Than Chung* [Morning Bell] (1929). Reprint, Saigon: Dan Toc, 1957.

Phuong Huu. *105 Ngay Khoi-Nghia Thai-Nguyen* [105 Days of the Thai Nguyen Uprising]. Saigon: Nam Viet, 1949.

Phuong Lan. *Nha Cach Mang Nguyen An Ninh* [Nguyen An Ninh, Revolutionary]. Saigon: Khai Tri, 1970.

———. *Nha Cach Mang Ta Thu Thau, 1906–1945* [Ta Thu Thau: Revolutionary, 1906–1945]. Sai Gon: Khai Tri, 1973.

Pike, Douglas. *Vietnam and the Soviet Union: Anatomy of an Alliance.* Boulder, Colo.: Westview Press, 1987.

Porter, Gareth. "Proletariat and Peasantry in Early Vietnamese Communism." *Asian Thought and Society* 1, no. 3 (December 1976): 333–46.

Rabinow, Paul. *French Modern: Norms and Forms of the Social Environment.* Chicago: Chicago University Press, 1989.

Robequain, Charles. *The Economic Development of French Indo-China.* Translated by Isabel A. Ward. London: Oxford University Press, 1944. Originally published as *L'Evolution économique de l'Indochine française* (Paris: Hartmann, 1939).

Rogers, John. "Hanoi Hilton Heads into History Books." Reuters News Service, November 15, 1994.

Rothman, David. *The Discovery of the Asylum: Social Order and Disorder in the New Republic.* Boston: Little, Brown, 1971.

Rousseau, Louis, Dr. *Un Médicin au bagne.* Paris: Fleury, 1930.

Roussenq, Paul. *Vingt-cinq ans au bagne.* Paris: La Defense, 1934.

Roux, J. B. "Les Prisons du vieux Hué." *Bulletin des amis du vieux Hué* 1 (January–March 1915): 51–58.

Salemink, Oscar. "Mois and Maquis: The Invention and Appropriation of Vietnam's Montagnards from Sabatier to the CIA." In *Colonial Situations: Essays on the Contextualization of Ethnographic Knowledge,* ed. George Stocking Jr., 243–79. Madison: University of Wisconsin Press, 1991.

Salman, Michael. "Nothing Without Labor: Penology, Discipline and Independence in the Philippines under United States Rule." In *Discrepant Histories: Translocal Essays on Filipino Cultures,* ed. Vicente L. Rafael. Philadelphia: Temple University Press, 1995.

Salvatore, Ricardo, and Carlos Aguirre, eds. *The Birth of the Penitentiary in Latin America: Essays on Criminology, Prison Reform and Social Control.* Austin: University of Texas Press, 1996.

Sampson, Cedric. "Nationalism and Communism in Vietnam, 1925–1931." Ph.D diss., University of California, Los Angeles, 1975.

San Ho. *Nhat Ky Tuyet Thuc 9 Ngay Ruoi: Mot Cuoc Tranh Dau Cua Tu Chinh Tri Con Lon* [Diary of a Nine-and-a-Half-Day Hunger Strike: A Struggle of Political Prisoners on Poulo Condore]. Nam Dinh: Su Thuc, 1939.

Schreiner, Alfred. *Les Institutions annamites en Basse-Cochinchine avant la conquête française.* 3 vols. Saigon: Claude, 1900–2. Reprint, Farnborough, Eng.: Gregg International, 1969.

Scott, James. *The Moral Economy of the Peasant: Rebellion and Subsistence in Southeast Asia.* New Haven, Conn.: Yale University Press, 1976.

Sellin, J. T. *Pioneering in Penology: The Amsterdam House of Correction in the Sixteenth and Seventeenth Century.* Philadelphia: University of Pennsylvania Press, 1944.

Shortland, John. *Persecutions of Annam: A History of Christianity in Cochin China and Tonking.* London: Burnes & Oates, 1875.

Smith, Alexander. *A Complete History of the Lives and Robberies of the Most Notorious Highwaymen.* Edited by Arthur Hayward. London: George Routledge & Sons, 1933.

Smith, Harvey, et al. *Area Handbook for North Vietnam.* Washington, D.C.: U.S. Government Printing Office, 1967.

Smith, Ralph. "The Development of Opposition to French Rule in Southern Vietnam 1880–1940." *Past and Present* 54 (December 1972): 94–129.

So Van Hoa Thong Tin Ha Noi and Vien Lich Su Dang. *Dau Tranh Cua Cac Chien Si Yeu Nuoc Va Cach Mang Tai Nha Tu Hoa Lo, 1899–1954* [The Struggle of Patriotic and Revolutionary Fighters in Hoa Lo Prison, 1899–1954]. Hanoi: Chinh Tri Quoc Gia, 1994.

Spierenburg, Pieter. *The Prison Experience: Disciplinary Institutions and Their Inmates in Early Modern Europe.* New Brunswick, N.J.: Rutgers University Press, 1991.

———. *The Spectacle of the Scaffold: Executions and the Evolution of Repression, from a Preindustrial Metropolis to the European Experience.* Cambridge: Cambridge University Press, 1984.

Stoler, Ann Laura. " 'In Cold Blood': Hierarchies of Credibility and the Politics of Colonial Narratives." *Representations* 37 (Winter 1992): 154–89.

Stuart-Fox, Martin. "The French in Laos, 1887–1945." *Modern Asian Studies* 29, no. 1 (1995): 111–39.

Ta Van Tai. *The Vietnamese Tradition of Human Rights.* Berkeley, Calif.: Institute of East Asian Studies, 1988.

Tabulet, Georges. *Le Geste français en Indochine.* 2 vols. Paris: Adrien-Maisonneuve, 1955.

Tana, Li. "An Alternative Vietnam? The Nguyen Kingdom in the Seventeenth and Eighteenth Centuries." *Journal of Southeast Asian Studies* 29, no. 1 (March 1998): 111–21.

Taylor, Keith. *The Birth of Vietnam.* Berkeley and Los Angeles: University of California, 1983.

———. "Nguyen Hoang and the Beginning of Viet Nam's Southward Expansion." In *Southeast Asia in the Early Modern Era,* ed. Anthony Reid. Ithaca, N.Y.: Cornell University Press, 1993.

Thompson, Virginia. *French Indochina.* New York: Octagon Books, 1968.

———. *Labor Problems in Southeast Asia.* New Haven, Conn.: Yale University Press, 1947.

Ton Quang Phiet. *Mot Ngay Ngan Thu (Lan Thu Nhat O Nha Nguc)* [The Eternal Day (My First Time in Prison)]. Hue: Phuc Long, 1935.

———. "Mot Vai Ky Niem Ve Phan Boi Chau" [Some Memories of Phan Boi Chau]. In *Ong Gia Ben Ngu: Hoi Ky.* Hue: Thuan Hoa, 1982.

―――. "Ve Dong Chi Phan Dang Luu: Mot Dong Chi Tri Thuc Cach Mang Kien Cuong" [Comrade Phan Dang Luu: A Steadfast Revolutionary Intellectual]. *Nghien Cuu Lich Su* 147 (November–December 1972): 61–64.

Tønnesson, Stein. *The Vietnamese Revolution of 1945: Roosevelt, Ho Chi Minh, and De Gaulle in a World at War.* Oslo: International Peace Research Institute; Newbury Park, Calif.: Sage Publications, 1991.

Tran Cung. "Tu Con Dao Tro Ve: Hoi Ky" [Returning from Con Dao: A Memoir]. *Nghien Cuu Lich Su* 134 (September–October 1970): 18–26.

Tran Dang Ninh. *Hai Lan Vuot Nguc* [Two Prison Escapes]. Hanoi: Van Hoc, 1970.

Tran Huy Lieu. "Con Lon Ky Su" [Con Lon Memoir]. In *Hoi Ky Tran Huy Lieu,* ed. Pham Nhu Thom. Hanoi: Khoa Hoc Xa Hoi, 1991.

―――. "Danh Gia Luu Vinh Phuc Va Quan Co Den Trong Cuoc Khang Phap O Viet Nam." [Assessing Luu Vinh Phuc and the Black Flags in the Anti-French Resistance in Vietnam]. *Nghien Cuu Lich Su* 42 (1961): 21–25.

―――. "Duoi ham Son La" [In the Son La Hole]. In *Hoi Ky Tran Huy Lieu,* ed. Pham Nhu Thom. Hanoi: Khoa Hoc Xa Hoi, 1991.

―――. *Lich Su Tam Muoi Nam Chong Phap, Tap I* [History of Eighty Years Against the French, vol. 1]. Hanoi: Su Hoc, 1961.

―――. *Loan Thai Nguyen* [The Thai Nguyen Rebellion]. Hanoi: Bao Ngoc Van Doan, 1935.

―――. *Mat Tran Dan Chu Dong Duong.* [The Popular Front in Indochina]. Hanoi: Su Hoc, 1960.

―――. "Nho Lai 'Ong Gia Ben Ngu'" [Recalling the Old Man of Ben Ngu]. In *Ong Gia Ben Ngu: Hoi Ky.* Hue: Thuan Hoa, 1982.

―――. "Phan Dau De Tro Nen Mot Dang Vien Cong San" [Striving to Become a Communist Party Member]. In *Hoi Ky Tran Huy Lieu,* ed. Pham Nhu Thom. Hanoi: Khoa Hoc Xa Hoi, 1991.

―――. "Tinh Trong Nguc Toi" [Love in the Dark Prison]. 1950. In *Hoi Ky Tran Huy Lieu,* ed. Pham Nhu Thom. Hanoi: Khoa Hoc Xa Hoi, 1991.

―――. "Tren Dao Hon Cau" [On Hon Cau Island]. In *Hoi Ky Tran Huy Lieu,* ed. Pham Nhu Thom. Hanoi: Khoa Hoc Xa Hoi, 1991.

―――. "Tu 'Tieng Suoi Reo,' den 'Dong Song Cong,' den 'Con Duong Nghia'" [From "The Bubbling Spring" to "The Cong River" to "The Path of Justice"]. In *Hoi Ky Tran Huy Lieu,* ed. Pham Nhu Thom. Hanoi: Khoa Hoc Xa Hoi, 1991.

―――. "Tu Hoc Trong Tu" [Self-Study in Prison]. In *Hoi Ky Tran Huy Lieu,* ed. Pham Nhu Thom. Hanoi: Khoa Hoc Xa Hoi, 1991.

―――. "Xuan No Trong Tu" [Spring Blooms in Prison]. In *Hoi Ky Tran Huy Lieu,* ed. Pham Nhu Thom. Hanoi: Khoa Hoc Xa Hoi, 1991.

Tran Huy Lieu, Nguyen Cong Binh, and Van Tao. *Tai Lieu Tham Khao Lich Su Cach Mang Can Dai Viet Nam: Khoi Nghia Yen The, Khoi Nghia Cua Cac Dan Toc Mien Nui Tap II* [Referential Documentary History of the Modern Vietnamese Revolution: The Uprisings of Yen The and of the Mountain People, vol. 2]. Hanoi: Van Su Dia, 1958.

Tran Huy Lieu, Nguyen Cong Binh, Phan Khoi, and Van Tao. *Tai Lieu Tham Khao Lich Su Cach Mang Can Dai Viet-Nam, Tap III* [Historical Documents on the Modern Vietnamese Revolution, vol. 3]. Hanoi: Ban Nghien Cuu Van Su Dia, 1955.

Tran Thanh Phuong. *Day, Cac Nha Tu My-Nguy* [Here, the Prisons of the American Puppets]. Ho Chi Minh City: Thanh Pho Ho Chi Minh, 1995.

Tran Van Cung. "Chi Bo Cong San Dau Tien Va Dong Duong Cong San Dang" [The First Communist Cell and the Indochinese Communist Party]. In *Buoc Ngoat Vi Dai Cua Lich Su Cach Mang Viet Nam* [The Glorious Turning Point of the History of the Vietnam Communist Party]. Hanoi: Van Hoc, 1960.

Tran Van Giau. *Giai Cap Cong Nhan Viet Nam Tu Dang Cong San Thanh Lap Den Cach Mang Thanh Cong, Tap II: 1936–1939* [The Vietnamese Working Class from the Founding of the Communist Party to the Victory of the Revolution, vol. 2: 1936–1939]. Hanoi: Vien Su Hoc, 1962.

———. "Lop Hoc Chu Nghia Mac-Lenin Va To Bao *Y Kien Chung* o Banh I, Con Lon, 1935–1936." [The Class of Marxism-Leninism and the Newspaper "Consensus" in Dormitory 1, Con Lon, 1935–1936]. *Tap Chi Lich Su Dang* 5, no. 33 (1990): 4–7.

Tran Van Que. *Con-Lon Quan-Dao Truoc Ngay 9–3–1945* [The Poulo Condore Archipelago Before March 9, 1945]. Saigon: Thanh-Huong Tung-Thu, 1961.

Truong Buu Lam. "Japan and the Disruption of the Vietnamese Nationalist Movement." In *Aspects of Vietnamese History*, ed. Walter Vella. Honolulu: University of Hawaii Press, 1973.

———. *Patterns of Vietnamese Response to Foreign Intervention, 1858–1900*. Southeast Asia Studies Monograph Series, no. 11. New Haven, Conn.: Yale University, 1967.

Truong Ngoc Phu. "Tu Vu Am Sat Bazin Nam 1929 Den Cuoc Khoi Nghia Yen Bay Nam 1930 Cua Viet Nam Quoc Dan Dang" [From the Assassination of Bazin in 1929 to the Yen Bay Uprising in 1930 of the Vietnamese Nationalist Party]. *Su Dia* 9, no. 26 (January–March 1974): 22–30.

Tuck, Patrick. *French Catholic Missionaries and the Politics of Imperialism in Vietnam, 1857–1914: A Documentary Survey*. Liverpool: Liverpool University Press, 1987.

Tucker, Robert, ed. *The Lenin Anthology*. New York: Norton, 1975.

Ty Van Hoa Thong Tin Son La. *Tho Ca Cach Mang Nha Tu Son La, 1930–1945* [Revolutionary Poetry from Son La Prison, 1930–1945]. Edited by Nguyen Anh Tuan. Son La: Ty Van Hoa Thong Tin Son La, 1980.

Uy Ban Khoa Hoc Xa Hoi. *Tong Tap Van Hoc Viet Nam, Tap 35* [Anthology of Vietnamese Literature, vol. 35]. Hanoi: Khoa Hoc Xa Hoi, 1985.

Van Tan [Tran Duc Sac]. "Journalist Tran Huy Lieu." *Vietnamese Studies* no. 15 (85) (1986): 89–93.

———. "Hoc Tap, Hoc Tap, Hoc Tap De Hoat Dong Tot Cho Dang" [Study, Study, Study to Work Effectively for the Party]. In *Truong Hoc Sau Song Sat: Hoi Ky Cach Mang*. Hanoi: Thanh Nien, 1969.

Van Tien Dung. "Niem Tin La Suc Manh" [Belief Is Strength]. In Bao Tang Cach Mang Viet Nam and Bao Tang Son La, *Suoi Reo Nam Ay: Hoi Ky Cach Mang* [The Bubbling Spring That Year: Revolutionary Memoirs]. Hanoi: Van Hoa–Thong Tin, 1993.

Vaughan, Megan. *Curing Their Ills: Colonial Power and African Illness.* Stanford, Calif.: Stanford University Press, 1991.

Vien Lich Su Dang and Tinh Uy Dak Lak. *Lich Su Nha Day Buon Ma Thuot, 1930–1945* [History of Buon Ma Thuot Penitentiary, 1930–1945]. Hanoi: Su That, 1991.

Vien Mac-Lenin and Vien Lich Su Dang. *Nguc Son La, Truong Hoc Dau Tranh Cach Mang* [Son La Prison, the School of Revolutionary Struggle]. Hanoi: Thong Tin Ly Luan, 1992.

Vien Van Hoc. *Tho Ca Cach Mang, 1925–1945* [Revolutionary Poetry, 1925–1945]. Hanoi: Khoa Hoc Xa Hoi, 1973.

Viollis, Andrée [Andrée Françoise Caroline d'Ardenne de Tizac]. *Indochine S.O.S.* 1935. Paris: Éditeurs français réunis, 1949.

Vo Van Truc, ed. *Tieng Hat Trong Tu, Tap I* [Songs Sung in Prison, vol. 1]. Hanoi: Thanh Nien, 1972.

———, ed. *Tieng Hat Trong Tu, Tap II* [Songs Sung in Prison, vol. 2]. Hanoi: Thanh Nien, 1974.

Vu Duc Bang. "The Dong Kinh Free School Movement, 1907–1908." In *Aspects of Vietnamese History,* ed. Walter Vella. Honolulu: University of Hawaii Press, 1973.

Vu Ngu Chieu. "The Other Side of the 1945 Vietnamese Revolution: The Empire of Viet-Nam (Mar.–Aug. 1945)." *Journal of Asian Studies* 45, no. 2 (February 1986): 293–328.

Vu Thuy. "Chi Bo Dac Biet, 1930–1945" [The Special Cell, 1930–1945]. *Tap Chi Lich Su Dang* 5, no. 33 (1990): 46–47, 58.

Vu Trong Phung. "Nguoi Tu Duoc Tha" [The Prisoner Released]. In *Tuyen Tap Vu Trong Phung, I* [Collected Works of Vu Trong Phung, vol. 1], ed. Nguyen Dang Manh and Tran Huy Ta. Hanoi: Van Hoc, 1996.

———. *So Do* [Dumb Luck]. 1936. Reprint, Hanoi: Van Hoc, 1988.

Vu Van Tinh. "Mot Chut Tai Lieu Ve Luong Ngoc Quyen" [A Few Documents about Luong Ngoc Quyen]. *Nghien Cuu Lich Su* 128 (November 1969): 61–62.

Waley-Cohen, Joanna. *Exile in Mid-Qing China, 1758–1820.* New Haven, Conn.: Yale University Press, 1991.

Werner, Jayne. "New Light on Vietnamese Marxism." *Bulletin of Concerned Asian Scholars* 10, no. 4 (1978): 42–48.

White, Christine. "The Vietnamese Revolutionary Alliance: Intellectuals, Workers and Peasants." In *Peasant Rebellion and Communist Revolution in Asia,* ed. John Lewis. Stanford, Calif.: Stanford University Press, 1974.

Woodside, Alexander B. *Community and Revolution in Modern Vietnam.* Boston: Houghton Mifflin, 1976.

———. *Vietnam and the Chinese Model: A Comparative Study of Vietnamese and Chinese Government in the First Half of the Nineteenth Century.* Cambridge, Mass.: Harvard University Press, 1971.

Wright, Gordon. *Between the Guillotine and Liberty: Two Centuries of the Crime Problem in France.* New York: Oxford University Press, 1983.

Wright, Gwendolyn. *The Politics of Design in French Colonial Urbanism.* Chicago: University of Chicago Press, 1991.

Xuan Thuy. "Suoi Reo Nam Ay" [The Bubbling Spring That Year]. *Tap Chi Van Hoc* 1 (1960). Reprinted in Bao Tang Cach Mang Viet Nam and Bao Tang Son La, *Suoi Reo Nam Ay: Hoi Ky Cach Mang* [The Bubbling Spring That Year: Revolutionary Memoirs]. Hanoi: Van Hoa–Thong Tin, 1993.

Yang, Anand. "Disciplining 'Natives': Prisons and Prisoners in Early Nineteenth-Century India." *South Asia* 10, no. 2 (1987): 29–45.

Zimring, Franklin E., and Gordon Hawkins. *The Scale of Imprisonment.* Chicago: University of Chicago Press, 1991.

Zinoman, Peter. "Beyond the Revolutionary Prison Memoir." *Vietnam Review* 1 (Autumn–Winter 1996): 256–72.

Index

Action committees, 267, 290–92
Administrative surveillance, 268,
281–86; by colonial state, 283–84;
failure of, 288; humiliation of, 293;
by the Sûreté, 282, 283, 284, 289,
290; *Le Travail* on, 282
Agricultural stations, 60, 88
Alcohol, state monopoly on, 102
Amnesties: Bao Dai's, 25, 276; celebra-
tions of, 287; colonial press on,
278–81; for female prisoners, 274;
and French Left, 268–78; Indochinese movement for, 272–73; legal
opposition on, 275, 280, 281; limitations on, 279; *La Lutte* on, 272,
273, 277; of 1936, 241; numbers of,
277–78; for Phan Boi Chau,
246–47, 250; for political prisoners,
255–56, 278, 286–87; Popular Front
policy on, 267; in Sino-Vietnamese
tradition, 25; Sûreté on, 273; at Tet,
258, 277; *Tieng Dan* on, 273, 276,
277; Tran Huy Lieu on, 126–27; *Le
Travail* on, 279–80
Amnesty Councils, 274, 275, 276
Anderson, Benedict, 4n, 67
Andouard, Lieutenant, 57, 144,
146–47
Anh chis (gang leaders), 118–19, 129;
tattoos of, 120

Annam: amnesties in, 25, 276, 277;
antitax movement in, 268; autonomy of, 38; colonial administration
of, 70; demonstrations in, 204; ex-
political prisoners in, 284; fiscal
framework of, 42; French annexation of, 29; Garde indigène, 47; ju-
diciary of, 40–41, 274n; missionaries in, 20n; penitentiaries of, 55–56;
political prisoners in, 41–42, 257;
precolonial prisons of, 20, 23,
24–25, 26; prisoner rebellions in,
137; prison population of, 205;
prison system of, 4; as protectorate,
39, 40, 62; provincial prisons of, 46;
residents superior of, 42, 274
Anticolonialism: in colonial prison
system, 5, 7–8; leadership of, 29,
287; media support for, 243; of
1930s, 2, 200, 267; party politics in,
139; regionalism in, 158; of released prisoners, 286–92; and Thai
Nguyen rebellion, 173, 199; traditionalism in, 159; during World
War II, 297–99. *See also* Nationalism, Vietnamese
Anticolonials: amnesties for, 278;
bonding among, 69; charges
against, 109; execution of, 31n; ex-
prisoners among, 289, 292; and

331

Text:	10/13 Aldus
Display:	Aldus
Composition:	Impressions Book and Journal Services, Inc.
Printing and binding:	Edwards Brothers, Inc.
Maps:	Bill Nelson